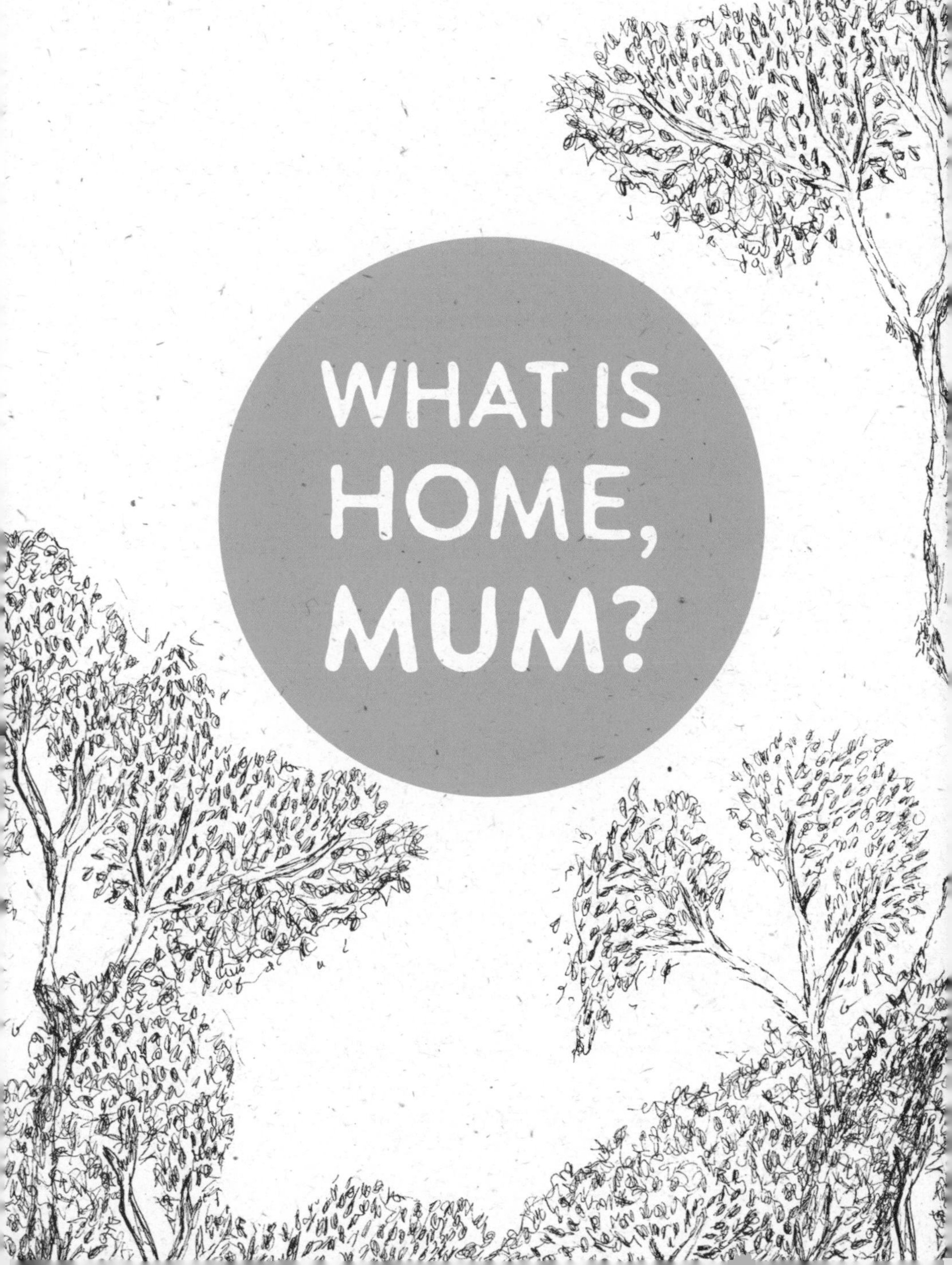
WHAT IS HOME, MUM?

WHAT IS HOME, MUM?

SABBA KHAN

STREET NOISE

Street Noise Books • Brooklyn, New York

Originally published as *The Roles We Play*
by Myriad Editions, An imprint of
New Internationalist Publications,
Oxford, UK, in 2021

Thank you to the following for kind permission
to use their words:
Tweet on page 7, © Bo Ren
The Gifts of Imperfection, page 84, © Brené Brown
Translation of "Manzil Talaash Kar" by Allama Iqbal,
page 269–70, © Shay Khan

ISBN 978-1951-491-17-8

Printed in South Korea

9 8 7 6 5 4 3 2 1

First Edition

For Mum, to see her.

For Mark, to show him.

And for me...

...mainly for me.
To find myself.

Please refer to the back of the
book for a full glossary of terms
that includes Pathwari, Urdu, and
Arabic words and phrases.

◆

Listening to music has been
an important part of creating
What is Home, Mum? Each chapter
is accompanied by a song.
The full playlist is on page 285 and
can be listened to here:

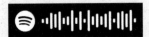

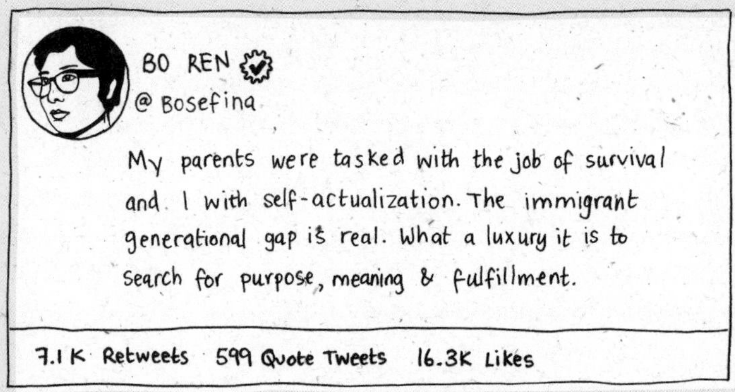
BO REN
@Bosefina
My parents were tasked with the job of survival and I with self-actualization. The immigrant generational gap is real. What a luxury it is to search for purpose, meaning & fulfillment.
7.1K Retweets 599 Quote Tweets 16.3K Likes

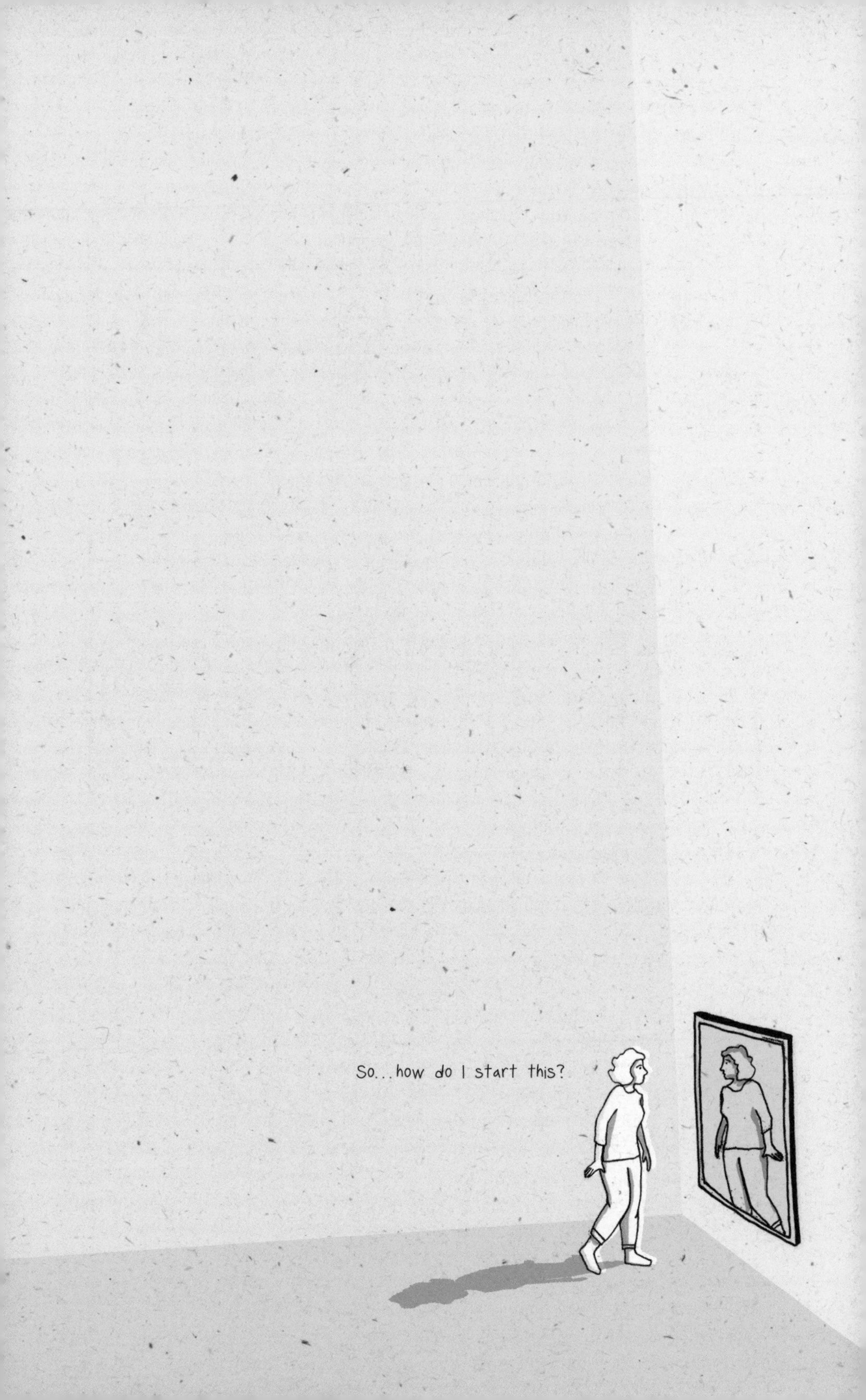
So...how do I start this?

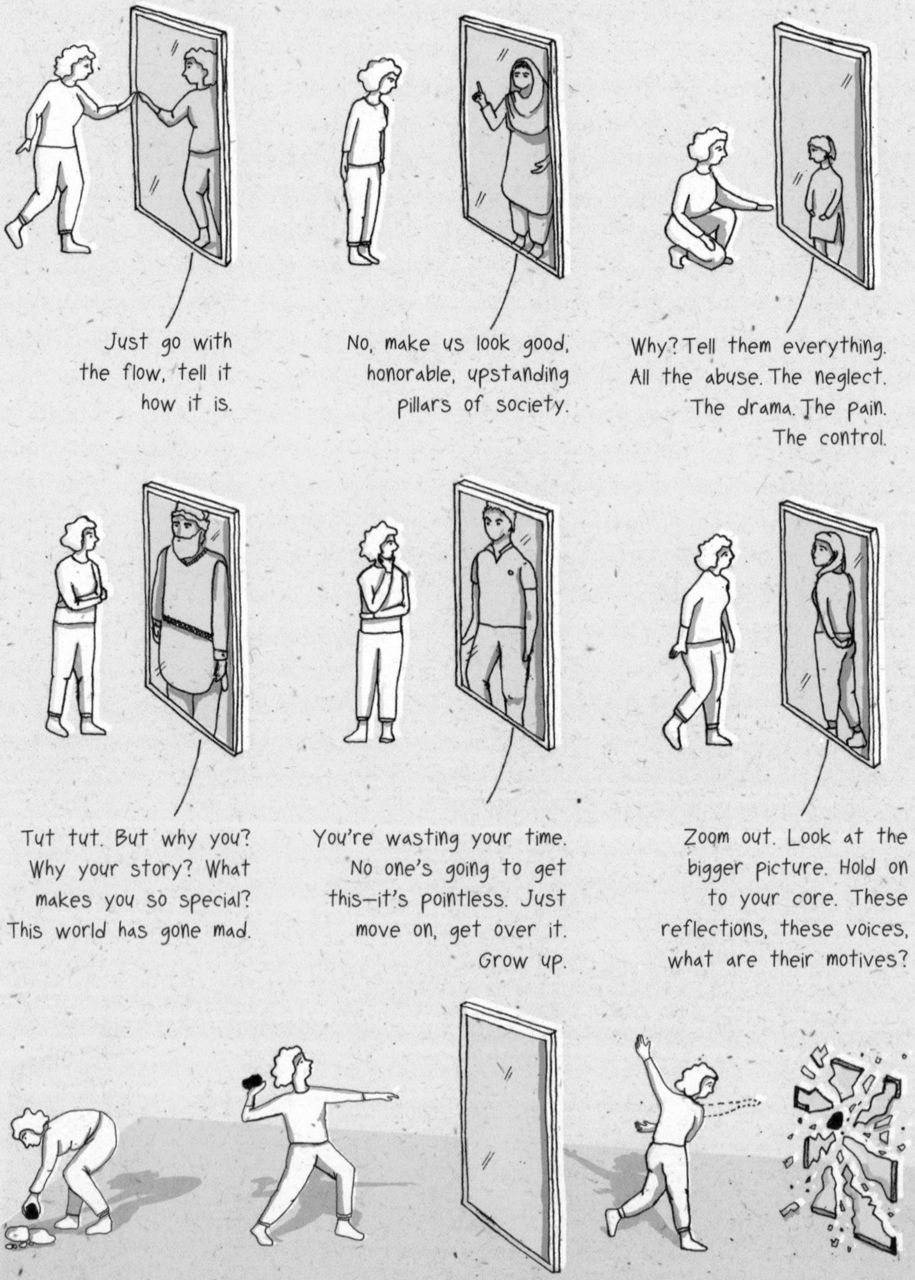

Just go with the flow, tell it how it is.
No, make us look good, honorable, upstanding pillars of society.
Why? Tell them everything. All the abuse. The neglect. The drama. The pain. The control.
Tut tut. But why you? Why your story? What makes you so special? This world has gone mad.
You're wasting your time. No one's going to get this—it's pointless. Just move on, get over it. Grow up.
Zoom out. Look at the bigger picture. Hold on to your core. These reflections, these voices, what are their motives?

Somewhere,
in these pieces,
she's here...

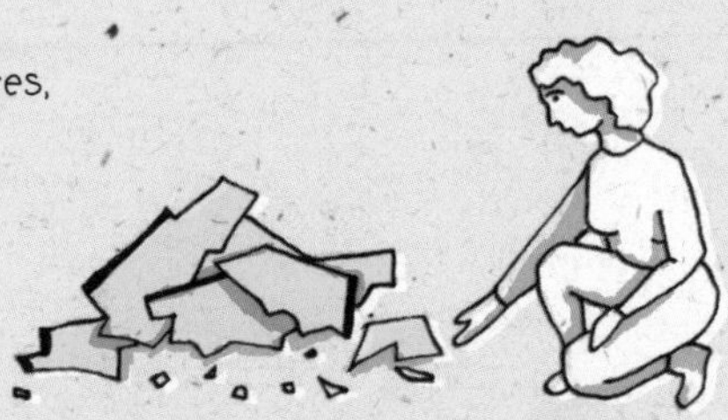

...unscathed by those
other voices,

my guide,
my gut.

I've just got to
hold on to her...

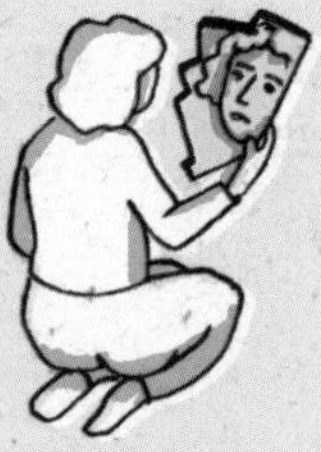

...and we'll talk, and
we'll find new ways
of seeing old memories...

...like the laser eye surgery I've
always wanted to get done.

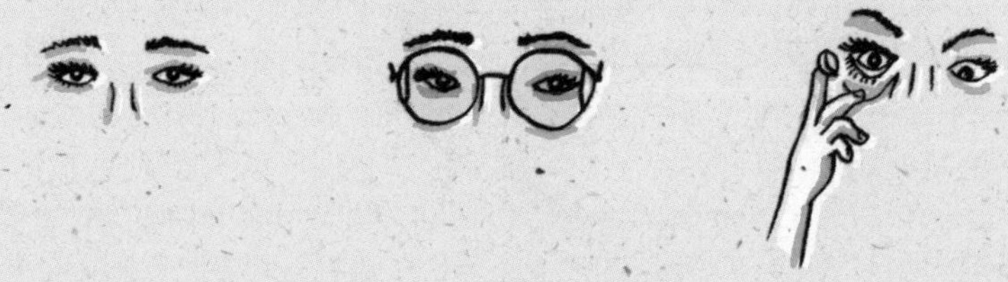

To see past experiences
sharper,
clearer,
brighter...

...my essence,

my soul,

my core,

ME.

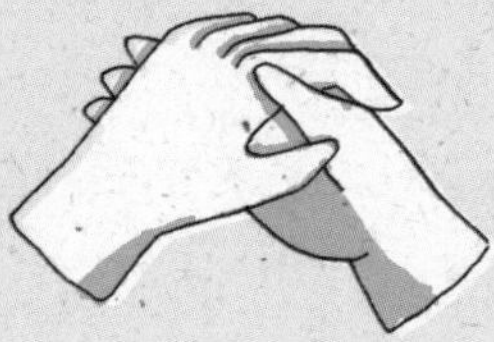

She'll hold my hand...

...and in the voice of a
therapist I saw last year,
she'll gently ask:

So, what does it feel
like to belong?

What does it
mean to belong?

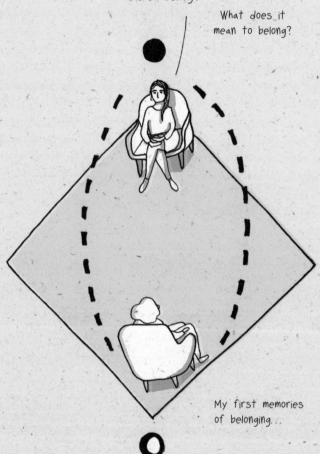

My first memories
of belonging...

...I'm seven years old.

one

01 | TOGETHER | ♫ Colleen "Everyone Alive Wants Answers"

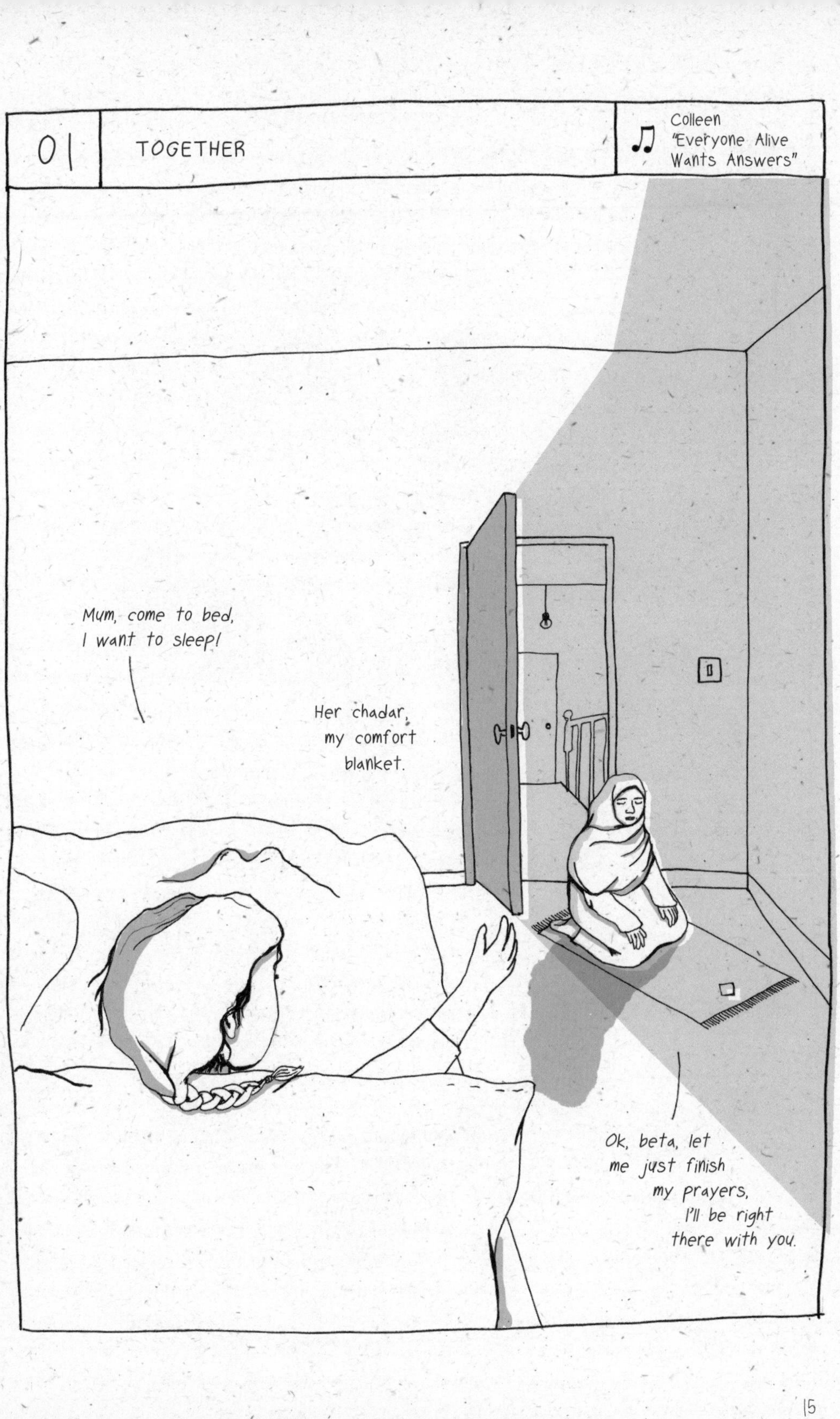
Mum, come to bed, I want to sleep!
Her chadar, my comfort blanket.
Ok, beta, let me just finish my prayers, I'll be right there with you.

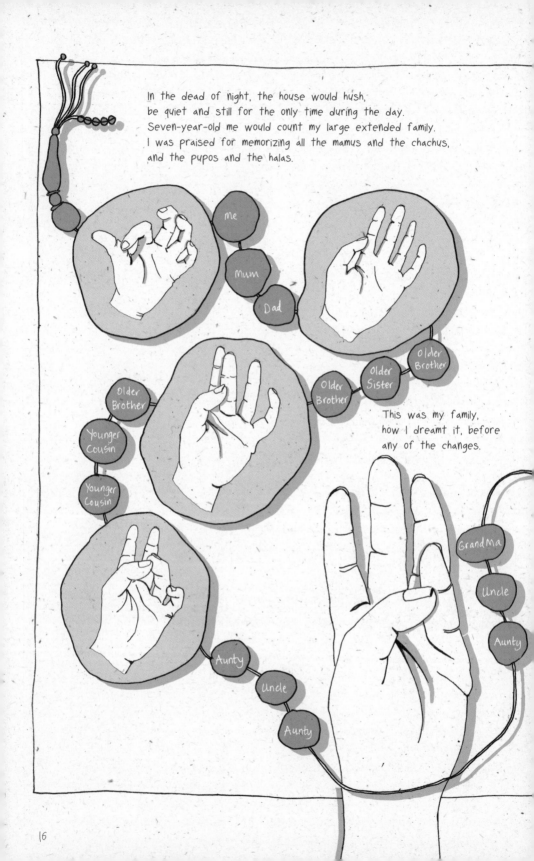

In the dead of night, the house would hush,
be quiet and still for the only time during the day.
Seven-year-old me would count my large extended family.
I was praised for memorizing all the mamus and the chachus,
and the pupos and the halas.

Me

Mum

Dad

Older Brother

Older Sister

Older Brother

This was my family,
how I dreamt it, before
any of the changes.

Older Brother

Younger Cousin

Younger Cousin

GrandMa

Uncle

Aunty

Aunty

Uncle

Aunty

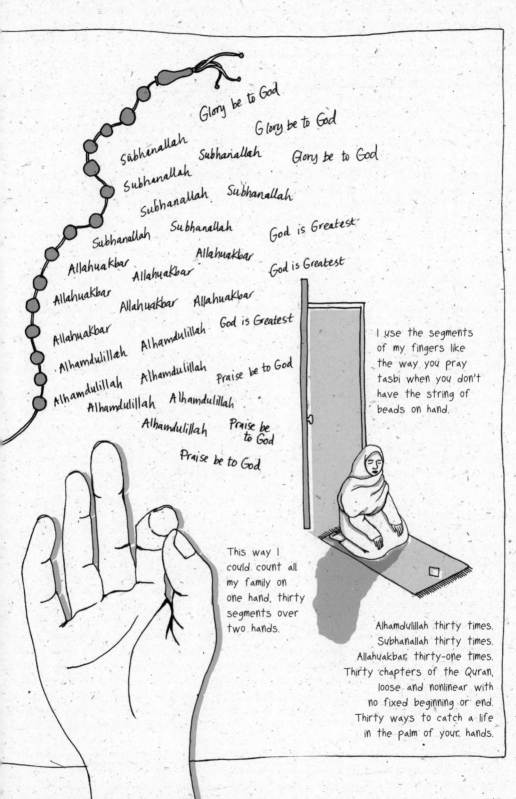

Glory be to God
Glory be to God
Glory be to God

Subhanallah
Subhanallah
Subhanallah
Subhanallah
Subhanallah
Subhanallah
Subhanallah

Allahuakbar
Allahuakbar
Allahuakbar
Allahuakbar
Allahuakbar
Allahuakbar
Allahuakbar
Allahuakbar

God is Greatest
God is Greatest
God is Greatest

Alhamdulillah
Alhamdulillah
Alhamdulillah
Alhamdulillah
Alhamdulillah
Alhamdulillah
Alhamdulillah

Praise be to God
Praise be to God
Praise be to God

I use the segments of my fingers like the way you pray tasbi when you don't have the string of beads on hand.

This way I could count all my family on one hand, thirty segments over two hands.

Alhamdulillah thirty times. Subhanallah thirty times. Allahuakbar thirty-one times. Thirty chapters of the Quran, loose and nonlinear with no fixed beginning or end. Thirty ways to catch a life in the palm of your hands.

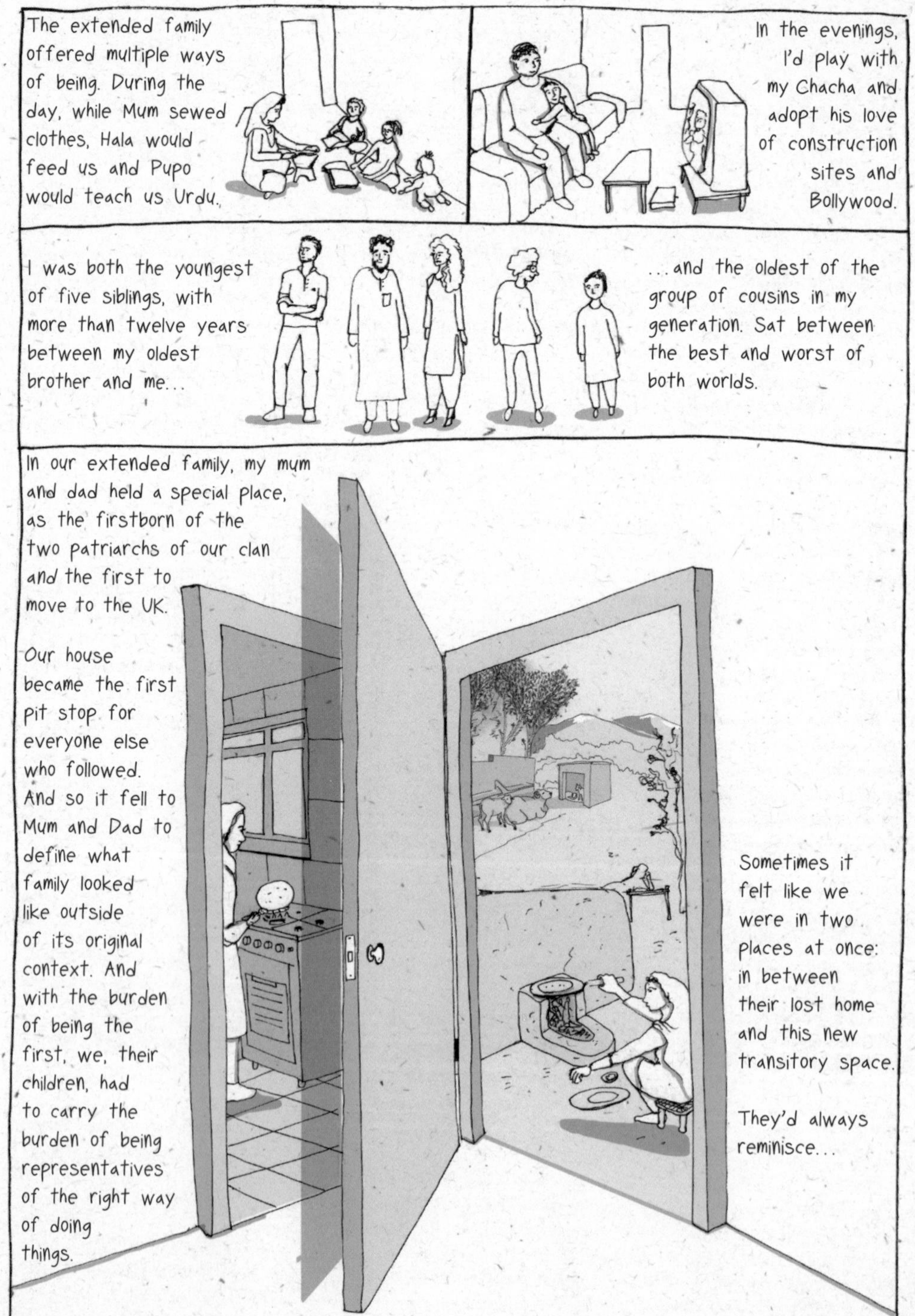
The extended family offered multiple ways of being. During the day, while Mum sewed clothes, Hala would feed us and Pupo would teach us Urdu.
In the evenings, I'd play with my Chacha and adopt his love of construction sites and Bollywood.
I was both the youngest of five siblings, with more than twelve years between my oldest brother and me...
...and the oldest of the group of cousins in my generation. Sat between the best and worst of both worlds.
In our extended family, my mum and dad held a special place, as the firstborn of the two patriarchs of our clan and the first to move to the UK.
Our house became the first pit stop for everyone else who followed. And so it fell to Mum and Dad to define what family looked like outside of its original context. And with the burden of being the first, we, their children, had to carry the burden of being representatives of the right way of doing things.
Sometimes it felt like we were in two places at once: in between their lost home and this new transitory space.
They'd always reminisce...

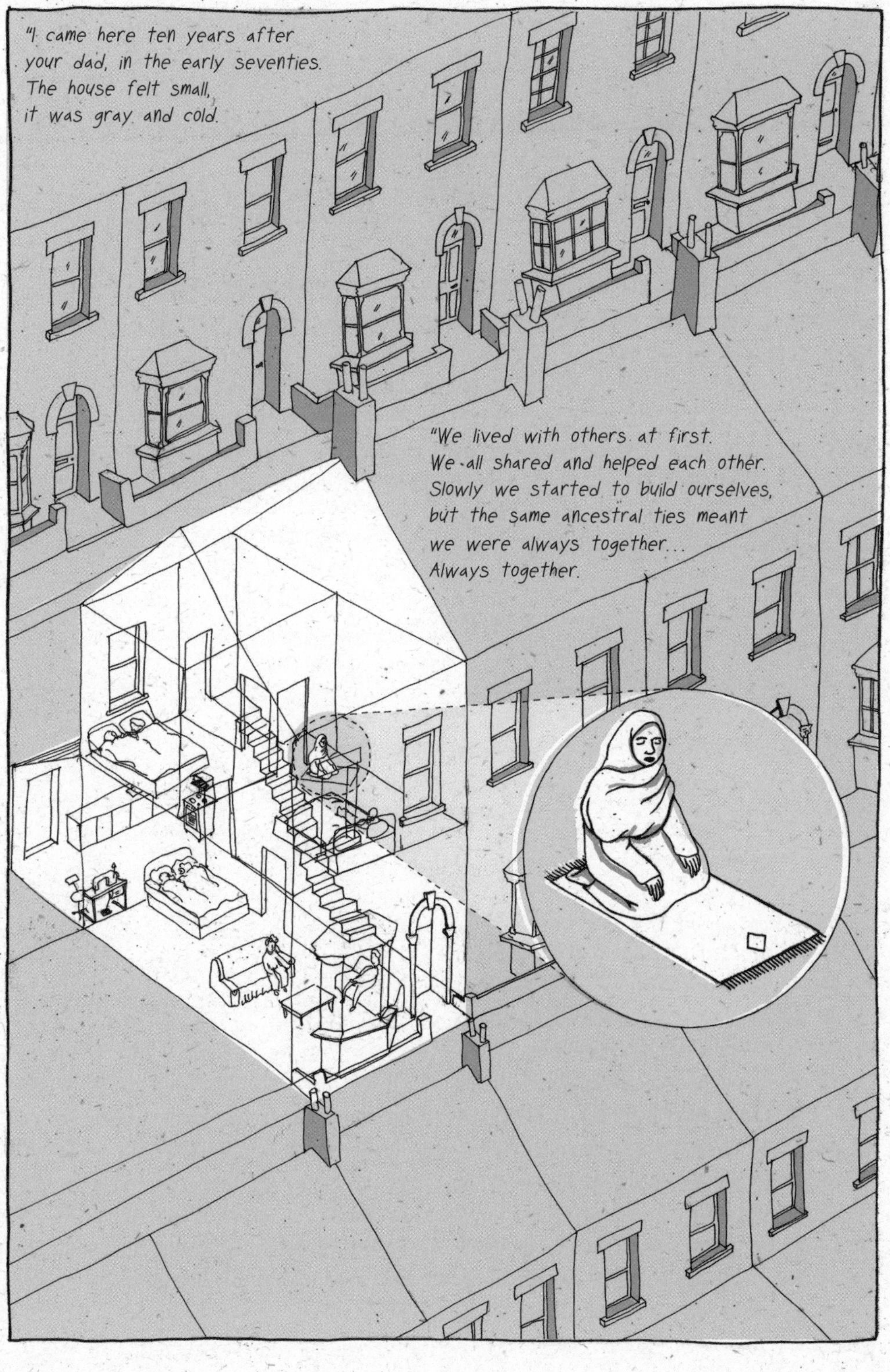
"I came here ten years after
your dad, in the early seventies.
The house felt small,
it was gray and cold.
"We lived with others at first.
We all shared and helped each other.
Slowly we started to build ourselves,
but the same ancestral ties meant
we were always together...
Always together.

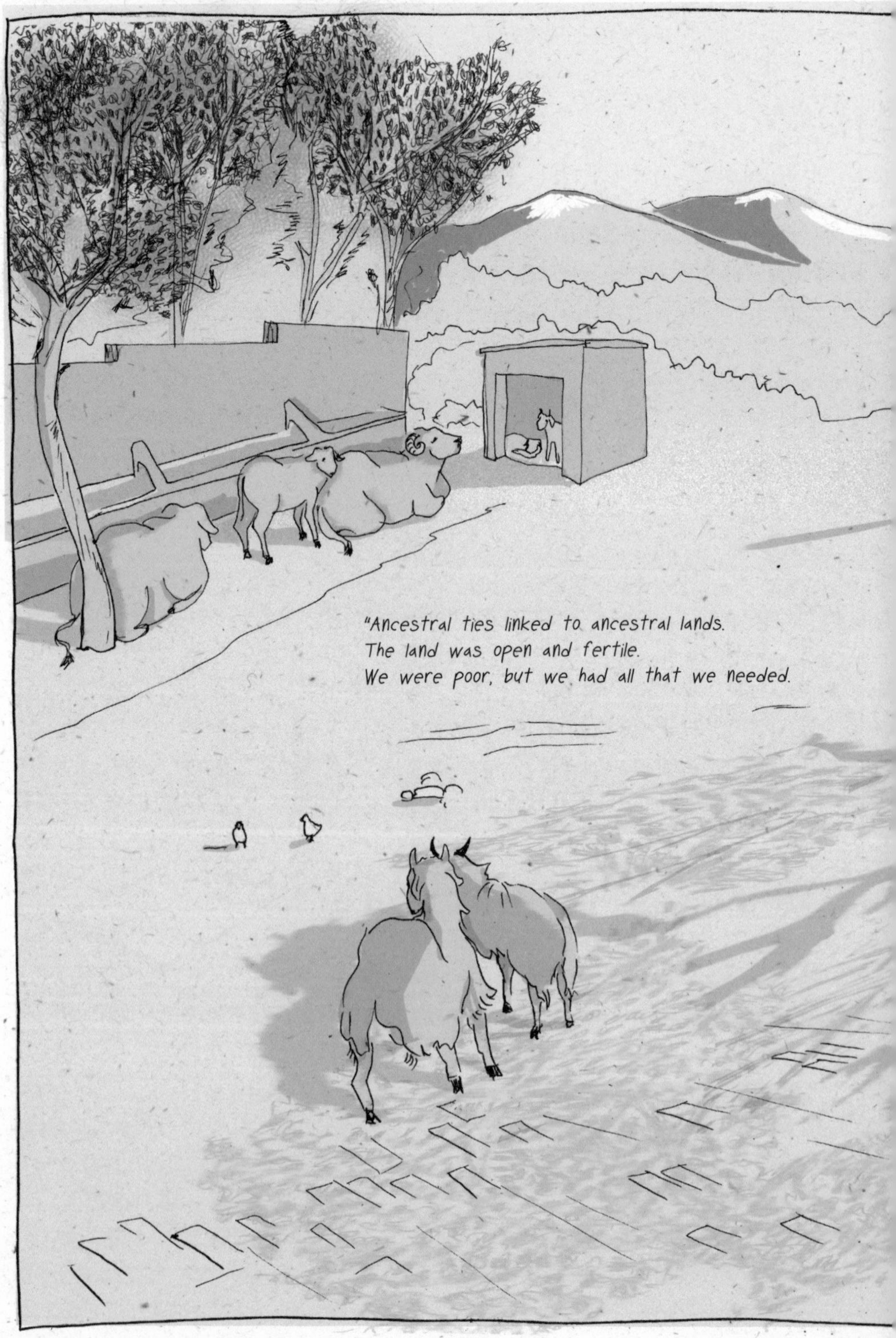
"Ancestral ties linked to ancestral lands.
The land was open and fertile.
We were poor, but we had all that we needed.

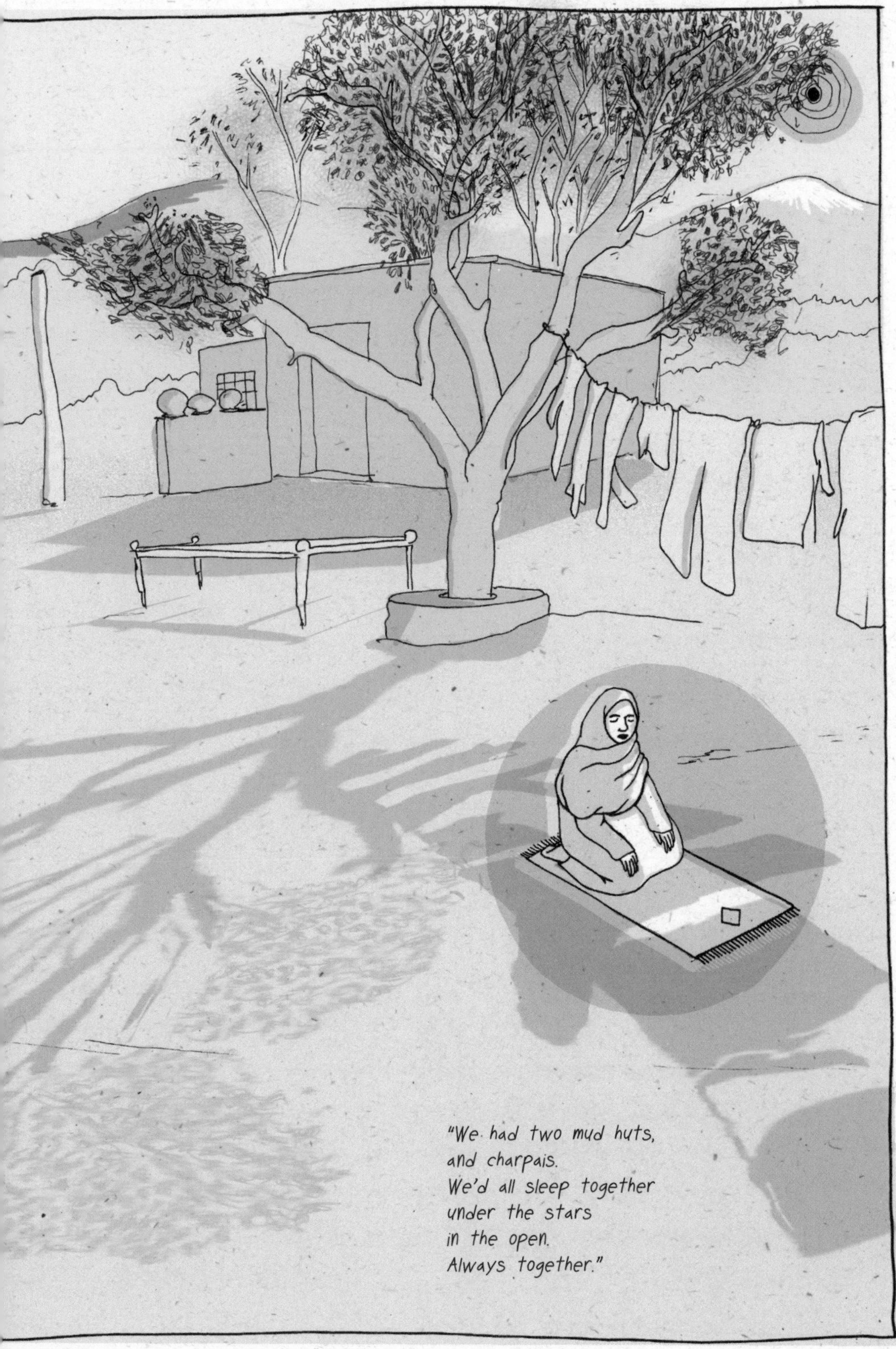
"We had two mud huts,
and charpais.
We'd all sleep together
under the stars
in the open.
Always together."

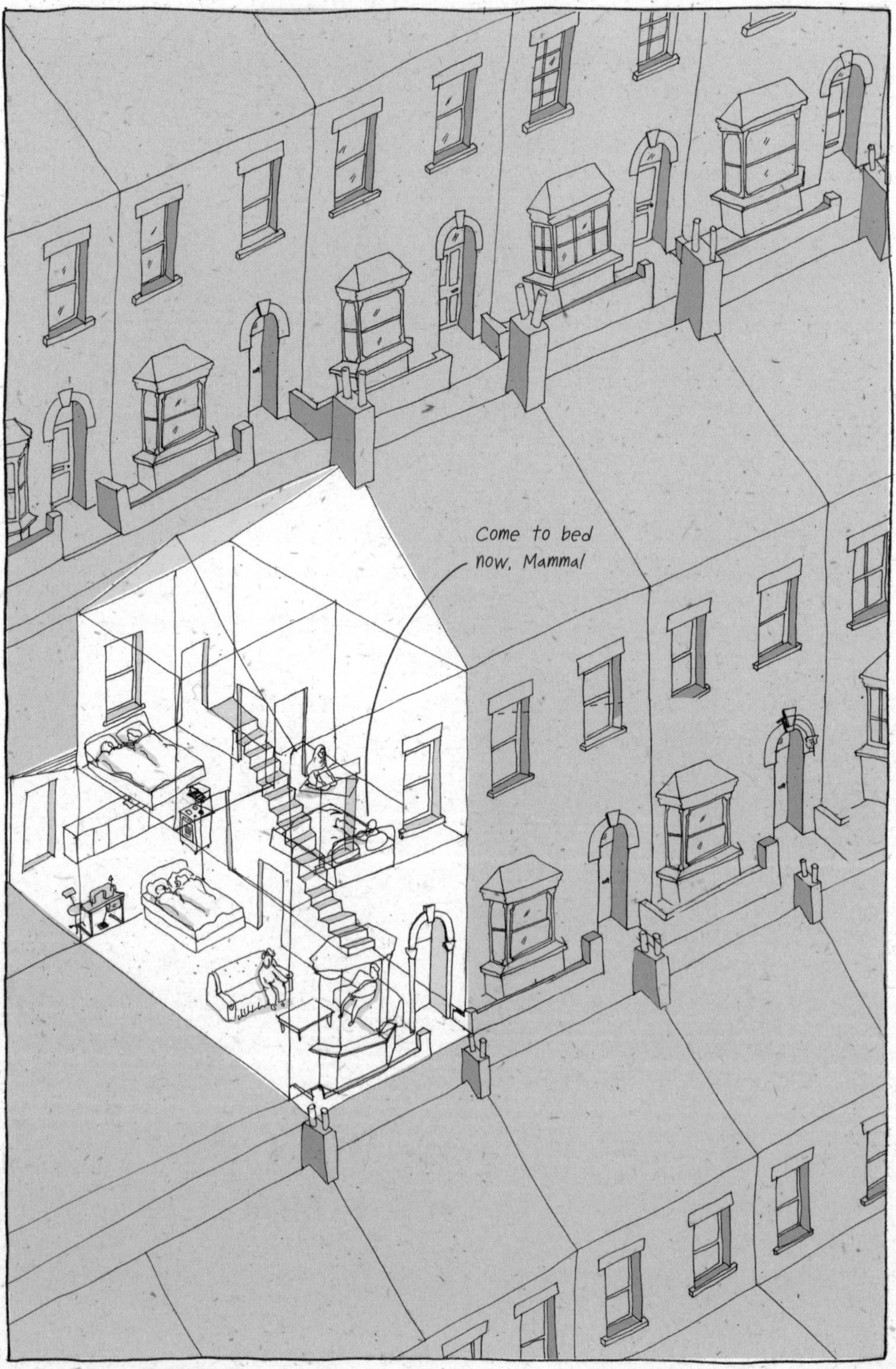
Come to bed now, Mamma!

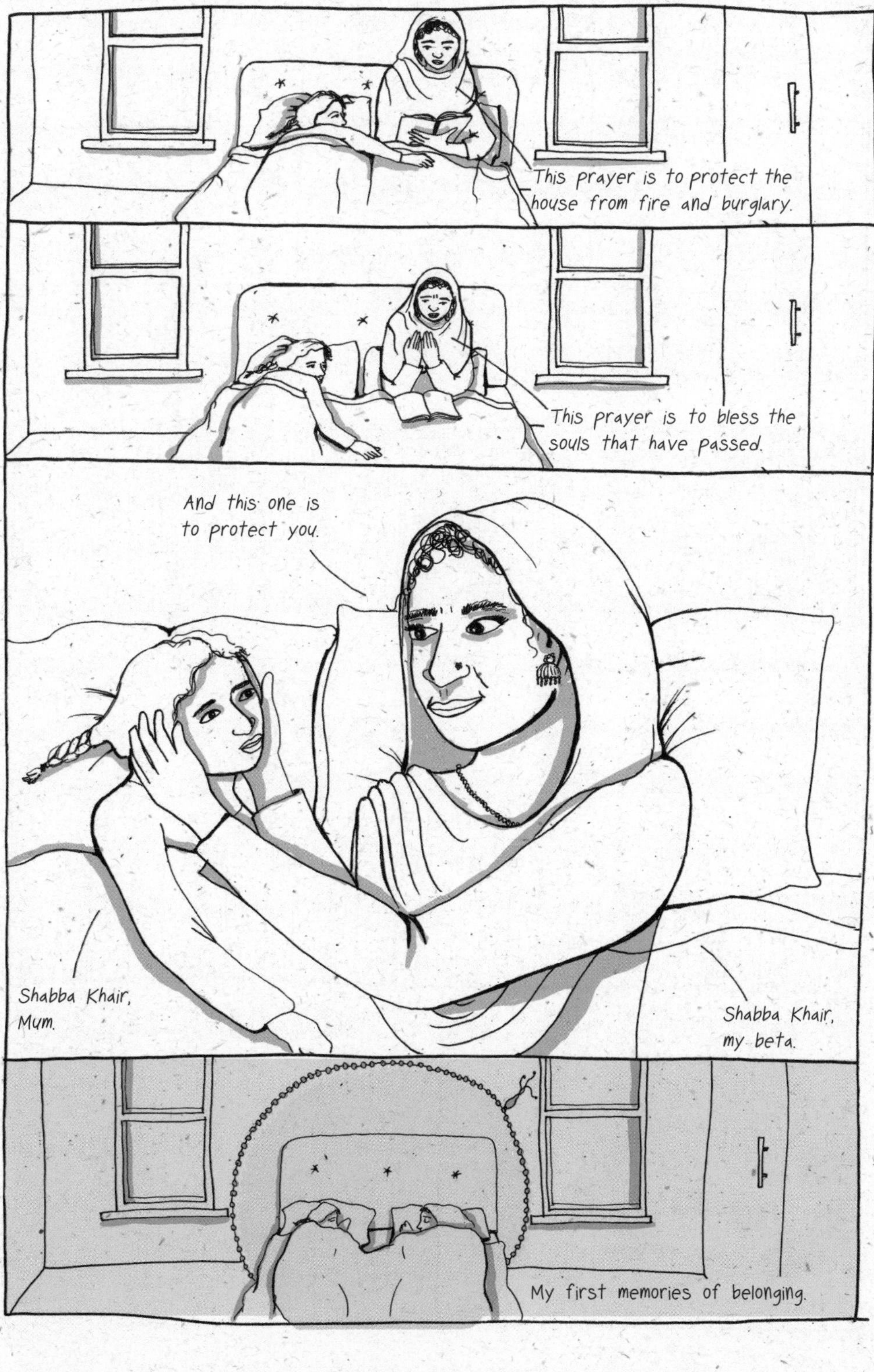
This prayer is to protect the house from fire and burglary.
This prayer is to bless the souls that have passed.
And this one is to protect you.
Shabba Khair, Mum.
Shabba Khair, my beta.
My first memories of belonging.

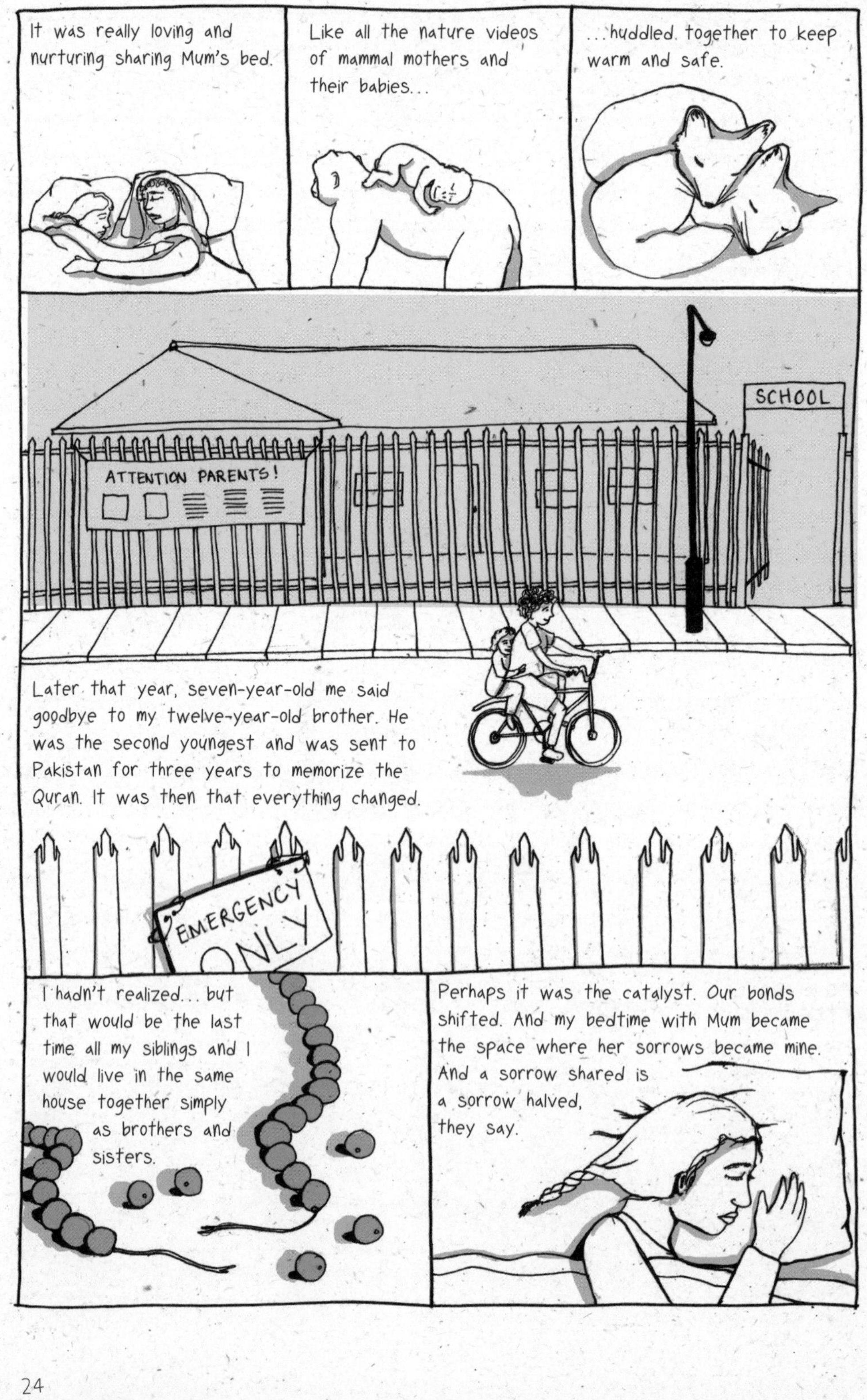
It was really loving and nurturing sharing Mum's bed.
Like all the nature videos of mammal mothers and their babies...
...huddled together to keep warm and safe.
SCHOOL
ATTENTION PARENTS!
Later that year, seven-year-old me said goodbye to my twelve-year-old brother. He was the second youngest and was sent to Pakistan for three years to memorize the Quran. It was then that everything changed.
EMERGENCY ONLY
I hadn't realized... but that would be the last time all my siblings and I would live in the same house together simply as brothers and sisters.
Perhaps it was the catalyst. Our bonds shifted. And my bedtime with Mum became the space where her sorrows became mine. And a sorrow shared is a sorrow halved, they say.

Sometimes that sorrow is so
sweet and so strong...

...it slips out at the mere
association of a memory.

I have to watch these
moments. They tell me my
wounds have not healed.

I've only learned to mask them,
flavor and perfume them,
to give the illusion
of being over it.

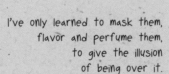

I'm far from over it.

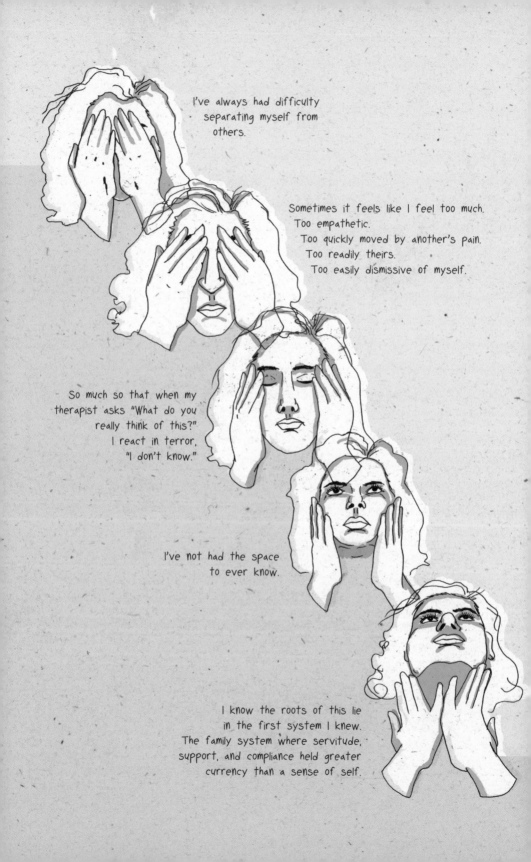

I've always had difficulty
separating myself from
others.

Sometimes it feels like I feel too much.
Too empathetic.
Too quickly moved by another's pain.
Too readily theirs.
Too easily dismissive of myself.

So much so that when my
therapist asks "What do you
really think of this?"
I react in terror,
"I don't know."

I've not had the space
to ever know.

I know the roots of this lie
in the first system I knew.
The family system where servitude,
support, and compliance held greater
currency than a sense of self.

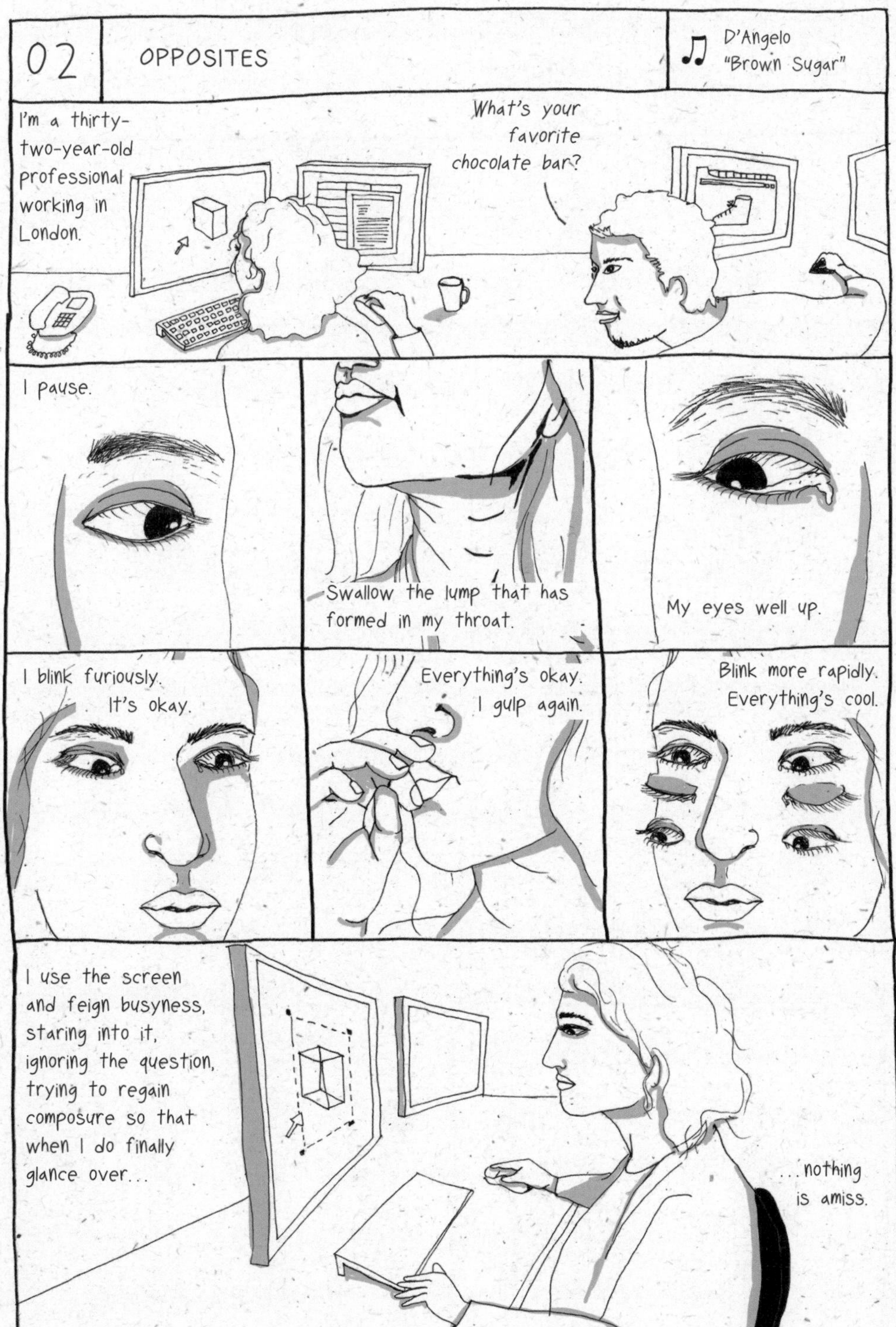

02
OPPOSITES
D'Angelo "Brown Sugar"
I'm a thirty-two-year-old professional working in London.
What's your favorite chocolate bar?
I pause.
Swallow the lump that has formed in my throat.
My eyes well up.
I blink furiously.
It's okay.
Everything's okay.
I gulp again.
Blink more rapidly.
Everything's cool.
I use the screen and feign busyness, staring into it, ignoring the question, trying to regain composure so that when I do finally glance over...
...nothing is amiss.

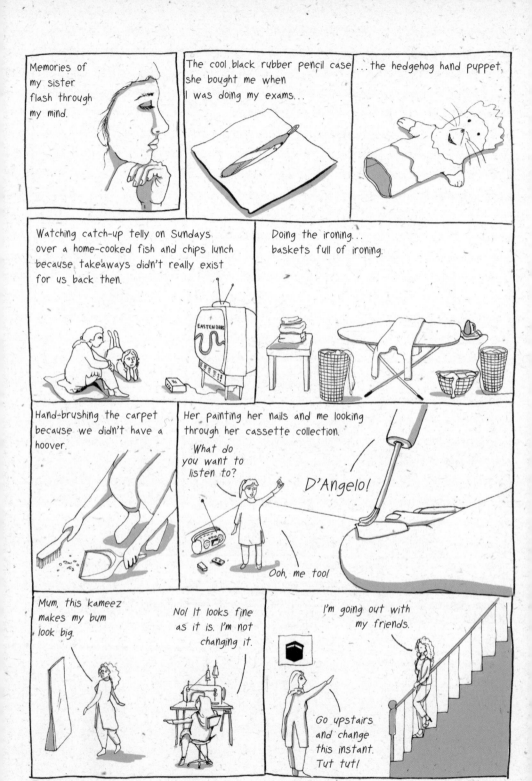

Memories of my sister flash through my mind.

The cool black rubber pencil case she bought me when I was doing my exams...

...the hedgehog hand puppet.

Watching catch-up telly on Sundays over a home-cooked fish and chips lunch because takeaways didn't really exist for us back then.

EASTENDERS

Doing the ironing... baskets full of ironing.

Hand-brushing the carpet because we didn't have a hoover.

Her painting her nails and me looking through her cassette collection.

What do you want to listen to?

D'Angelo!

Ooh, me too!

Mum, this kameez makes my bum look big.

No! It looks fine as it is. I'm not changing it.

I'm going out with my friends.

Go upstairs and change this instant. Tut tut!

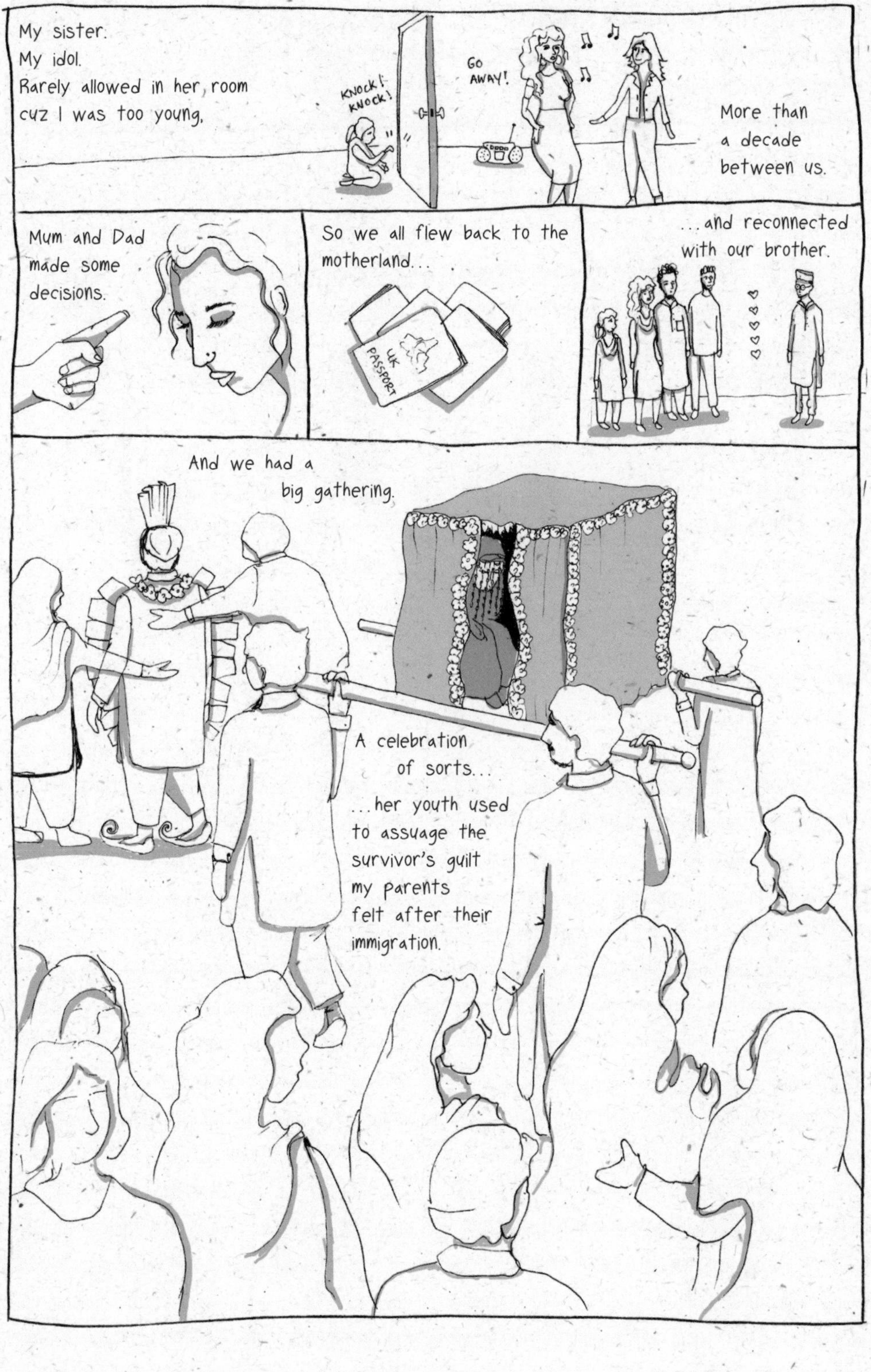
My sister.
My idol.
Rarely allowed in her room
cuz I was too young,
KNOCK! KNOCK!
GO AWAY!
More than
a decade
between us.
Mum and Dad
made some
decisions.
So we all flew back to the
motherland...
UK
PASSPORT
...and reconnected
with our brother.
And we had a
big gathering.
A celebration
of sorts...
...her youth used
to assuage the
survivor's guilt
my parents
felt after their
immigration.

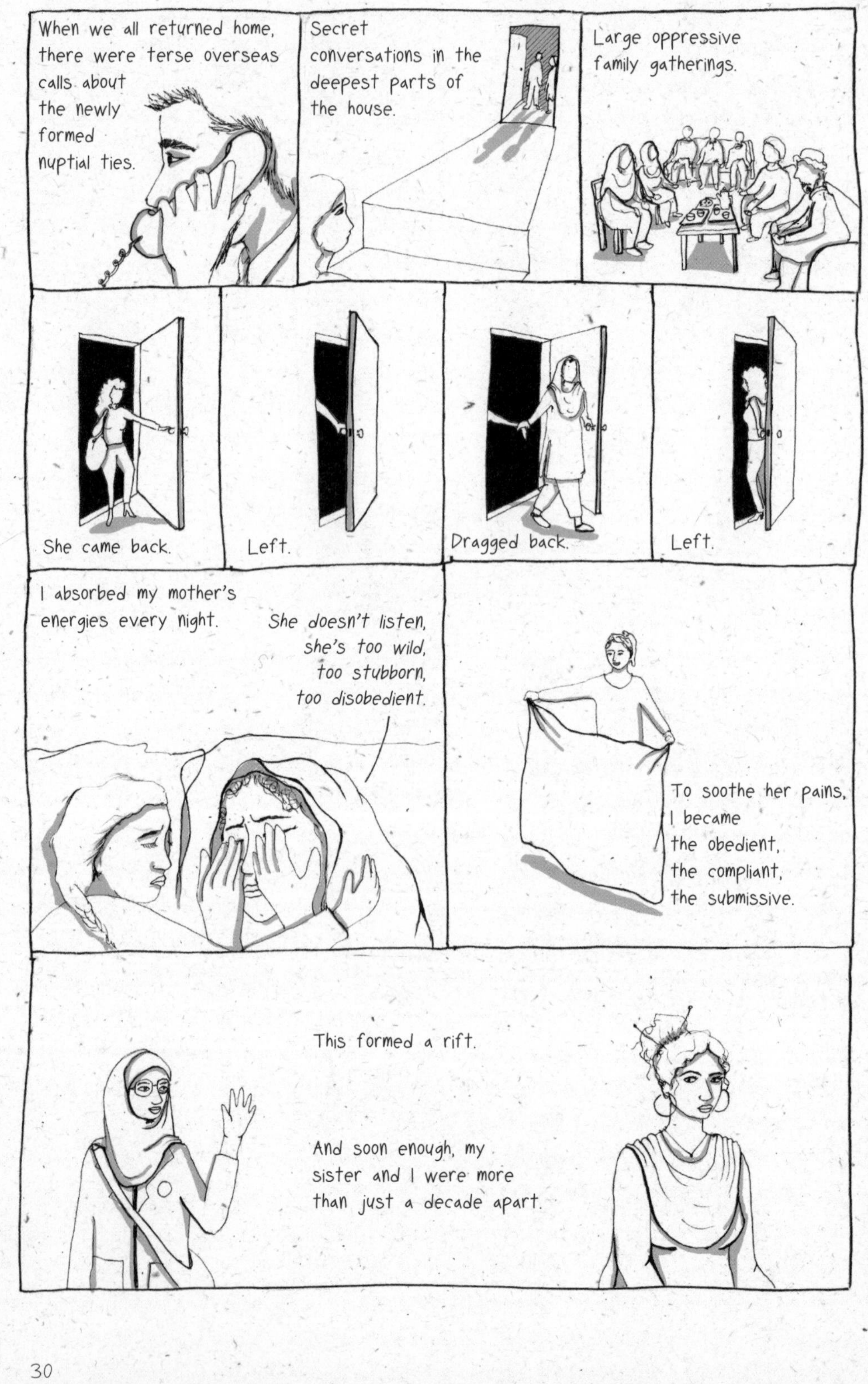
When we all returned home, there were terse overseas calls about the newly formed nuptial ties.
Secret conversations in the deepest parts of the house.
Large oppressive family gatherings.
She came back.
Left.
Dragged back.
Left.
I absorbed my mother's energies every night.
She doesn't listen, she's too wild, too stubborn, too disobedient.
To soothe her pains, I became the obedient, the compliant, the submissive.
This formed a rift.
And soon enough, my sister and I were more than just a decade apart.

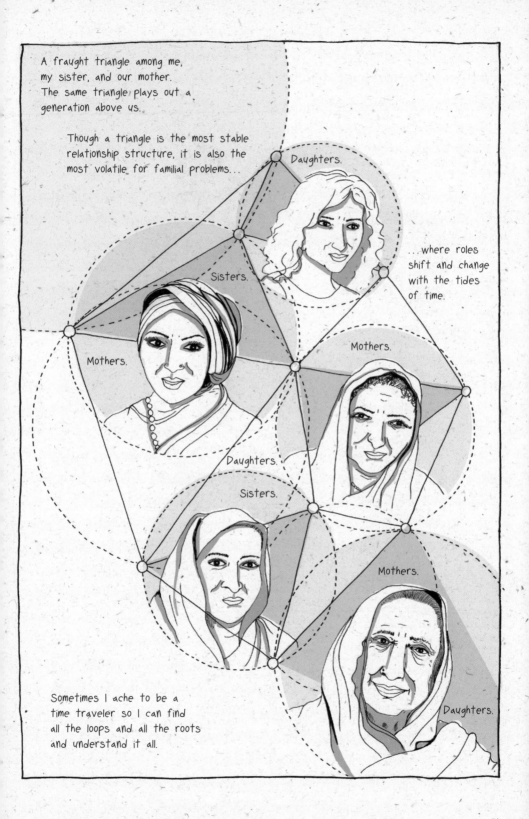

A fraught triangle among me, my sister, and our mother. The same triangle plays out a generation above us.

Though a triangle is the most stable relationship structure, it is also the most volatile for familial problems...

Daughters.

...where roles shift and change with the tides of time.

Sisters.

Mothers.

Mothers.

Daughters.

Sisters.

Mothers.

Sometimes I ache to be a time traveler so I can find all the loops and all the roots and understand it all.

Daughters.

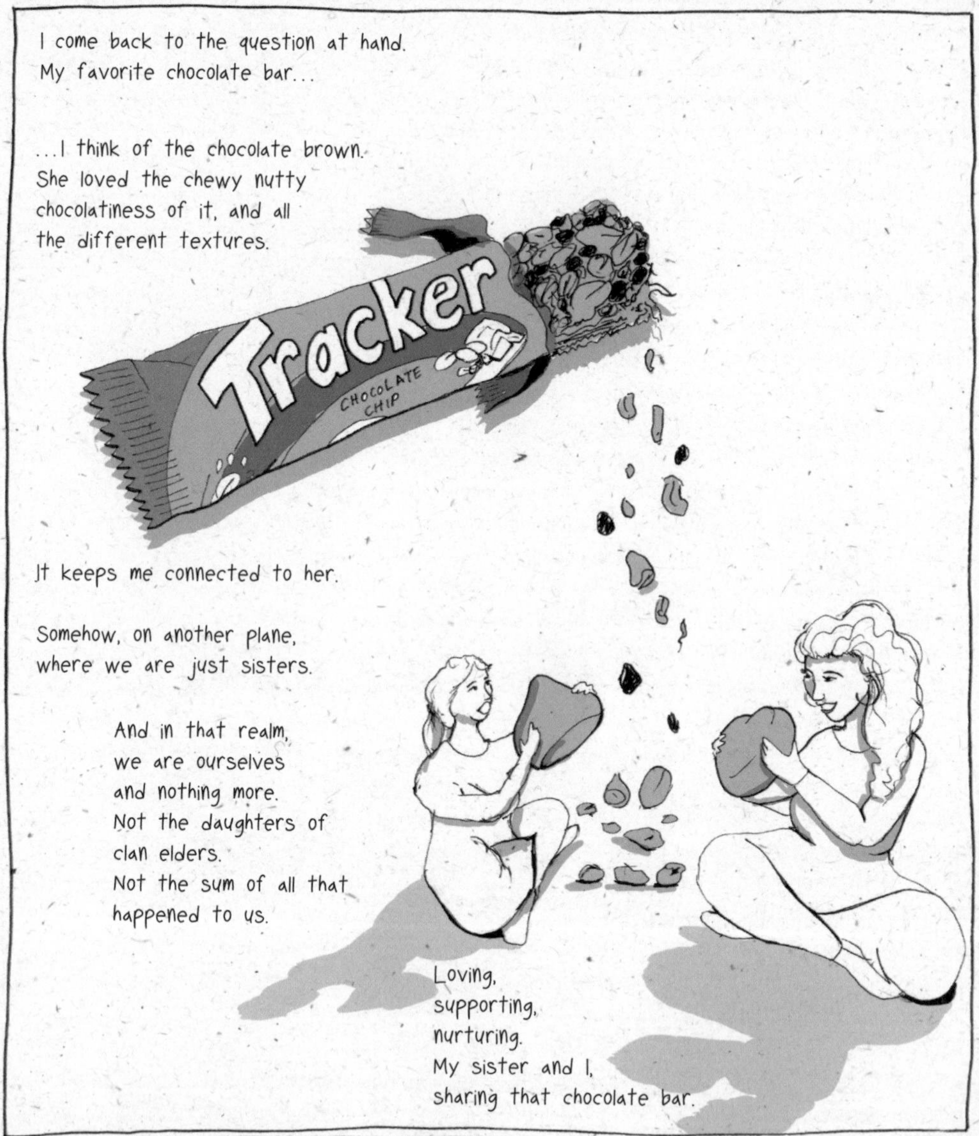
I come back to the question at hand.
My favorite chocolate bar...
...I think of the chocolate brown.
She loved the chewy nutty
chocolatiness of it, and all
the different textures.
Tracker
CHOCOLATE CHIP
It keeps me connected to her.
Somehow, on another plane,
where we are just sisters.
And in that realm,
we are ourselves
and nothing more.
Not the daughters of
clan elders.
Not the sum of all that
happened to us.
Loving,
supporting,
nurturing.
My sister and I,
sharing that chocolate bar.

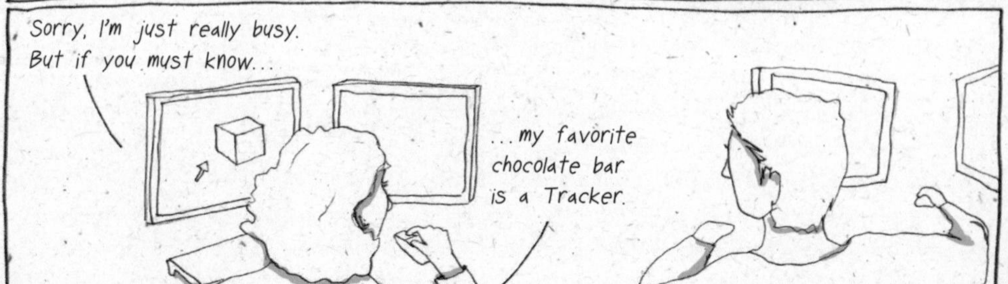
Sorry, I'm just really busy.
But if you must know...
...my favorite
chocolate bar
is a Tracker.

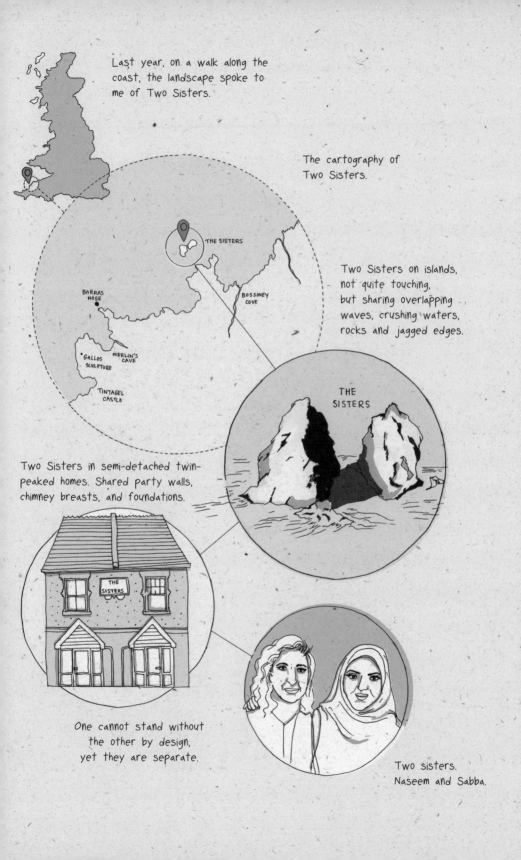

Last year, on a walk along the coast, the landscape spoke to me of Two Sisters.

The cartography of Two Sisters.

THE SISTERS

BARRAS NOSE

BOSSINEY COVE

GALLOS SCULPTURE

MERLIN'S CAVE

TINTAGEL CASTLE

Two Sisters on islands, not quite touching, but sharing overlapping waves, crushing waters, rocks and jagged edges.

THE SISTERS

Two Sisters in semi-detached twin-peaked homes. Shared party walls, chimney breasts, and foundations.

THE SISTERS

One cannot stand without the other by design, yet they are separate.

Two sisters. Naseem and Sabba.

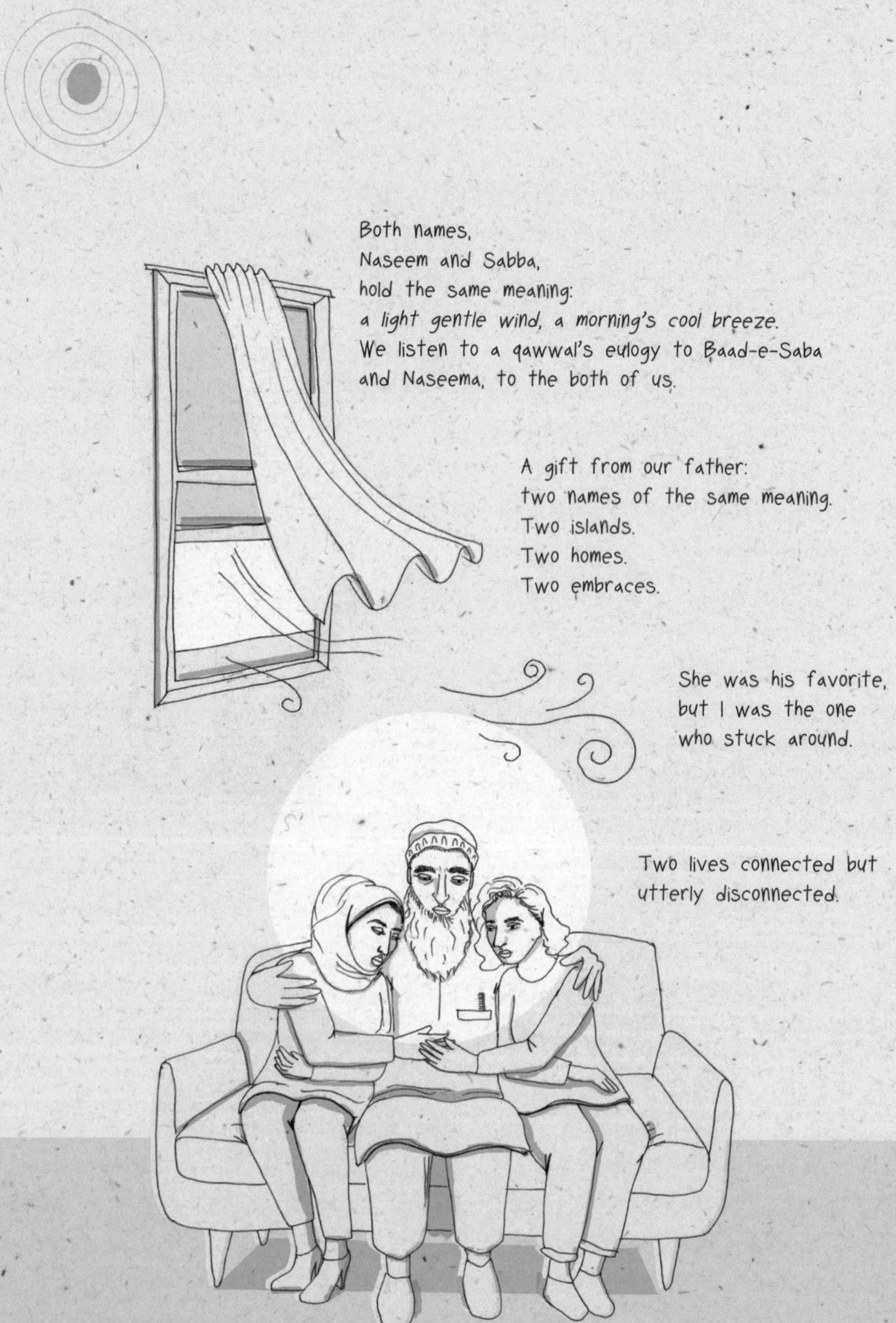
Both names,
Naseem and Sabba,
hold the same meaning:
a light gentle wind, a morning's cool breeze.
We listen to a qawwal's eulogy to Baad-e-Saba
and Naseema, to the both of us.
A gift from our father:
two names of the same meaning.
Two islands.
Two homes.
Two embraces.
She was his favorite,
but I was the one
who stuck around.
Two lives connected but
utterly disconnected.

♫ Fugees
"Killing Me Softly With His Song"

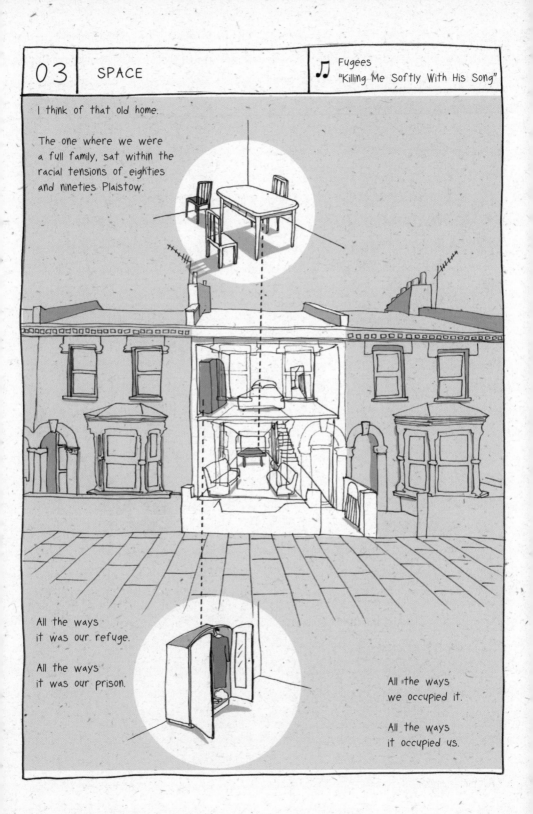

I think of that old home.

The one where we were a full family, sat within the racial tensions of eighties and nineties Plaistow.

All the ways
it was our refuge.

All the ways
it was our prison.

All the ways
we occupied it.

All the ways
it occupied us.

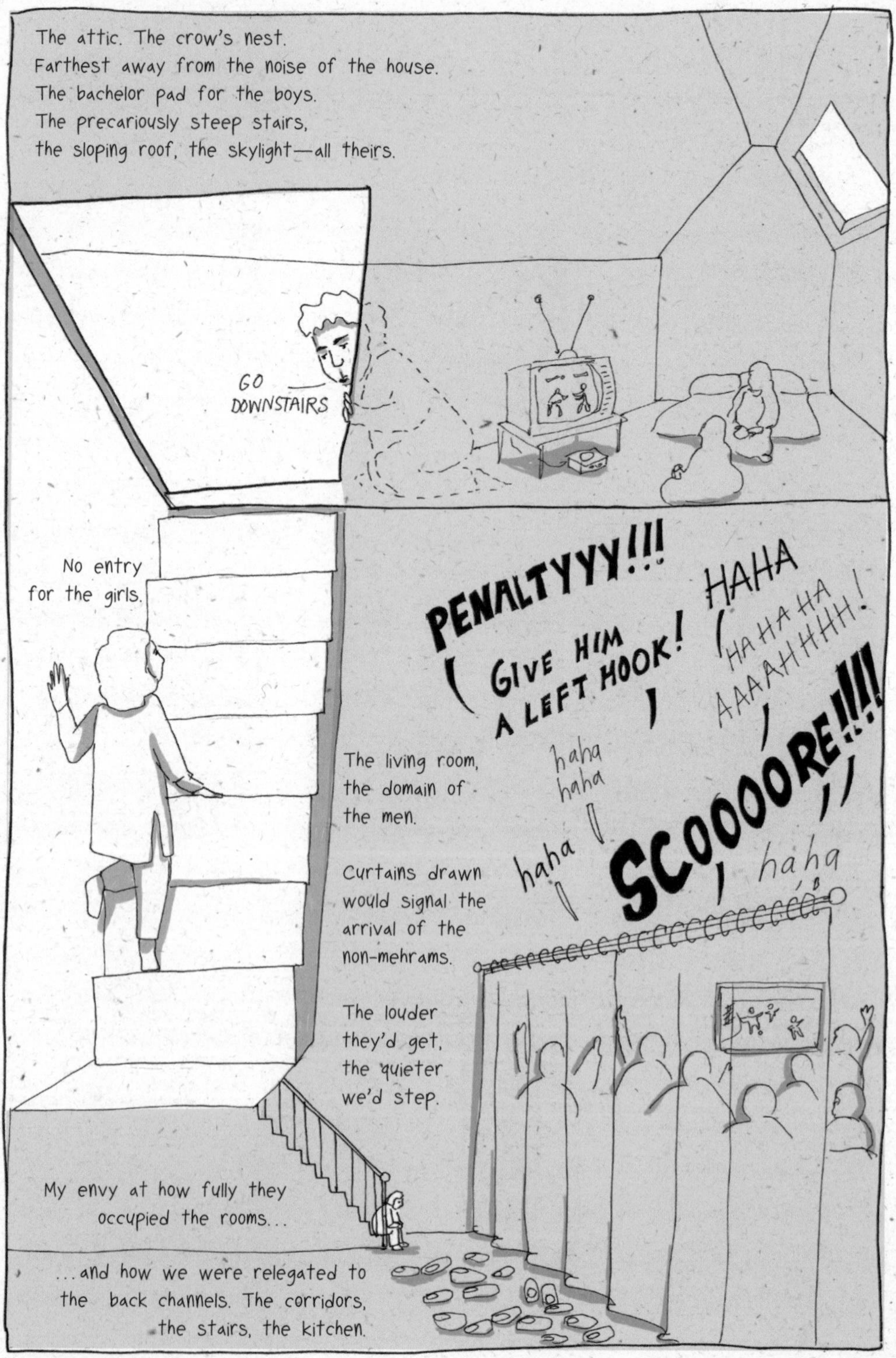
The attic. The crow's nest.
Farthest away from the noise of the house.
The bachelor pad for the boys.
The precariously steep stairs,
the sloping roof, the skylight—all theirs.
GO DOWNSTAIRS
No entry for the girls.
PENALTYYY!!!
GIVE HIM A LEFT HOOK!
HAHA
HA HA HA HA AAAAHHHH!
SCOOOORE!!!!
haha haha
haha
haha
The living room, the domain of the men.
Curtains drawn would signal the arrival of the non-mehrams.
The louder they'd get, the quieter we'd step.
My envy at how fully they occupied the rooms...
...and how we were relegated to the back channels. The corridors, the stairs, the kitchen.

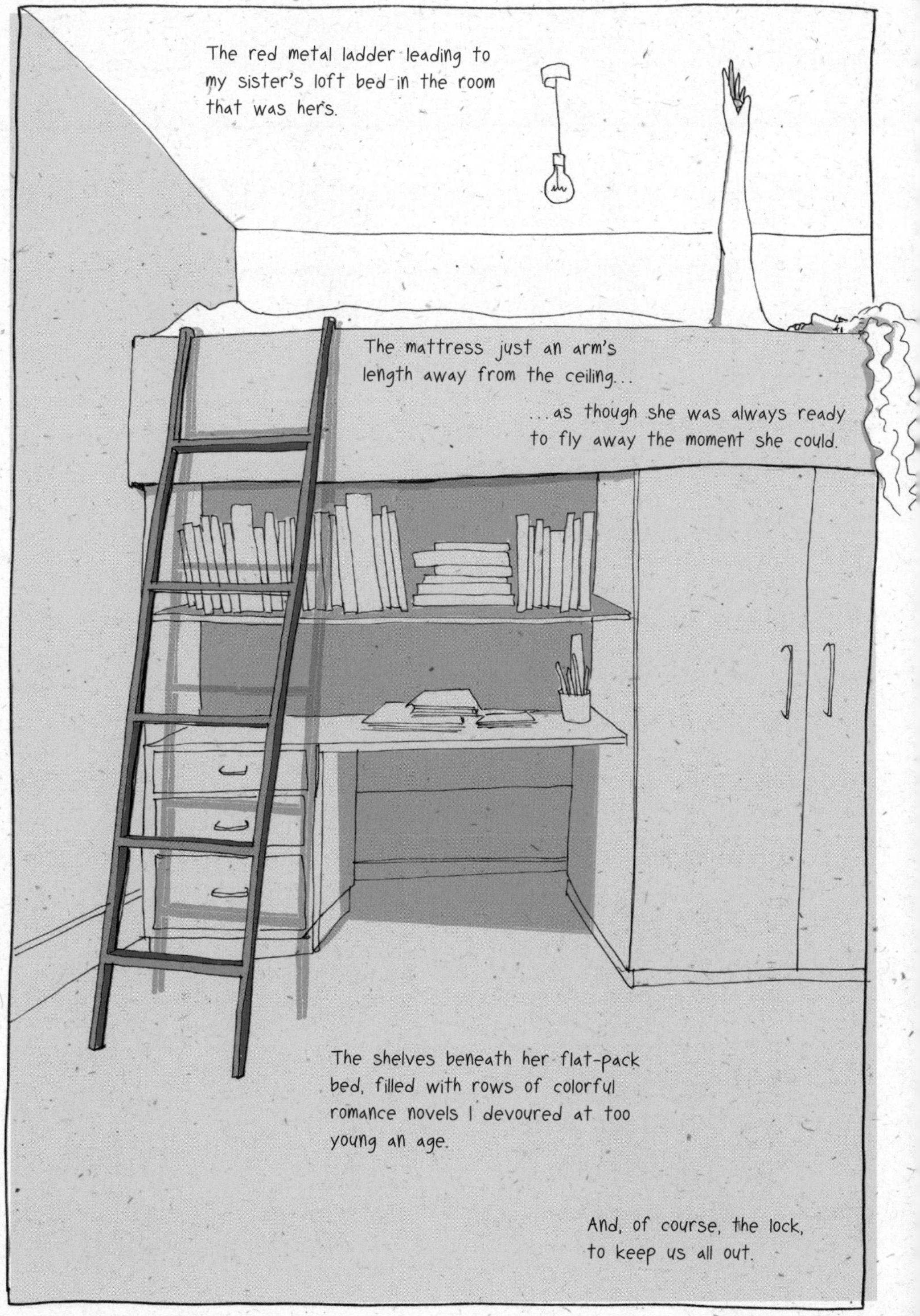
The red metal ladder leading to my sister's loft bed in the room that was hers.
The mattress just an arm's length away from the ceiling...
...as though she was always ready to fly away the moment she could.
The shelves beneath her flat-pack bed, filled with rows of colorful romance novels I devoured at too young an age.
And, of course, the lock, to keep us all out.

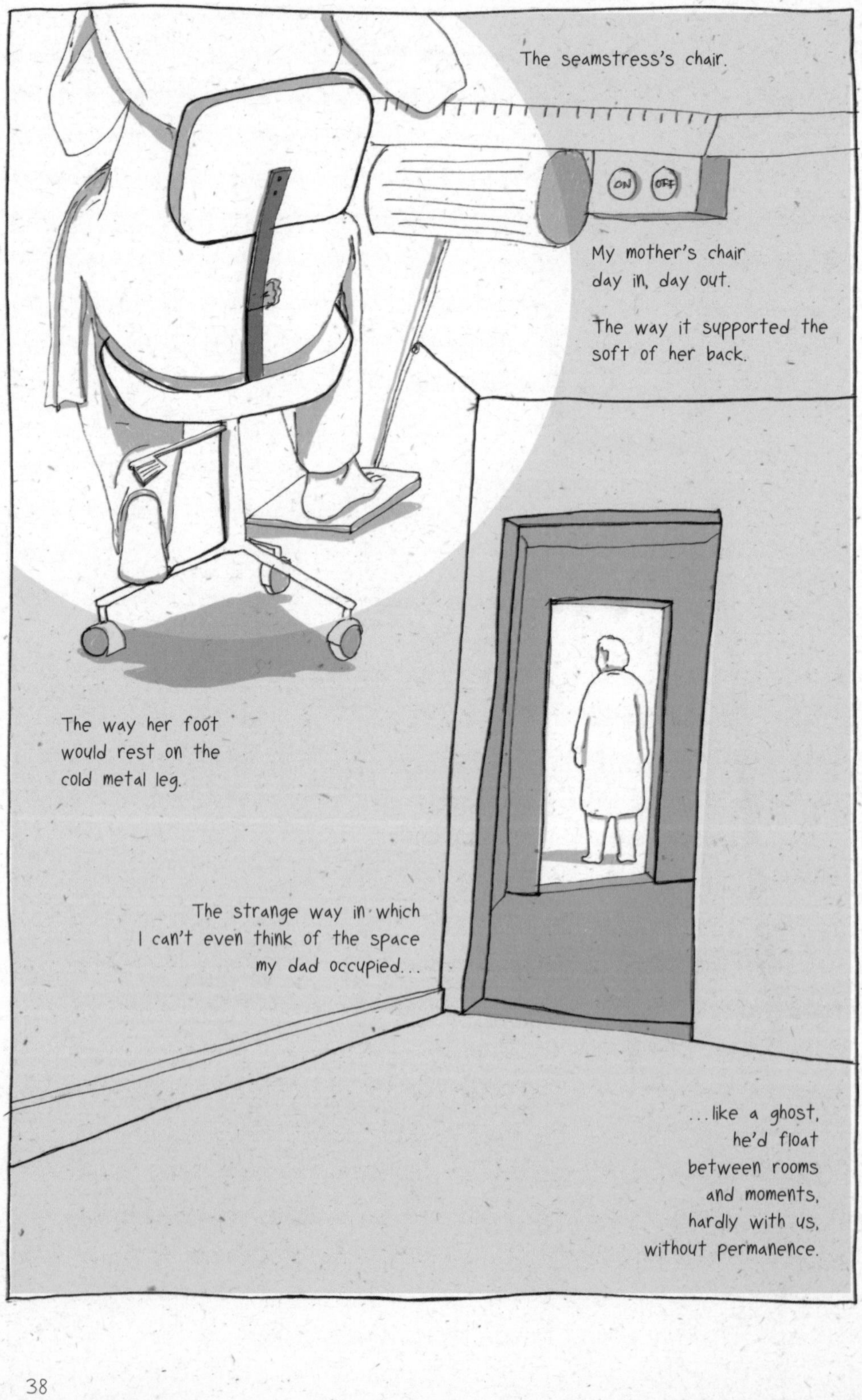
The seamstress's chair.
ON
OFF
My mother's chair
day in, day out.
The way it supported the
soft of her back.
The way her foot
would rest on the
cold metal leg.
The strange way in which
I can't even think of the space
my dad occupied...
...like a ghost,
he'd float
between rooms
and moments,
hardly with us,
without permanence.

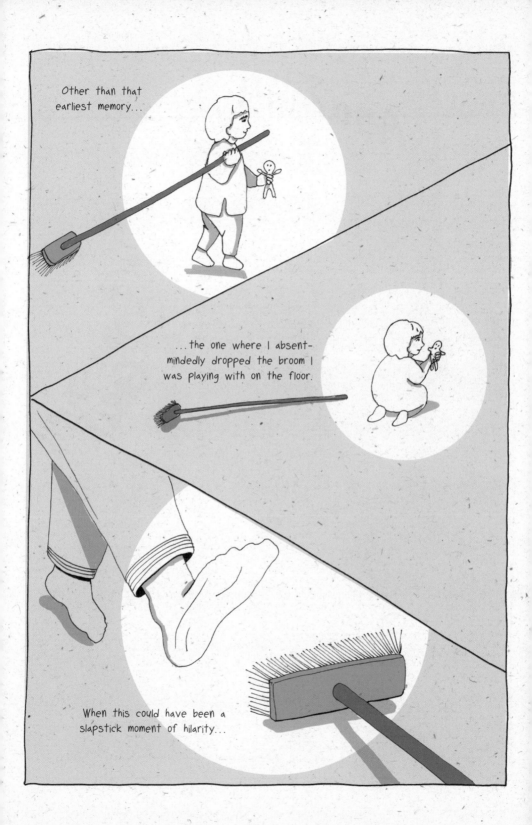

Other than that earliest memory...

...the one where I absent-mindedly dropped the broom I was playing with on the floor.

When this could have been a slapstick moment of hilarity...

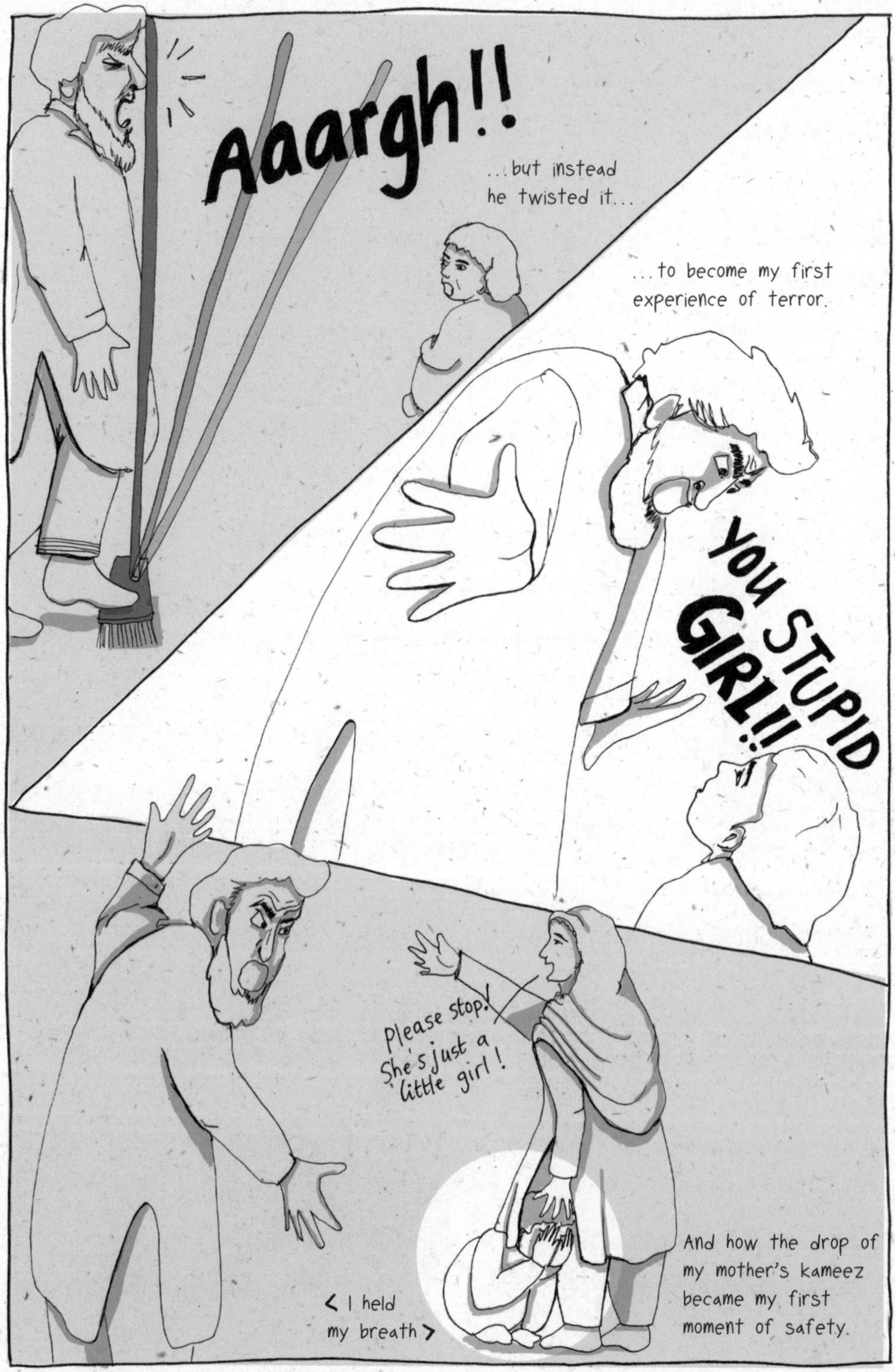
Aaargh!!
...but instead he twisted it...
...to become my first experience of terror.
YOU STUPID GIRL!!
Please stop! She's just a little girl!
< I held my breath >
And how the drop of my mother's kameez became my first moment of safety.

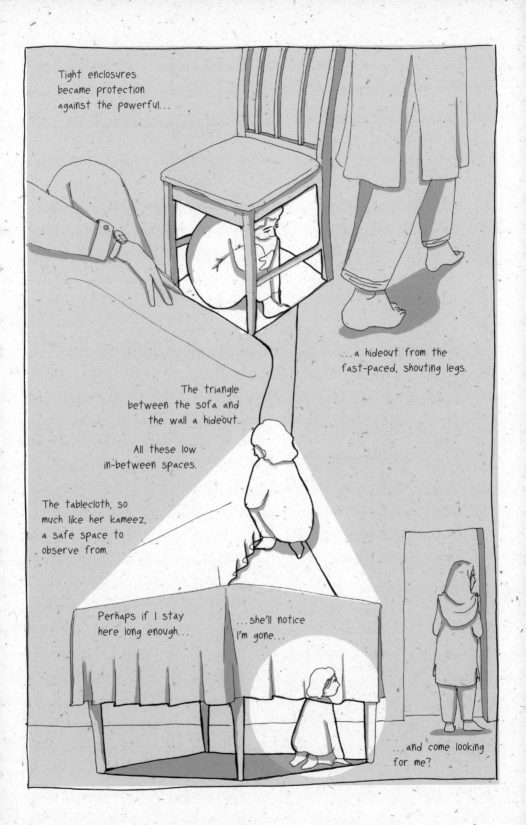

Tight enclosures became protection against the powerful...

...a hideout from the fast-paced, shouting legs.

The triangle between the sofa and the wall a hideout.

All these low in-between spaces.

The tablecloth, so much like her kameez, a safe space to observe from.

Perhaps if I stay here long enough...

...she'll notice I'm gone...

...and come looking for me?

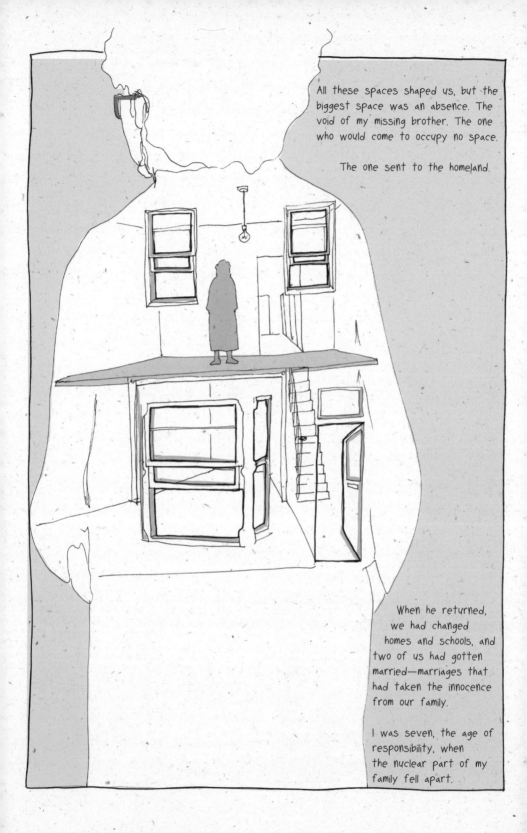

All these spaces shaped us, but the biggest space was an absence. The void of my missing brother. The one who would come to occupy no space.

The one sent to the homeland.

When he returned, we had changed homes and schools, and two of us had gotten married—marriages that had taken the innocence from our family.

I was seven, the age of responsibility, when the nuclear part of my family fell apart.

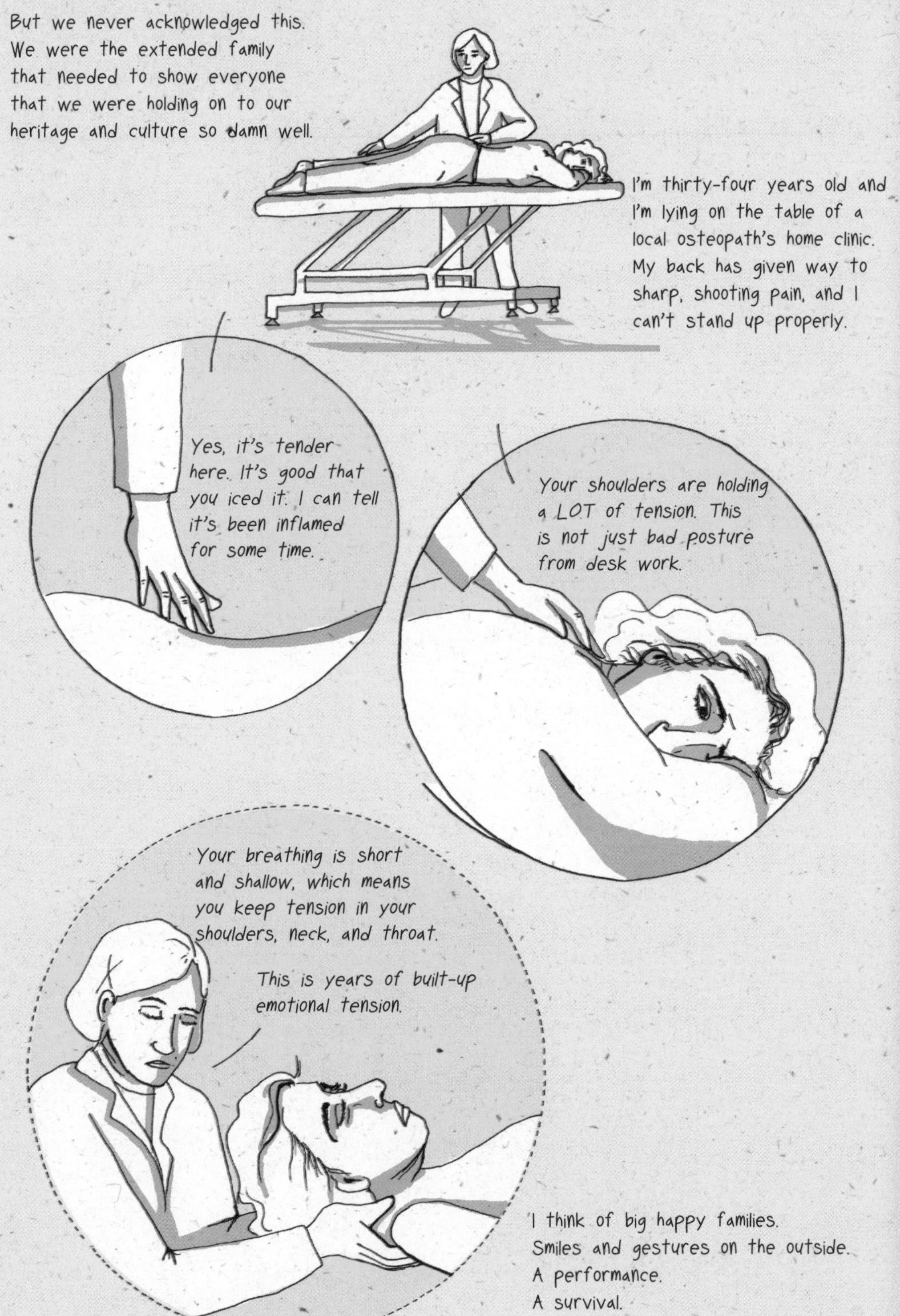
But we never acknowledged this. We were the extended family that needed to show everyone that we were holding on to our heritage and culture so damn well.
I'm thirty-four years old and I'm lying on the table of a local osteopath's home clinic. My back has given way to sharp, shooting pain, and I can't stand up properly.
Yes, it's tender here. It's good that you iced it. I can tell it's been inflamed for some time.
Your shoulders are holding a LOT of tension. This is not just bad posture from desk work.
Your breathing is short and shallow, which means you keep tension in your shoulders, neck, and throat.
This is years of built-up emotional tension.
I think of big happy families. Smiles and gestures on the outside. A performance. A survival.

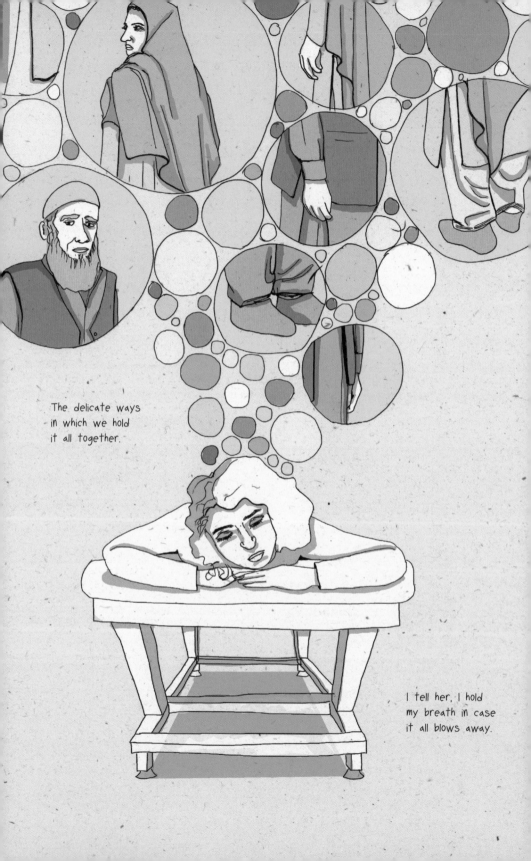

The delicate ways in which we hold it all together.

I tell her, I hold my breath in case it all blows away.

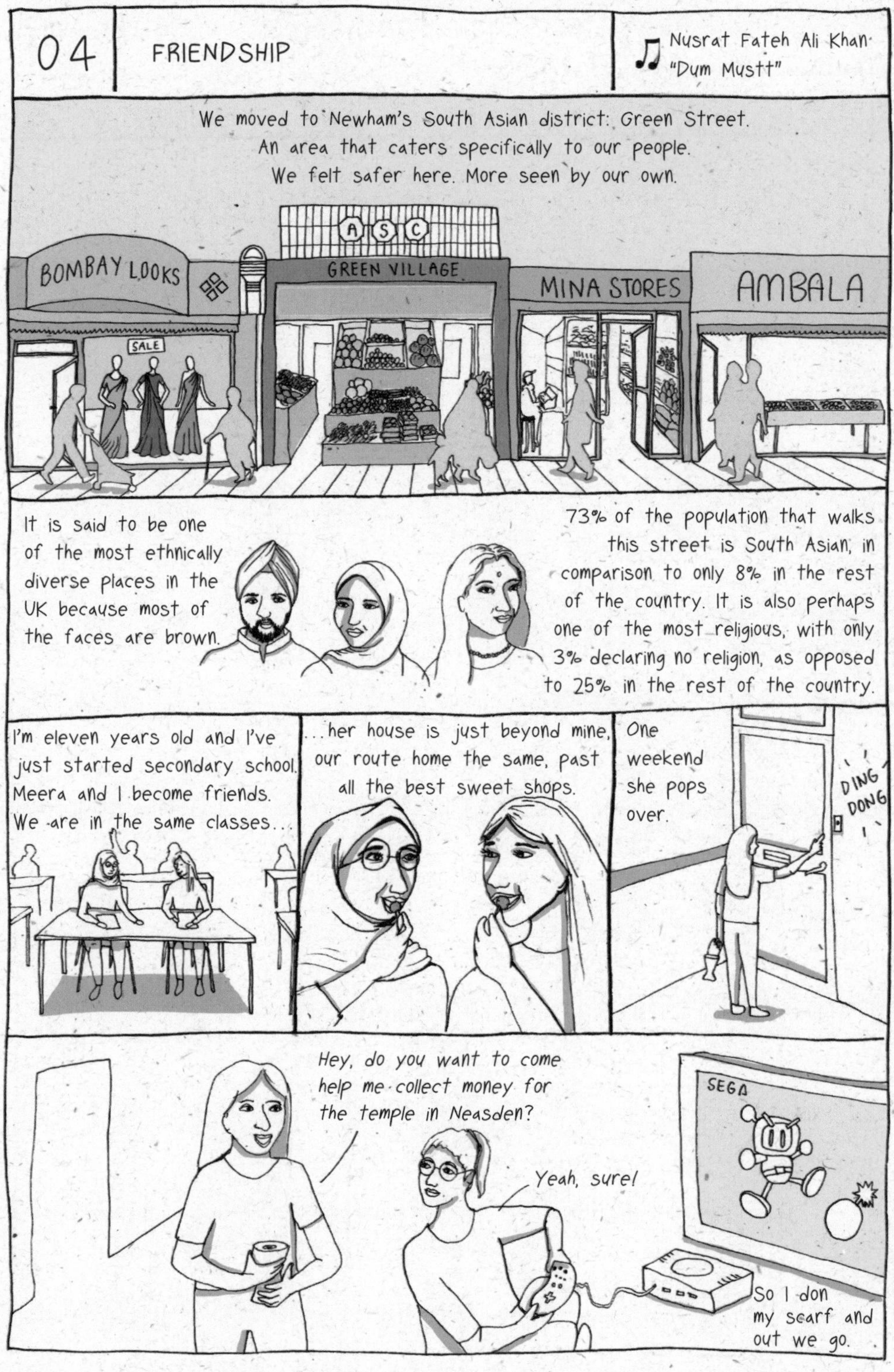
04
FRIENDSHIP
Nusrat Fateh Ali Khan
"Dum Mustt"
We moved to Newham's South Asian district: Green Street.
An area that caters specifically to our people.
We felt safer here. More seen by our own.
BOMBAY LOOKS
SALE
A S C
GREEN VILLAGE
MINA STORES
AMBALA
It is said to be one of the most ethnically diverse places in the UK because most of the faces are brown.
73% of the population that walks this street is South Asian, in comparison to only 8% in the rest of the country. It is also perhaps one of the most religious, with only 3% declaring no religion, as opposed to 25% in the rest of the country.
I'm eleven years old and I've just started secondary school. Meera and I become friends. We are in the same classes...
...her house is just beyond mine, our route home the same, past all the best sweet shops.
One weekend she pops over.
DING DONG
Hey, do you want to come help me collect money for the temple in Neasden?
Yeah, sure!
SEGA
So I don my scarf and out we go.

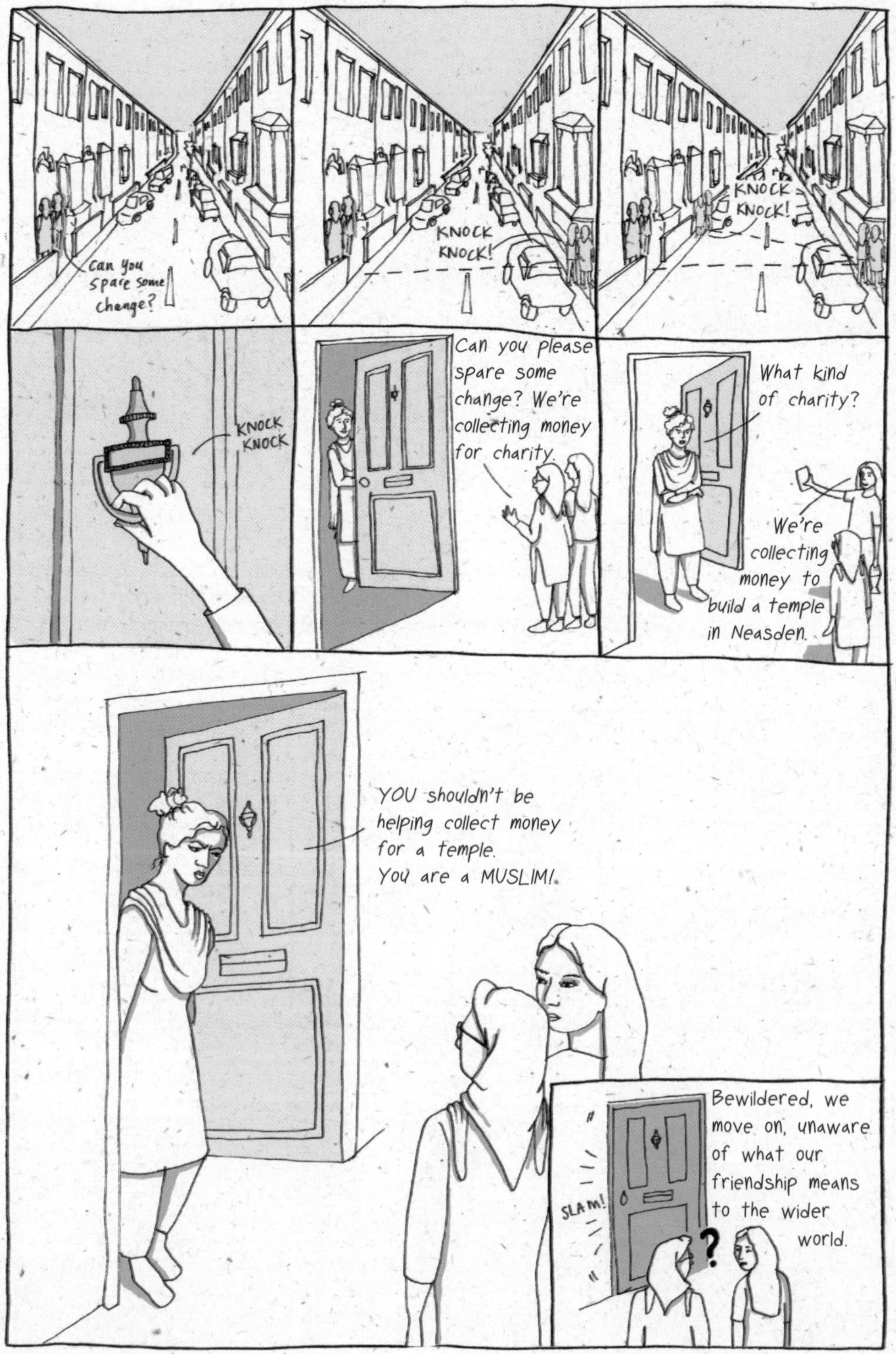
Can you spare some change?
KNOCK KNOCK!
KNOCK KNOCK!
KNOCK KNOCK
Can you please spare some change? We're collecting money for charity.
What kind of charity?
We're collecting money to build a temple in Neasden.
YOU shouldn't be helping collect money for a temple. You are a MUSLIM!
SLAM!
?
Bewildered, we move on, unaware of what our friendship means to the wider world.

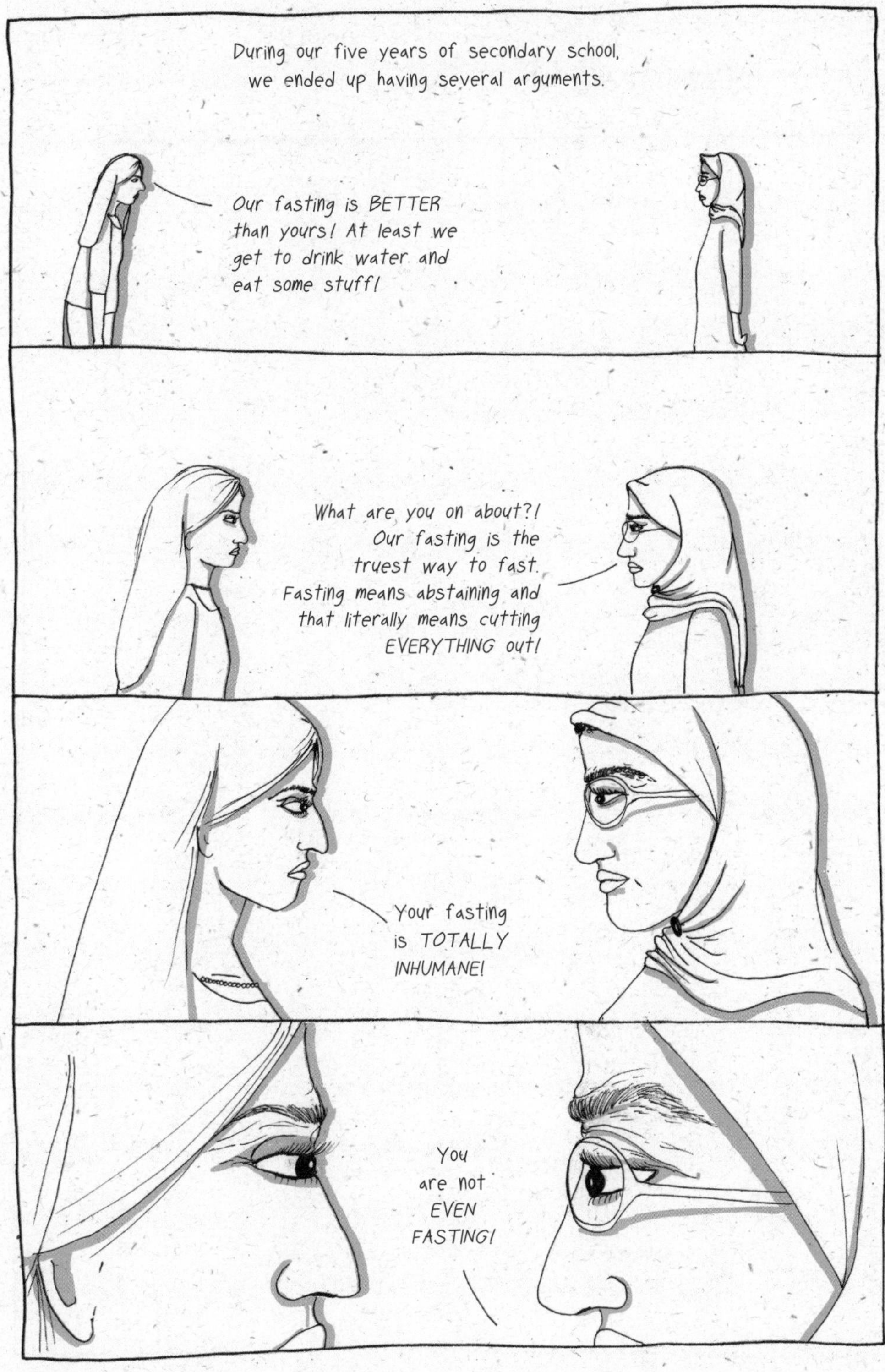
During our five years of secondary school, we ended up having several arguments.
Our fasting is BETTER than yours! At least we get to drink water and eat some stuff!
What are you on about?! Our fasting is the truest way to fast. Fasting means abstaining and that literally means cutting EVERYTHING out!
Your fasting is TOTALLY INHUMANE!
You are not EVEN FASTING!

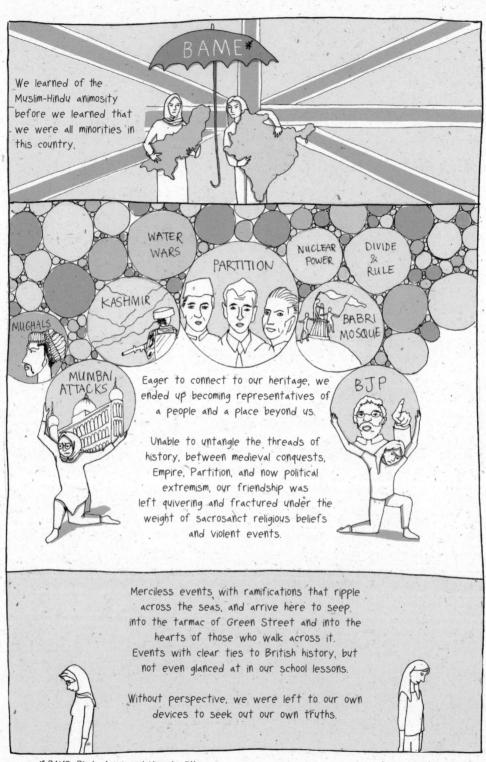

We learned of the Muslim-Hindu animosity before we learned that we were all minorities in this country.

BAME*

WATER WARS

PARTITION

NUCLEAR POWER

DIVIDE & RULE

KASHMIR

MUGHALS

BABRI MOSQUE

MUMBAI ATTACKS

BJP

Eager to connect to our heritage, we ended up becoming representatives of a people and a place beyond us.

Unable to untangle the threads of history, between medieval conquests, Empire, Partition, and now political extremism, our friendship was left quivering and fractured under the weight of sacrosanct religious beliefs and violent events.

Merciless events with ramifications that ripple across the seas, and arrive here to seep into the tarmac of Green Street and into the hearts of those who walk across it. Events with clear ties to British history, but not even glanced at in our school lessons.

Without perspective, we were left to our own devices to seek out our own truths.

* BAME: Black, Asian, and Minority Ethnic

48

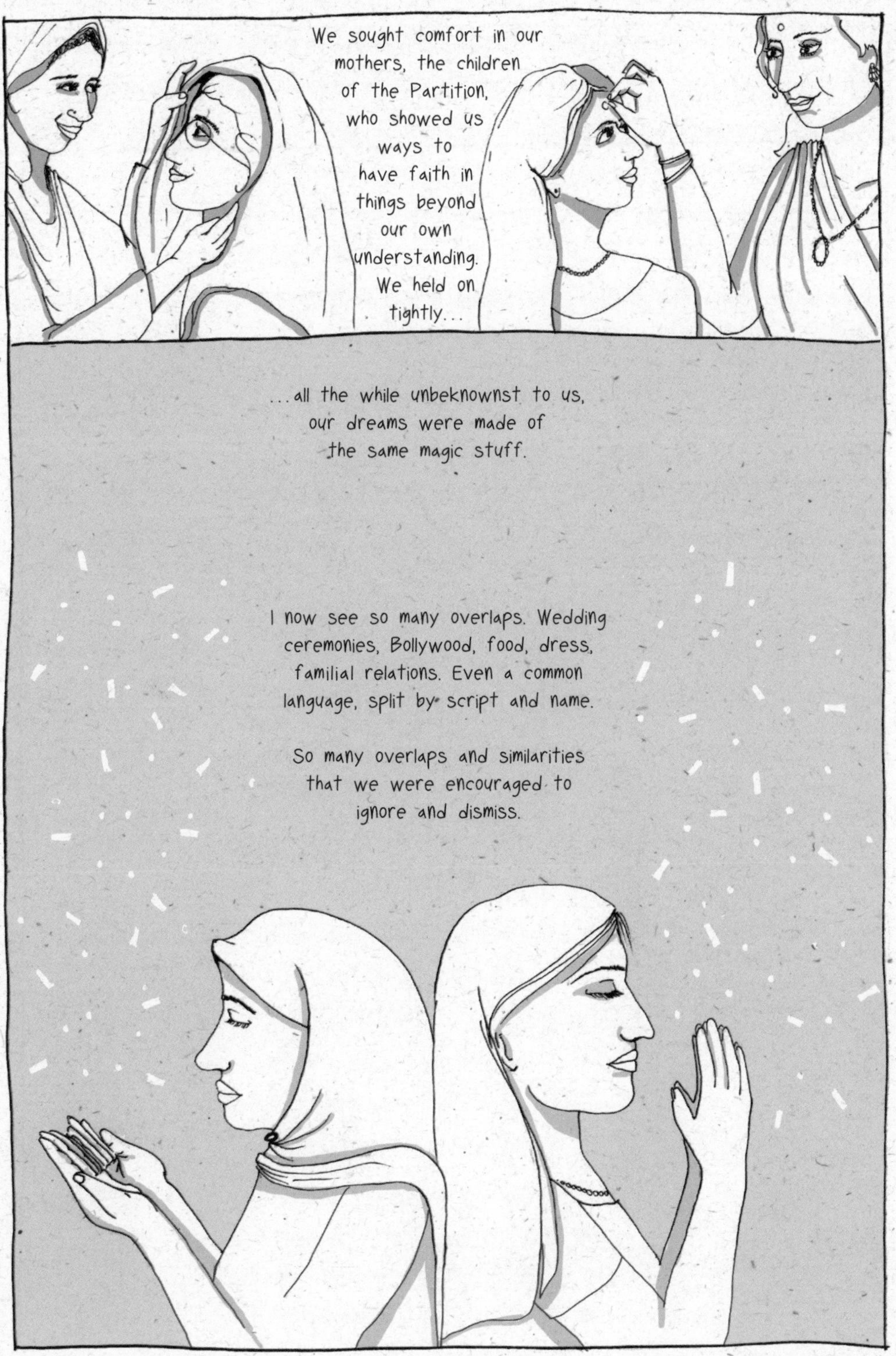
We sought comfort in our mothers, the children of the Partition, who showed us ways to have faith in things beyond our own understanding. We held on tightly...
...all the while unbeknownst to us, our dreams were made of the same magic stuff.
I now see so many overlaps. Wedding ceremonies, Bollywood, food, dress, familial relations. Even a common language, split by script and name.
So many overlaps and similarities that we were encouraged to ignore and dismiss.

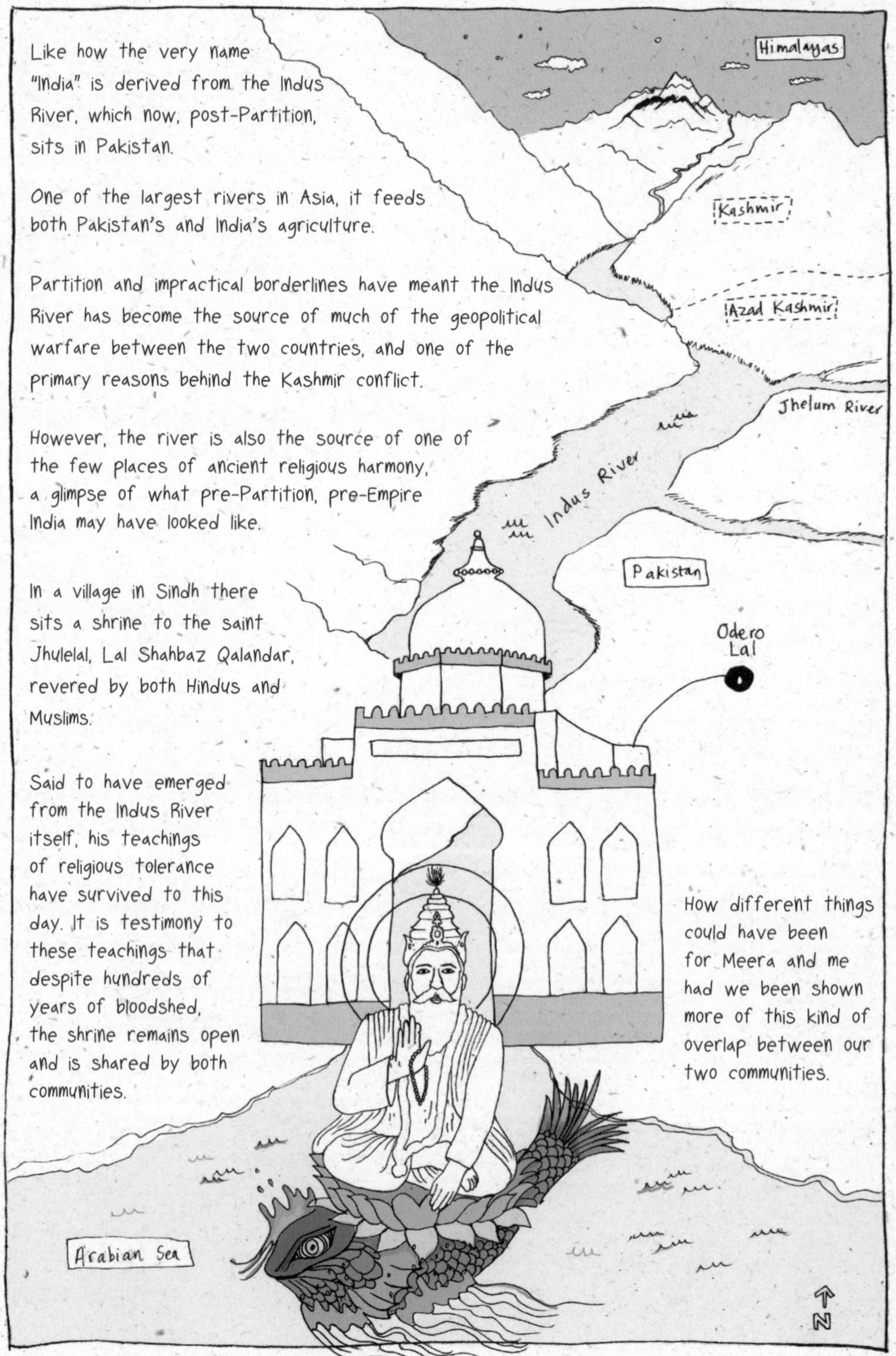
Like how the very name "India" is derived from the Indus River, which now, post-Partition, sits in Pakistan.
One of the largest rivers in Asia, it feeds both Pakistan's and India's agriculture.
Partition and impractical borderlines have meant the Indus River has become the source of much of the geopolitical warfare between the two countries, and one of the primary reasons behind the Kashmir conflict.
However, the river is also the source of one of the few places of ancient religious harmony, a glimpse of what pre-Partition, pre-Empire India may have looked like.
In a village in Sindh there sits a shrine to the saint Jhulelal, Lal Shahbaz Qalandar, revered by both Hindus and Muslims.
Said to have emerged from the Indus River itself, his teachings of religious tolerance have survived to this day. It is testimony to these teachings that despite hundreds of years of bloodshed, the shrine remains open and is shared by both communities.
Himalayas
Kashmir
Azad Kashmir
Jhelum River
Indus River
Pakistan
Odero Lal
How different things could have been for Meera and me had we been shown more of this kind of overlap between our two communities.
Arabian Sea
N

How did we stay in this
bubble for so long?

If Newham is one of the
most diverse boroughs in
the country...

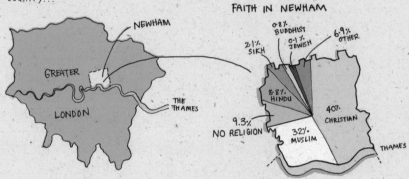

FAITH IN NEWHAM

0.8% BUDDHIST
6.9% OTHER
2.1% SIKH
0.1% JEWISH
8.8% HINDU
40% CHRISTIAN
9.3% NO RELIGION
32% MUSLIM
THAMES

GREATER
LONDON
NEWHAM
THE THAMES

...why did it take until going to
university for this South Asian
diaspora bubble to burst for me?

And what of those
who never get to go
to university, like so many
of the people in my family?

I often wondered why my year group was predominantly brown, with a sprinkling of black and white kids.

Where'd they all go? I'd ask myself...

Our home was walking distance from six different schools.

SARAH BONNELL
ST. ANGELA'S
STRATFORD
FOREST GATE
ST. BON'S
LISTER

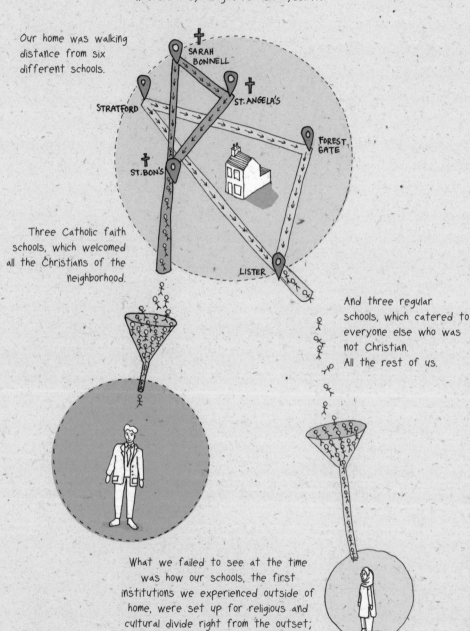

Three Catholic faith schools, which welcomed all the Christians of the neighborhood.

And three regular schools, which catered to everyone else who was not Christian.
All the rest of us.

What we failed to see at the time was how our schools, the first institutions we experienced outside of home, were set up for religious and cultural divide right from the outset; we lived side by side, but worlds apart in one of the most diverse boroughs of the country.

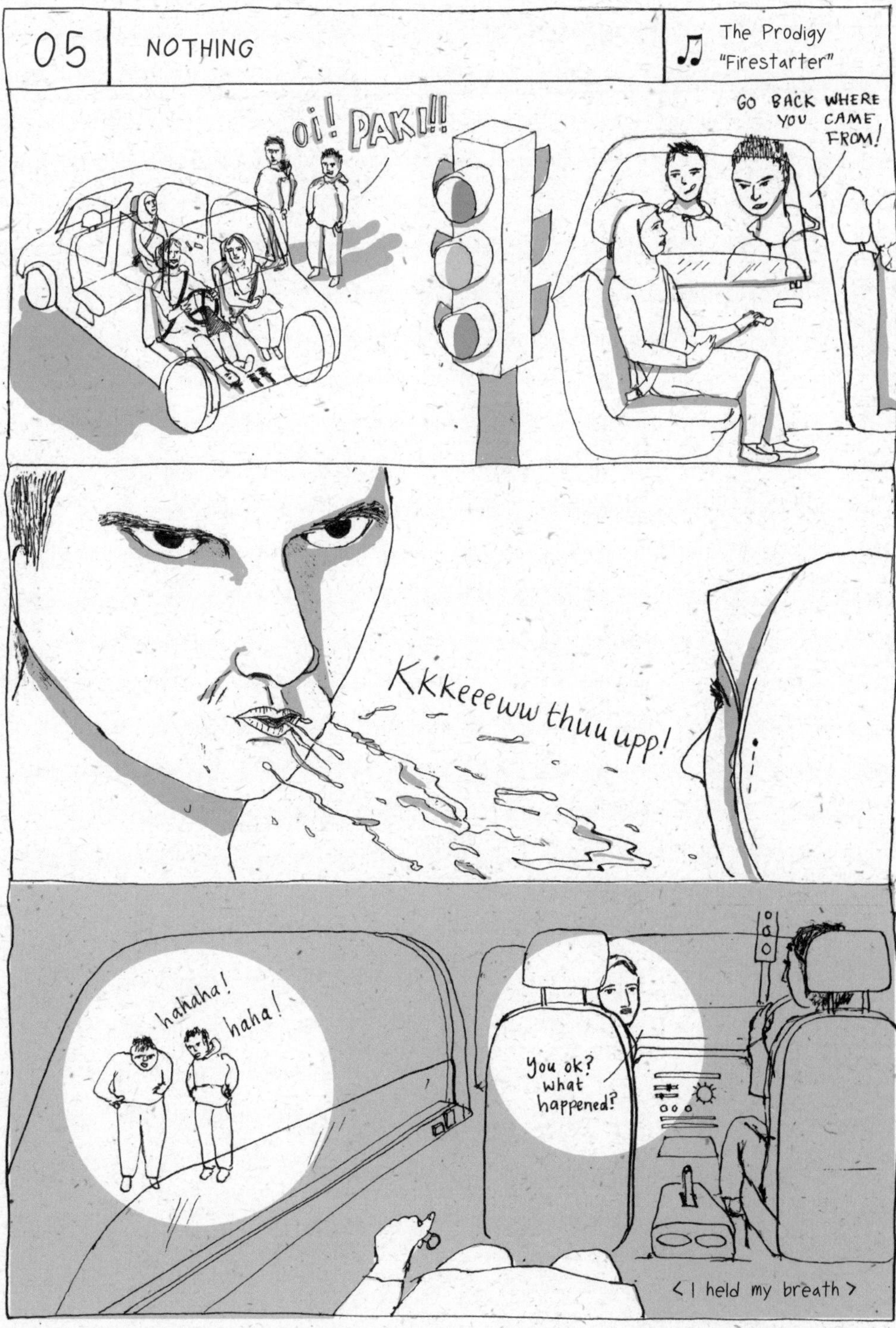
05
NOTHING
The Prodigy
"Firestarter"
oi! PAKI!!
GO BACK WHERE YOU CAME FROM!
Kkkeeeww thuu upp!
hahaha!
haha!
You ok? what happened?
< I held my breath >

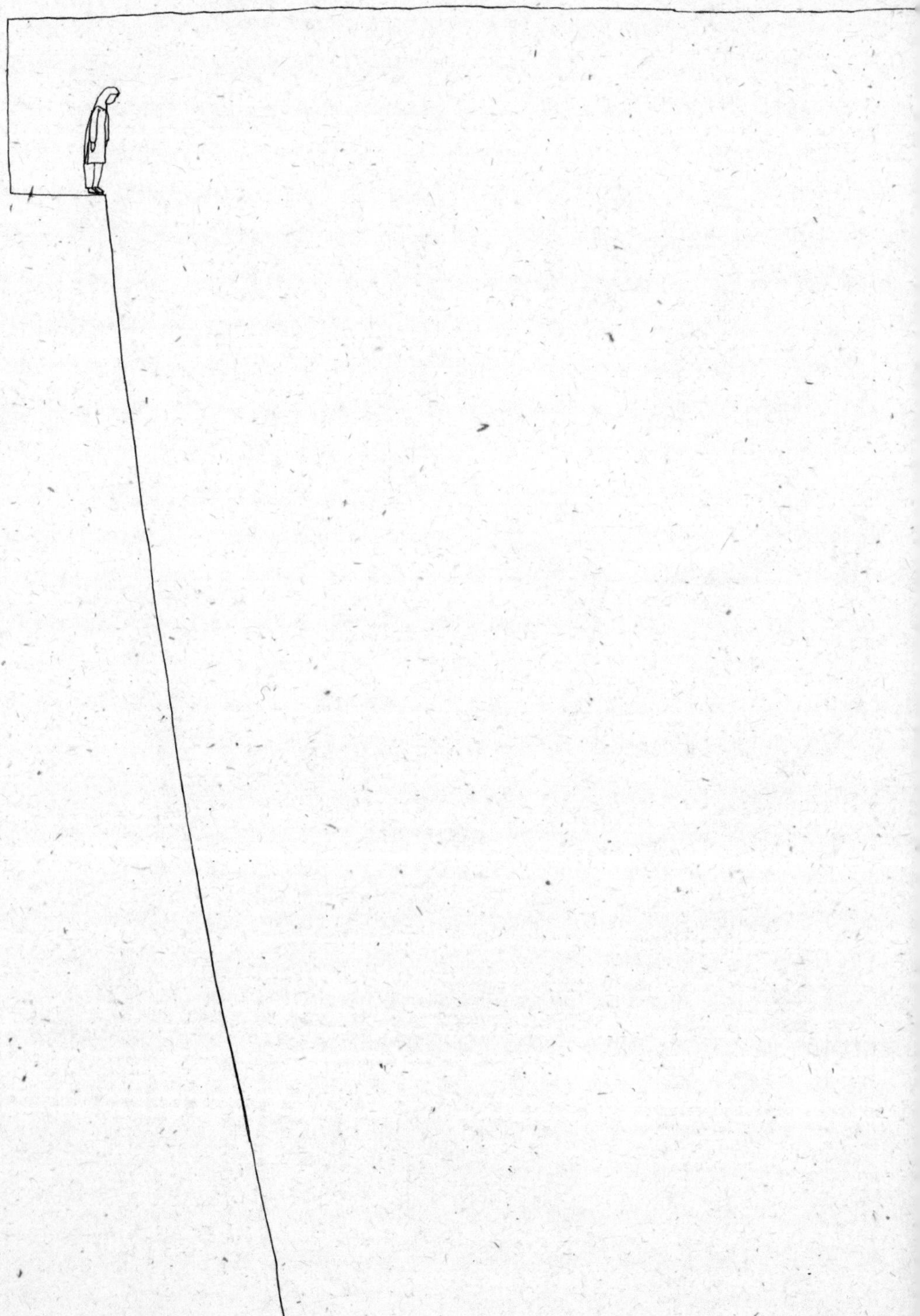

Nothing.

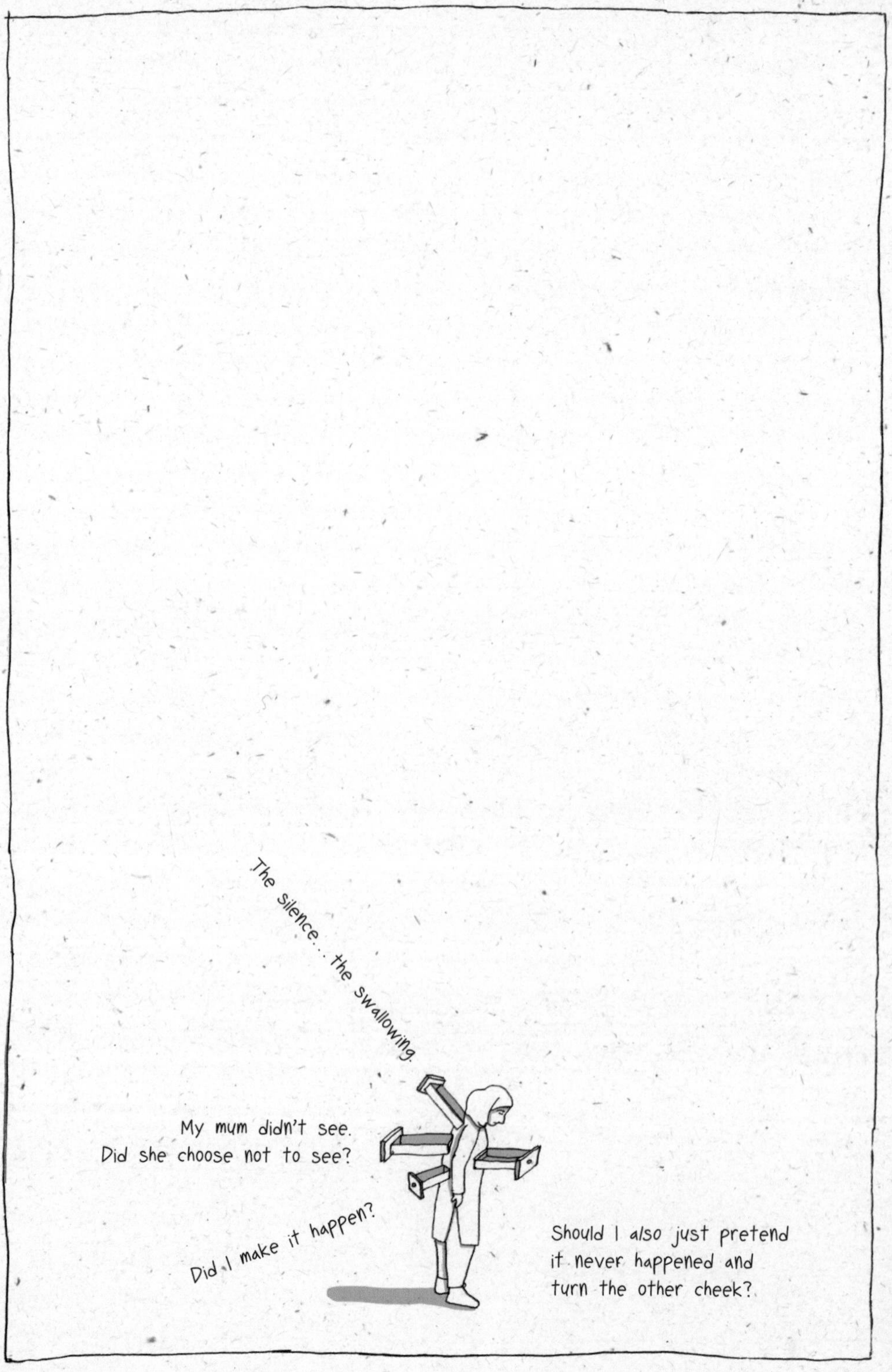
The silence... the swallowing.
My mum didn't see.
Did she choose not to see?
Did I make it happen?
Should I also just pretend
it never happened and
turn the other cheek?

My mother,
my home.

The home they tell
me to go back to.

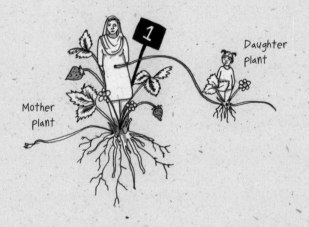

Mother
Plant

Daughter
Plant

Like strawberries,
we grow...

...offshoots of
each other.

Am I the second generation of growth? Or the first generation within this host culture?

Is it the legacy of the journey or the act of assimilation that is of most value to our sense of self?

Am I looking back to her, my roots, or looking forward to this new, alien, hostile space?

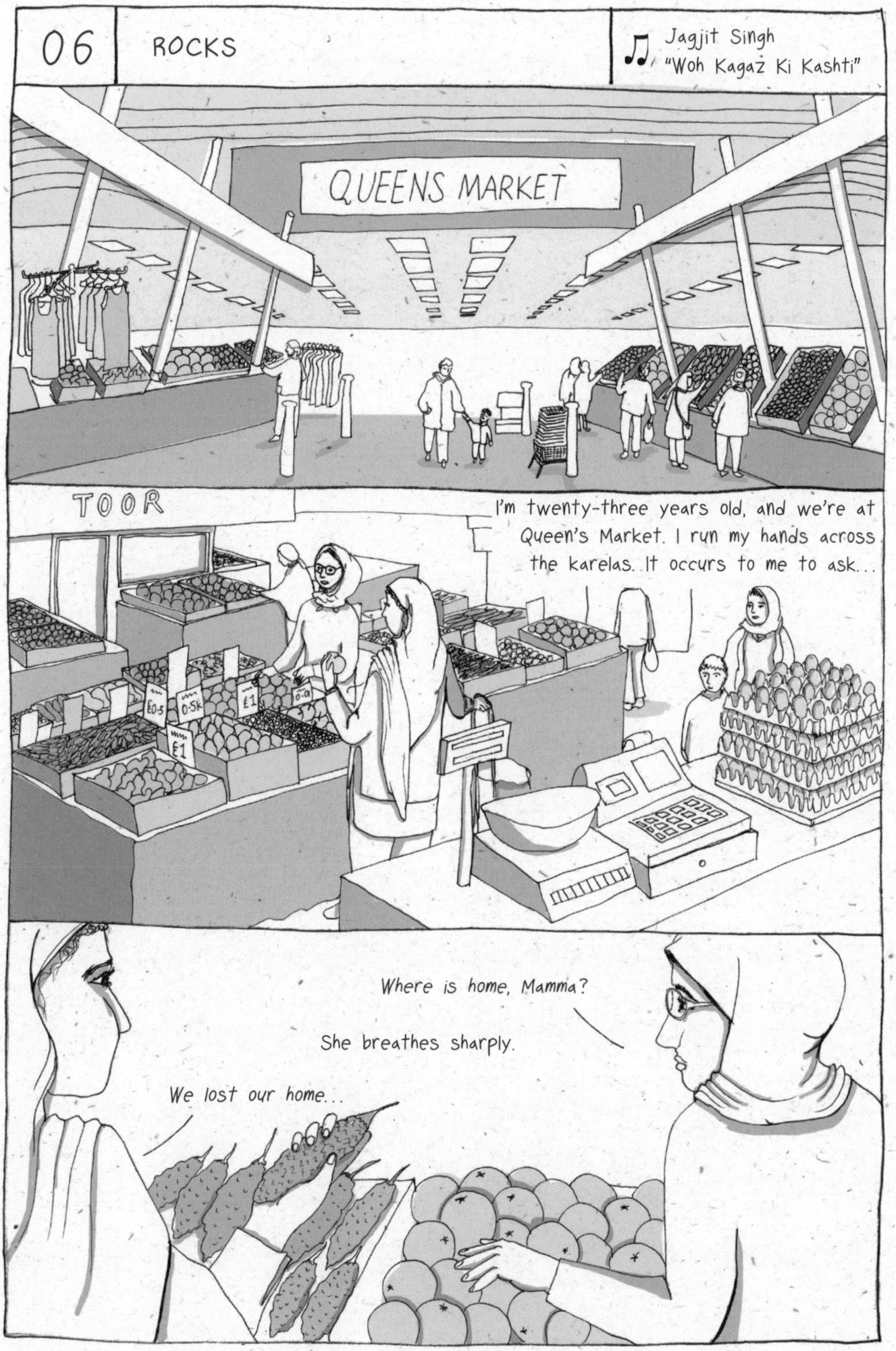
06
ROCKS
Jagjit Singh
"Woh Kagaz Ki Kashti"
QUEENS MARKET
TOOR
I'm twenty-three years old, and we're at Queen's Market. I run my hands across the karelas. It occurs to me to ask...
£0.5
0.5k
£1
£1
Where is home, Mamma?
She breathes sharply.
We lost our home...

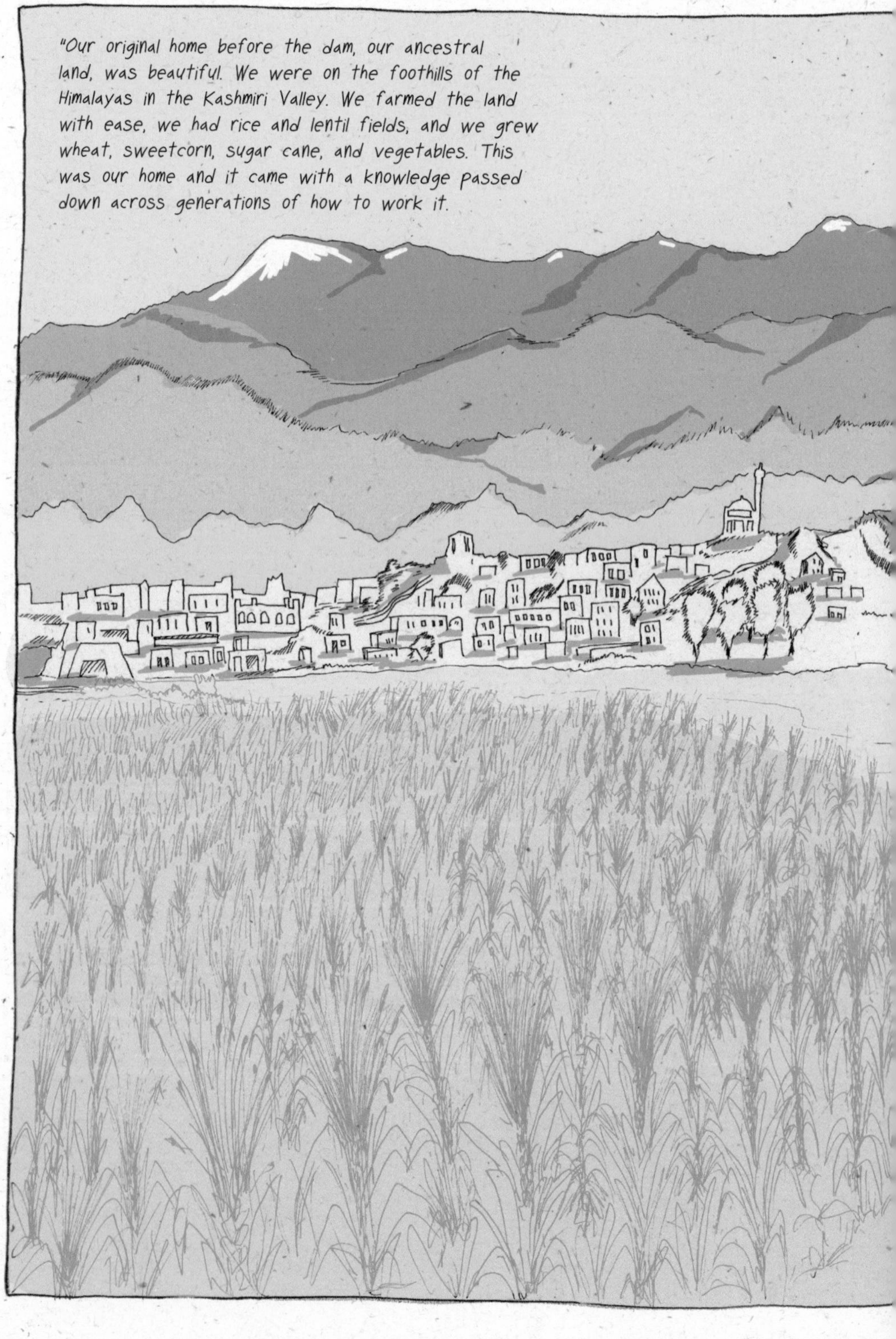
"Our original home before the dam, our ancestral land, was beautiful. We were on the foothills of the Himalayas in the Kashmiri Valley. We farmed the land with ease, we had rice and lentil fields, and we grew wheat, sweetcorn, sugar cane, and vegetables. This was our home and it came with a knowledge passed down across generations of how to work it.

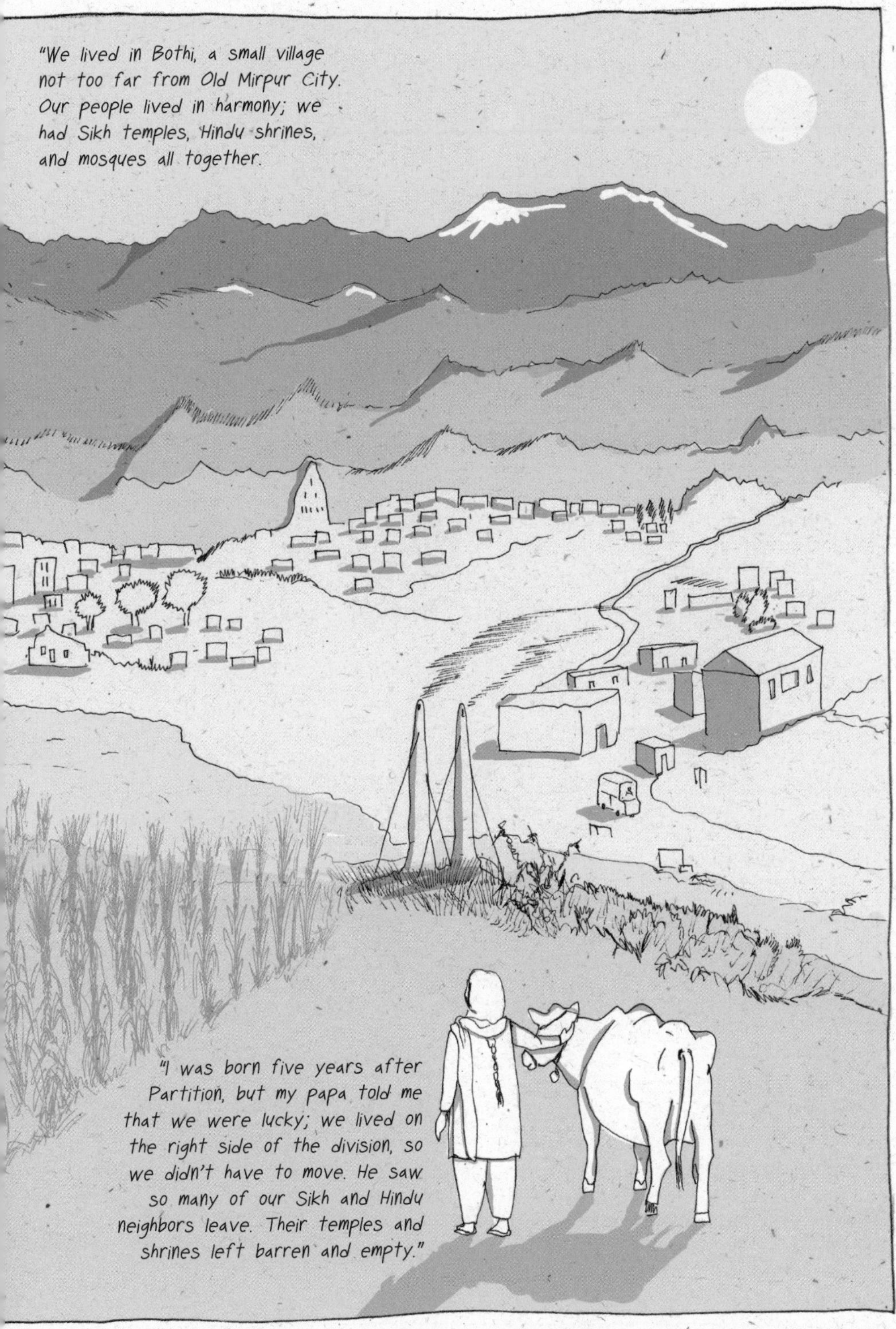
"We lived in Bothi, a small village not too far from Old Mirpur City. Our people lived in harmony; we had Sikh temples, Hindu shrines, and mosques all together.
"I was born five years after Partition, but my papa told me that we were lucky; we lived on the right side of the division, so we didn't have to move. He saw so many of our Sikh and Hindu neighbors leave. Their temples and shrines left barren and empty."

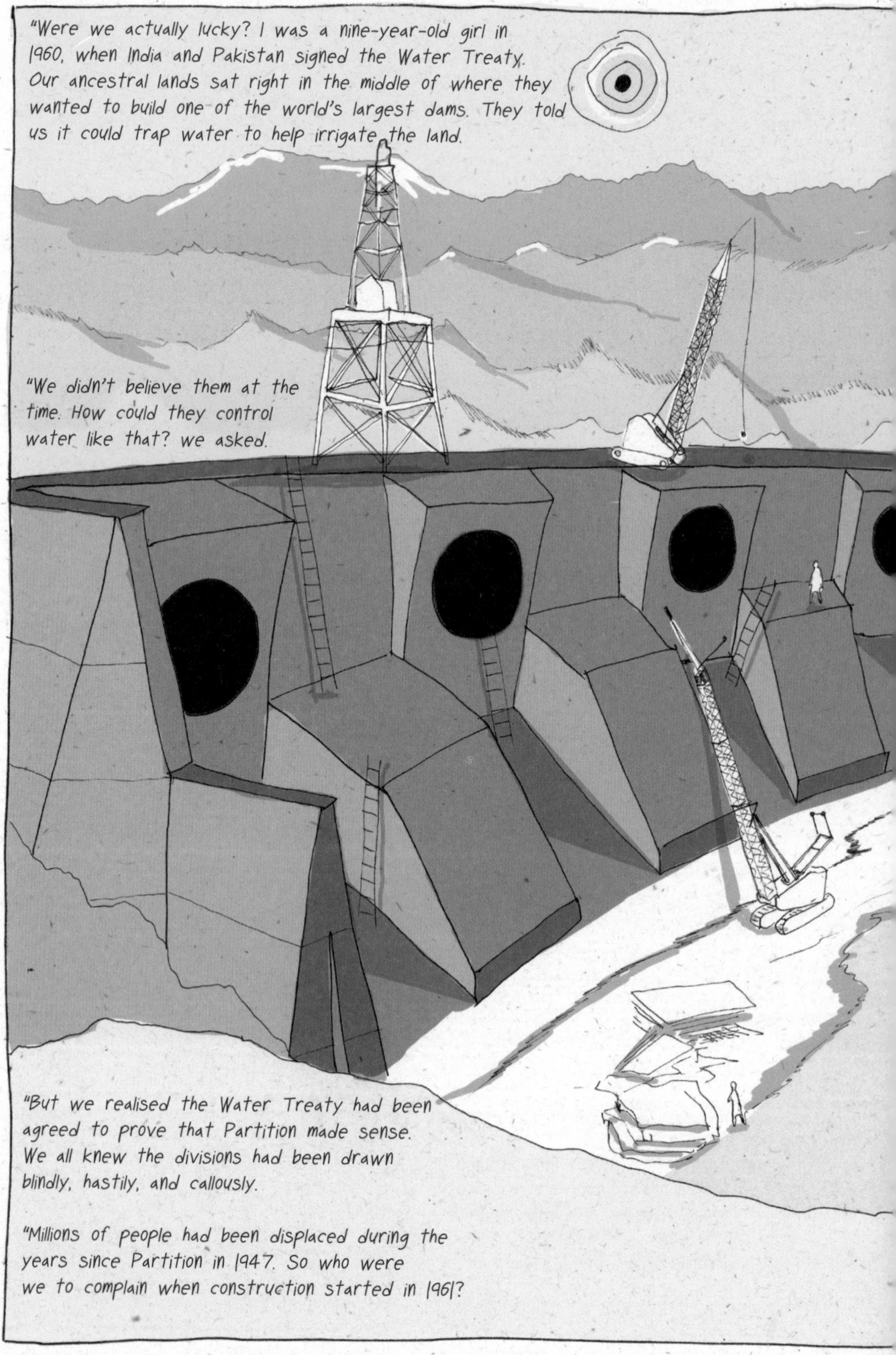
"Were we actually lucky? I was a nine-year-old girl in 1960, when India and Pakistan signed the Water Treaty. Our ancestral lands sat right in the middle of where they wanted to build one of the world's largest dams. They told us it could trap water to help irrigate the land.
"We didn't believe them at the time. How could they control water like that? we asked.
"But we realised the Water Treaty had been agreed to prove that Partition made sense. We all knew the divisions had been drawn blindly, hastily, and callously.
"Millions of people had been displaced during the years since Partition in 1947. So who were we to complain when construction started in 1961?

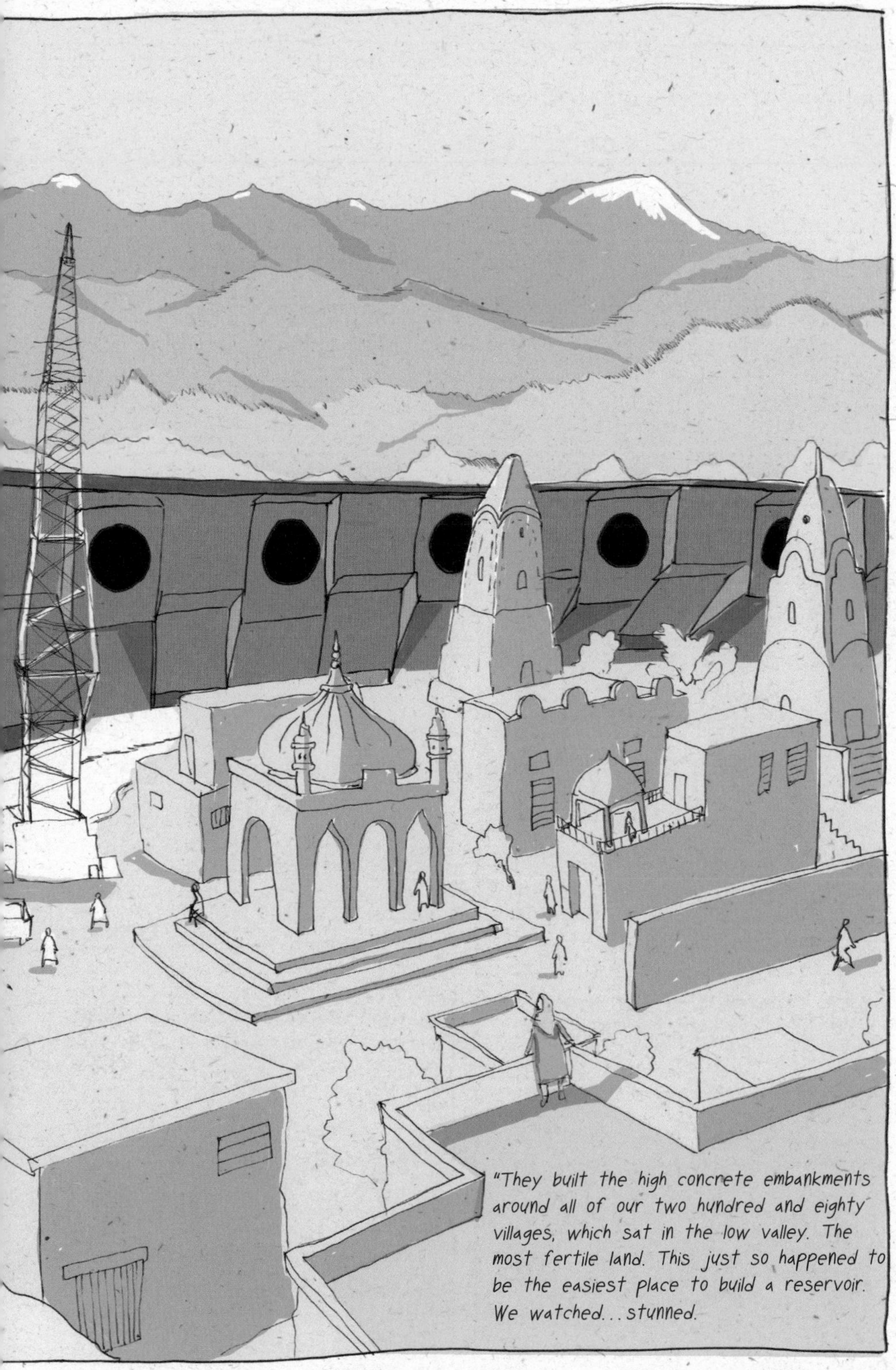
"They built the high concrete embankments around all of our two hundred and eighty villages, which sat in the low valley. The most fertile land. This just so happened to be the easiest place to build a reservoir. We watched... stunned.

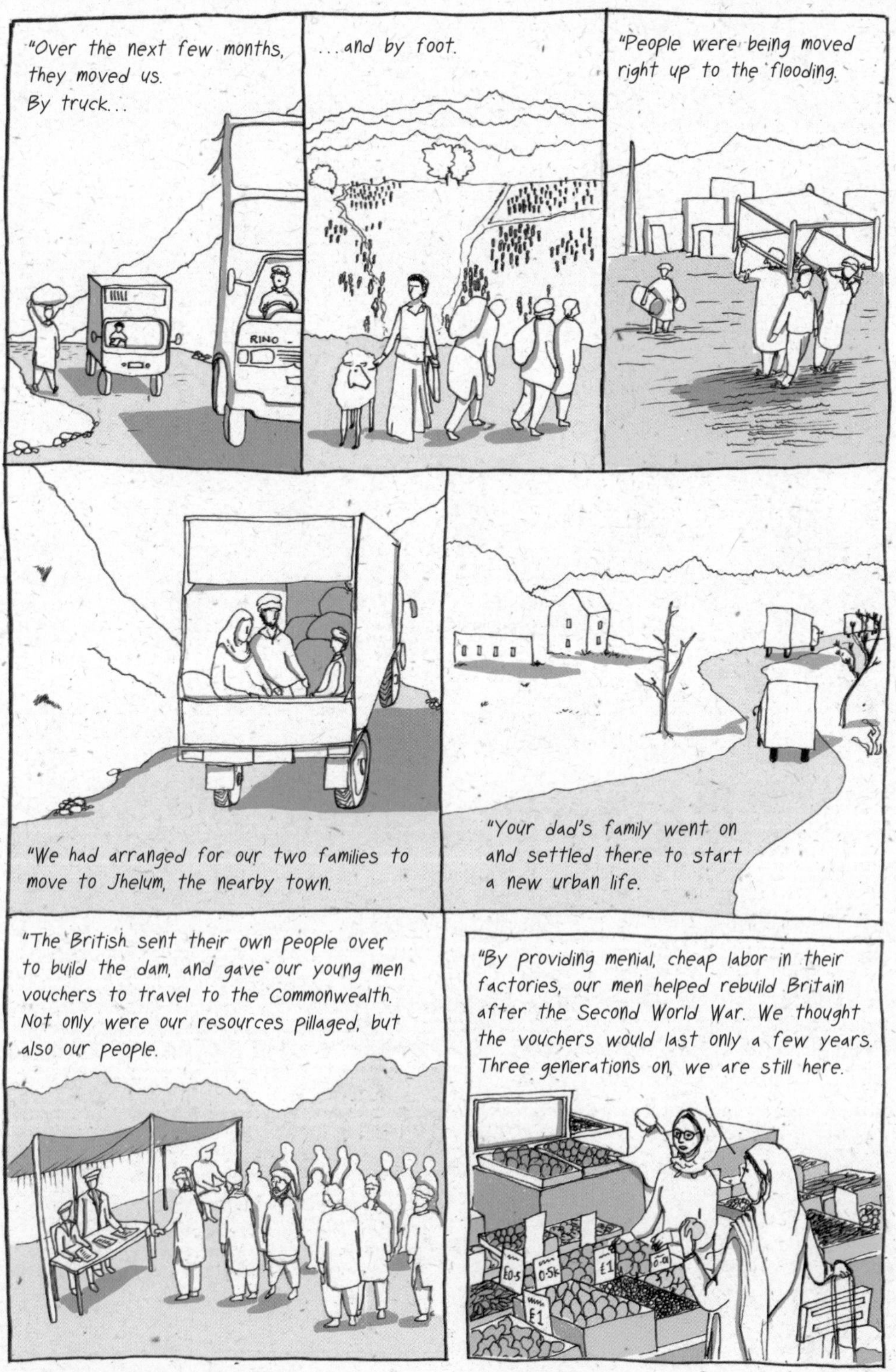
"Over the next few months, they moved us. By truck...
RINO
...and by foot.
"People were being moved right up to the flooding.
"We had arranged for our two families to move to Jhelum, the nearby town.
"Your dad's family went on and settled there to start a new urban life.
"The British sent their own people over to build the dam, and gave our young men vouchers to travel to the Commonwealth. Not only were our resources pillaged, but also our people.
"By providing menial, cheap labor in their factories, our men helped rebuild Britain after the Second World War. We thought the vouchers would last only a few years. Three generations on, we are still here.
£0.5
£1
£1

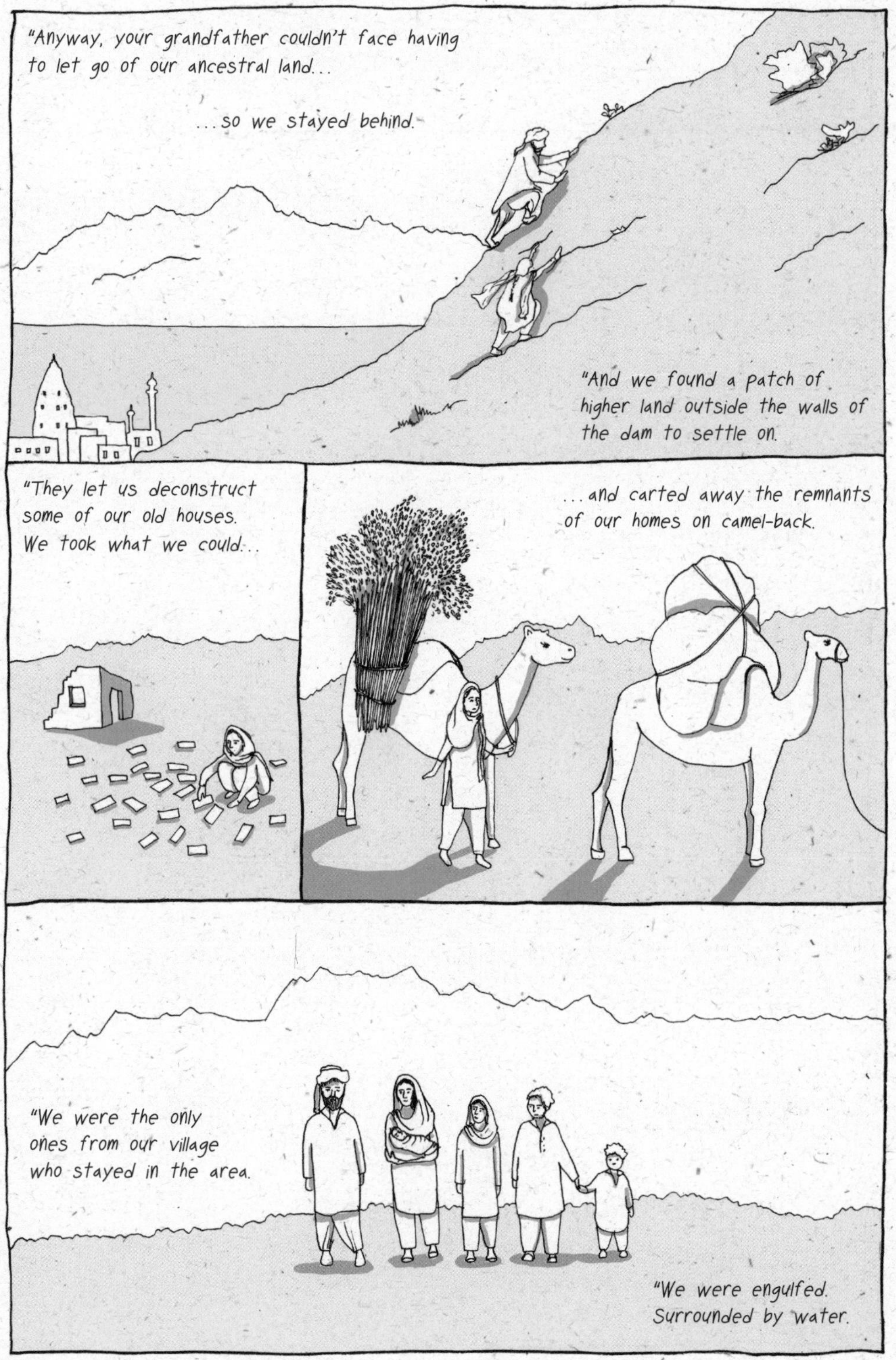
"Anyway, your grandfather couldn't face having to let go of our ancestral land...
...so we stayed behind.
"And we found a patch of higher land outside the walls of the dam to settle on.
"They let us deconstruct some of our old houses. We took what we could...
...and carted away the remnants of our homes on camel-back.
"We were the only ones from our village who stayed in the area.
"We were engulfed. Surrounded by water.

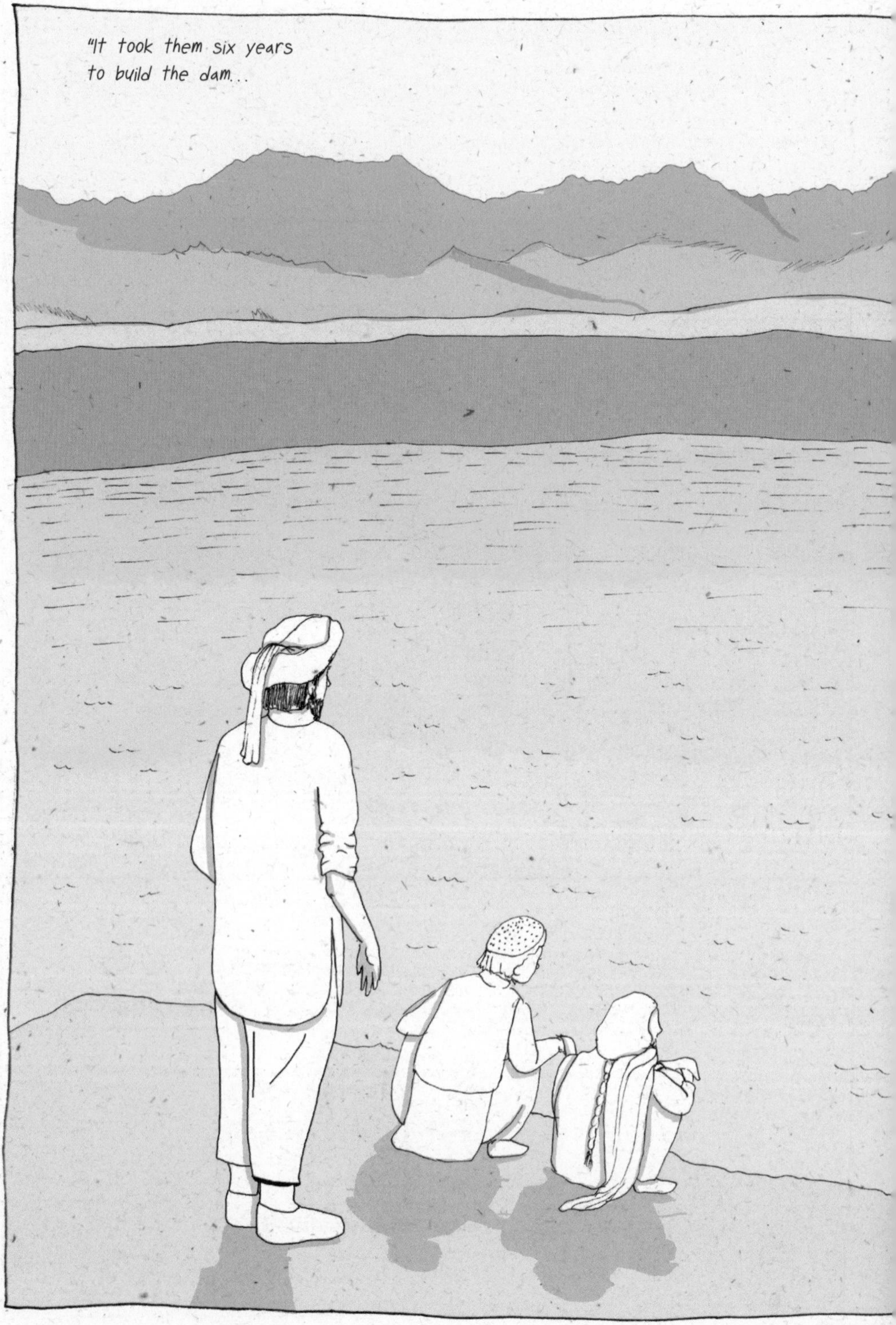
"It took them six years
to build the dam...

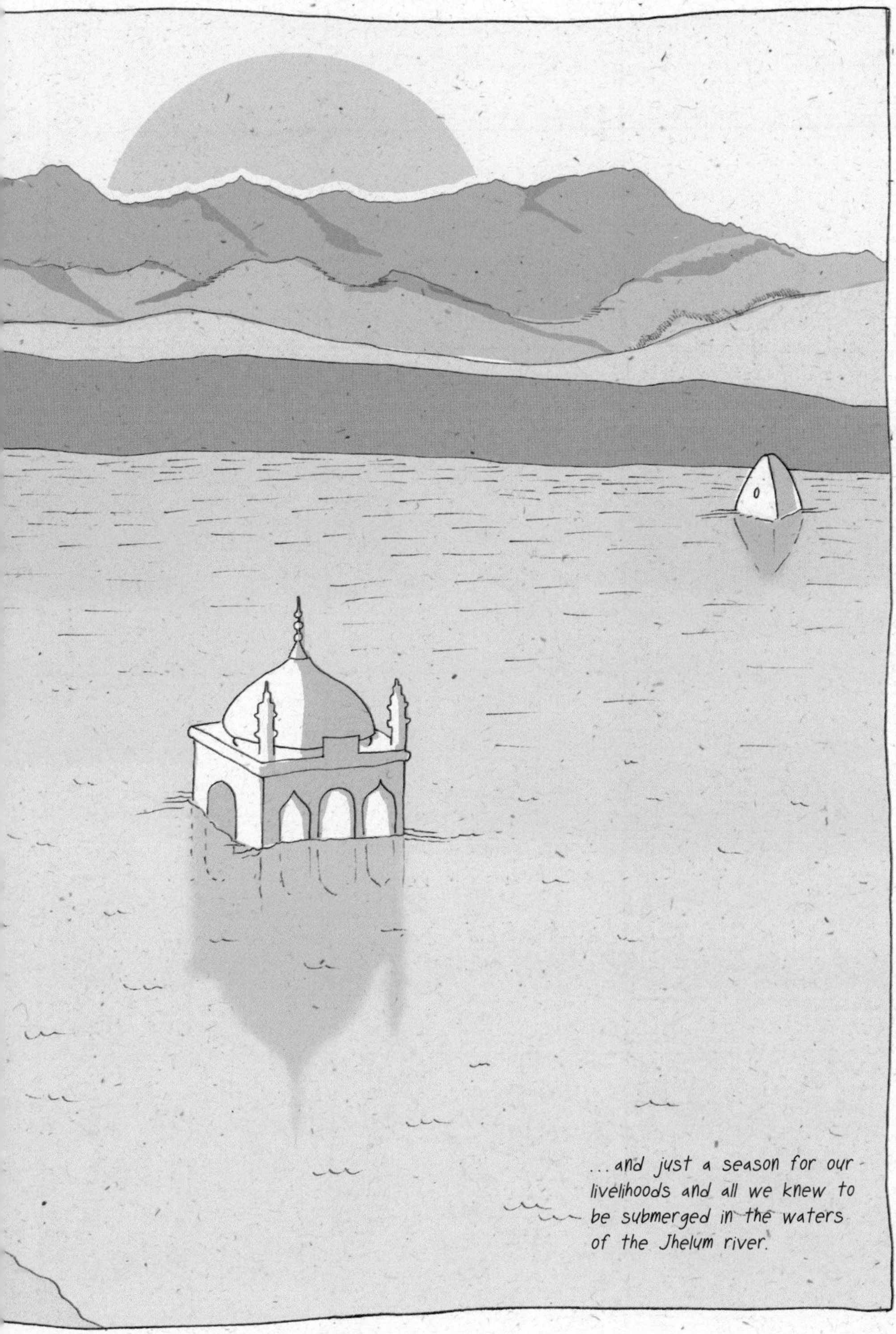
...and just a season for our livelihoods and all we knew to be submerged in the waters of the Jhelum river.

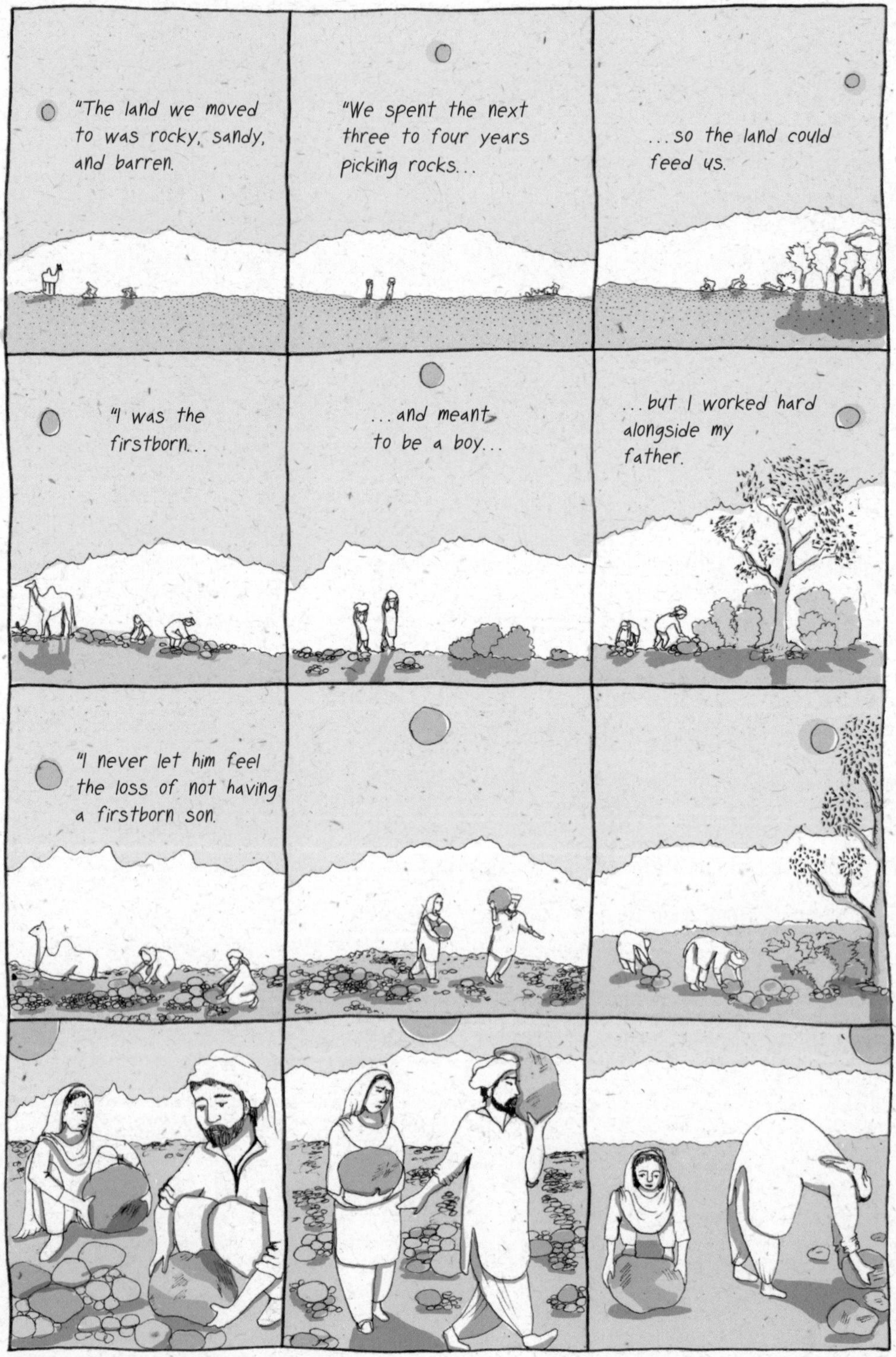
"The land we moved to was rocky, sandy, and barren.
"We spent the next three to four years picking rocks...
...so the land could feed us.
"I was the firstborn...
...and meant to be a boy...
...but I worked hard alongside my father.
"I never let him feel the loss of not having a firstborn son.

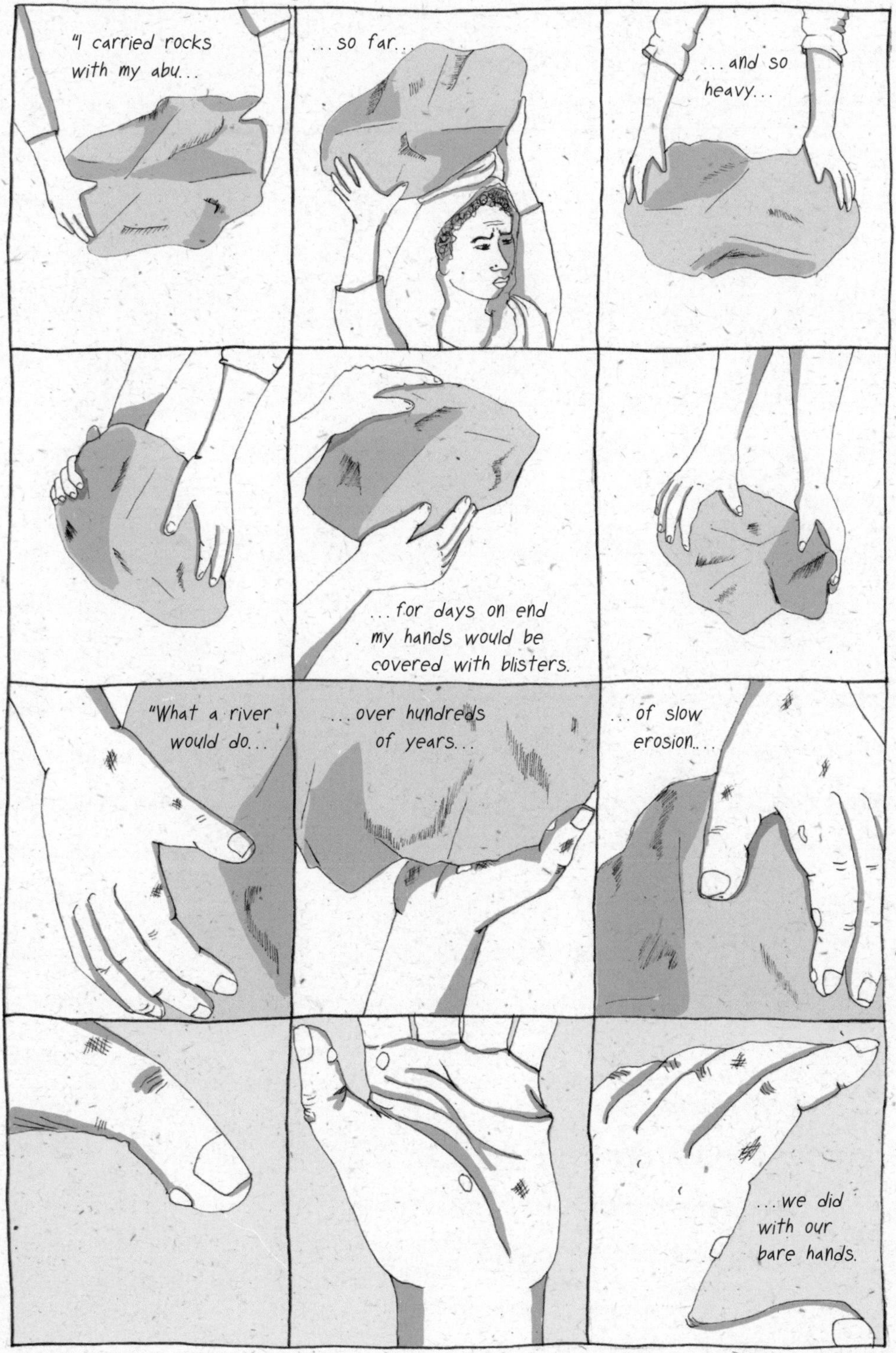
"I carried rocks with my abu...
...so far...
...and so heavy...
...for days on end my hands would be covered with blisters.
"What a river would do...
...over hundreds of years...
...of slow erosion...
...we did with our bare hands.

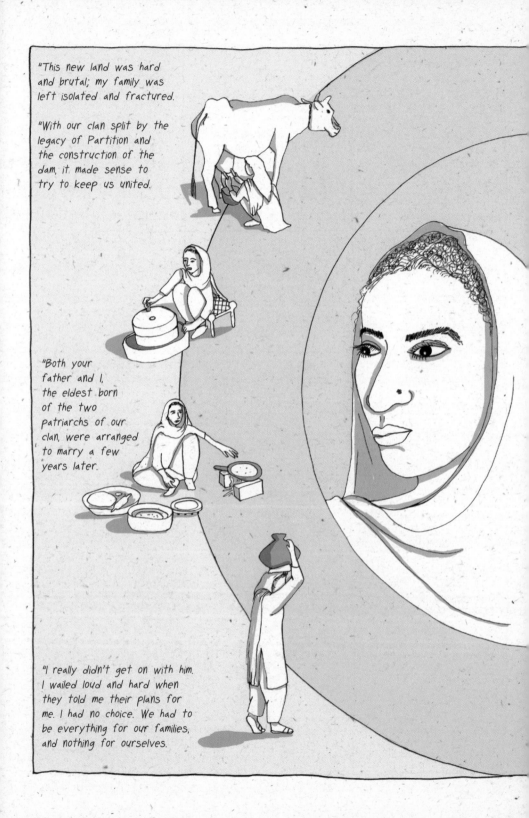

"This new land was hard and brutal; my family was left isolated and fractured.

"With our clan split by the legacy of Partition and the construction of the dam, it made sense to try to keep us united.

"Both your father and I, the eldest born of the two patriarchs of our clan, were arranged to marry a few years later.

"I really didn't get on with him. I wailed loud and hard when they told me their plans for me. I had no choice. We had to be everything for our families, and nothing for ourselves.

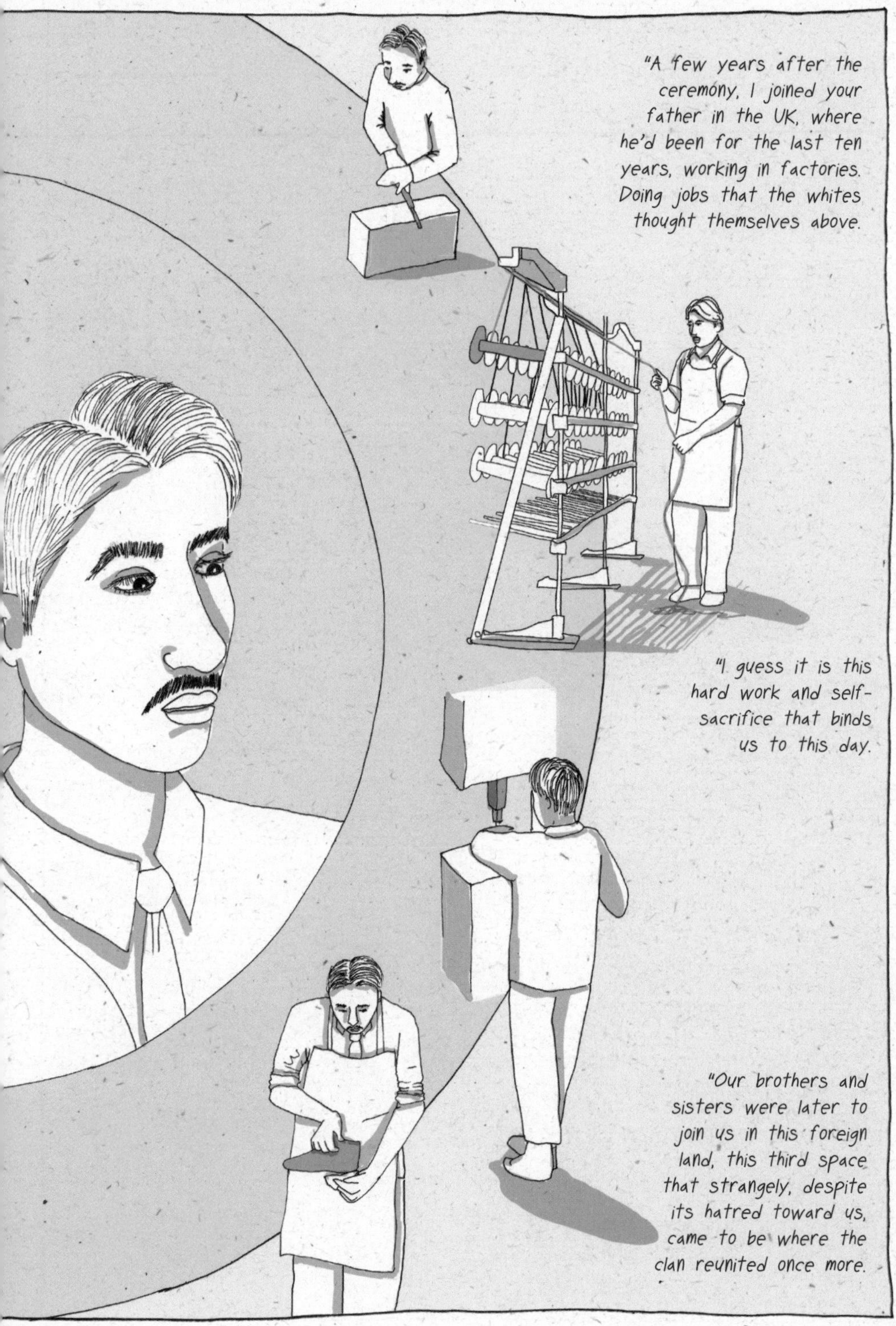
"A few years after the ceremony, I joined your father in the UK, where he'd been for the last ten years, working in factories. Doing jobs that the whites thought themselves above.
"I guess it is this hard work and self-sacrifice that binds us to this day.
"Our brothers and sisters were later to join us in this foreign land, this third space that strangely, despite its hatred toward us, came to be where the clan reunited once more.

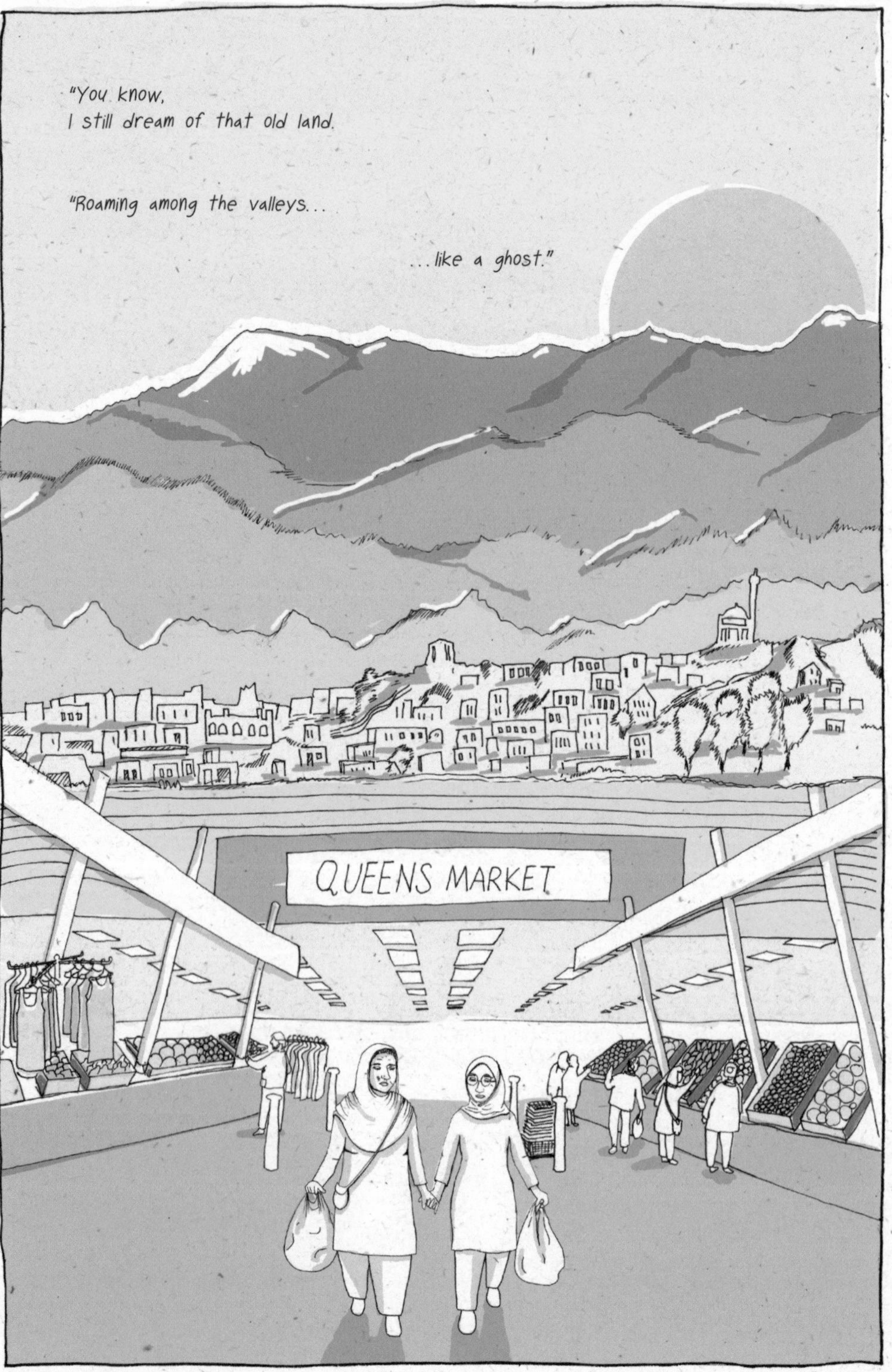
"You know,
I still dream of that old land.
"Roaming among the valleys...
...like a ghost."
QUEENS MARKET

The Partition was the biggest forced migration of contemporary times. It resulted in the mass movement of fifteen million people, and the death of over one million.

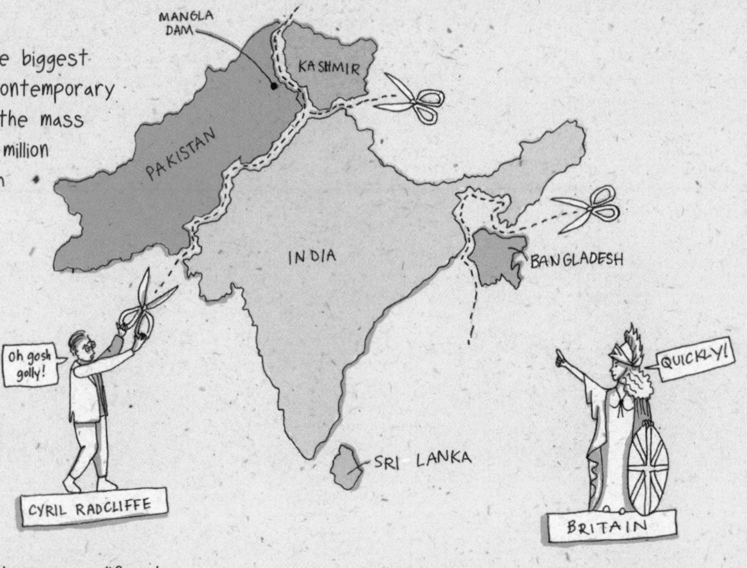
MANGLA DAM
KASHMIR
PAKISTAN
INDIA
BANGLADESH
SRI LANKA
Oh gosh golly!
CYRIL RADCLIFFE
QUICKLY!
BRITAIN

The dividing line was drawn up by a lawyer who had never been to South Asia before.

He was tasked with bringing a "fresh pair of eyes" to the job of defining the line that would go on to affect eighty million people—and was given just five weeks to do it.

This was just after the Second World War, and the Empire needed to cut its losses.

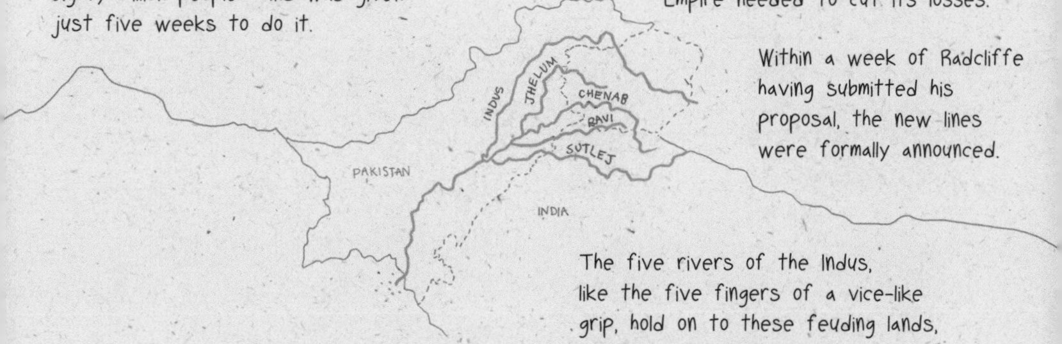
INDUS
JHELUM
CHENAB
RAVI
SUTLEJ
PAKISTAN
INDIA

Within a week of Radcliffe having submitted his proposal, the new lines were formally announced.

The five rivers of the Indus, like the five fingers of a vice-like grip, hold on to these feuding lands, running between the divisions.

Scarred ley lines and sacred tributaries, like the folds on the palm of my hand, tell our histories and our fortunes.

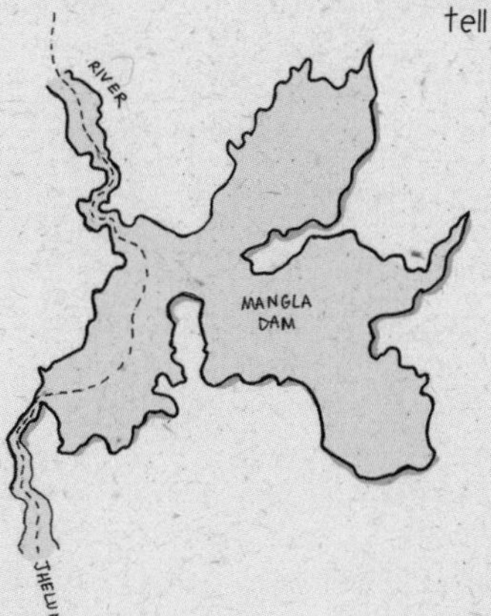
RIVER
MANGLA DAM
JHELUM

These movements in time and space overlap with who we are now.

Mangla Dam the same size as eight boroughs in London.

I shiver at the thought of all those homes lost, all those lives altered.

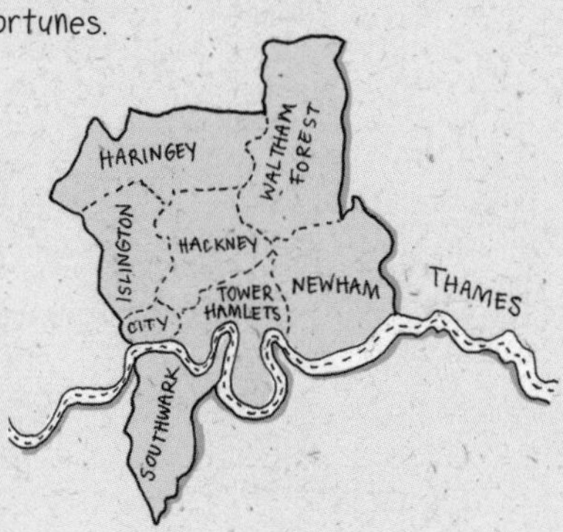
HARINGEY
WALTHAM FOREST
ISLINGTON
HACKNEY
TOWER HAMLETS
NEWHAM
CITY
SOUTHWARK
THAMES

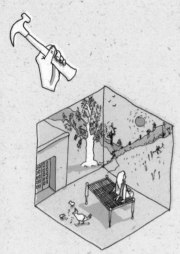

What is a displaced person?

A person who is forced to leave their home...

...because of war, persecution, or a natural disaster.

What is a diaspora?

The movement, migration, or scattering of a people...

...away from an established or ancestral homeland.

What is an immigrant?

A person who comes to a country to take up permanent residence...

...and is focused on the act of settling.

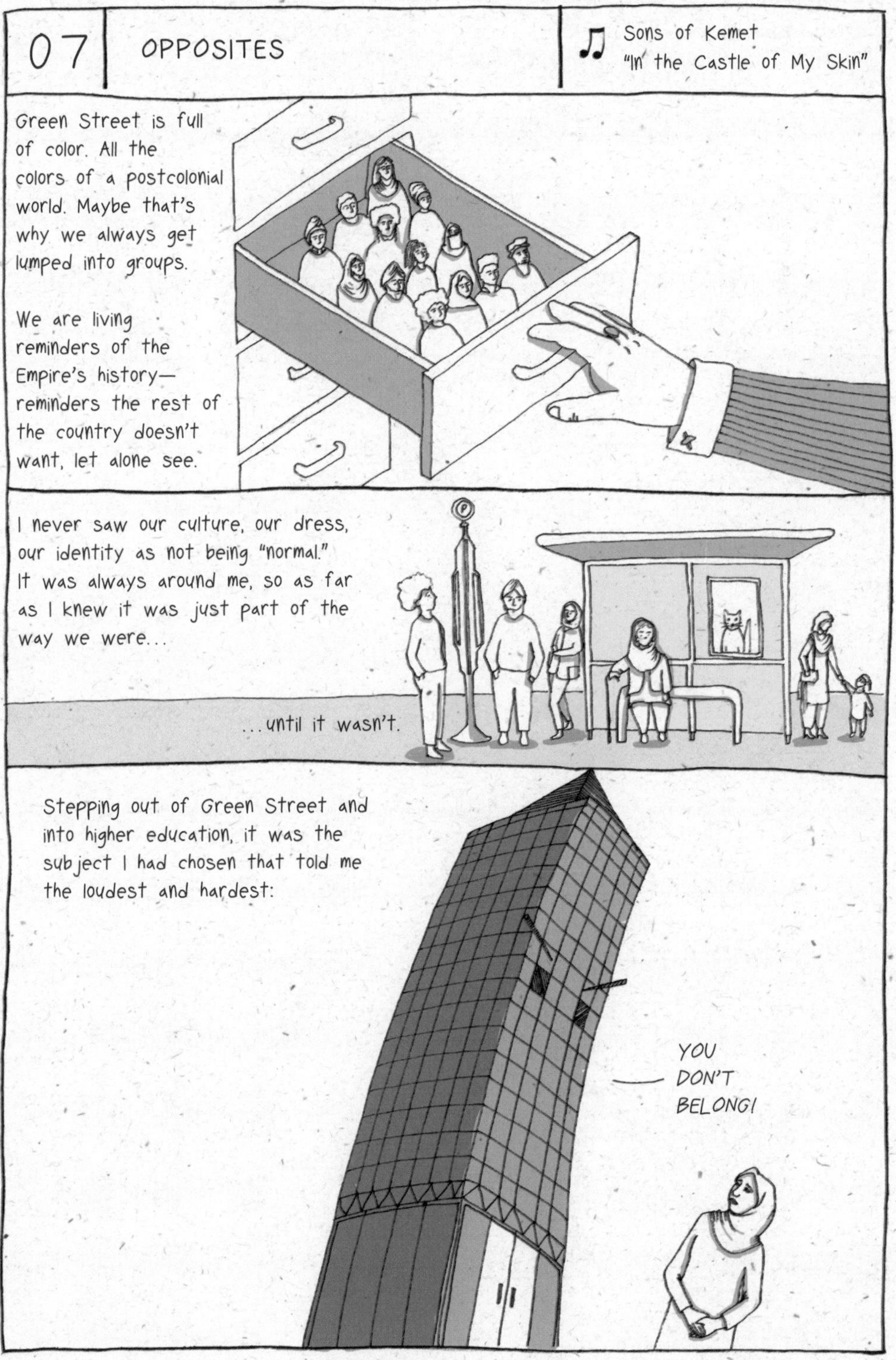
07
OPPOSITES
Sons of Kemet
"In the Castle of My Skin"
Green Street is full of color. All the colors of a postcolonial world. Maybe that's why we always get lumped into groups.
We are living reminders of the Empire's history—reminders the rest of the country doesn't want, let alone see.
I never saw our culture, our dress, our identity as not being "normal." It was always around me, so as far as I knew it was just part of the way we were...
...until it wasn't.
Stepping out of Green Street and into higher education, it was the subject I had chosen that told me the loudest and hardest:
YOU DON'T BELONG!

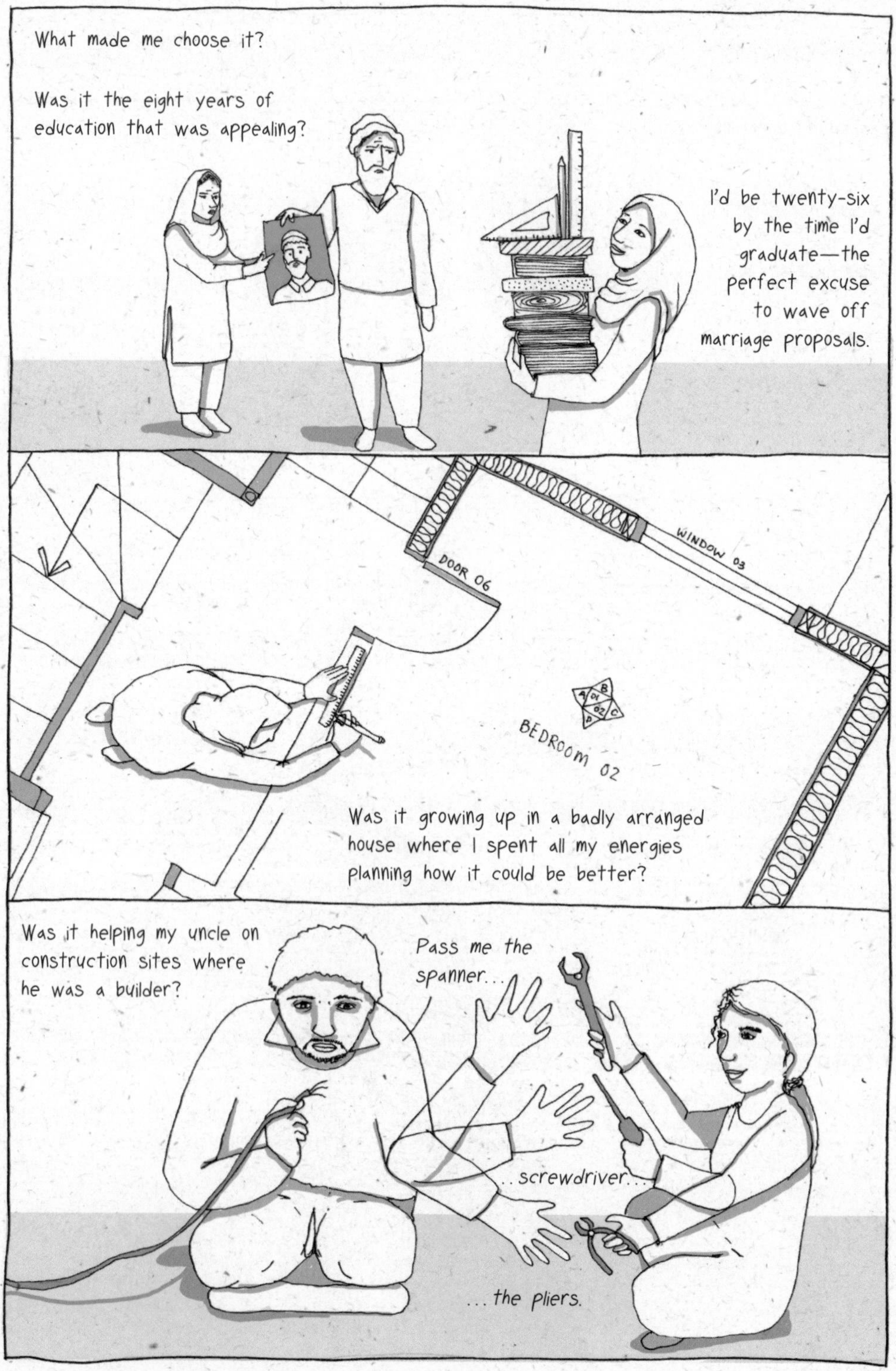
What made me choose it?
Was it the eight years of education that was appealing?
I'd be twenty-six by the time I'd graduate—the perfect excuse to wave off marriage proposals.
DOOR 06
WINDOW 03
BEDROOM 02
Was it growing up in a badly arranged house where I spent all my energies planning how it could be better?
Was it helping my uncle on construction sites where he was a builder?
Pass me the spanner...
...screwdriver...
...the pliers.

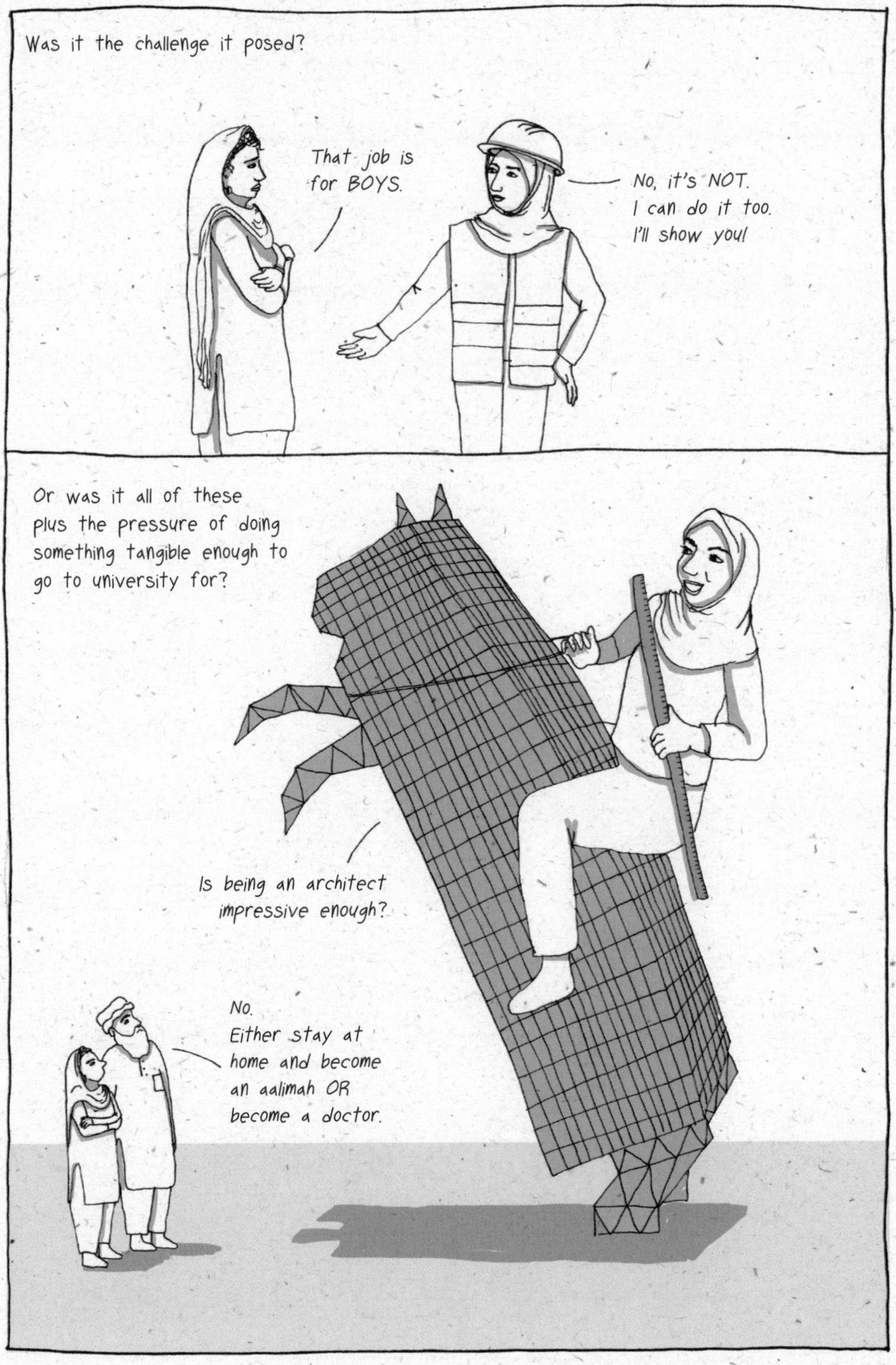
Was it the challenge it posed?
That job is for BOYS.
No, it's NOT. I can do it too. I'll show you!
Or was it all of these plus the pressure of doing something tangible enough to go to university for?
Is being an architect impressive enough?
No. Either stay at home and become an aalimah OR become a doctor.

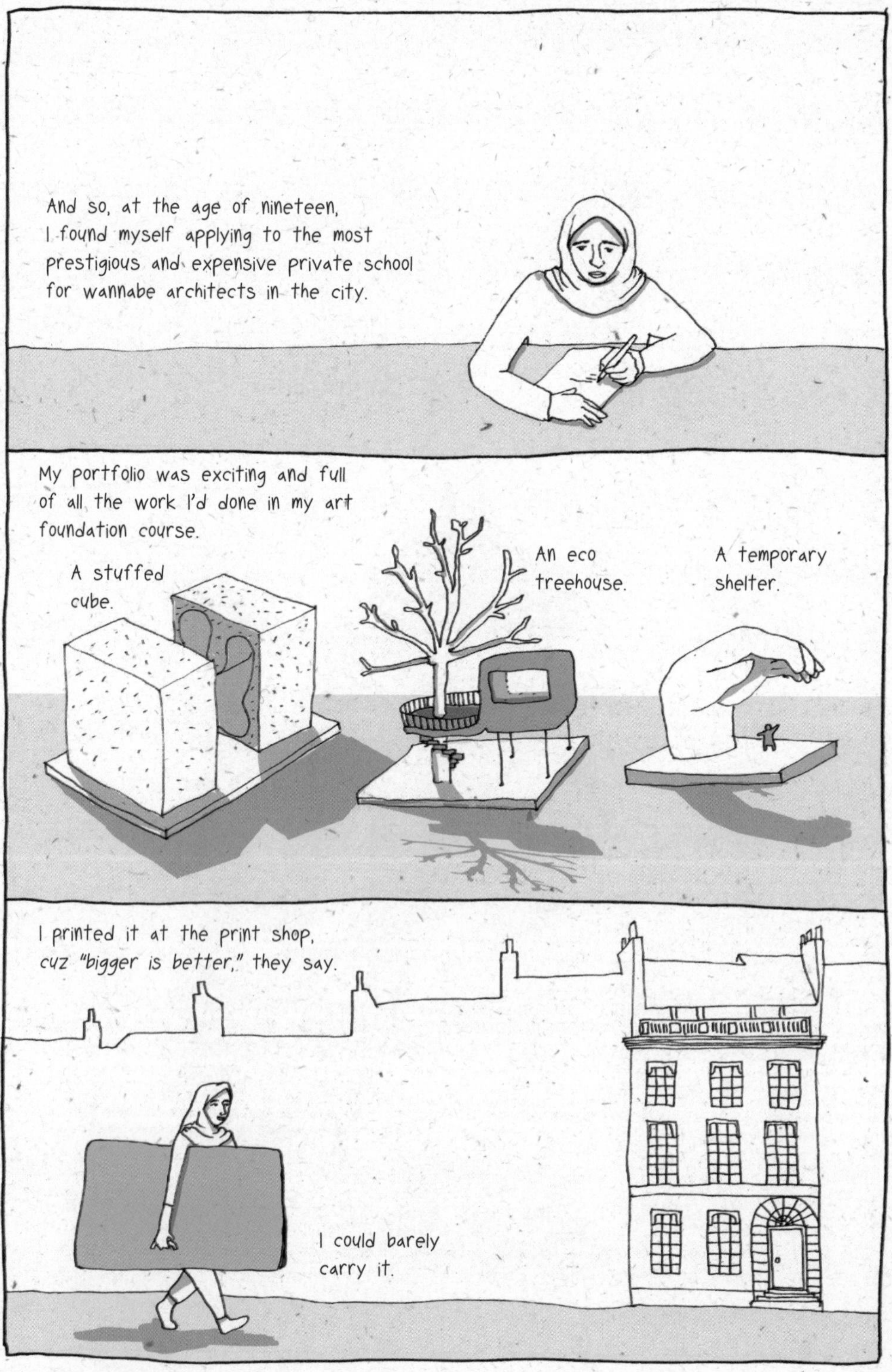
And so, at the age of nineteen, I found myself applying to the most prestigious and expensive private school for wannabe architects in the city.
My portfolio was exciting and full of all the work I'd done in my art foundation course.
A stuffed cube.
An eco treehouse.
A temporary shelter.
I printed it at the print shop, cuz "bigger is better," they say.
I could barely carry it.

My interviewer had a lean, hard face.
He flicked to the stuffed cube.

This is interesting. Tell me what you're saying with this?

Ah yes, well, the brief here was to take a two meter by two meter by two meter cube and make it into a habitable space for one person.

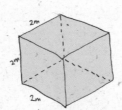

2m
2m
2m

Yes, but what are you trying to say with these images?

Um... I've taken pictures of the model I made and I'm showing how the spaces would be used.

Yes, but you have a lady in traditional Indian dress. Why???

Ahhh, yeah, that's my sister-in-law, and um, actually, we're Pakistani...

But what are you trying to say with her clothing?

Um...nothing really... that's just what she wears.

He stared at me, unimpressed.

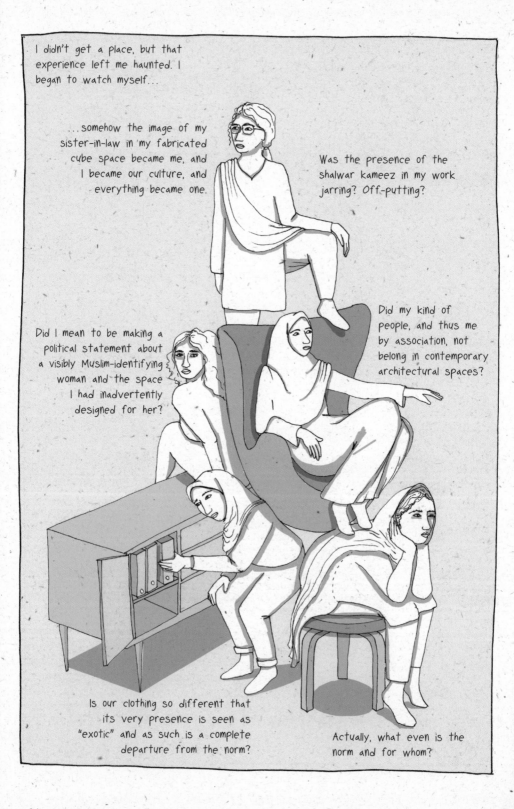

I didn't get a place, but that experience left me haunted. I began to watch myself...

...somehow the image of my sister-in-law in my fabricated cube space became me, and I became our culture, and everything became one.

Was the presence of the shalwar kameez in my work jarring? Off-putting?

Did my kind of people, and thus me by association, not belong in contemporary architectural spaces?

Did I mean to be making a political statement about a visibly Muslim-identifying woman and the space I had inadvertently designed for her?

Is our clothing so different that its very presence is seen as "exotic" and as such is a complete departure from the norm?

Actually, what even is the norm and for whom?

It took me a while to recognize the industry I had chosen did not really want me.

You see, the thing with architecture is that it doesn't just deal with the present.

It taps into people's aspirations for their environment, to a sense of their future, to notions of safety and types of society.

These are big, beautiful concepts, which all of us should have the power to engage with and shape for ourselves.

But, as architecture is linked to construction, which in turn is linked to private development and "property as profit," sadly the ability to affect our environment stays within the confines of those who can afford to.

And those who can afford to also get to dictate what home, shelter, and comfort look like.

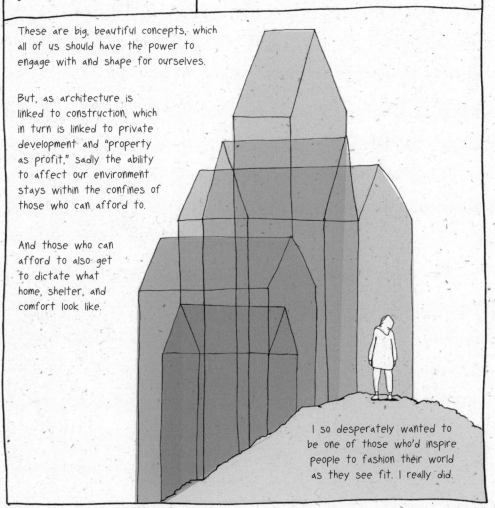

I so desperately wanted to be one of those who'd inspire people to fashion their world as they see fit. I really did.

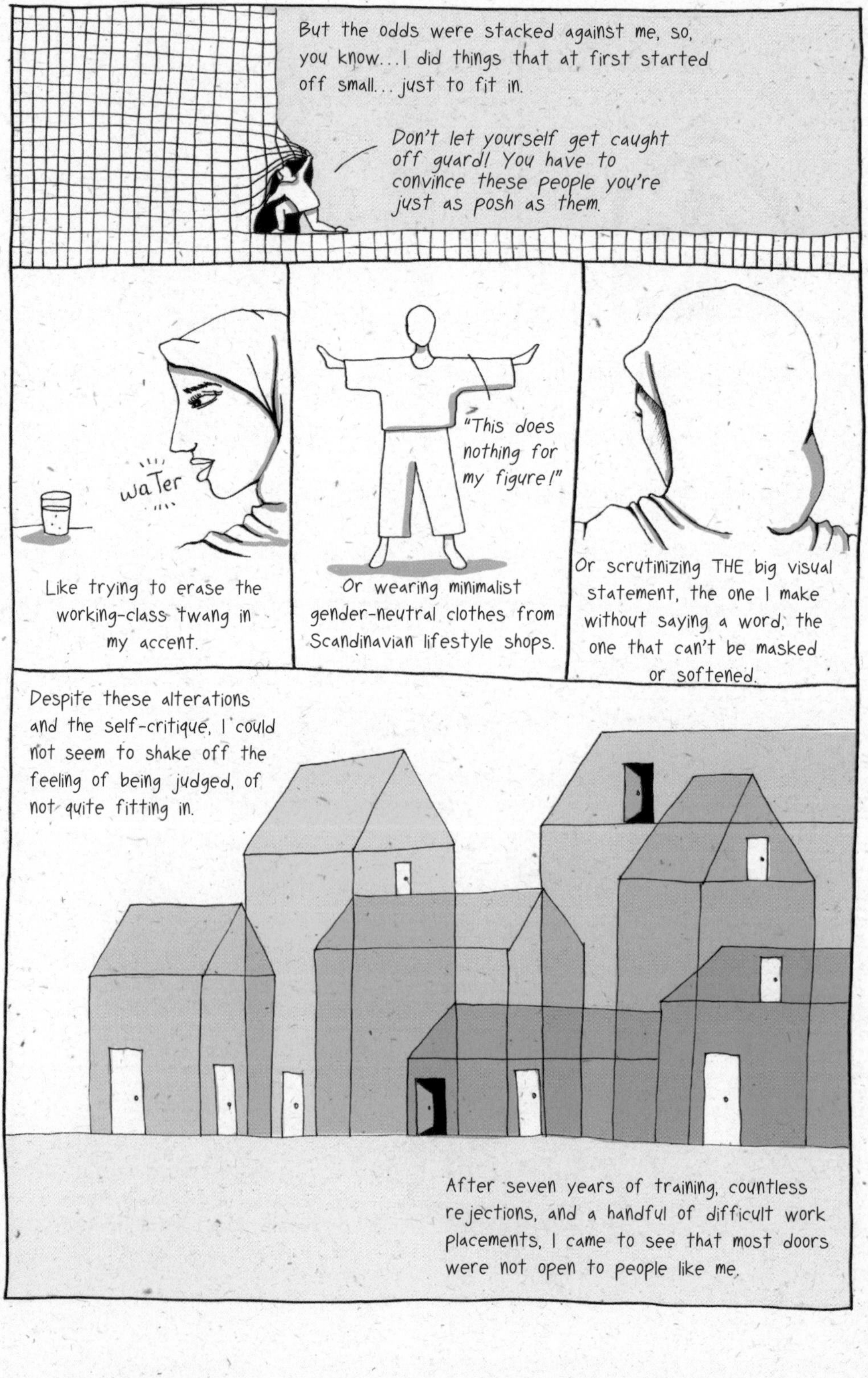
But the odds were stacked against me, so, you know... I did things that at first started off small... just to fit in.
Don't let yourself get caught off guard! You have to convince these people you're just as posh as them.
waTer
Like trying to erase the working-class twang in my accent.
"This does nothing for my figure!"
Or wearing minimalist gender-neutral clothes from Scandinavian lifestyle shops.
Or scrutinizing THE big visual statement, the one I make without saying a word, the one that can't be masked or softened.
Despite these alterations and the self-critique, I could not seem to shake off the feeling of being judged, of not quite fitting in.
After seven years of training, countless rejections, and a handful of difficult work placements, I came to see that most doors were not open to people like me.

It can be hard to be
gentle on ourselves in the
face of such othering.

We are, at the end of the
day, social creatures seeking
love, comfort, and validation...

...but I see
all those years of
trying to fit in...

SPEAK
RIGHT

...of a shape-shifting...

Hi, hi!
Nice to
meet you!

...assessing...

hmmm...

...molding...

...inherited from parents whose survival was...

...buckle down...

ssshhh!!

...stay quiet...

...eyes down.

And I wonder how we
can break this cycle,
of tippy toes,
not complaining,
and "yes, sirs."

Brené Brown
tells me...

"Fitting in is about assessing a situation and becoming who you need to be in order to be accepted.

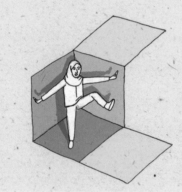

Belonging, on the other hand, doesn't require us to change who we are;

it requires us to be who we are."

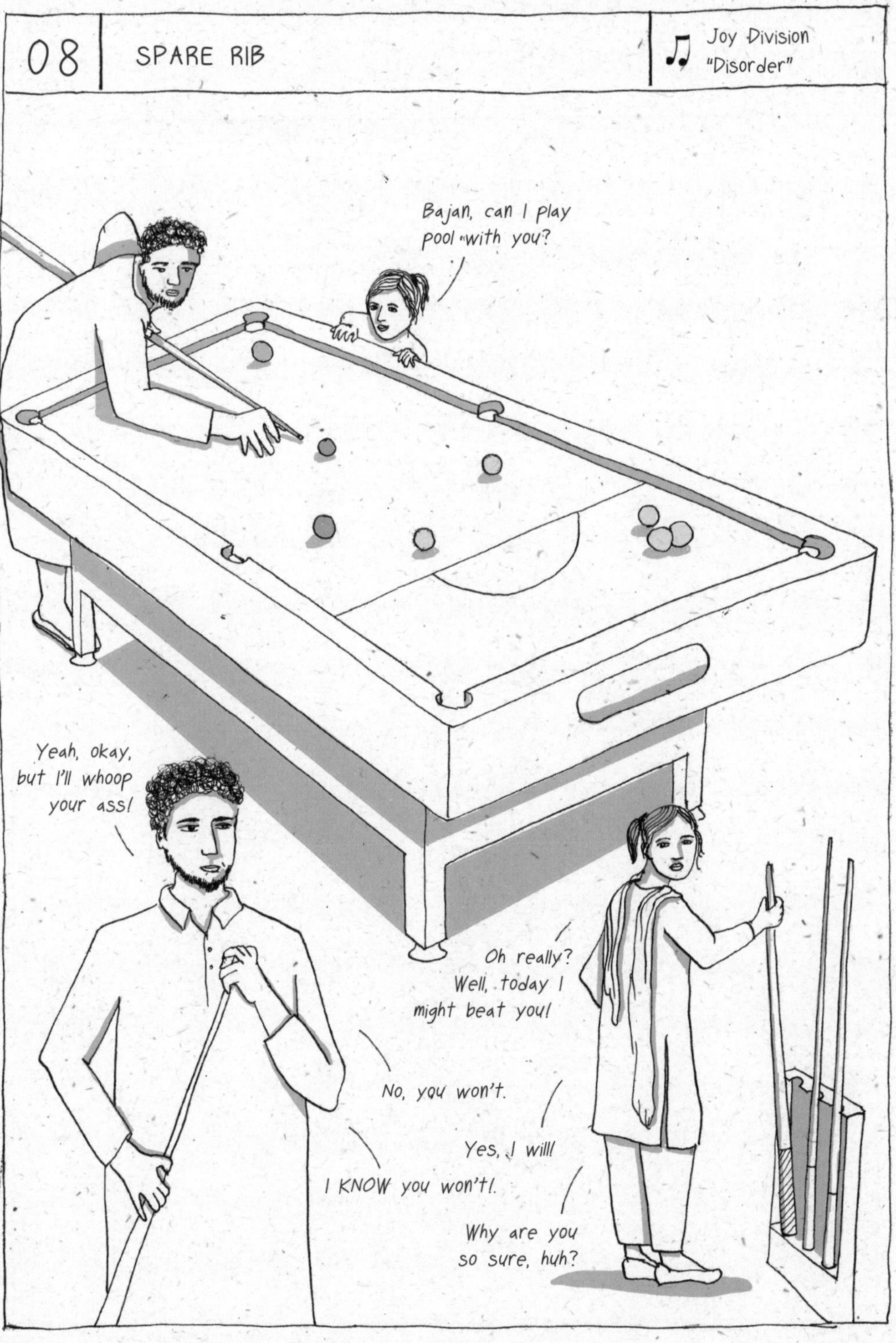
08
SPARE RIB
Joy Division
"Disorder"
Bajan, can I play pool with you?
Yeah, okay, but I'll whoop your ass!
Oh really? Well, today I might beat you!
No, you won't.
Yes, I will!
I KNOW you won't!.
Why are you so sure, huh?

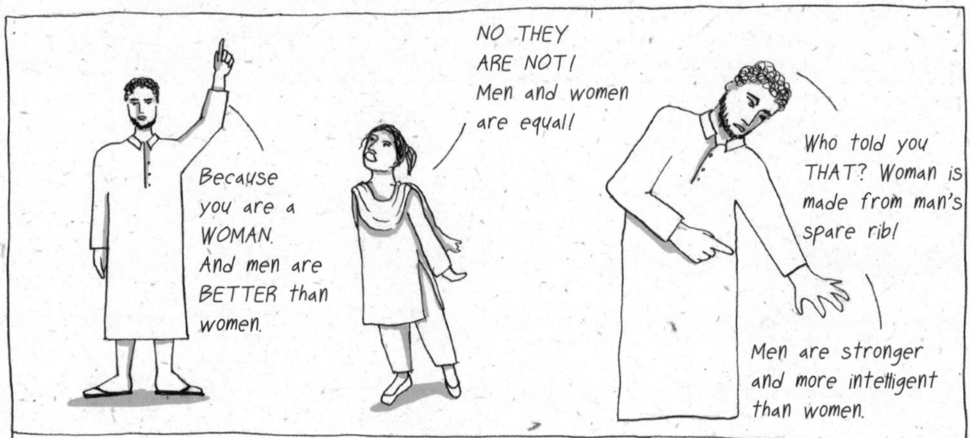
Because you are a WOMAN. And men are BETTER than women.
NO THEY ARE NOT! Men and women are equal!
Who told you THAT? Woman is made from man's spare rib!
Men are stronger and more intelligent than women.

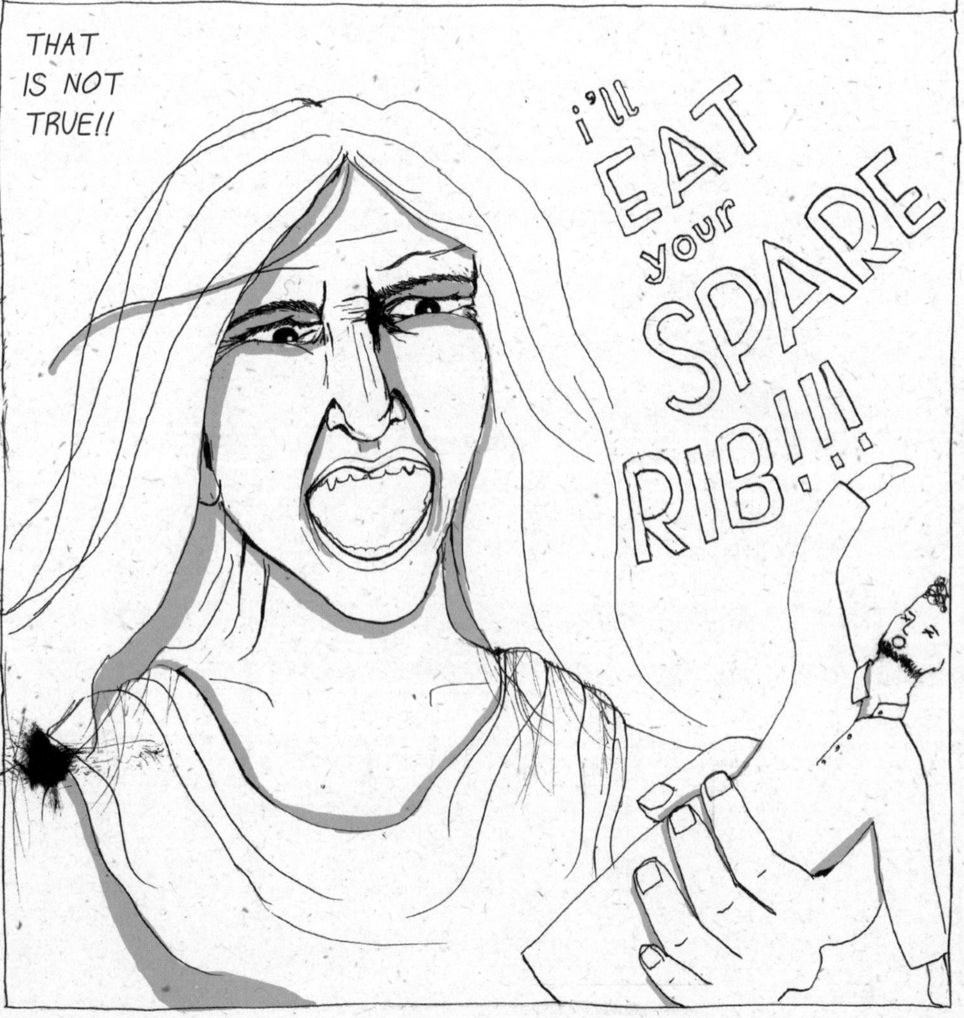
THAT IS NOT TRUE!!
i'll EAT your SPARE RIB!!!

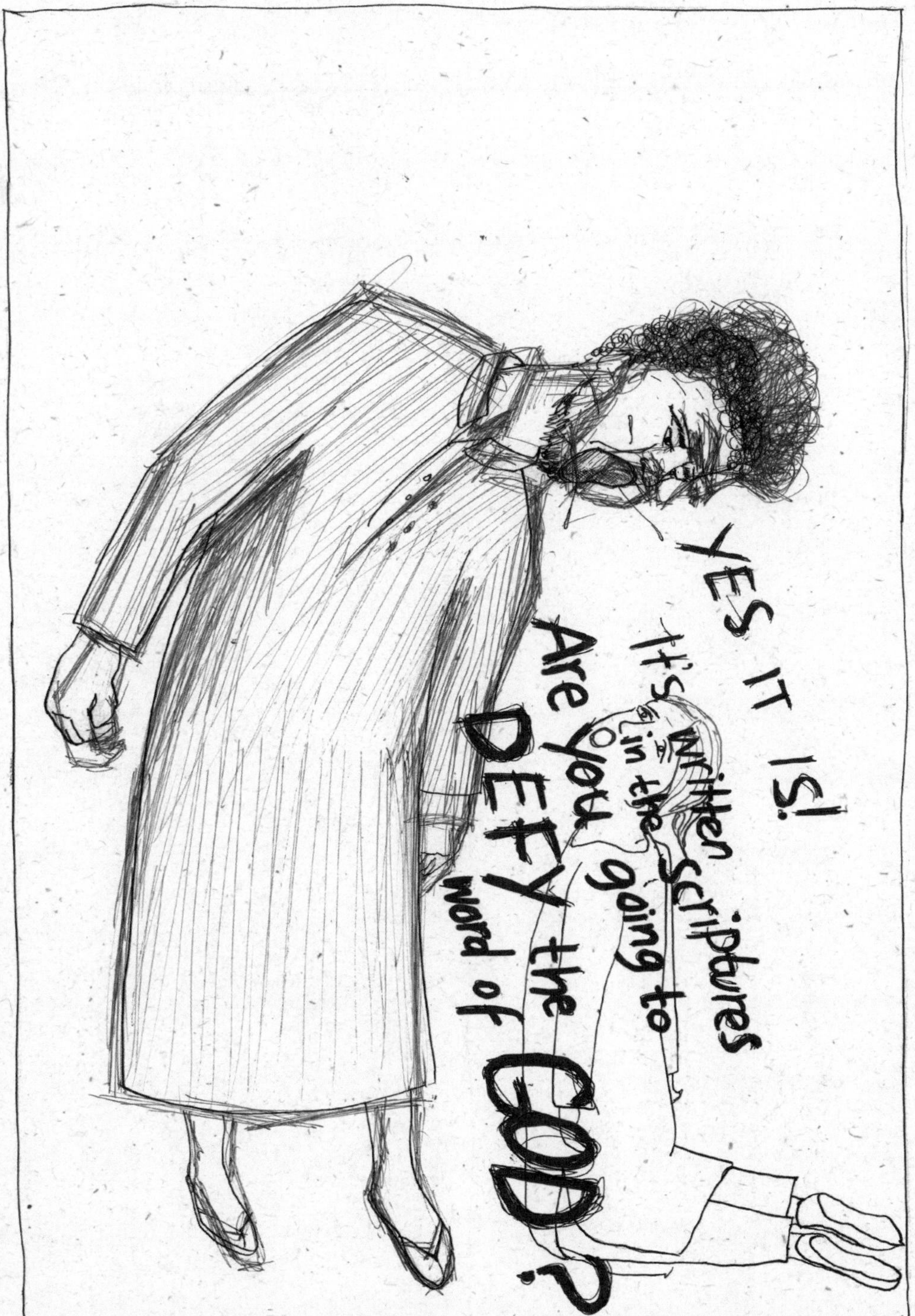
YES IT IS!
It's written in the scriptures
Are you going to DEFY the word of GOD?

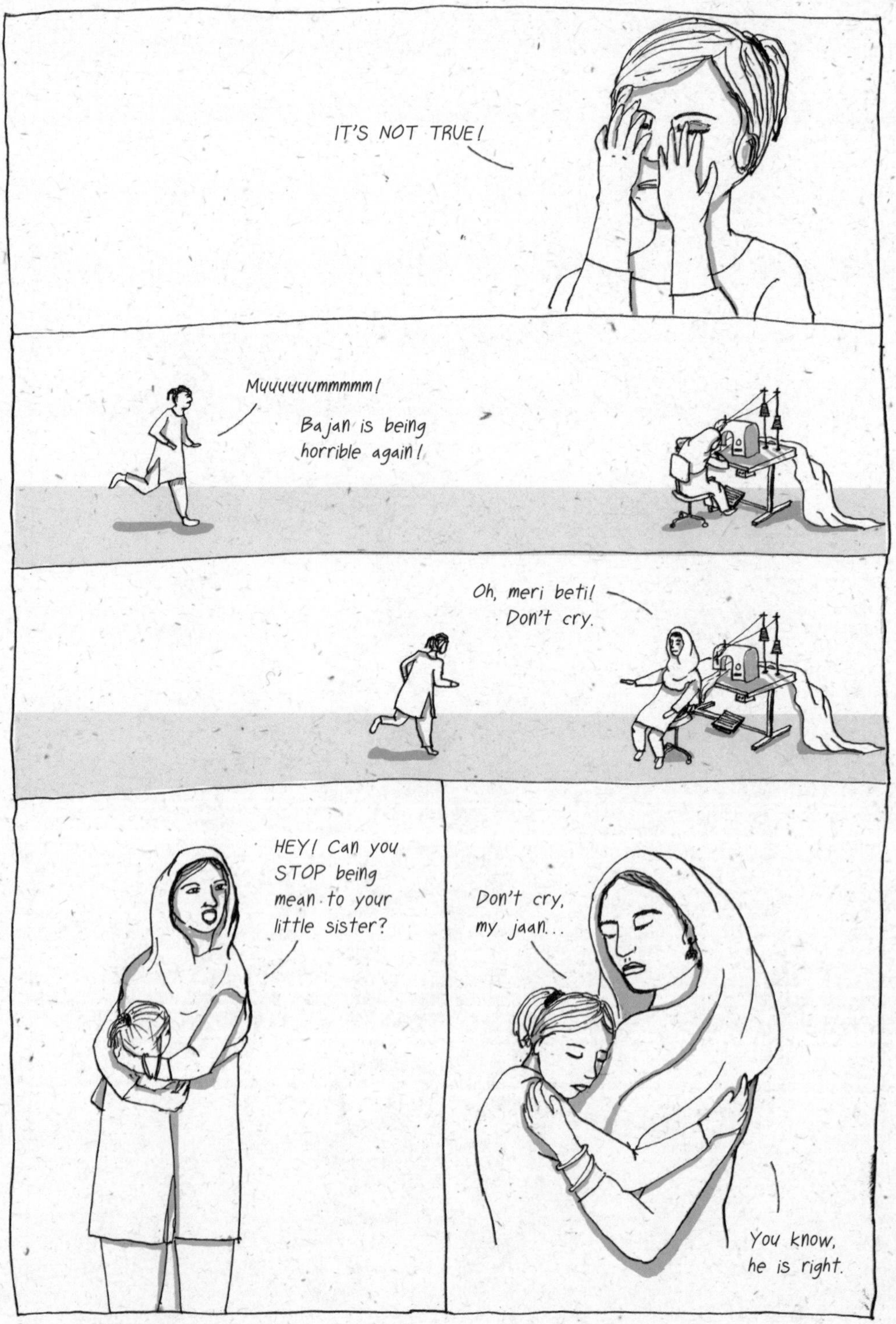
IT'S NOT TRUE!
Muuuuuummmmm!
Bajan is being horrible again!
Oh, meri beti! Don't cry.
HEY! Can you STOP being mean to your little sister?
Don't cry, my jaan...
You know, he is right.

Was belonging ever even offered in the family space?

The home, the only place to exercise control and domination.

This idealized microcosm, where the migrant man holds his historic power, his wife/mother/sister/daughter his subordinates.

The home, an offering of salvation for our men, loathed in society, emasculated and demonized in this hostile land.

Low-paid and low-skilled with very little chance of promotion, Pakistani and Bangladeshi men have some of the highest rates of unemployment in the country.

Ugly statistics that speak only of low chances, slim pickings—a clutching-of-straws kind of survival.

Us girls, really the harbingers of modernity, with its progressive feminist values...

...have been afforded small opportunities, and encouraged to seek emancipation, while the boys helped Mum and Dad survive.

Statistically, we were more able to "fit in," adapting to team dynamics and favored by the policies of change.

Bizarre, how this capitalist
patriarchy pits one gender against
the other to maintain its control.

Mothers, with their heightened protective
instincts, left to create a safe space for their
sons where they can play out being stronger,
smarter, more visible in the only place left.

Daughters, accused of fraternizing
with the host culture.

Families now torn between
tradition, religion, and
social progression.

Gender roles
torn asunder.

What a bargain with patriarchy, when
we women reinforce the values that
continue to undermine us. Look how
it thrives when we let it fester
among us.

The only way to dismantle this
centuries-old stronghold is for all
genders to work together.

09 MONSTROUS

♫ Kishore Kumar
"Roop Tera Mastana"

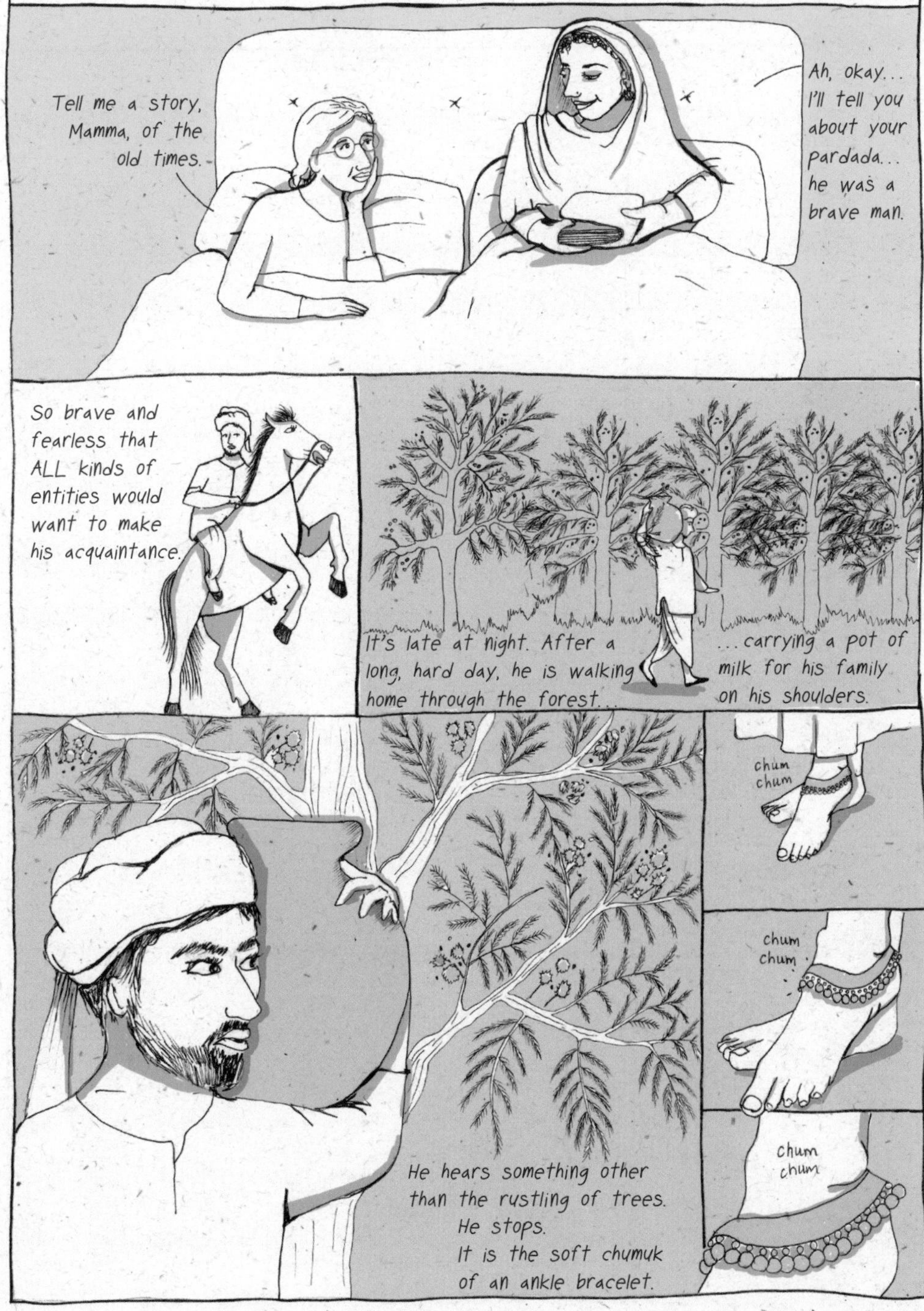
Tell me a story, Mamma, of the old times.
Ah, okay... I'll tell you about your pardada... he was a brave man.
So brave and fearless that ALL kinds of entities would want to make his acquaintance.
It's late at night. After a long, hard day, he is walking home through the forest...
...carrying a pot of milk for his family on his shoulders.
chum chum
chum chum
chum chum
He hears something other than the rustling of trees.
He stops.
It is the soft chumuk of an ankle bracelet.

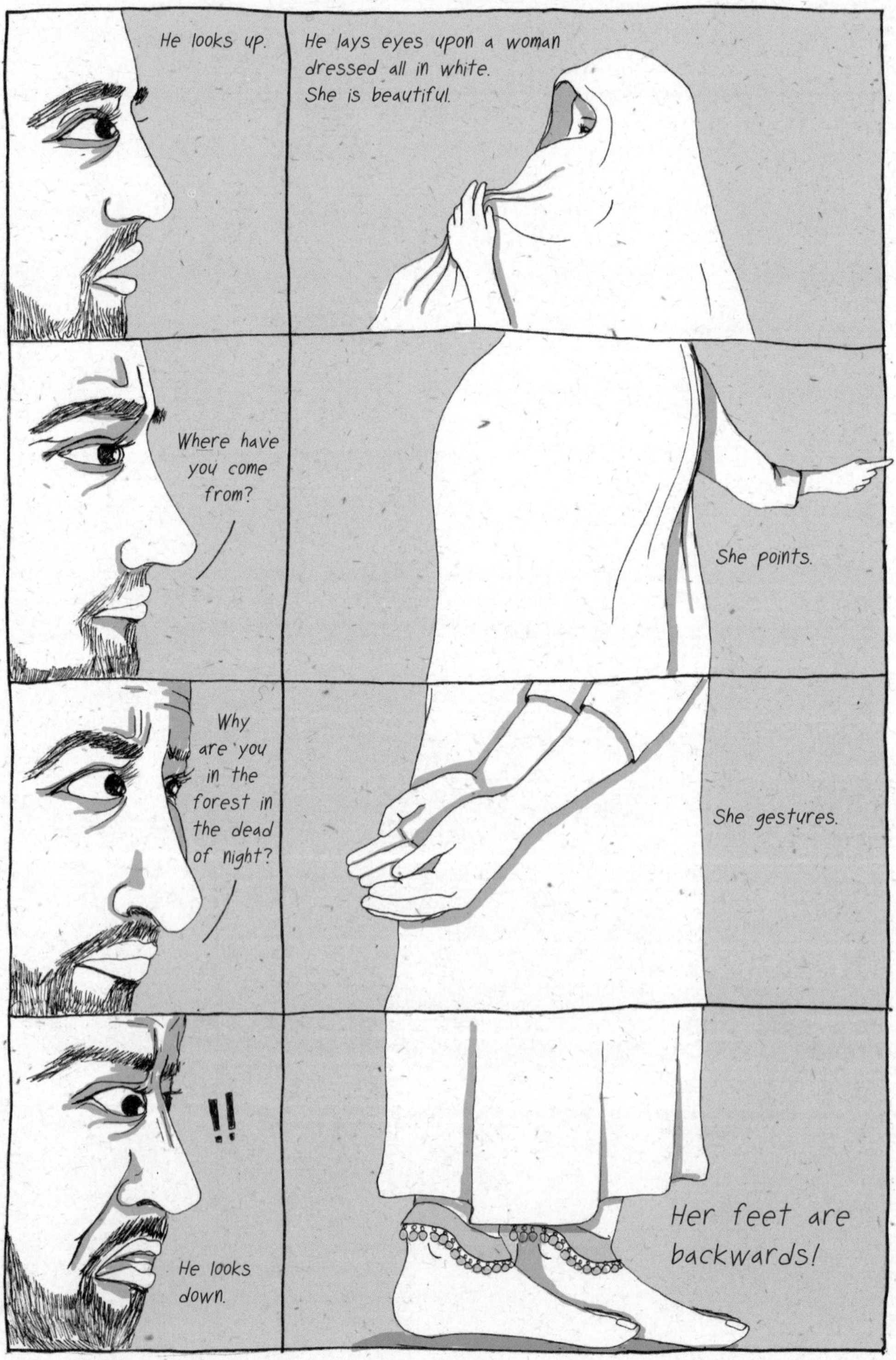
He looks up.
He lays eyes upon a woman dressed all in white. She is beautiful.
Where have you come from?
She points.
Why are you in the forest in the dead of night?
She gestures.
!!
He looks down.
Her feet are backwards!

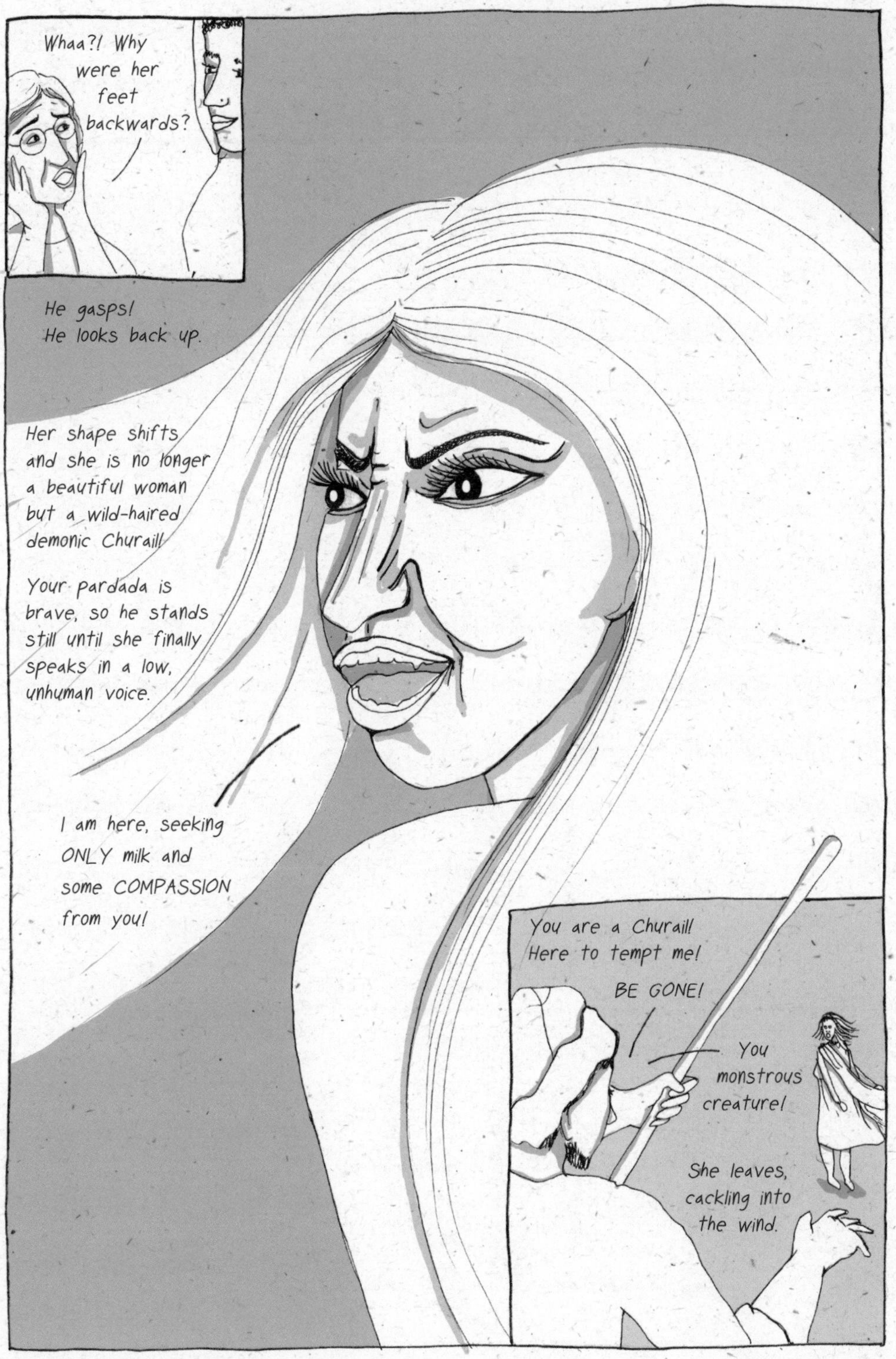
Whaa?! Why were her feet backwards?
He gasps! He looks back up.
Her shape shifts and she is no longer a beautiful woman but a wild-haired demonic Churail!
Your pardada is brave, so he stands still until she finally speaks in a low, unhuman voice.
I am here, seeking ONLY milk and some COMPASSION from you!
You are a Churail! Here to tempt me!
BE GONE!
You monstrous creature!
She leaves, cackling into the wind.

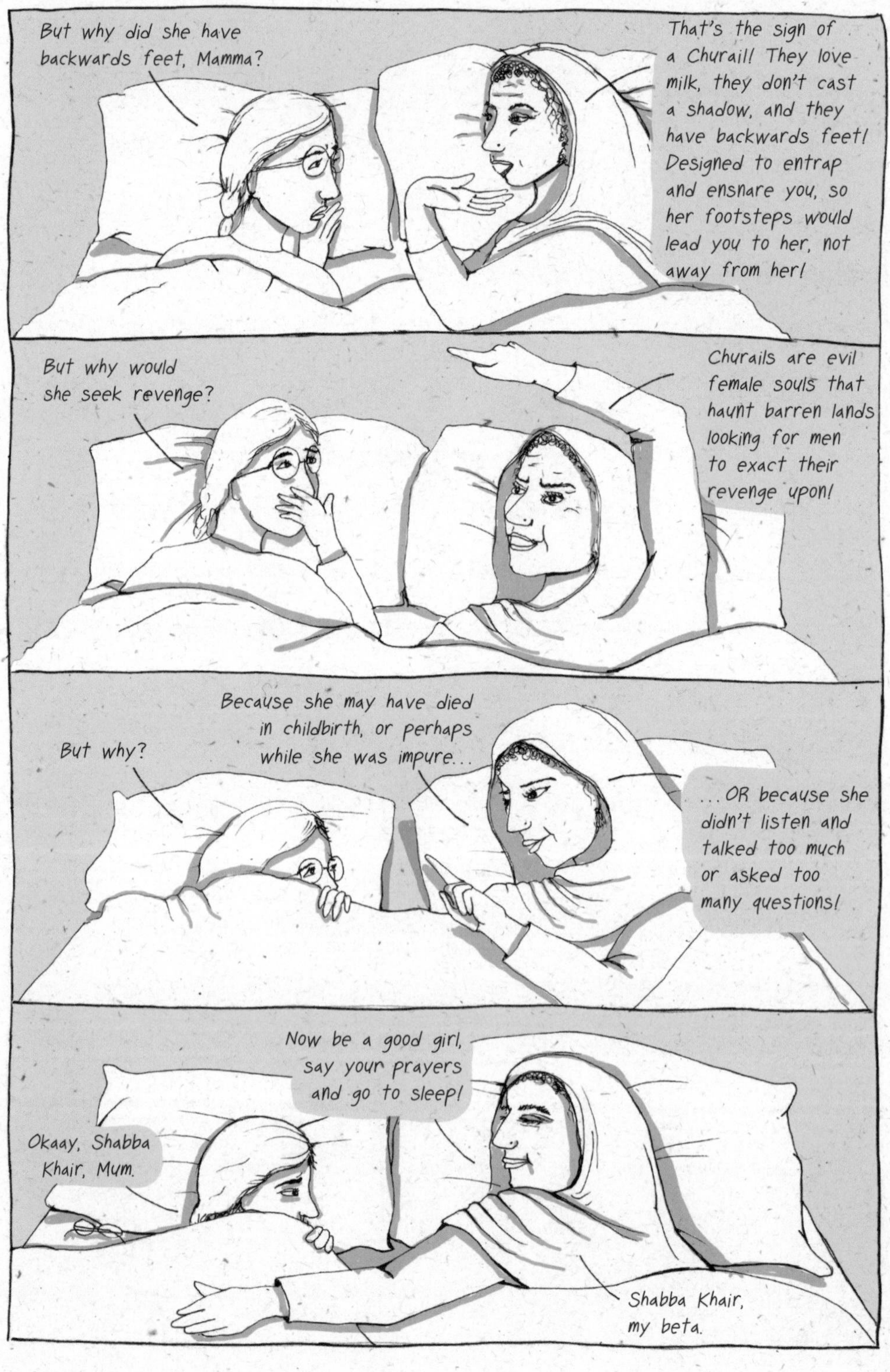
But why did she have backwards feet, Mamma?
That's the sign of a Churail! They love milk, they don't cast a shadow, and they have backwards feet! Designed to entrap and ensnare you, so her footsteps would lead you to her, not away from her!
But why would she seek revenge?
Churails are evil female souls that haunt barren lands looking for men to exact their revenge upon!
But why?
Because she may have died in childbirth, or perhaps while she was impure...
...OR because she didn't listen and talked too much or asked too many questions!
Now be a good girl, say your prayers and go to sleep!
Okaay, Shabba Khair, Mum.
Shabba Khair, my beta.

Those stories were exciting and thrilling when we were younger.

We'd all huddle around listening eagerly to tales of evil spirits and ancient forests.

They were the first lessons on the monstrous feminine.

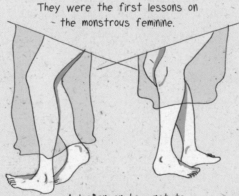

The beautiful virgin dressed in white...

...turned evil and demonic.

A lesson on how not to be as a female.

Her demands, wild hair, cackling laugh, her right to roam around at night, seen as abject... other... rejected... nonhuman.

Even my mother gave her no sympathy in the story. Though she may have been wronged, we were taught to loathe her, and honor the man instead.

And yet the Churail
spoke out against
injustice, against being
wronged. And survived.

It was her rage,
her indignation,
her perserverance...

...that would come to find
me much later.

Every time I needed
to eat the spare rib.

Every time I needed to become
the monstrous to fight back.

She became my archaic knowledge,
and I welcomed her.

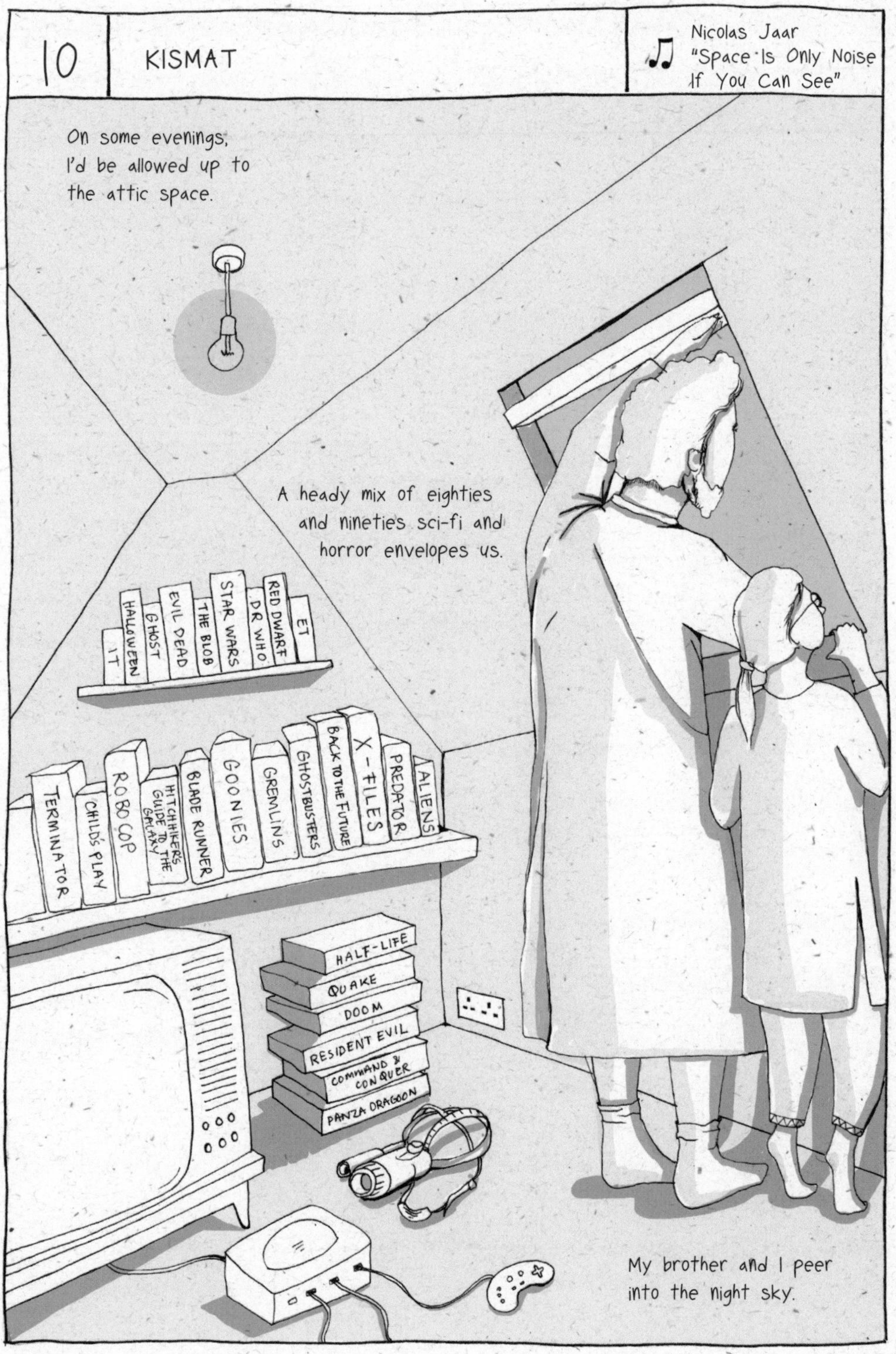
10
KISMAT
Nicolas Jaar
"Space Is Only Noise If You Can See"
On some evenings, I'd be allowed up to the attic space.
A heady mix of eighties and nineties sci-fi and horror envelopes us.
IT
HALLOWEEN
GHOST
EVIL DEAD
THE BLOB
STAR WARS
DR WHO
RED DWARF
ET
TERMINATOR
CHILD'S PLAY
ROBOCOP
HITCHHIKER'S GUIDE TO THE GALAXY
BLADE RUNNER
GOONIES
GREMLINS
GHOSTBUSTERS
BACK TO THE FUTURE
X-FILES
PREDATOR
ALIENS
HALF-LIFE
QUAKE
DOOM
RESIDENT EVIL
COMMAND & CONQUER
PANZA DRAGOON
My brother and I peer into the night sky.

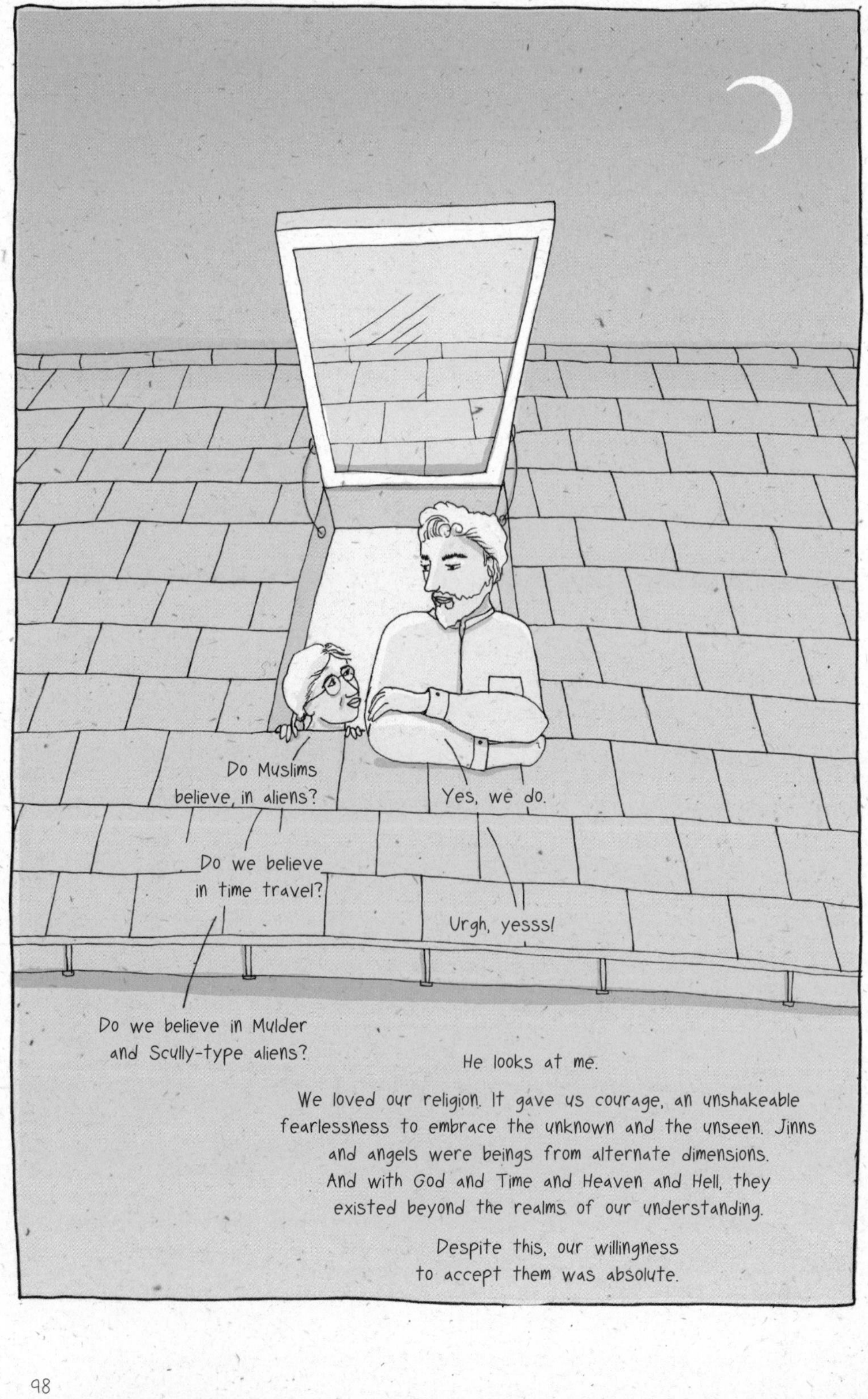
Do Muslims believe, in aliens?
Yes, we do.
Do we believe in time travel?
Urgh, yesss!
Do we believe in Mulder and Scully-type aliens?
He looks at me.
We loved our religion. It gave us courage, an unshakeable fearlessness to embrace the unknown and the unseen. Jinns and angels were beings from alternate dimensions. And with God and Time and Heaven and Hell, they existed beyond the realms of our understanding.
Despite this, our willingness to accept them was absolute.

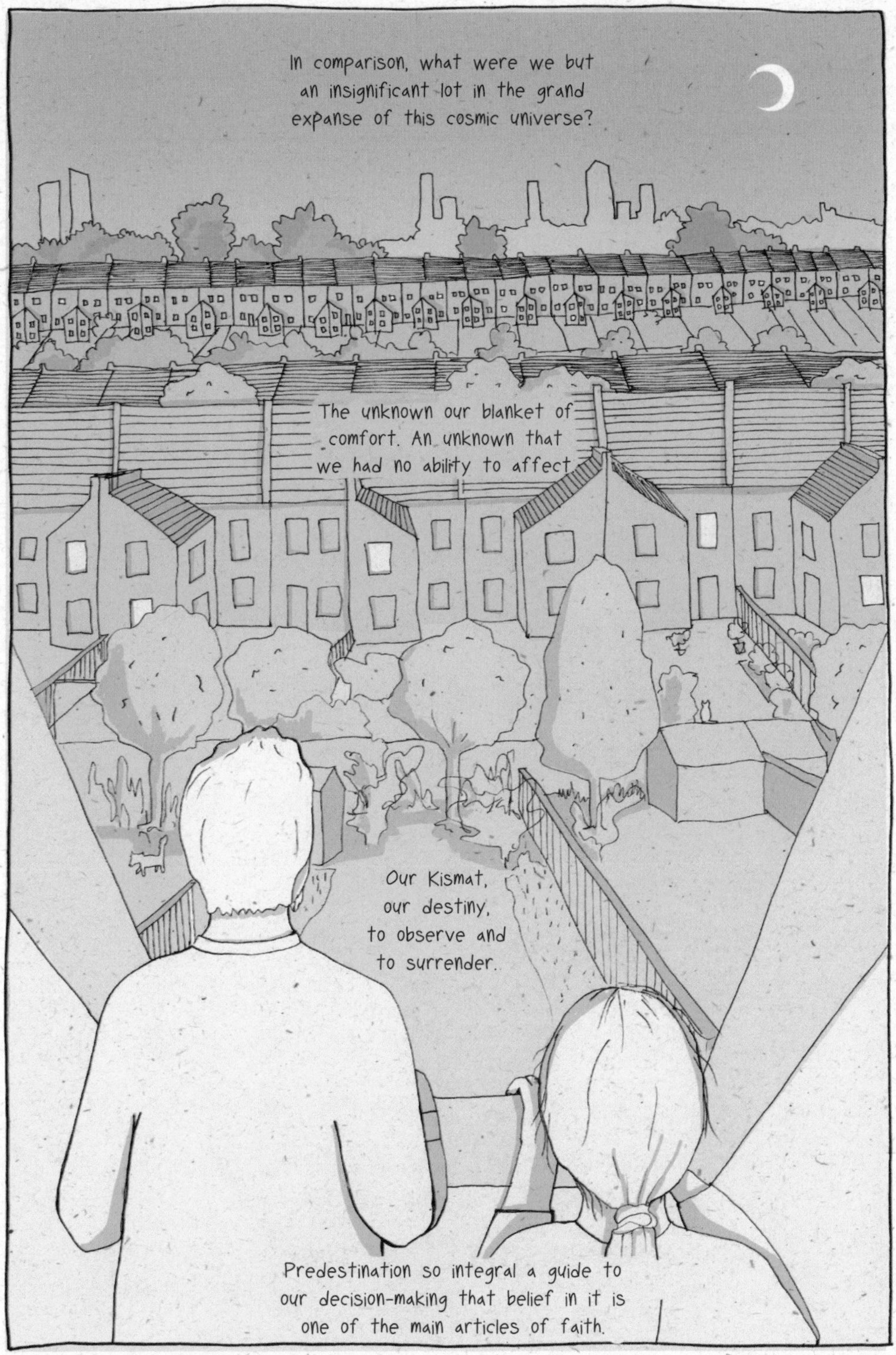
In comparison, what were we but an insignificant lot in the grand expanse of this cosmic universe?
The unknown our blanket of comfort. An unknown that we had no ability to affect.
Our Kismat, our destiny, to observe and to surrender.
Predestination so integral a guide to our decision-making that belief in it is one of the main articles of faith.

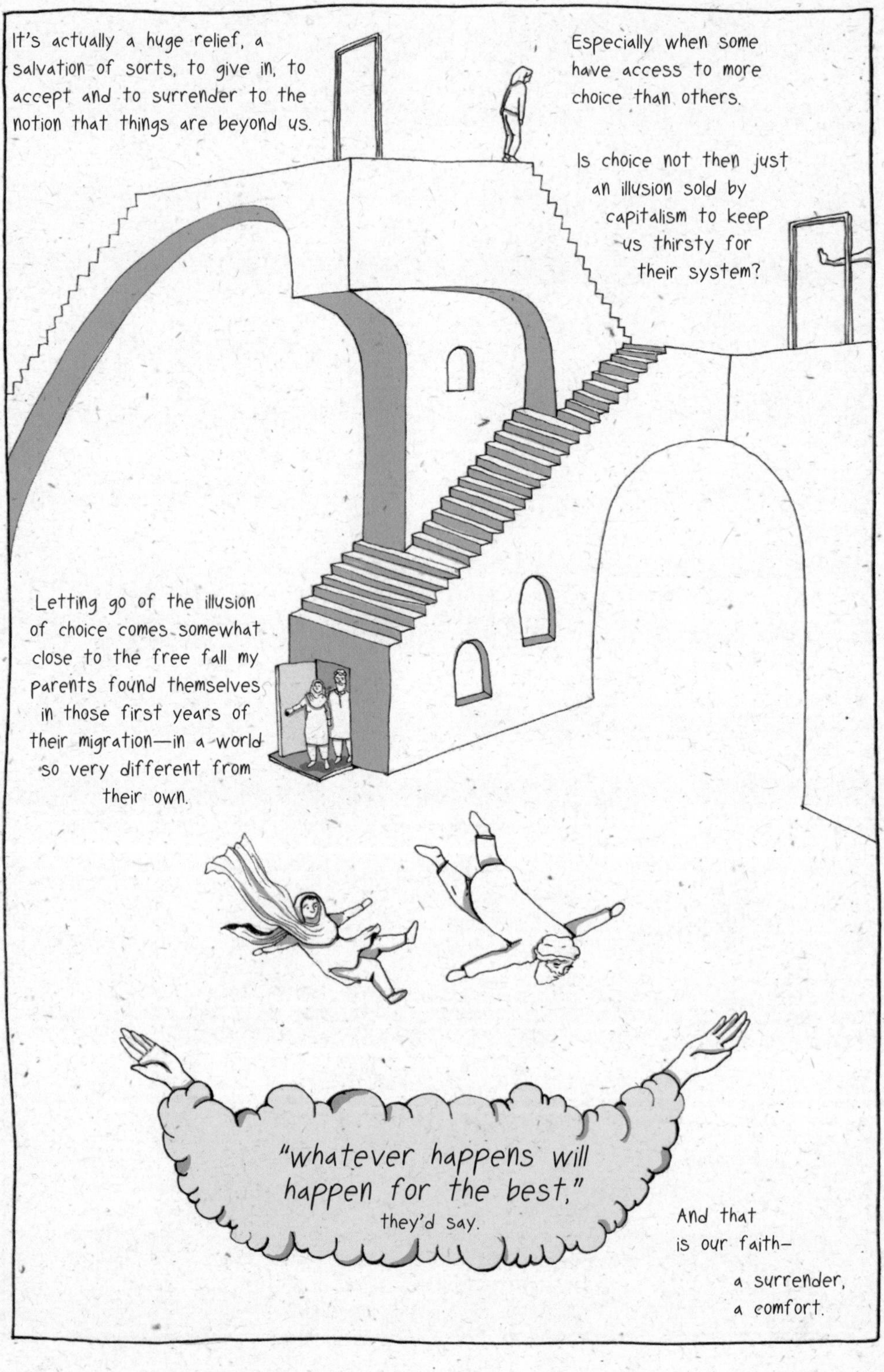

It's actually a huge relief, a salvation of sorts, to give in, to accept and to surrender to the notion that things are beyond us.
Especially when some have access to more choice than others.
Is choice not then just an illusion sold by capitalism to keep us thirsty for their system?
Letting go of the illusion of choice comes somewhat close to the free fall my parents found themselves in those first years of their migration—in a world so very different from their own.
"whatever happens will happen for the best,"
they'd say.
And that is our faith–
a surrender,
a comfort.

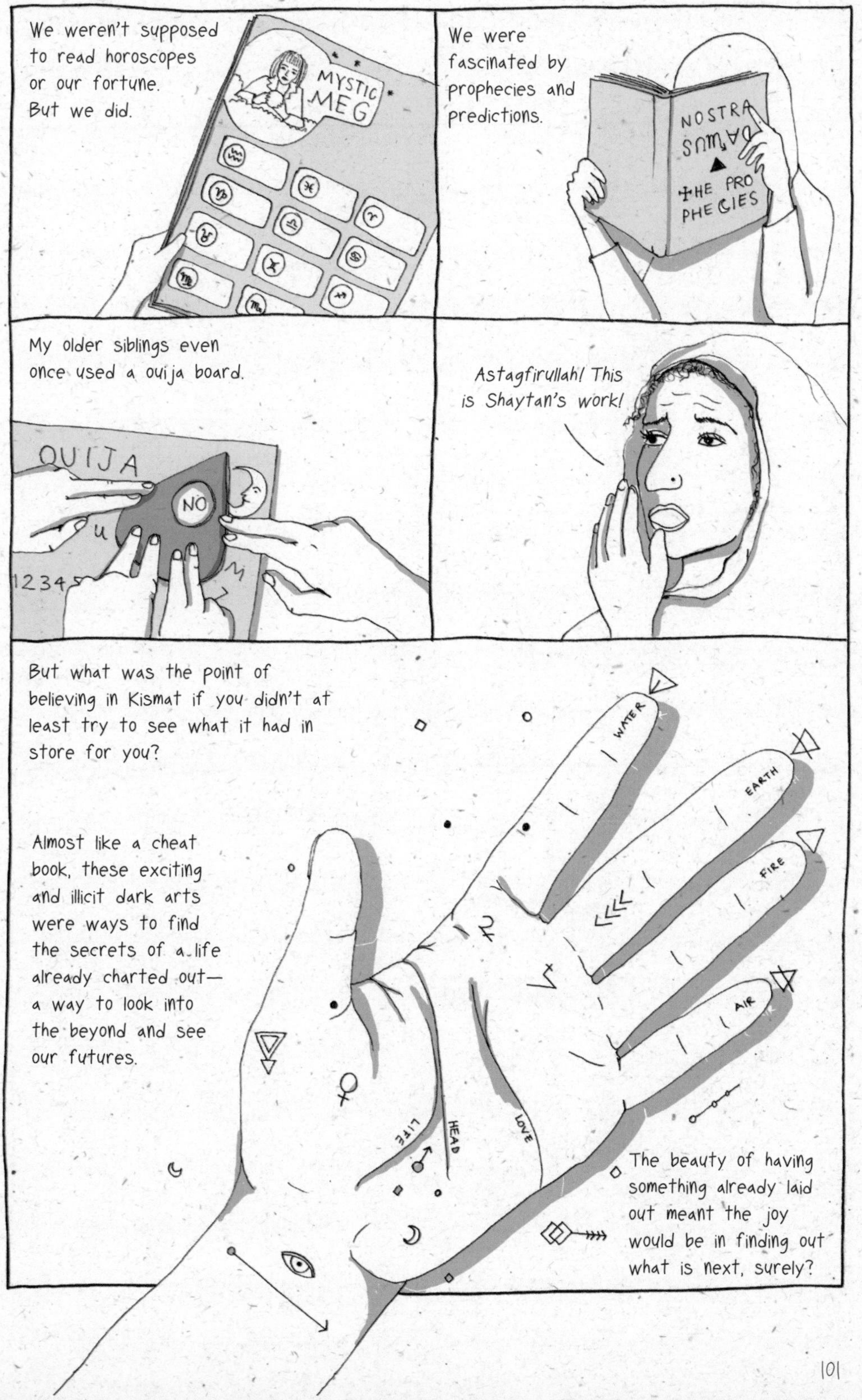
We weren't supposed to read horoscopes or our fortune. But we did.
MYSTIC MEG
We were fascinated by prophecies and predictions.
NOSTRADAMUS
THE PROPHECIES
My older siblings even once used a ouija board.
OUIJA
NO
12345
Astagfirullah! This is Shaytan's work!
But what was the point of believing in Kismat if you didn't at least try to see what it had in store for you?
Almost like a cheat book, these exciting and illicit dark arts were ways to find the secrets of a life already charted out— a way to look into the beyond and see our futures.
WATER
EARTH
FIRE
AIR
LIFE
HEAD
LOVE
The beauty of having something already laid out meant the joy would be in finding out what is next, surely?

But why would the angels record our deeds if they are known already?

And what of one's agency?

Does it mean every well-made decision is not mine?

And does it absolve me of every decision wrongly made?

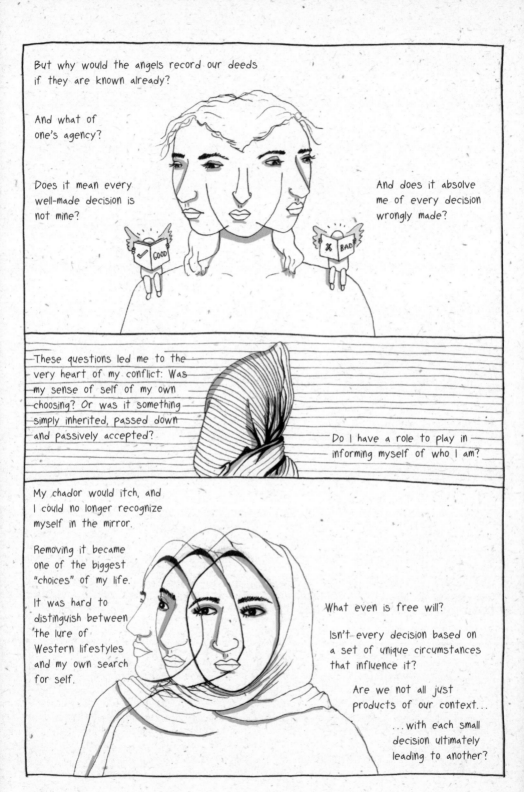

These questions led me to the very heart of my conflict: Was my sense of self of my own choosing? Or was it something simply inherited, passed down and passively accepted?

Do I have a role to play in informing myself of who I am?

My chador would itch, and I could no longer recognize myself in the mirror.

Removing it became one of the biggest "choices" of my life.

It was hard to distinguish between the lure of Western lifestyles and my own search for self.

What even is free will?

Isn't every decision based on a set of unique circumstances that influence it?

Are we not all just products of our context...

...with each small decision ultimately leading to another?

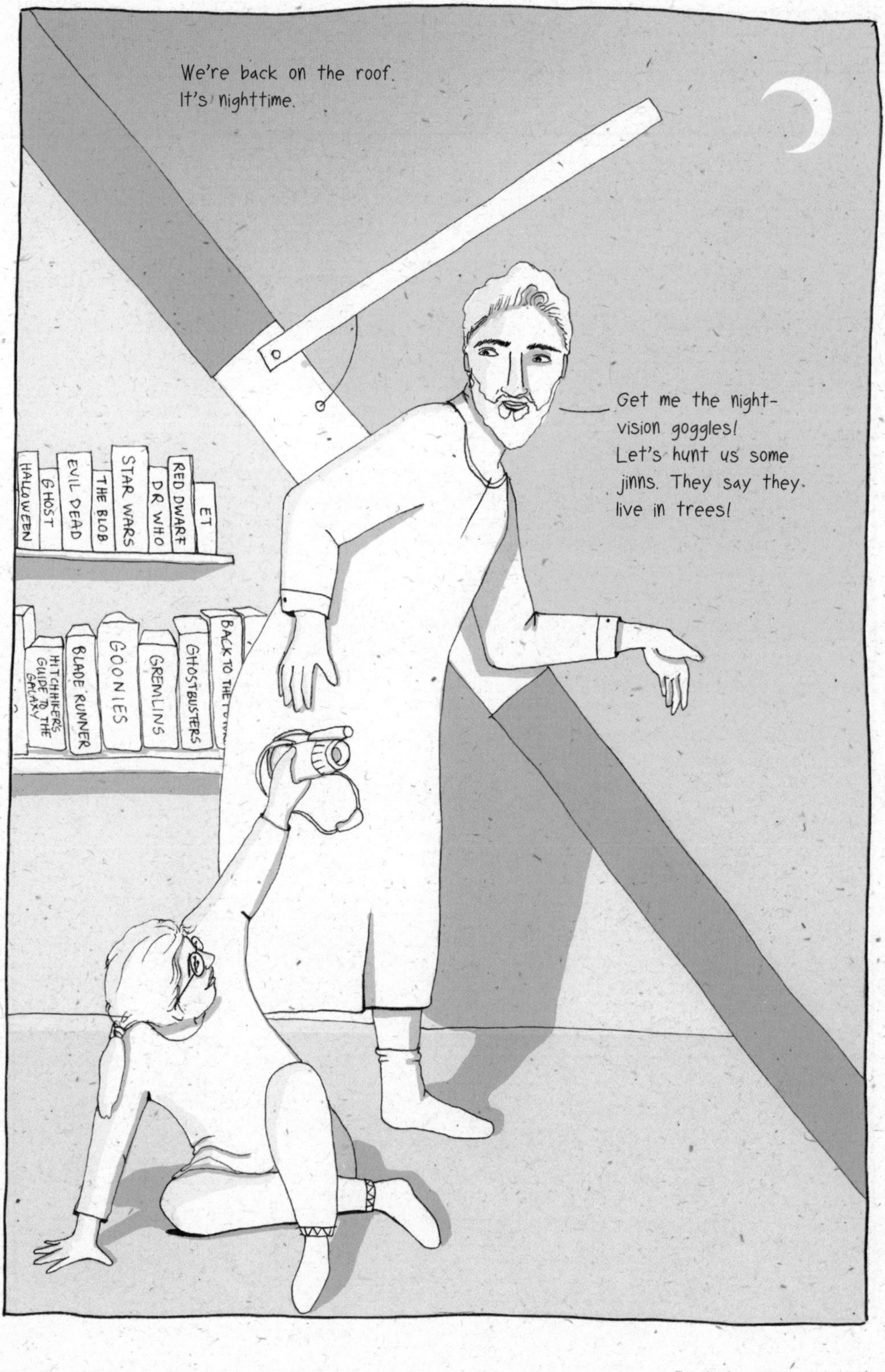
We're back on the roof.
It's nighttime.
Get me the night-vision goggles!
Let's hunt us some jinns. They say they live in trees!
HALLOWEEN
GHOST
EVIL DEAD
THE BLOB
STAR WARS
DR WHO
RED DWARF
ET
HITCHHIKER'S GUIDE TO THE GALAXY
BLADE RUNNER
GOONIES
GREMLINS
GHOSTBUSTERS

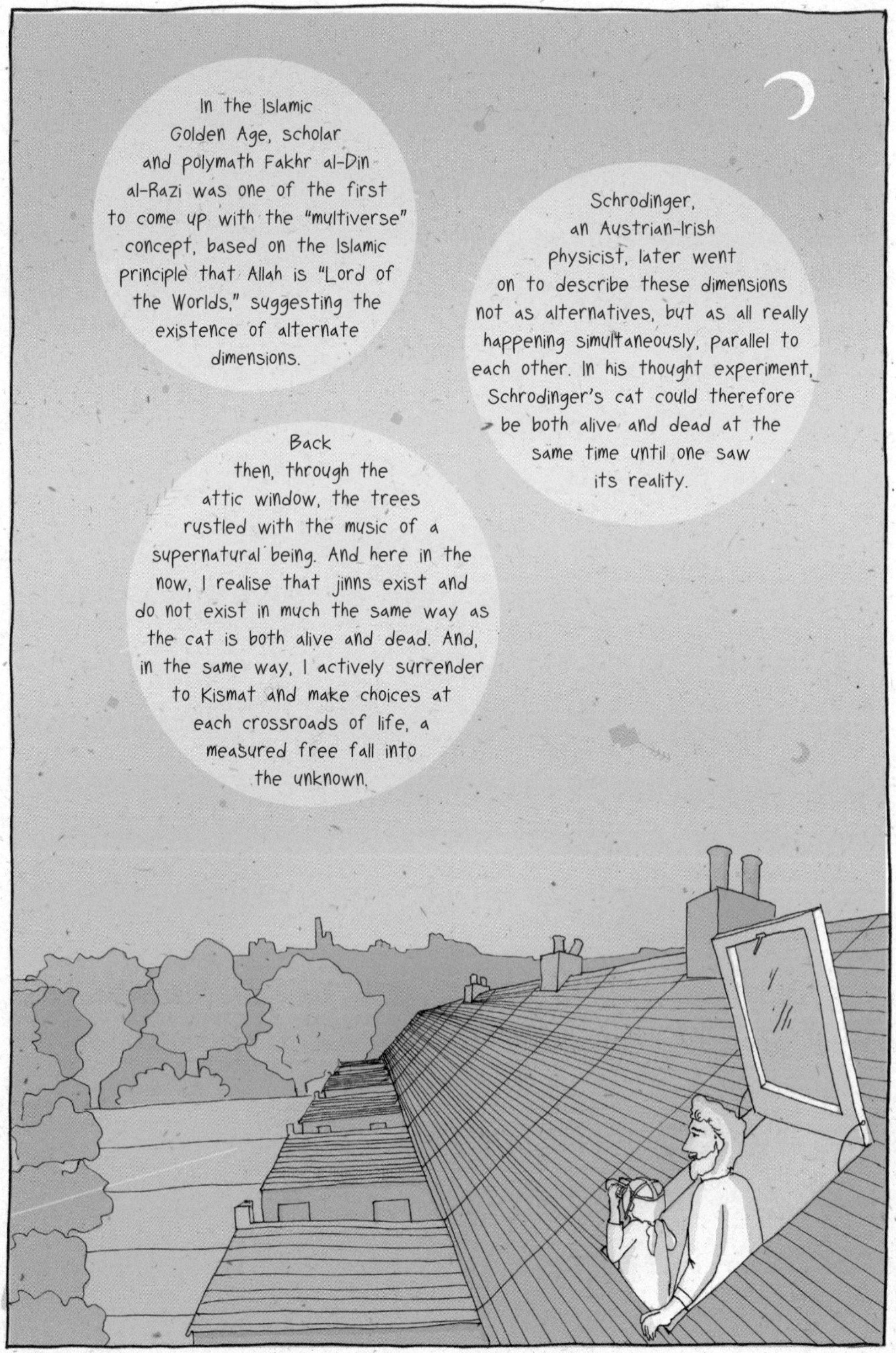
In the Islamic Golden Age, scholar and polymath Fakhr al-Din al-Razi was one of the first to come up with the "multiverse" concept, based on the Islamic principle that Allah is "Lord of the Worlds," suggesting the existence of alternate dimensions.
Schrodinger, an Austrian-Irish physicist, later went on to describe these dimensions not as alternatives, but as all really happening simultaneously, parallel to each other. In his thought experiment, Schrodinger's cat could therefore be both alive and dead at the same time until one saw its reality.
Back then, through the attic window, the trees rustled with the music of a supernatural being. And here in the now, I realise that jinns exist and do not exist in much the same way as the cat is both alive and dead. And, in the same way, I actively surrender to Kismat and make choices at each crossroads of life, a measured free fall into the unknown.

According to philosopher Carl Jung,

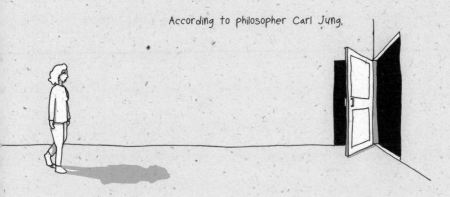

until we make the unconscious

conscious, it will direct our lives

SLAM

and we will call it fate.

And then we realize...

the

personal

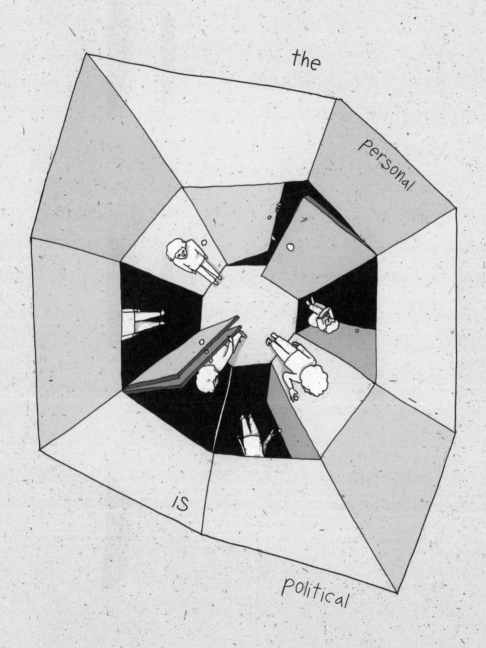

is

political

...and everything is connected.

two

11	PUNCTURED	♫ PJ Harvey "Let England Shake"

The 7/7 London attacks happened on a Thursday in 2005.
Fifty-two people were killed that day.

Inna Lillahi wa inna ilayhi raj'iun.

Two days later, I was travelling on the
tube to my weekend retail job.
I was twenty years old.

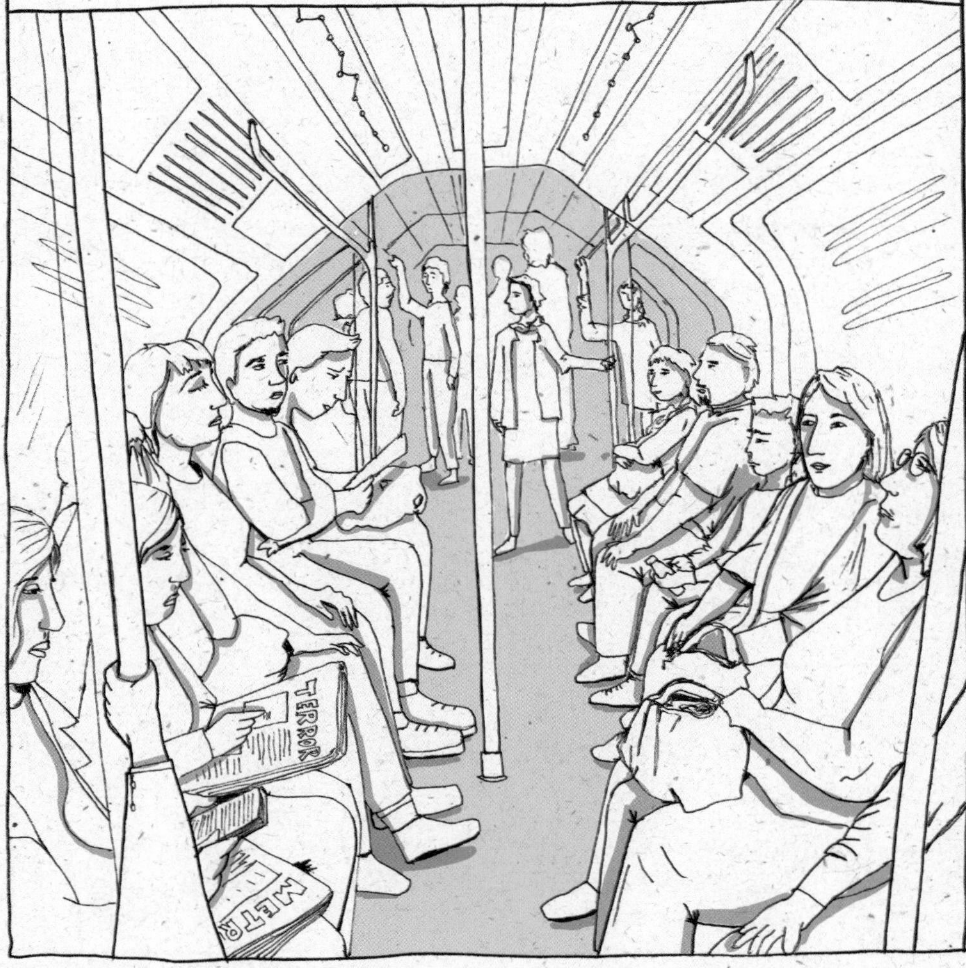
TERROR
METR

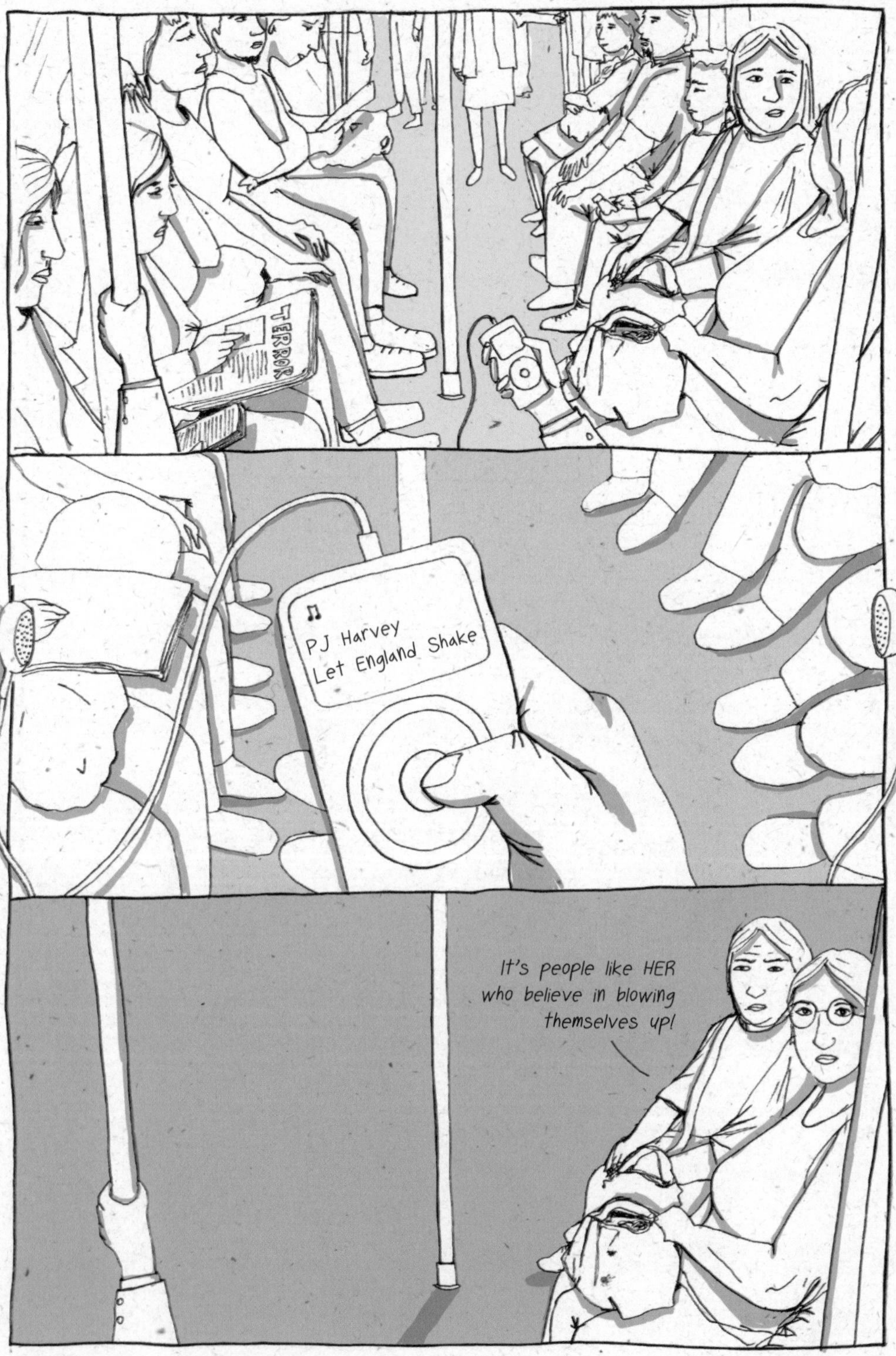
TERROR
PJ Harvey
Let England Shake
It's people like HER who believe in blowing themselves up!

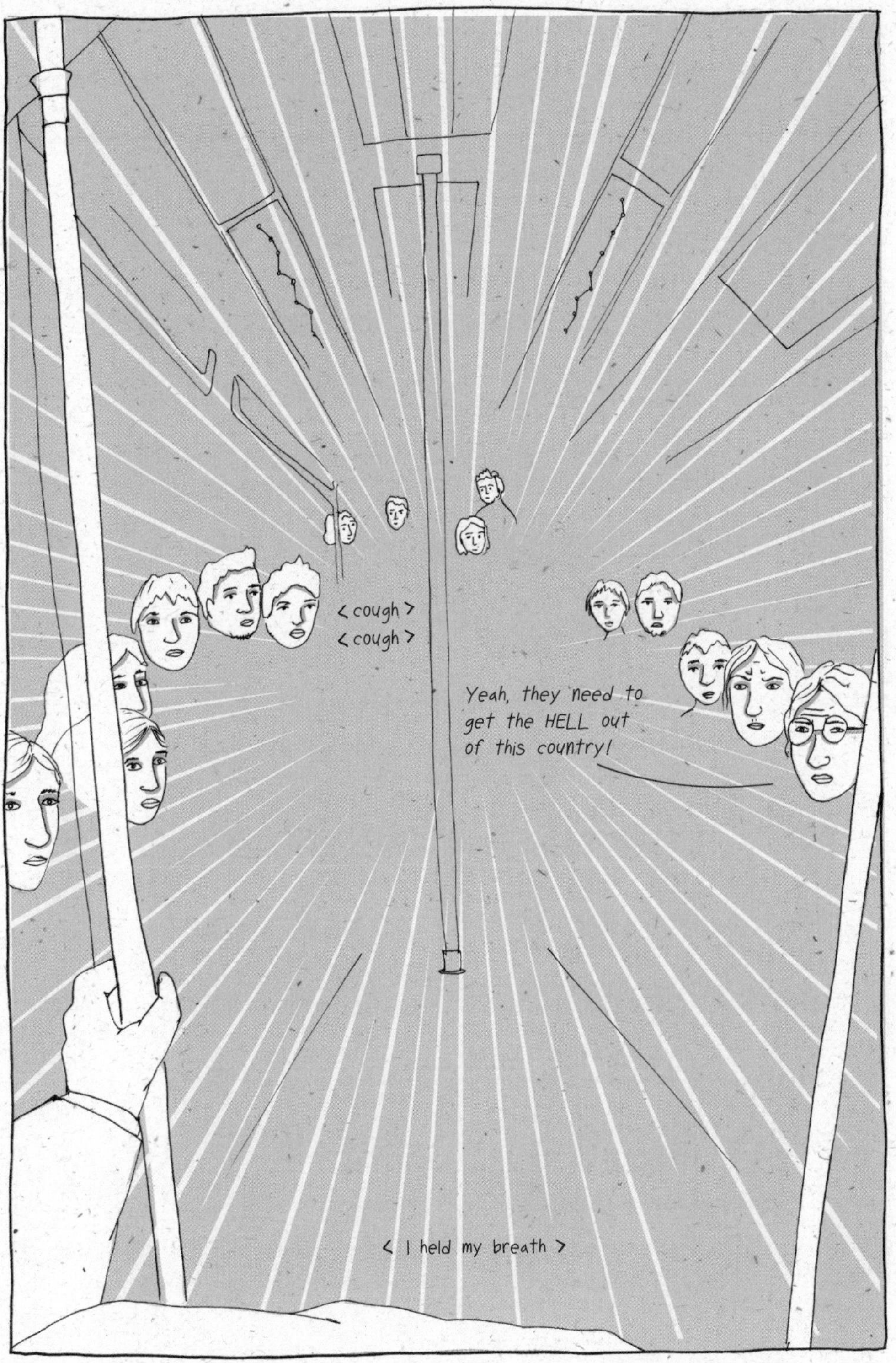
< cough >
< cough >
Yeah, they need to get the HELL out of this country!
< I held my breath >

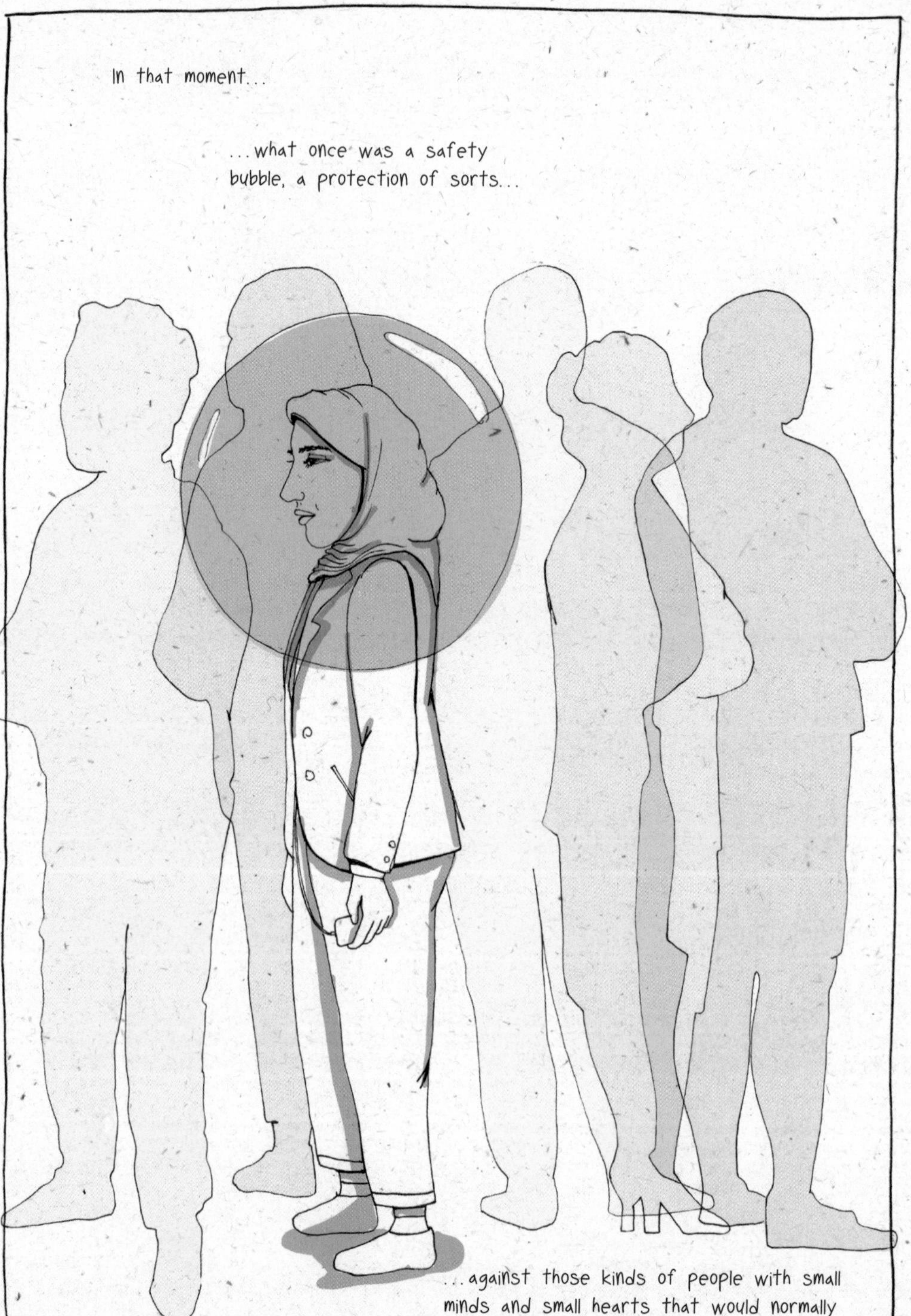
In that moment...
...what once was a safety bubble, a protection of sorts...
...against those kinds of people with small minds and small hearts that would normally ignore me or at best "tolerate" me...

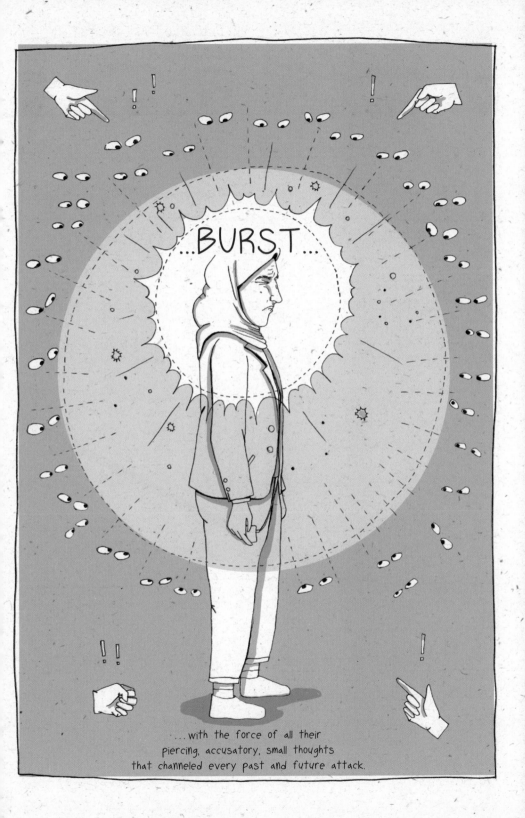

...with the force of all their
piercing, accusatory, small thoughts
that channeled every past and future attack.

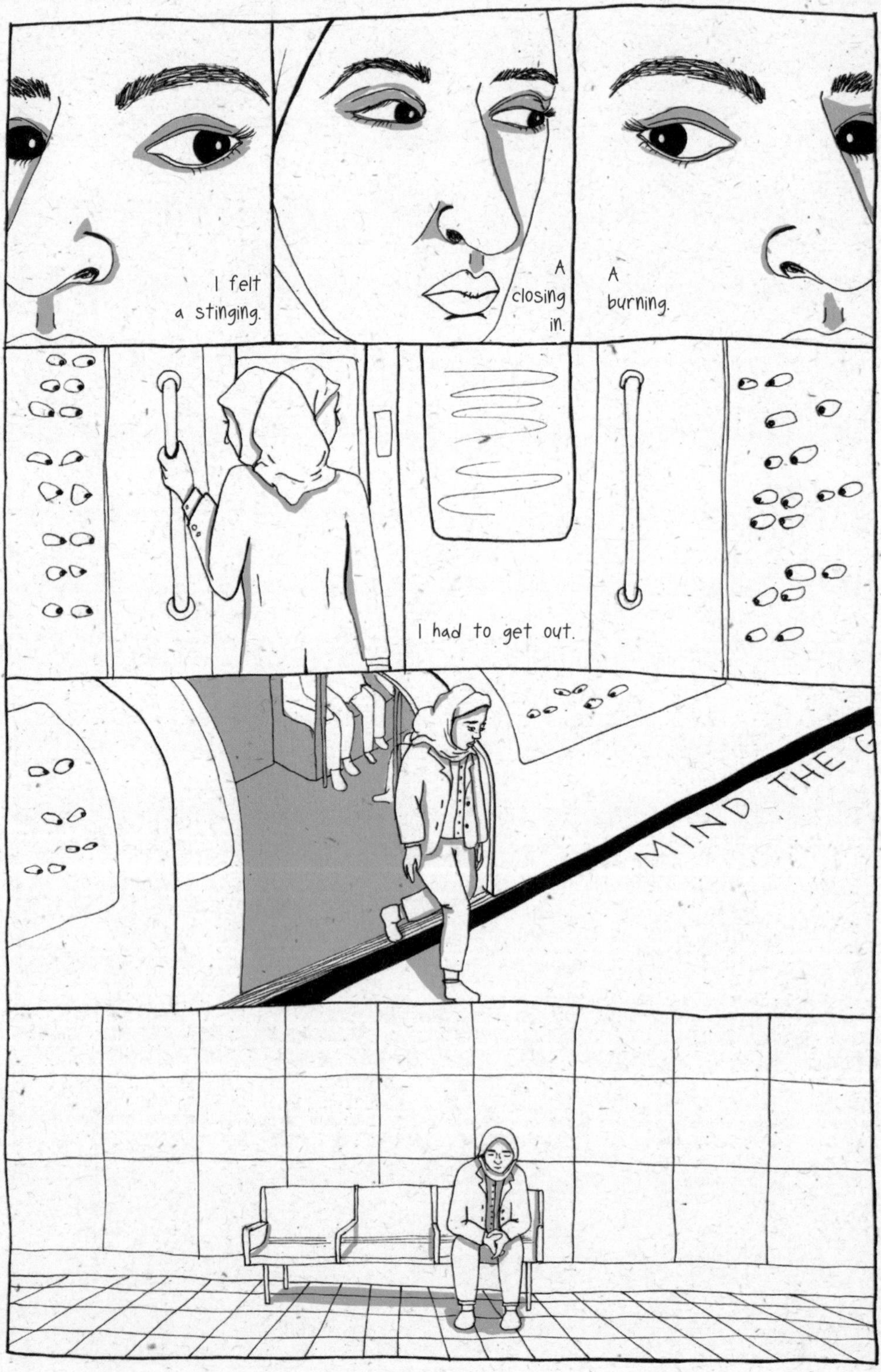
I felt a stinging.
A closing in.
A burning.
I had to get out.
MIND THE G

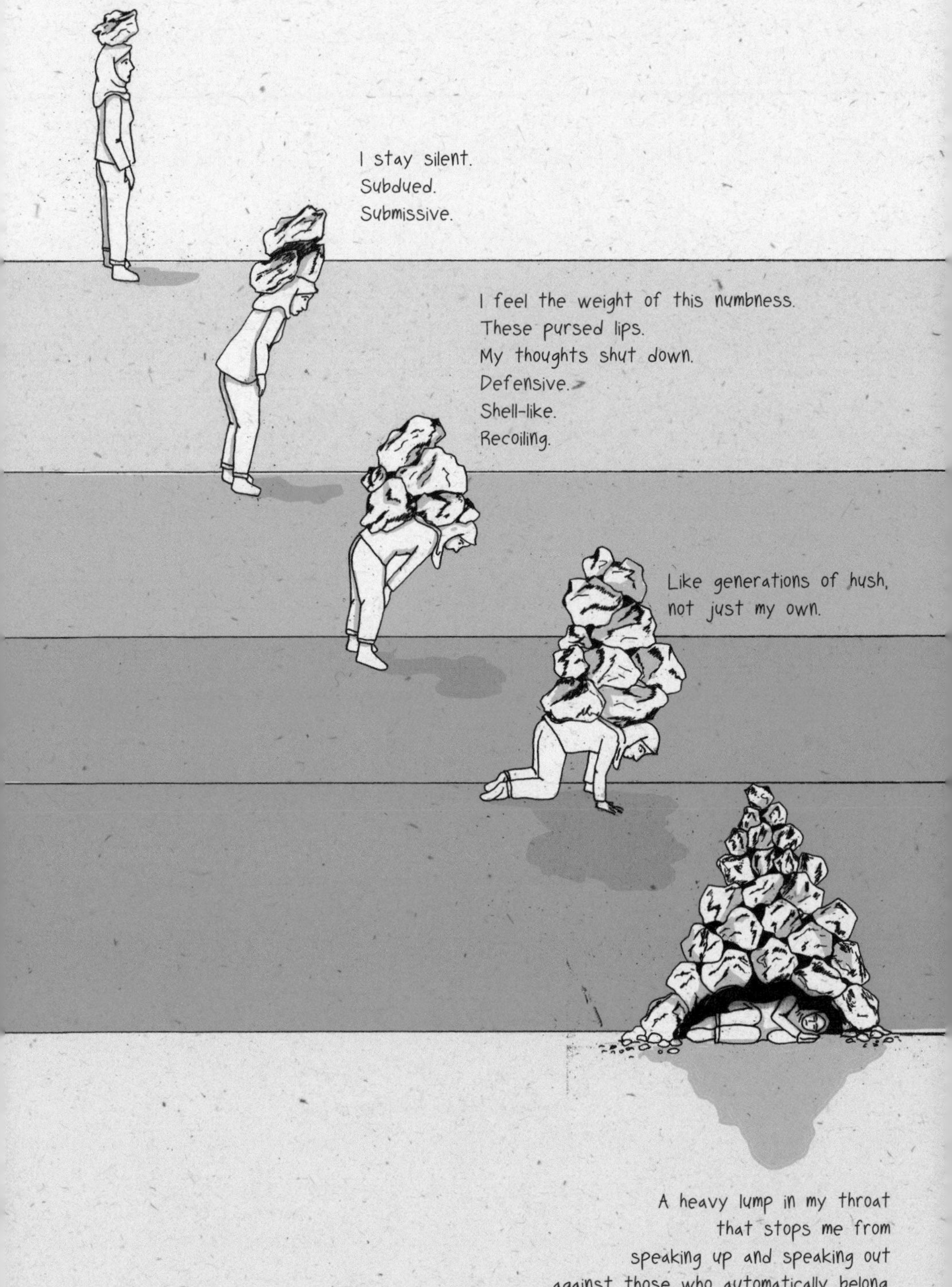
I stay silent.
Subdued.
Submissive.
I feel the weight of this numbness.
These pursed lips.
My thoughts shut down.
Defensive.
Shell-like.
Recoiling.
Like generations of hush,
not just my own.
A heavy lump in my throat
that stops me from
speaking up and speaking out
against those who automatically belong.

How do I begin to find my voice?

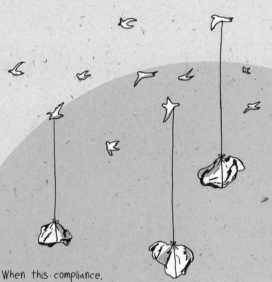

When this compliance, this silence has haunted me for most of my life.

A voice so quivering, so croaky, it has never had the space to speak.

She answers: Slowly and with practice. Start small, start every day. In the shops, over the phone.

I marvel at what belonging offers...

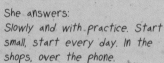

...a space to speak freely without fear.

12 QUESTIONS

♫ David Byrne & Brian Eno
"Strange Overtones"

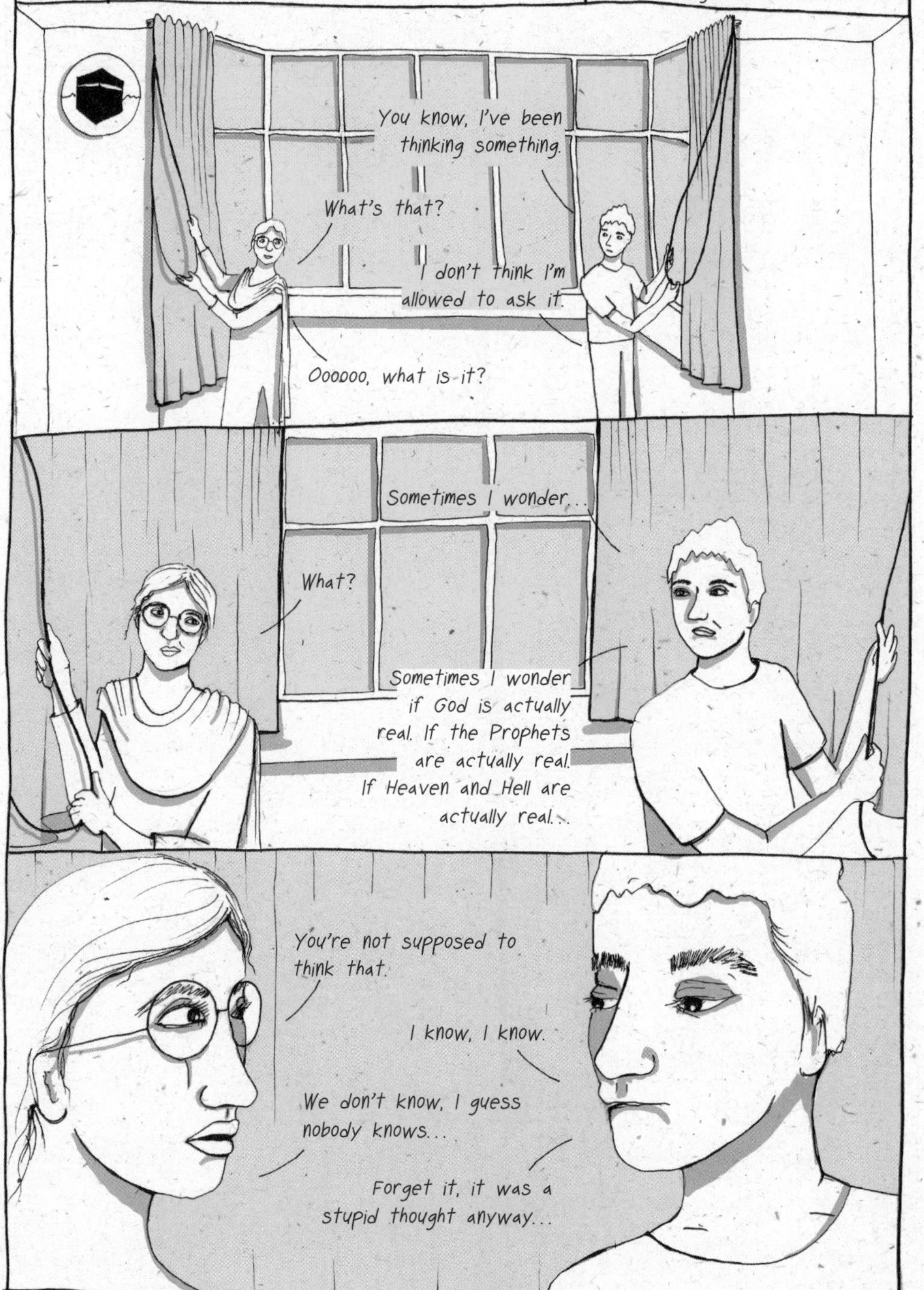
You know, I've been thinking something.
What's that?
I don't think I'm allowed to ask it.
Oooooo, what is it?
Sometimes I wonder...
What?
Sometimes I wonder if God is actually real. If the Prophets are actually real. If Heaven and Hell are actually real...
You're not supposed to think that.
I know, I know.
We don't know, I guess nobody knows...
Forget it, it was a stupid thought anyway...

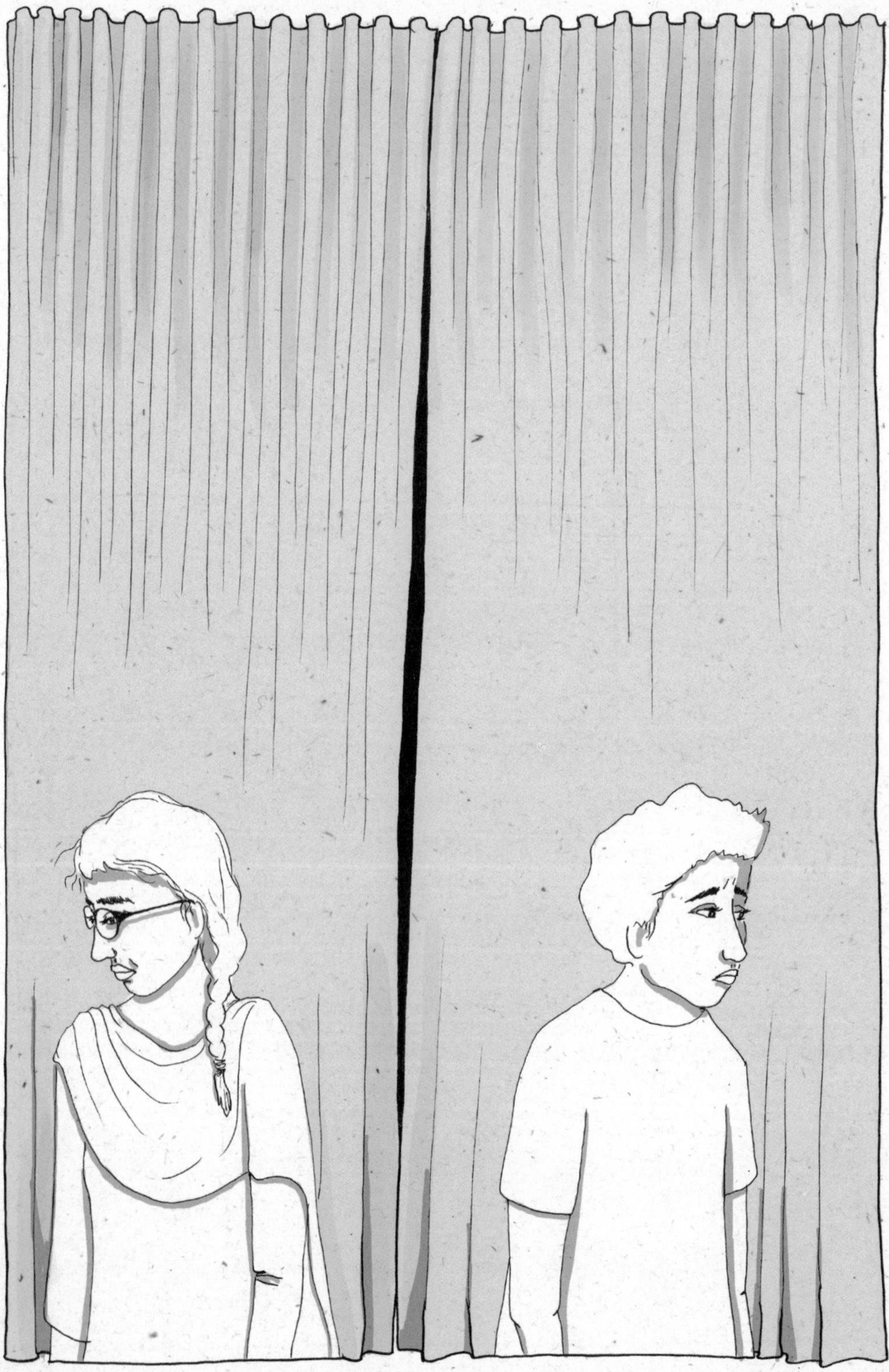

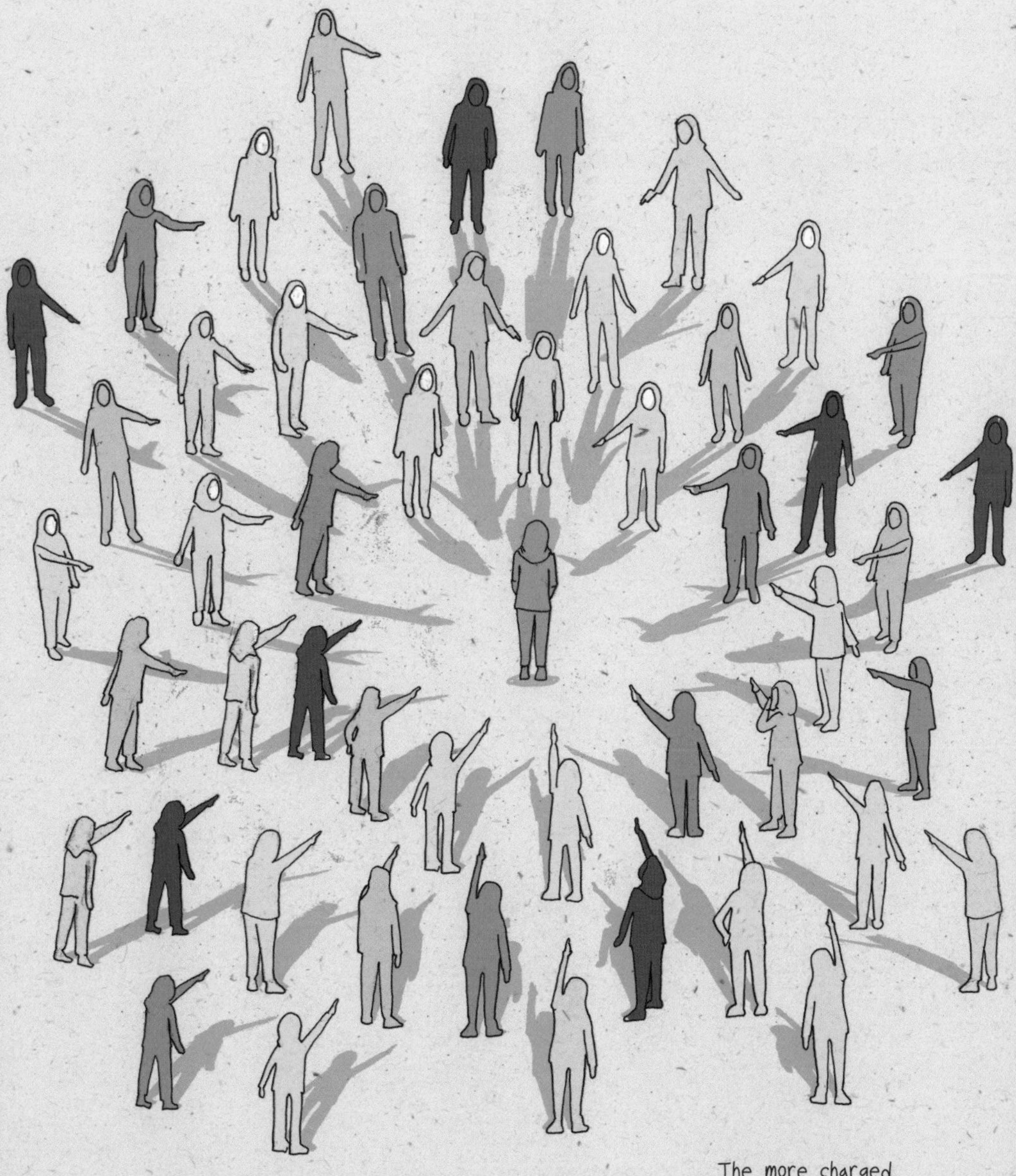

The more charged,
accusatory, and
ferocious the
world outside became...

...the more we tried to hold on
with visible gestures
and outward performances
of piety and righteousness.

The deep spirituality
and personal self-reflection
offered by faith
lost to playing ambassador.

So entangled now, in generations of
role-playing, it can be hard to tell if this
is who we are, or if it is actually
a response to power dynamics.

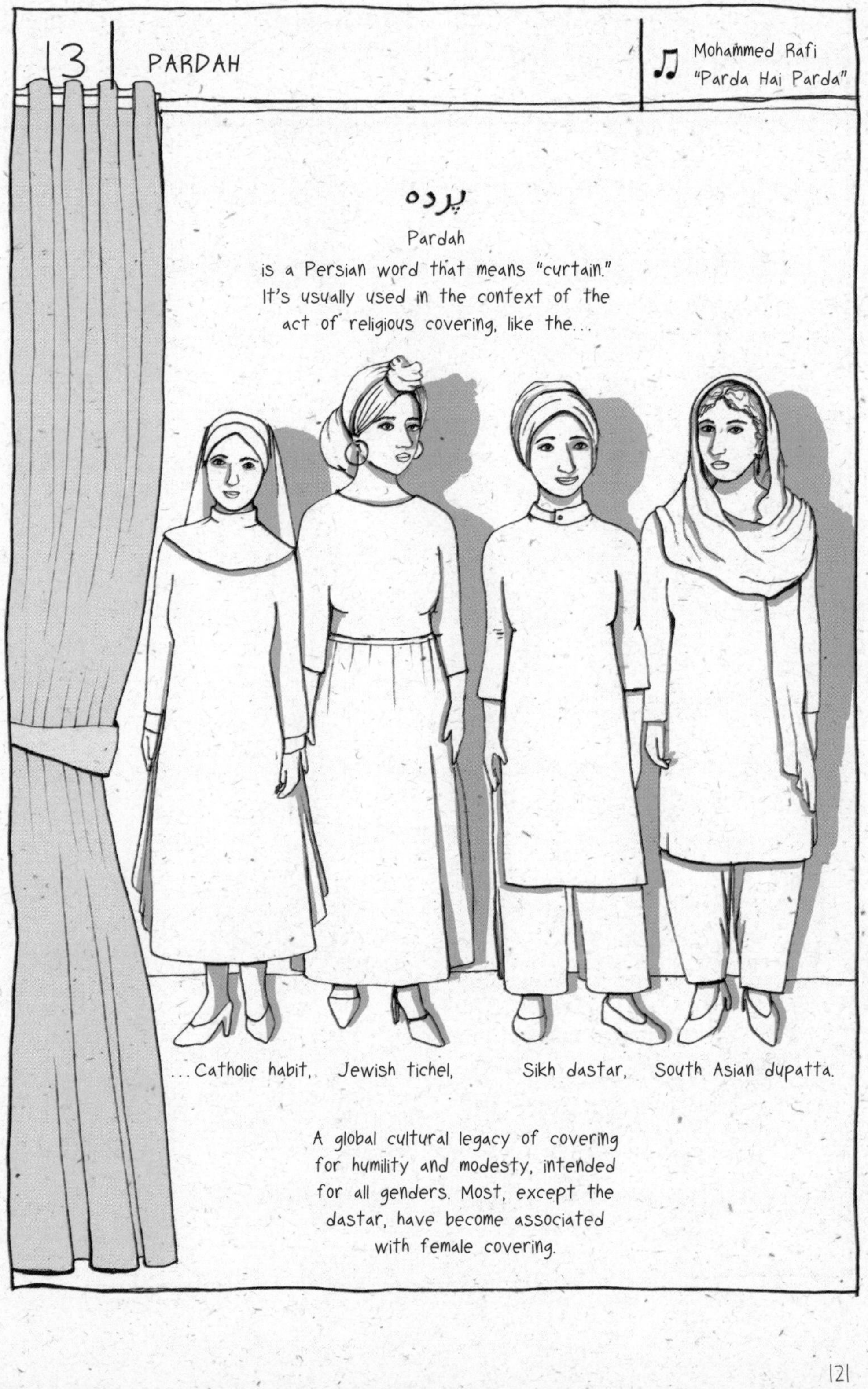
13
PARDAH
Mohammed Rafi
"Parda Hai Parda"
پرده
Pardah
is a Persian word that means "curtain."
It's usually used in the context of the
act of religious covering, like the...
...Catholic habit,
Jewish tichel,
Sikh dastar,
South Asian dupatta.
A global cultural legacy of covering
for humility and modesty, intended
for all genders. Most, except the
dastar, have become associated
with female covering.

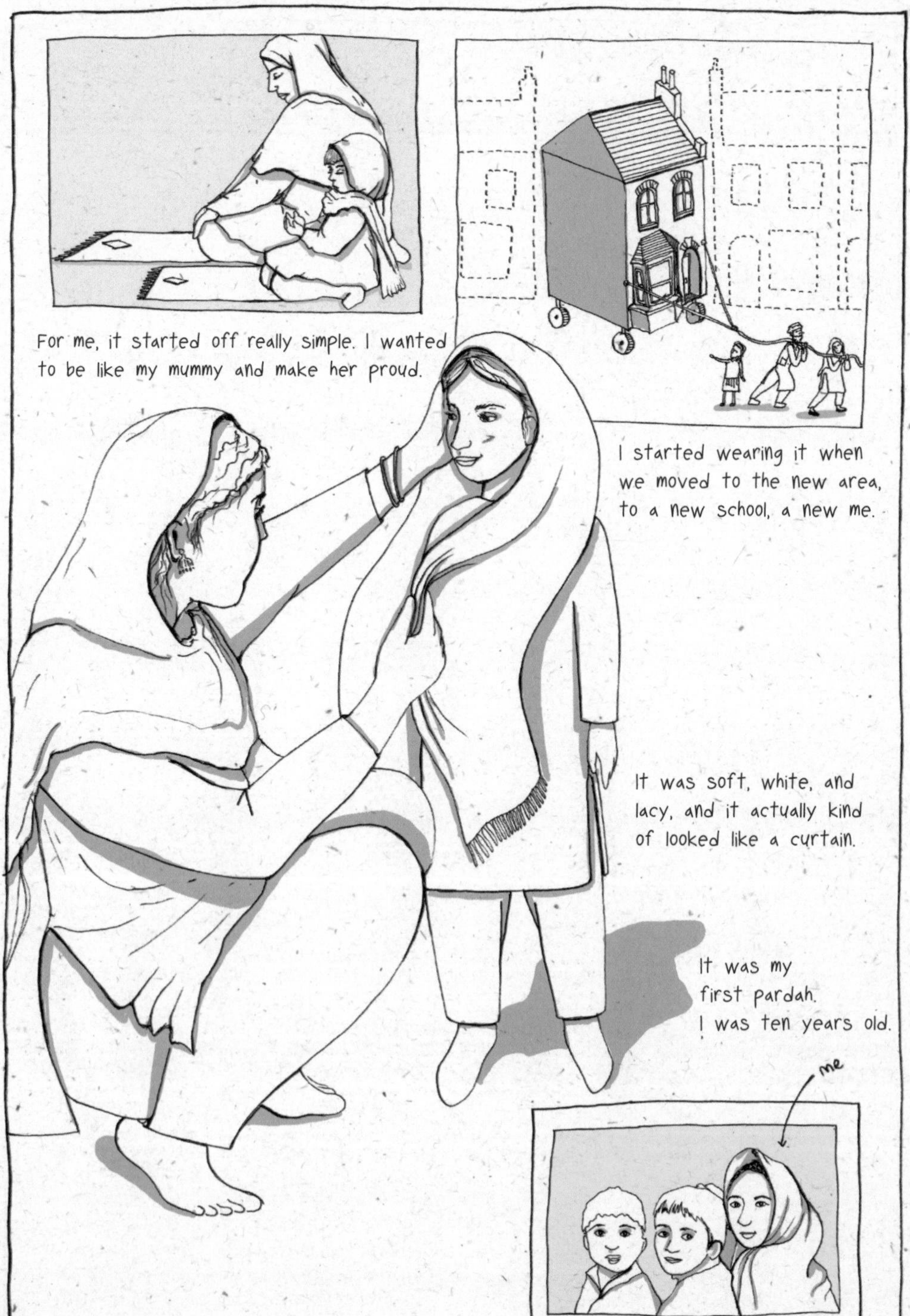
For me, it started off really simple. I wanted to be like my mummy and make her proud.
I started wearing it when we moved to the new area, to a new school, a new me.
It was soft, white, and lacy, and it actually kind of looked like a curtain.
It was my first pardah. I was ten years old.
me

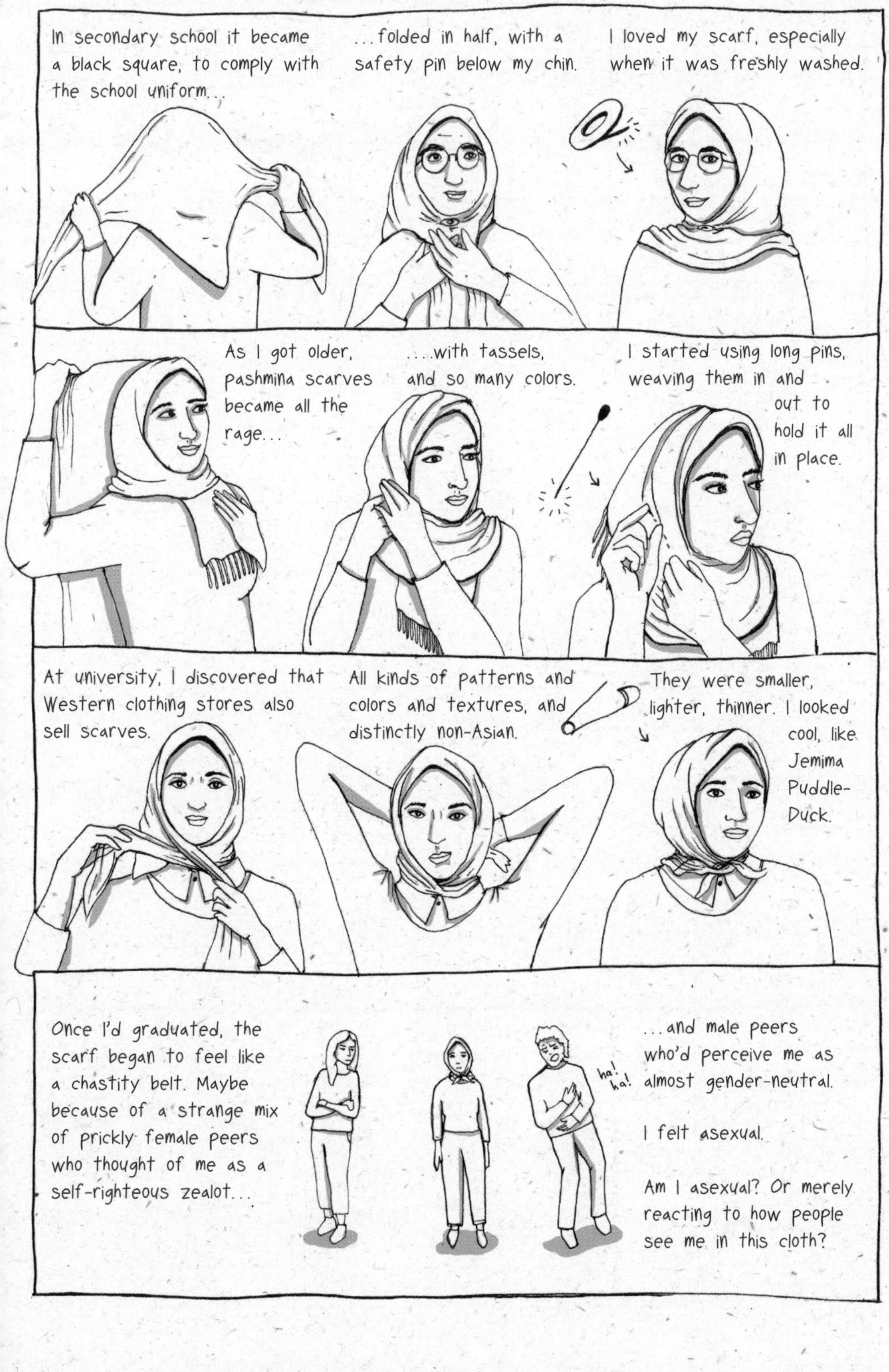
In secondary school it became a black square, to comply with the school uniform...
...folded in half, with a safety pin below my chin.
I loved my scarf, especially when it was freshly washed.
As I got older, pashmina scarves became all the rage...
....with tassels, and so many colors.
I started using long pins, weaving them in and out to hold it all in place.
At university, I discovered that Western clothing stores also sell scarves.
All kinds of patterns and colors and textures, and distinctly non-Asian.
They were smaller, lighter, thinner. I looked cool, like Jemima Puddle-Duck.
Once I'd graduated, the scarf began to feel like a chastity belt. Maybe because of a strange mix of prickly female peers who thought of me as a self-righteous zealot...
ha! ha!
...and male peers who'd perceive me as almost gender-neutral.
I felt asexual.
Am I asexual? Or merely reacting to how people see me in this cloth?

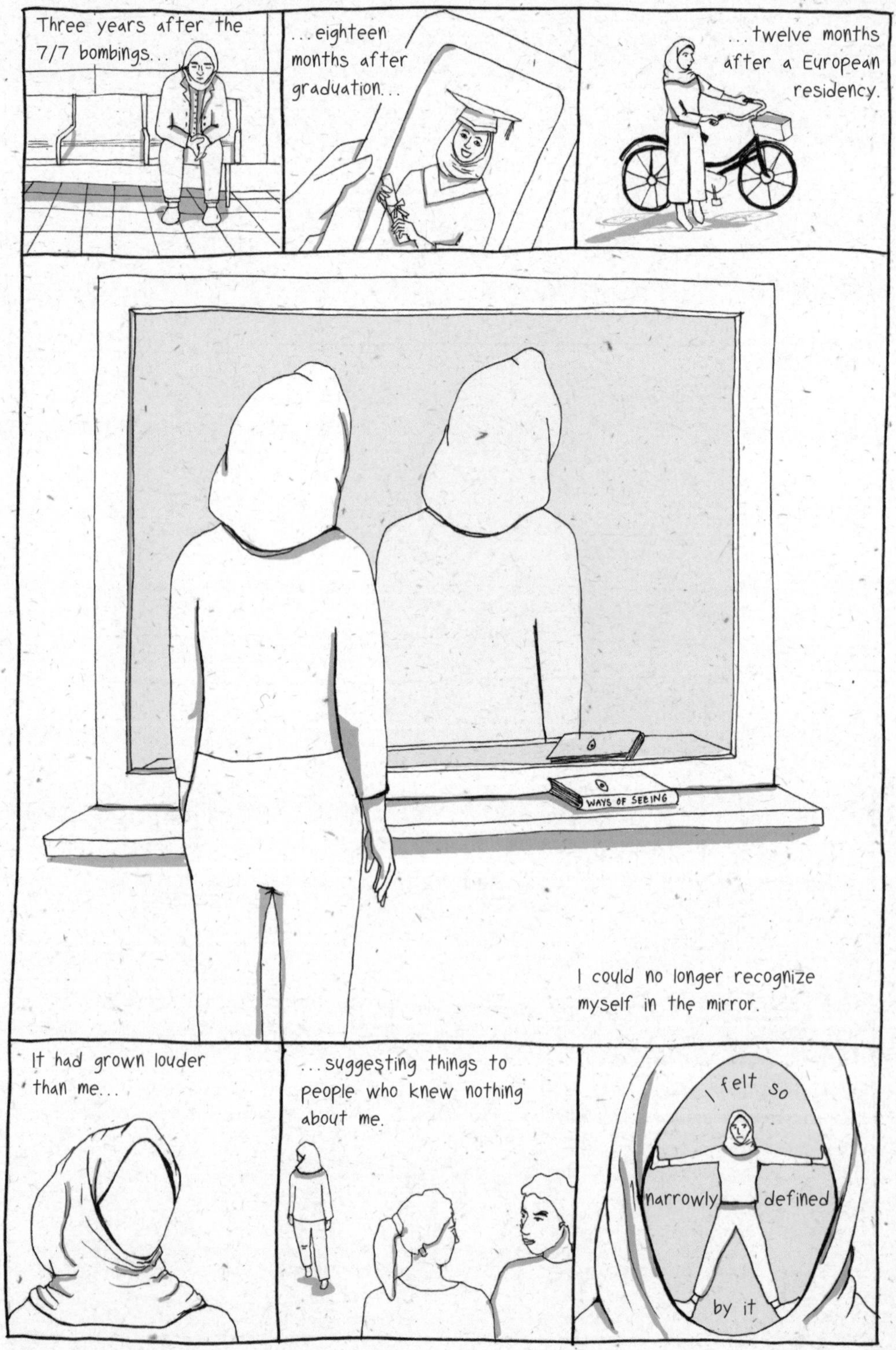
Three years after the 7/7 bombings...
...eighteen months after graduation...
...twelve months after a European residency.
WAYS OF SEEING
I could no longer recognize myself in the mirror.
It had grown louder than me...
...suggesting things to people who knew nothing about me.
I felt so
narrowly
defined
by it

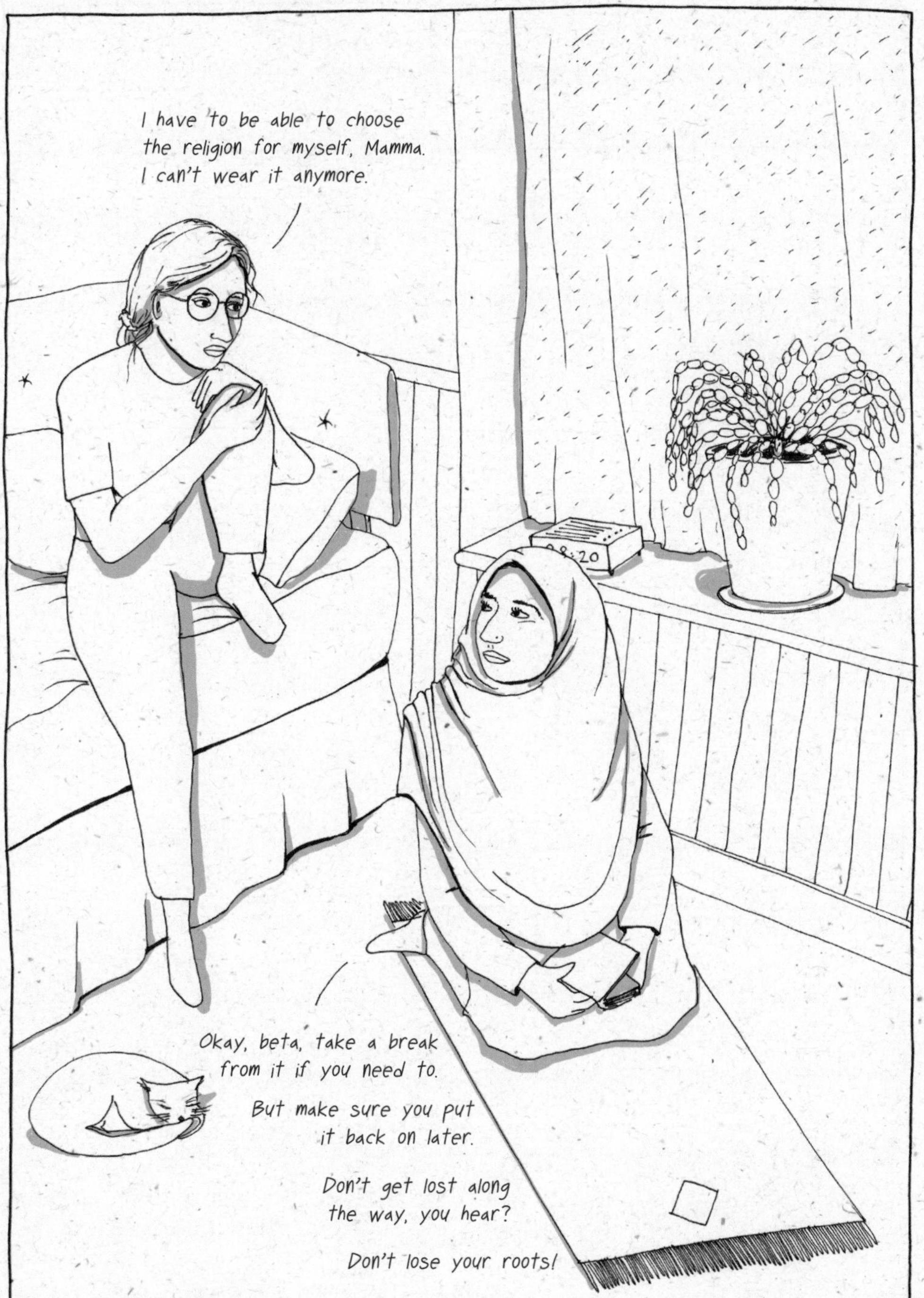
I have to be able to choose the religion for myself, Mamma. I can't wear it anymore.
Okay, beta, take a break from it if you need to.
But make sure you put it back on later.
Don't get lost along the way, you hear?
Don't lose your roots!
We'll see, Mamma. You have to let me see.

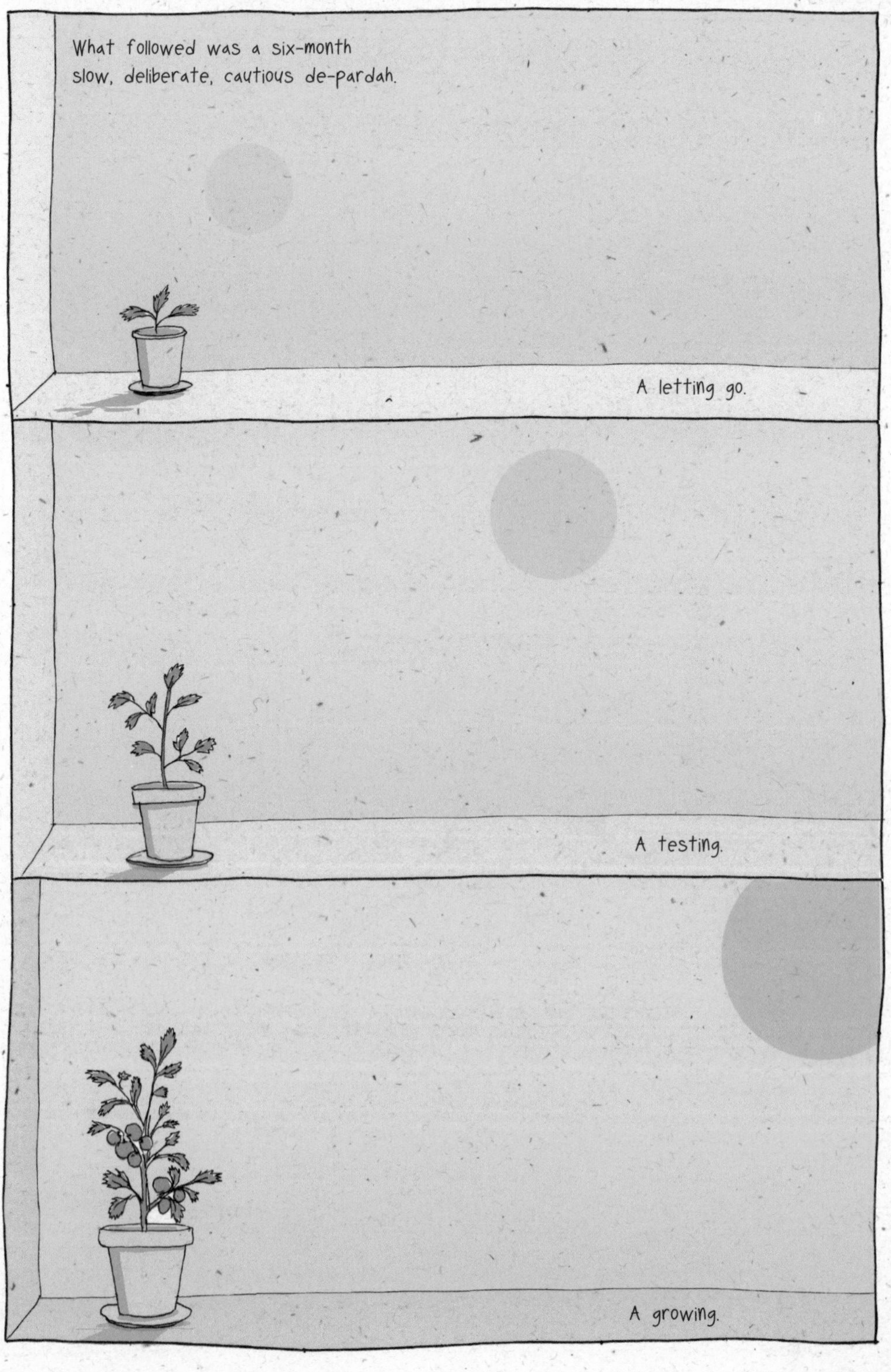
What followed was a six-month slow, deliberate, cautious de-pardah.
A letting go.
A testing.
A growing.

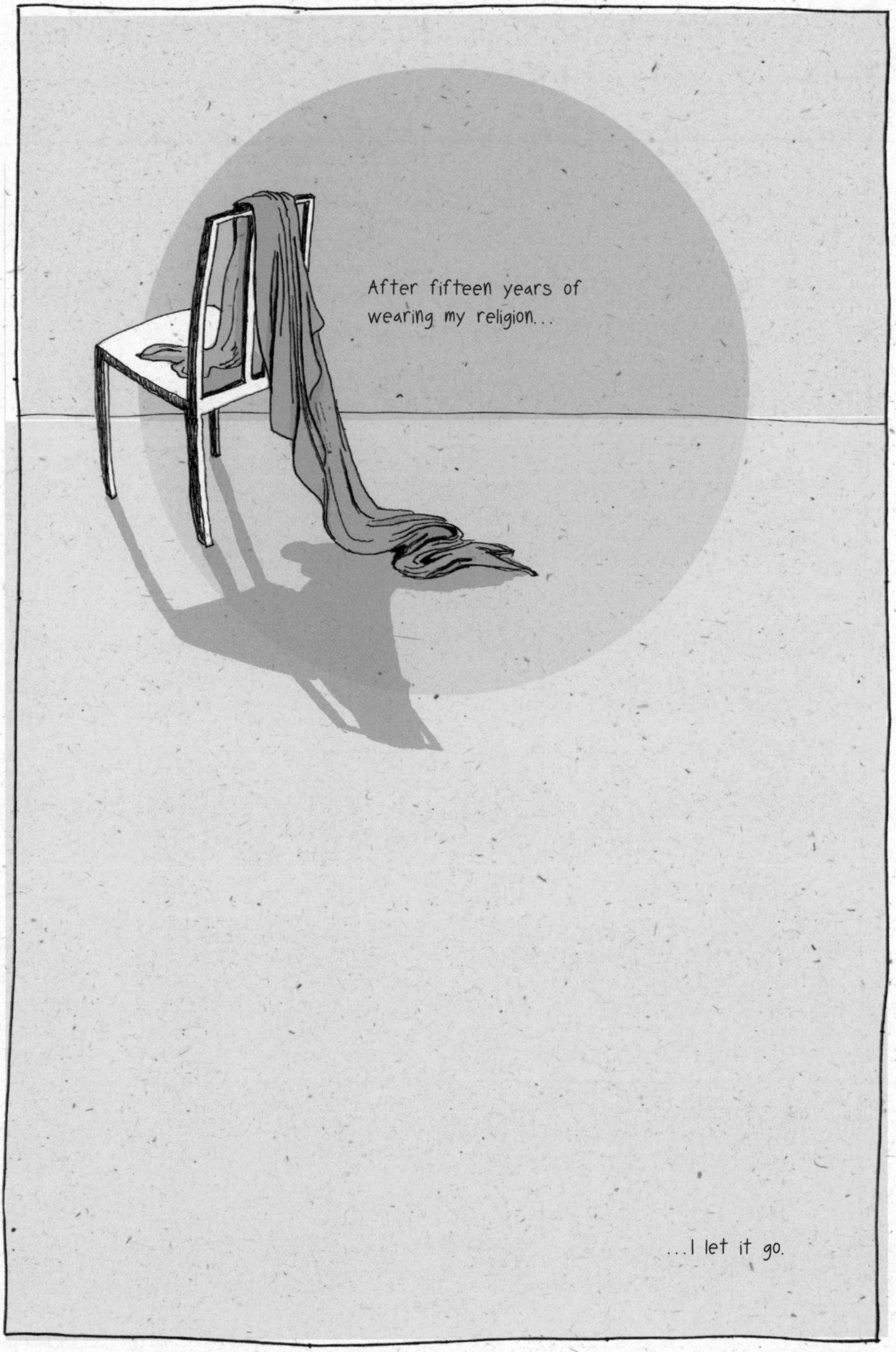
After fifteen years of wearing my religion...
...I let it go.

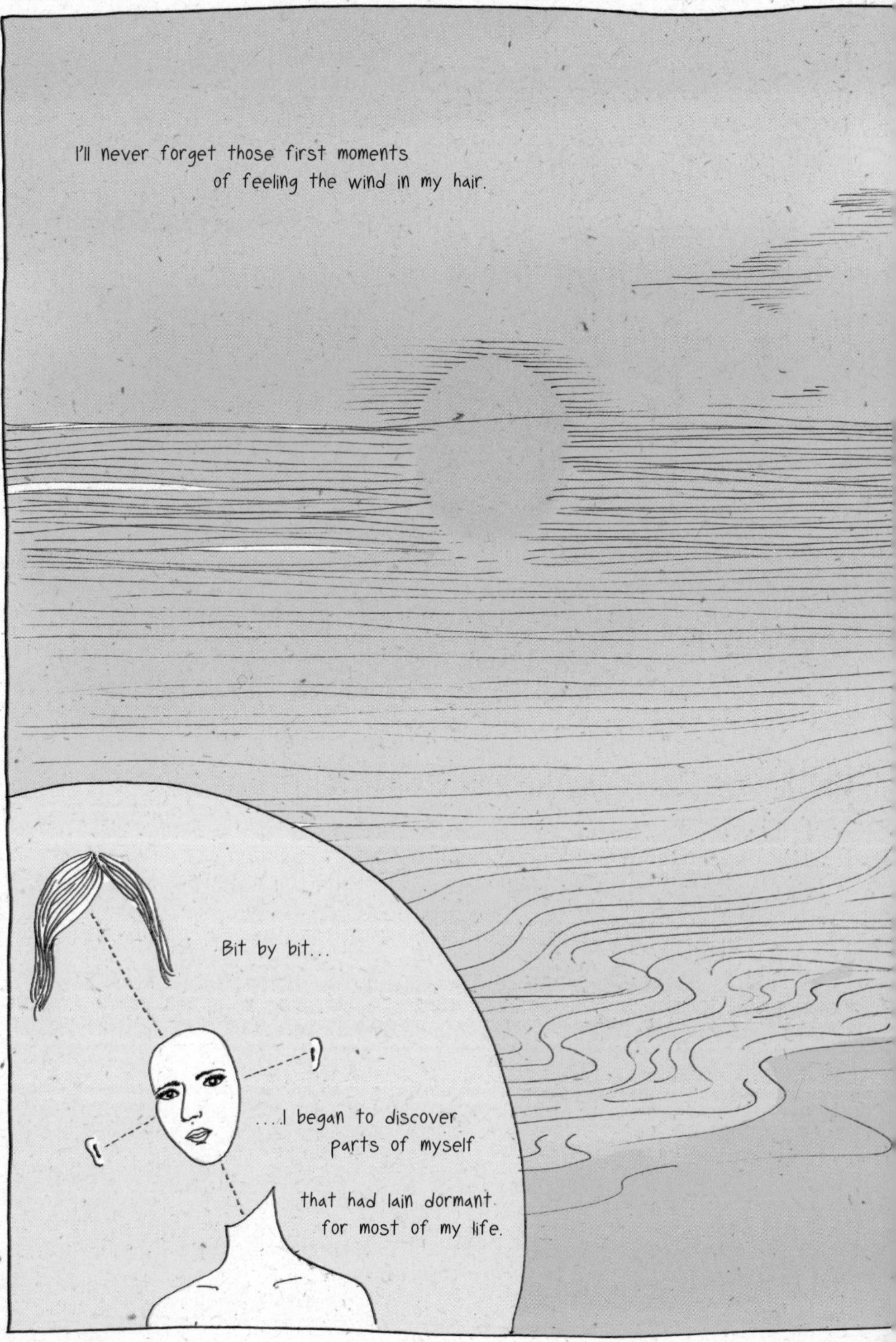
I'll never forget those first moments of feeling the wind in my hair.
Bit by bit...
...I began to discover parts of myself
that had lain dormant for most of my life.

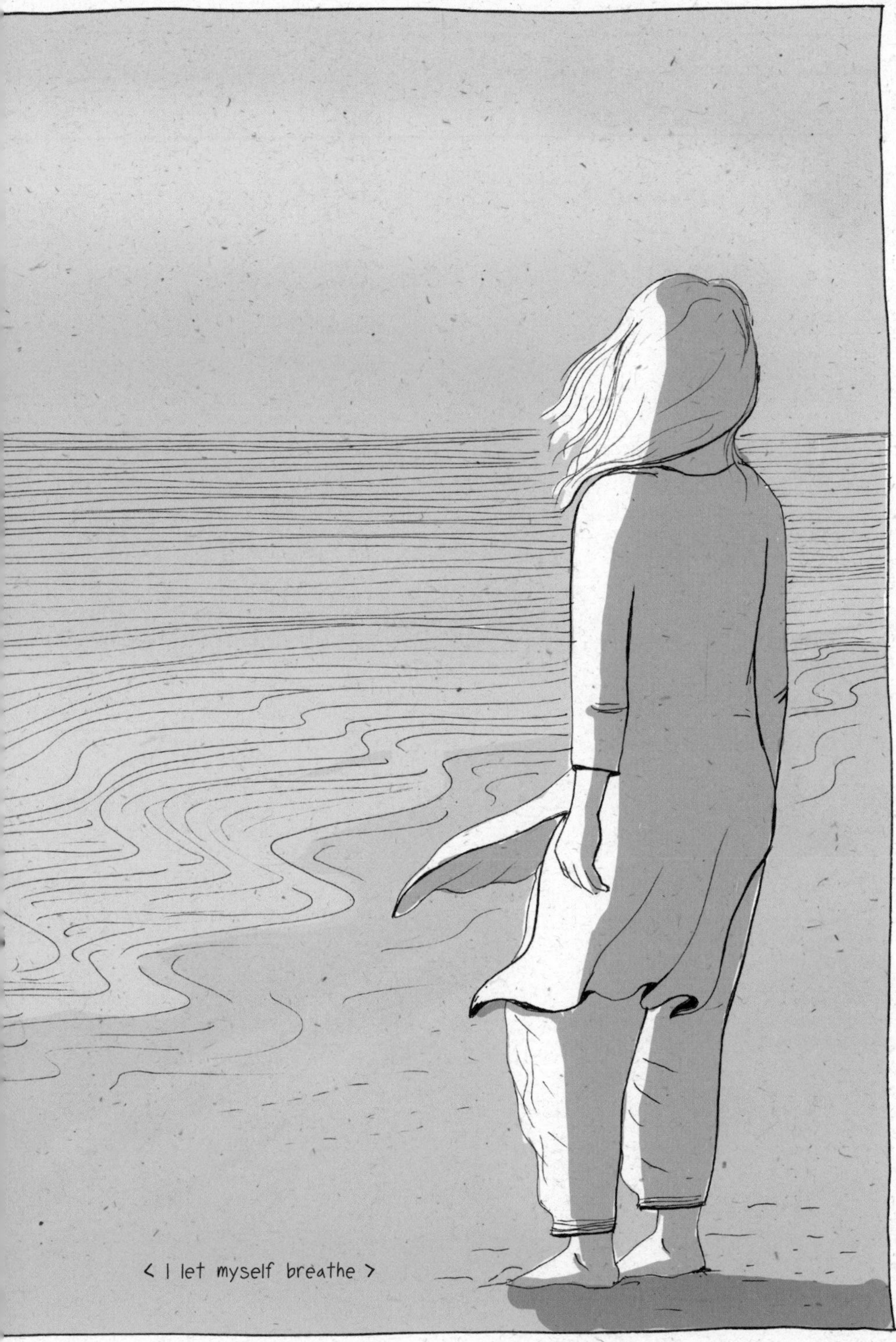
< I let myself breathe >

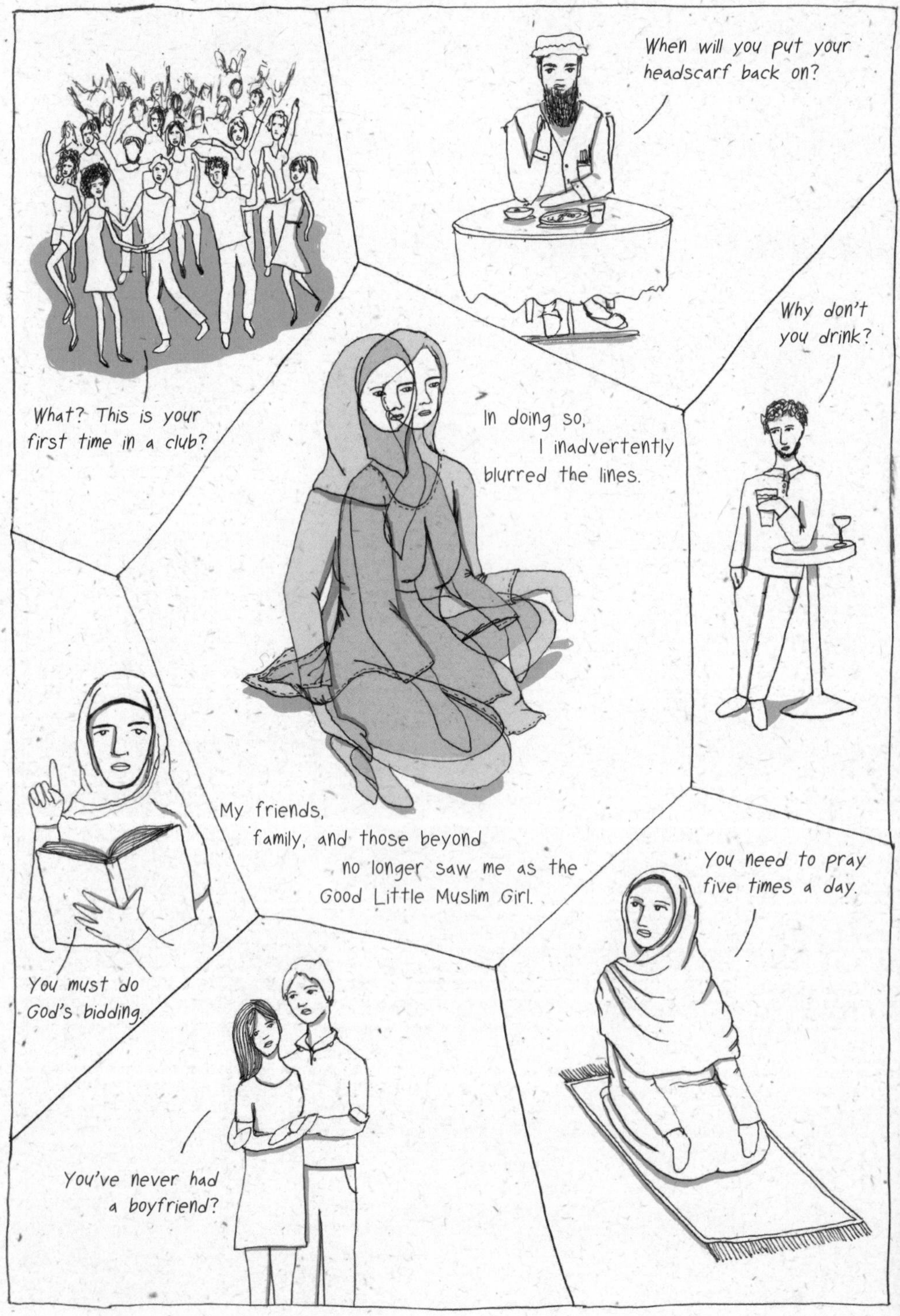
What? This is your first time in a club?
When will you put your headscarf back on?
In doing so, I inadvertently blurred the lines.
Why don't you drink?
My friends, family, and those beyond no longer saw me as the Good Little Muslim Girl.
You need to pray five times a day.
You must do God's bidding.
You've never had a boyfriend?

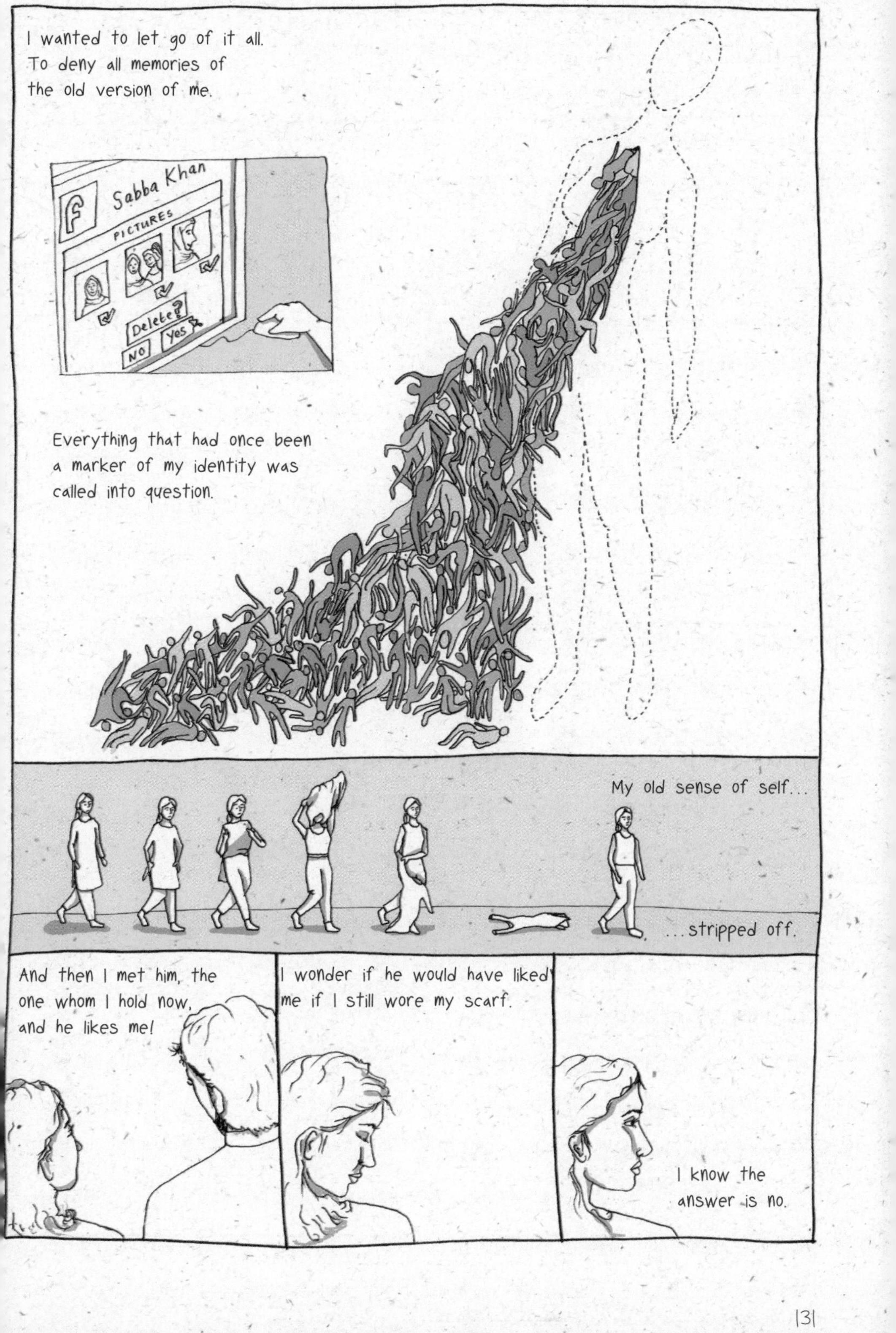
I wanted to let go of it all. To deny all memories of the old version of me.
Sabba Khan
PICTURES
Delete?
NO
Yes
Everything that had once been a marker of my identity was called into question.
My old sense of self...
...stripped off.
And then I met him, the one whom I hold now, and he likes me!
I wonder if he would have liked me if I still wore my scarf.
I know the answer is no.

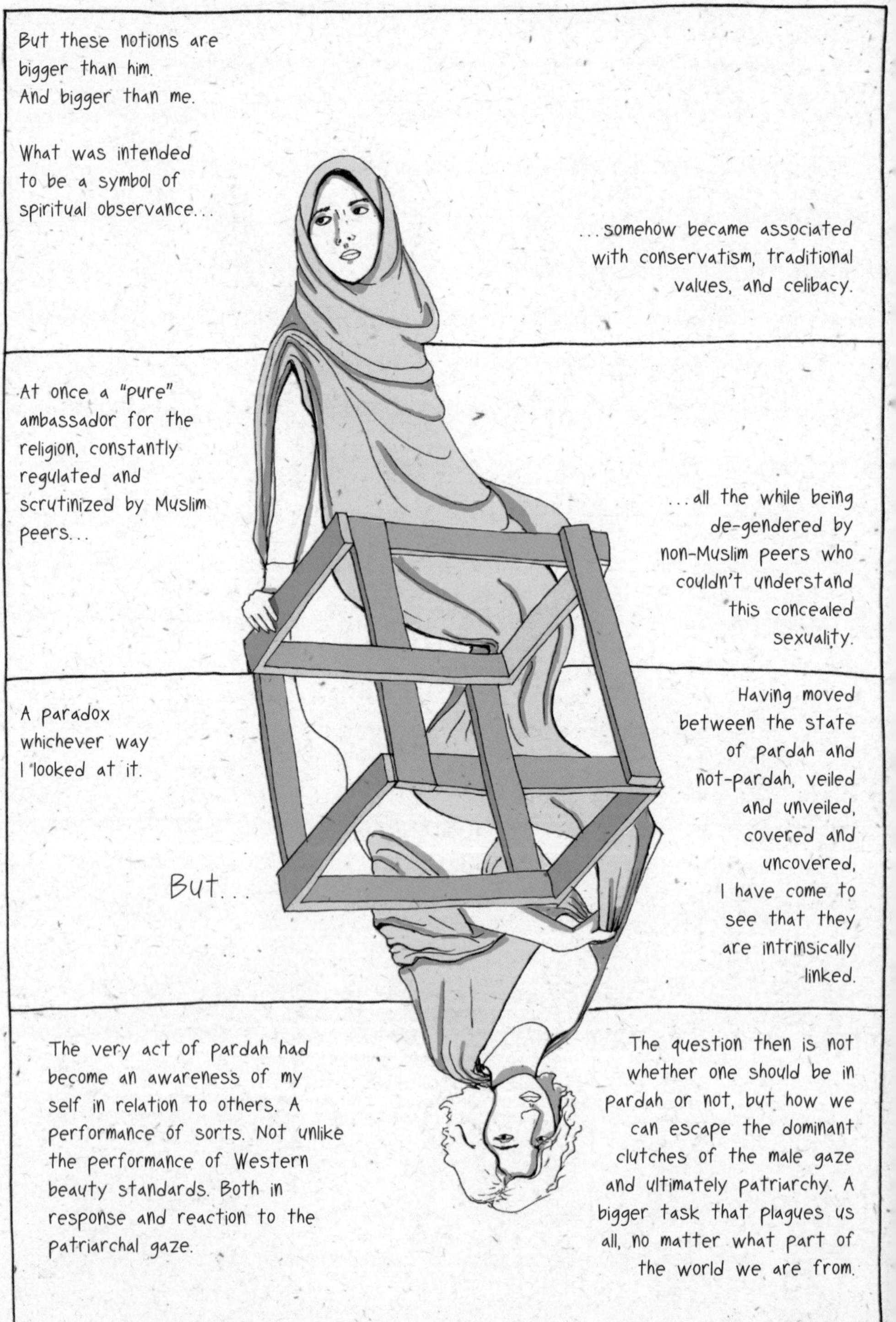
But these notions are bigger than him. And bigger than me.
What was intended to be a symbol of spiritual observance...
...somehow became associated with conservatism, traditional values, and celibacy.
At once a "pure" ambassador for the religion, constantly regulated and scrutinized by Muslim peers...
...all the while being de-gendered by non-Muslim peers who couldn't understand this concealed sexuality.
A paradox whichever way I looked at it.
Having moved between the state of pardah and not-pardah, veiled and unveiled, covered and uncovered,
But...
I have come to see that they are intrinsically linked.
The very act of pardah had become an awareness of my self in relation to others. A performance of sorts. Not unlike the performance of Western beauty standards. Both in response and reaction to the patriarchal gaze.
The question then is not whether one should be in pardah or not, but how we can escape the dominant clutches of the male gaze and ultimately patriarchy. A bigger task that plagues us all, no matter what part of the world we are from.

They say that children who grow up in homes where appearance is everything become adults who perform.

All the tools at our disposal

to fashion ourselves

into fixed ideals

of beauty,

of being attractive,

of being valuable.

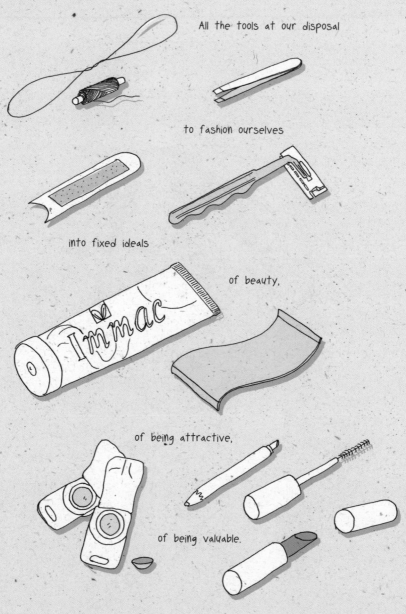

One of the few things both the outside and inside worlds have in common—a fixation with what you look like and how you dress.

I started rapidly losing my eyesight at
the age of nine, which meant thick-rimmed
glasses and lots of bullying from siblings
and schoolchildren.
I became the geeky, nerdy one.

So when I turned sixteen and
was legally allowed to choose
contacts for myself, I embraced them
and did not look back.

I went on to wear contacts almost
every day of my life from then on,
until I got a horrible eye infection in
my late twenties and had to stop.

Glasses on or off, hijab on or off,
shalwar kameez or tops and trousers,
hair up or hair down, makeup or natural,
red lipstick or not... all the ways in
which we are perceived. All the
ways in which we perform.

14 OTHER

♫ Letherette "After Dawn"

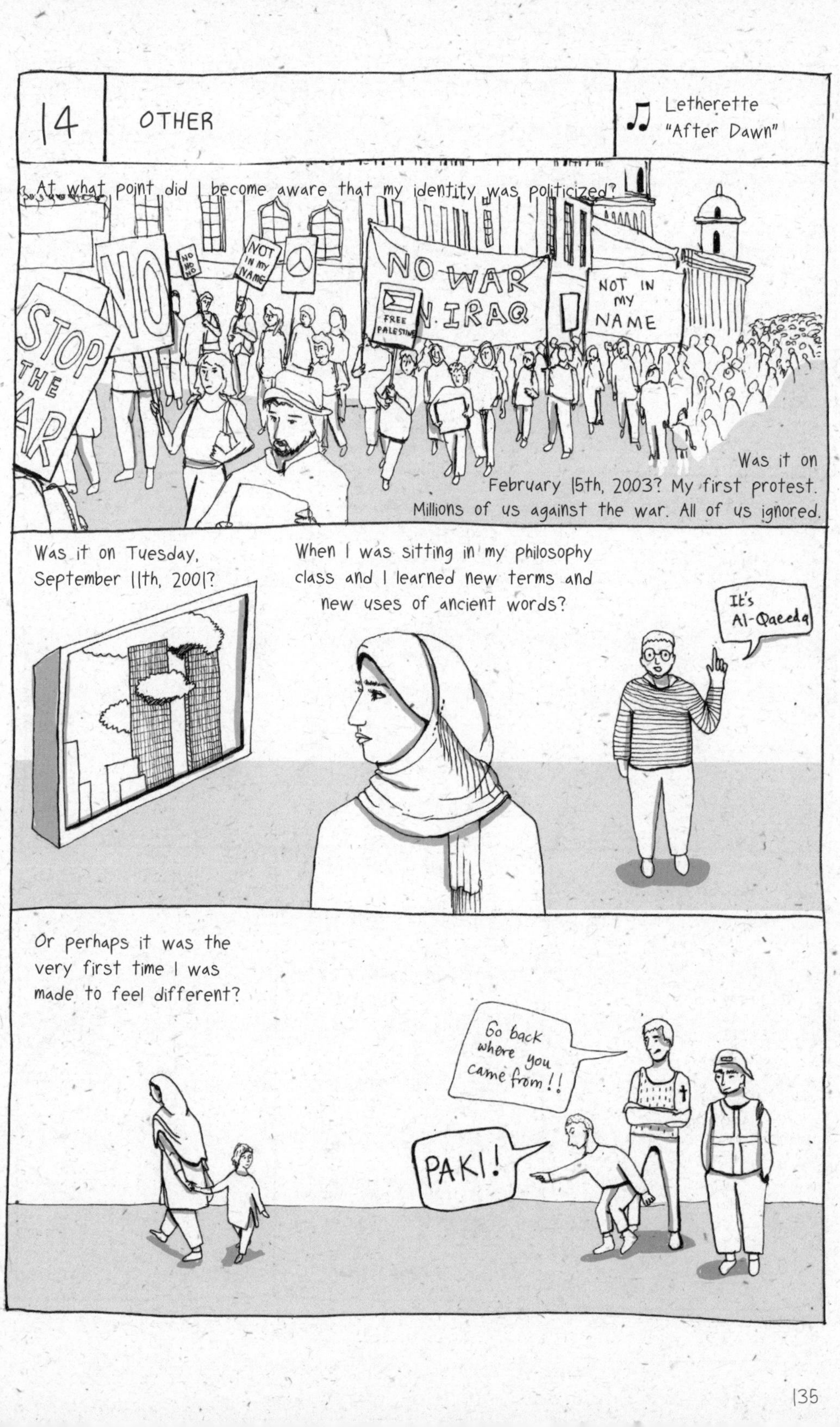
At what point did I become aware that my identity was politicized?
NO
NOT IN MY NAME
STOP THE WAR
NO WAR IN IRAQ
FREE PALESTINE
NOT IN MY NAME
Was it on February 15th, 2003? My first protest. Millions of us against the war. All of us ignored.
Was it on Tuesday, September 11th, 2001?
When I was sitting in my philosophy class and I learned new terms and new uses of ancient words?
It's Al-Qaeda
Or perhaps it was the very first time I was made to feel different?
Go back where you came from!!
PAKI!

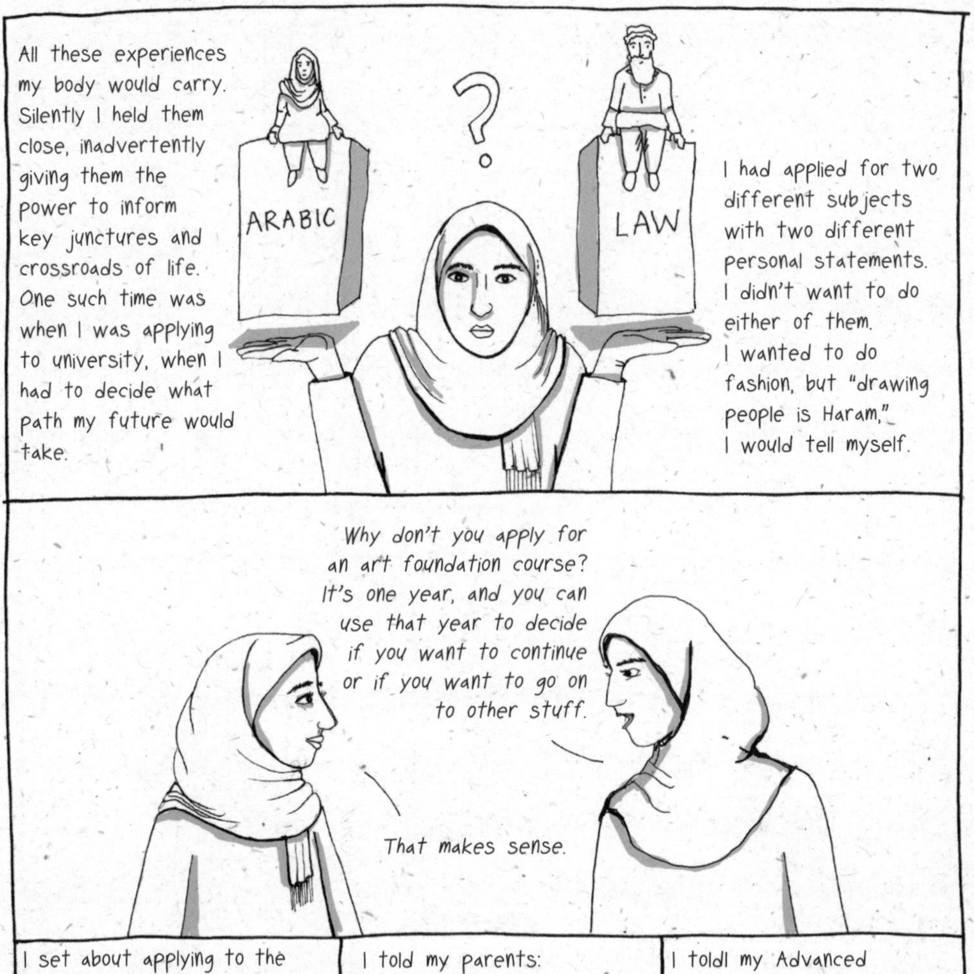
All these experiences my body would carry. Silently I held them close, inadvertently giving them the power to inform key junctures and crossroads of life. One such time was when I was applying to university, when I had to decide what path my future would take.
ARABIC
?
LAW
I had applied for two different subjects with two different personal statements. I didn't want to do either of them. I wanted to do fashion, but "drawing people is Haram," I would tell myself.
Why don't you apply for an art foundation course? It's one year, and you can use that year to decide if you want to continue or if you want to go on to other stuff.
That makes sense.
I set about applying to the same art foundation my friend was aiming for.
APPLY FOR PRESTIGIOUS ART SCHOOL HERE
I told my parents:
I've spent my life making clothes, I want a better life for you!
But I need a lawyer!
I toldl my Advanced Textiles teacher my plans...
You're going to apply to THAT art school? Good luck!

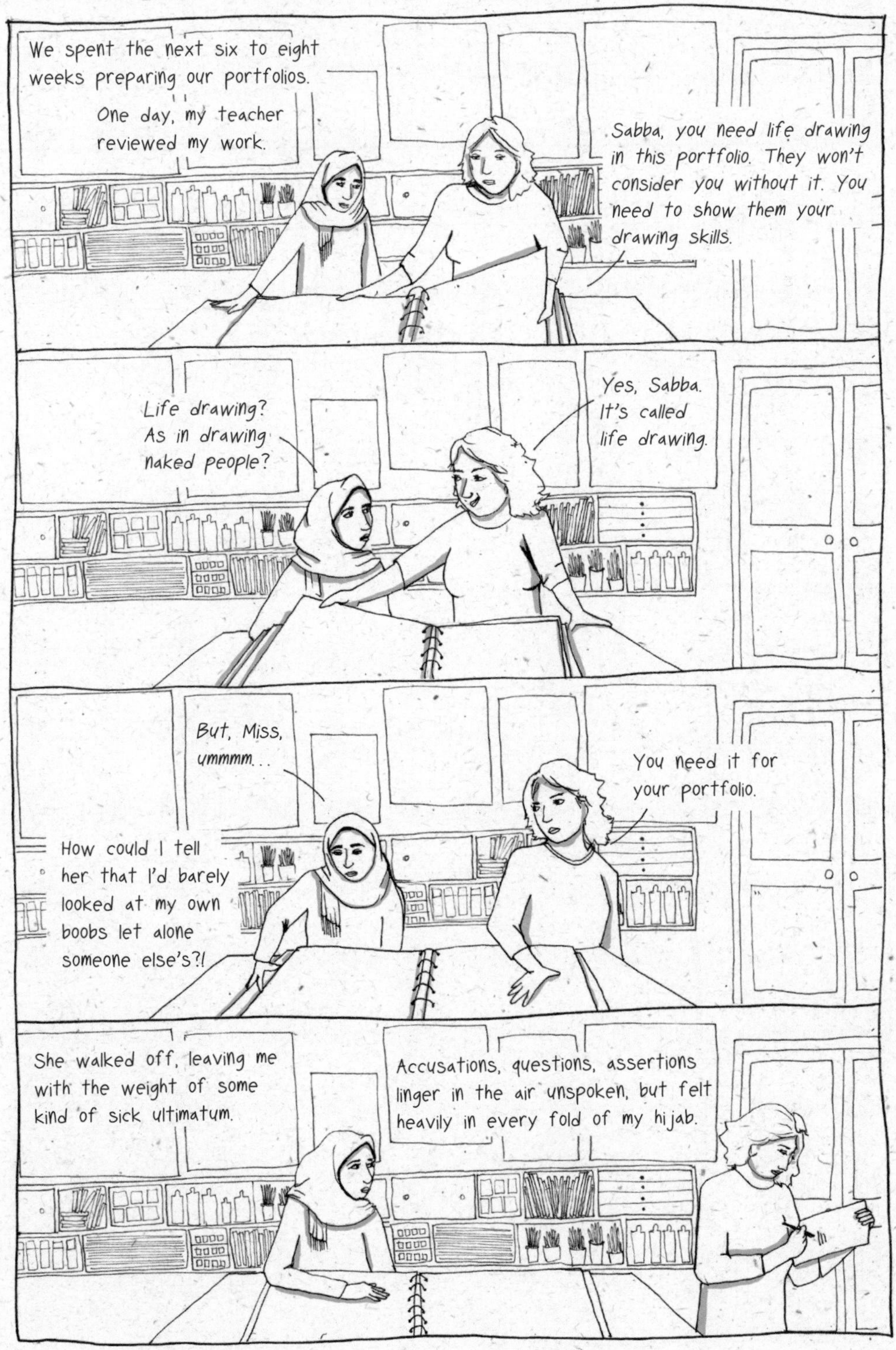
We spent the next six to eight weeks preparing our portfolios.
One day, my teacher reviewed my work.
Sabba, you need life drawing in this portfolio. They won't consider you without it. You need to show them your drawing skills.
Life drawing? As in drawing naked people?
Yes, Sabba. It's called life drawing.
But, Miss, ummmm...
You need it for your portfolio.
How could I tell her that I'd barely looked at my own boobs let alone someone else's?!
She walked off, leaving me with the weight of some kind of sick ultimatum.
Accusations, questions, assertions linger in the air unspoken, but felt heavily in every fold of my hijab.

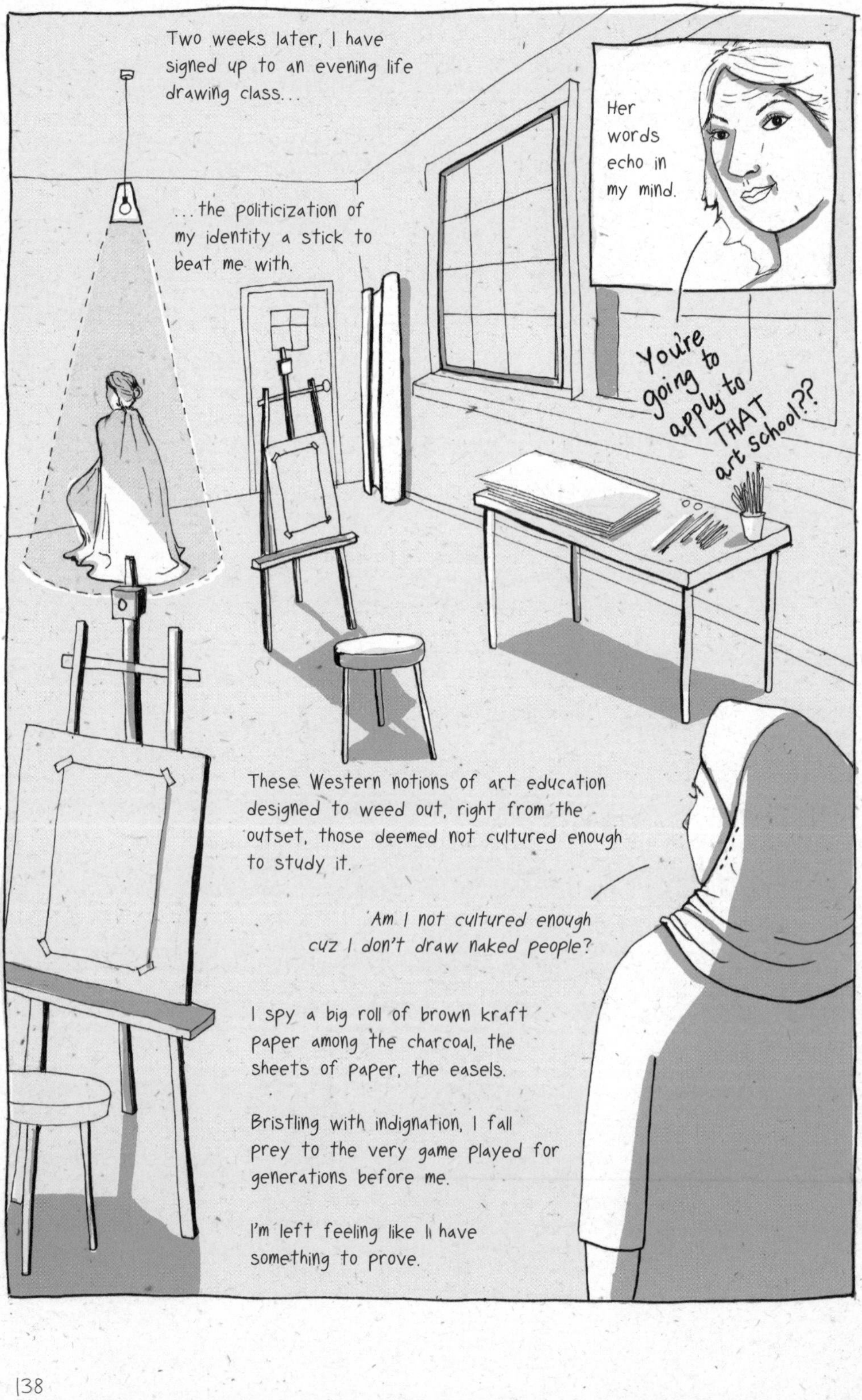
Two weeks later, I have signed up to an evening life drawing class...
...the politicization of my identity a stick to beat me with.
Her words echo in my mind.
You're going to apply to THAT art school??
These Western notions of art education designed to weed out, right from the outset, those deemed not cultured enough to study it.
Am I not cultured enough cuz I don't draw naked people?
I spy a big roll of brown kraft paper among the charcoal, the sheets of paper, the easels.
Bristling with indignation, I fall prey to the very game played for generations before me.
I'm left feeling like I have something to prove.

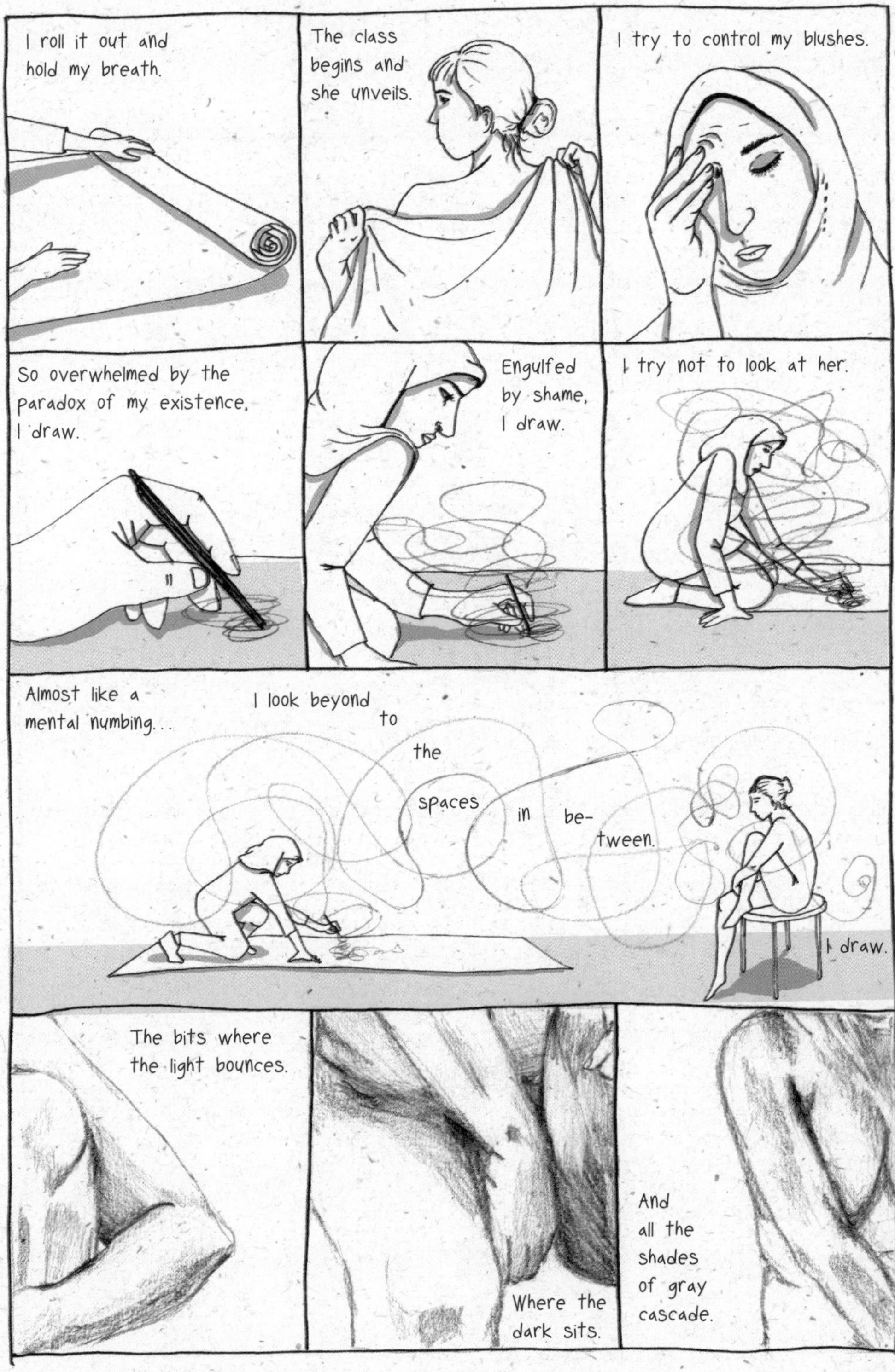

I roll it out and hold my breath.
The class begins and she unveils.
I try to control my blushes.
So overwhelmed by the paradox of my existence, I draw.
Engulfed by shame, I draw.
I try not to look at her.
Almost like a mental numbing...
I look beyond to the spaces in be- tween.
I draw.
The bits where the light bounces.
Where the dark sits.
And all the shades of gray cascade.

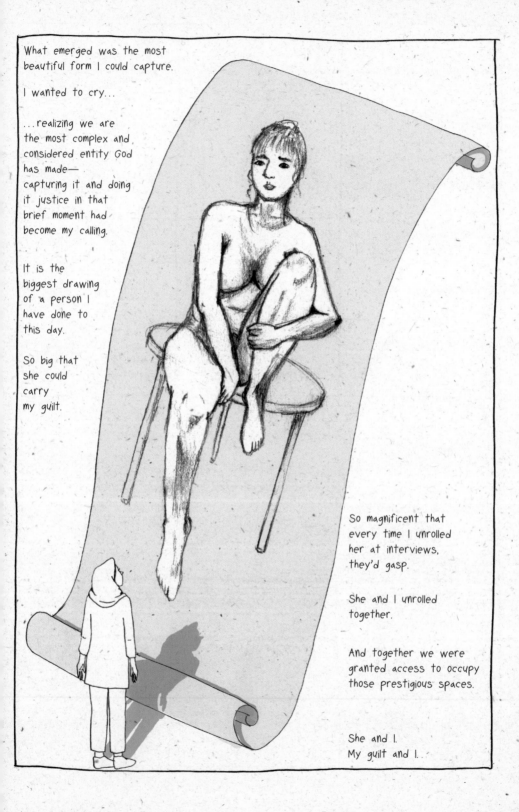

What emerged was the most
beautiful form I could capture.

I wanted to cry...

...realizing we are
the most complex and
considered entity God
has made—
capturing it and doing
it justice in that
brief moment had
become my calling.

It is the
biggest drawing
of a person I
have done to
this day.

So big that
she could
carry
my guilt.

So magnificent that
every time I unrolled
her at interviews,
they'd gasp.

She and I unrolled
together.

And together we were
granted access to occupy
those prestigious spaces.

She and I.
My guilt and I.

They call it imposter syndrome.
That niggly, cyclical voice of self-doubt, the fear of being found out, when you suddenly find yourself in a position of standing or influence.

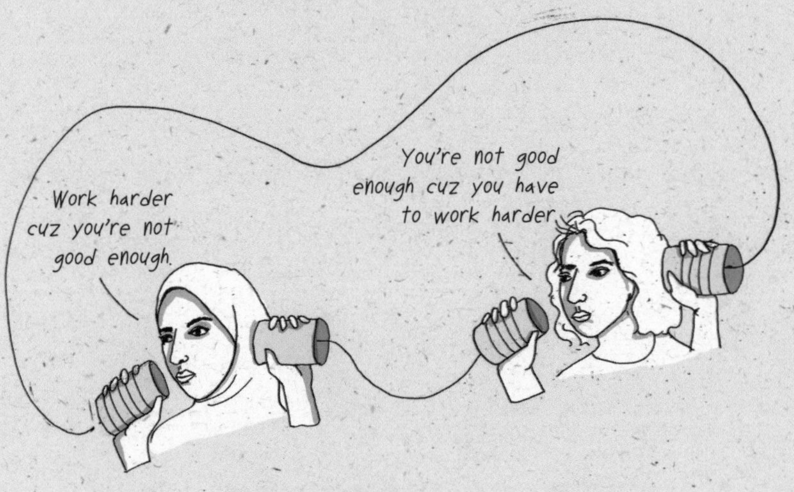
Work harder cuz you're not good enough.
You're not good enough cuz you have to work harder.

Where does it come from? Have I inherited it from my mother as an extension of her own inadequacies?

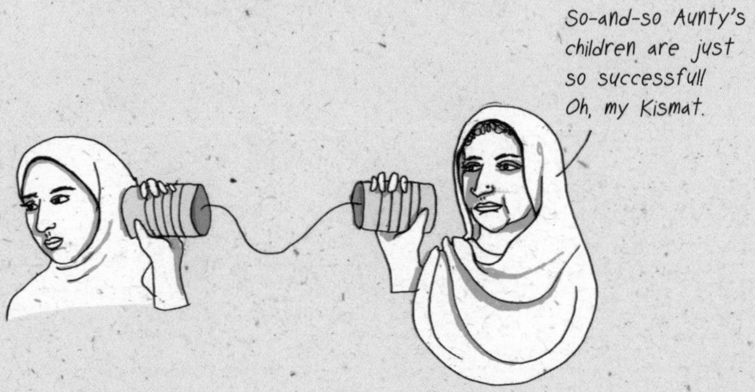
So-and-so Aunty's children are just so successful! Oh, my Kismat.

Or is it much deeper than her and me?

An echo chamber of wider societal norms to reinforce the idea that some are destined for more influential roles than others.

"Testimonial injustice" is when a person's thoughts and opinions are consistently ignored or mistrusted because of their identity.

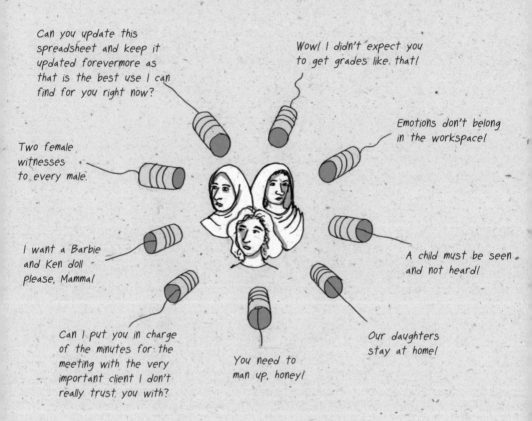

Can you update this spreadsheet and keep it updated forevermore as that is the best use I can find for you right now?

Wow! I didn't expect you to get grades like that!

Emotions don't belong in the workspace!

Two female witnesses to every male.

I want a Barbie and Ken doll please, Mamma!

A child must be seen and not heard!

Can I put you in charge of the minutes for the meeting with the very important client I don't really trust you with?

You need to man up, honey!

Our daughters stay at home!

It speaks of a conditioning beyond my own. Gender roles in a Victorian-style upbringing? White feminism? Toxic workplaces? Prejudiced teachers? What is it that has resulted in an internalized sense of othering, where I'm left punishing myself for my very existence?

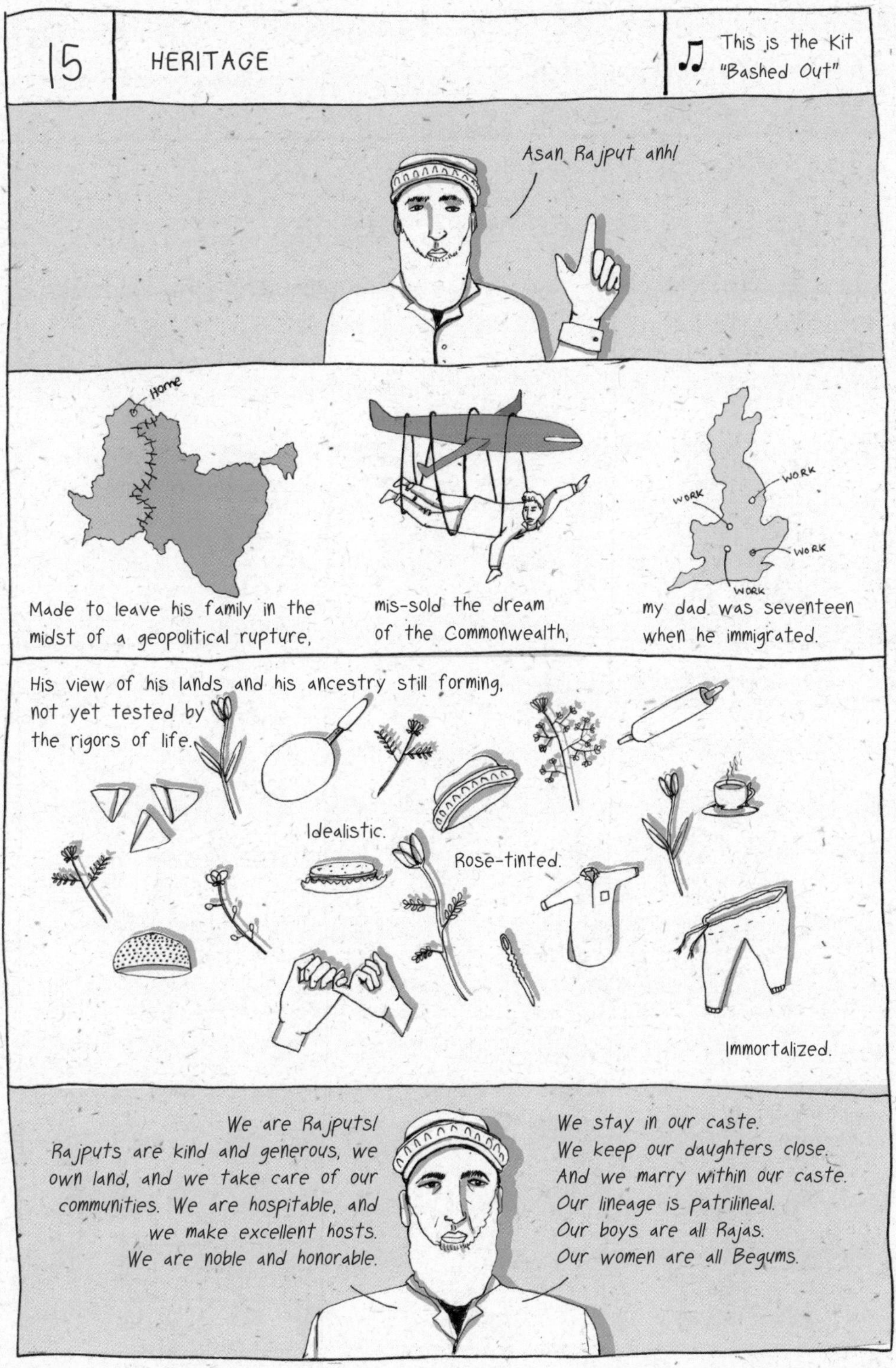
15
HERITAGE
This is the Kit
"Bashed Out"
Asan Rajput anh!
Home
WORK
WORK
WORK
WORK
Made to leave his family in the midst of a geopolitical rupture,
mis-sold the dream of the Commonwealth,
my dad was seventeen when he immigrated.
His view of his lands and his ancestry still forming, not yet tested by the rigors of life.
Idealistic.
Rose-tinted.
Immortalized.
We are Rajputs!
Rajputs are kind and generous, we own land, and we take care of our communities. We are hospitable, and we make excellent hosts.
We are noble and honorable.
We stay in our caste.
We keep our daughters close.
And we marry within our caste.
Our lineage is patrilineal.
Our boys are all Rajas.
Our women are all Begums.

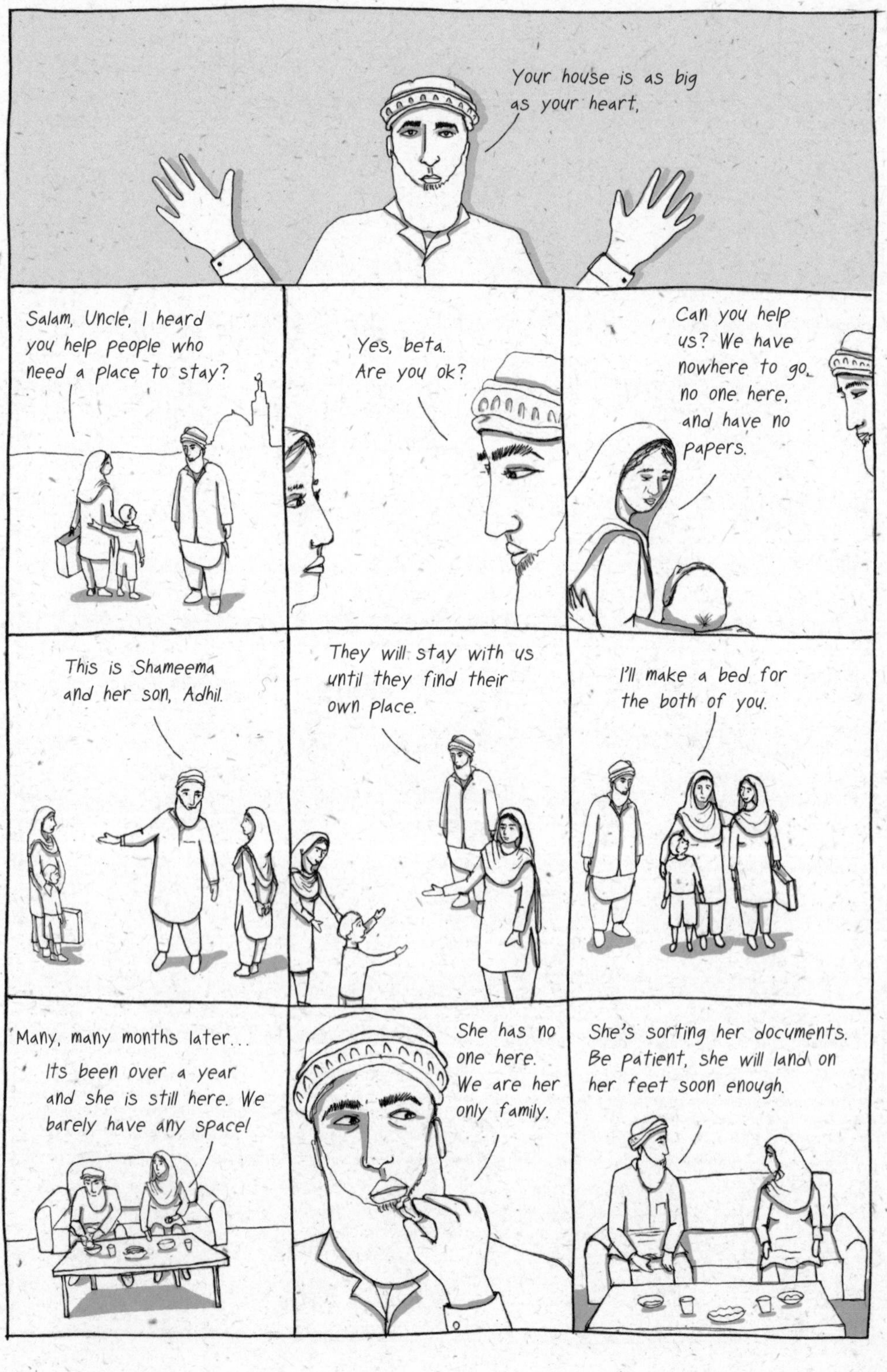

Your house is as big as your heart.
Salam, Uncle, I heard you help people who need a place to stay?
Yes, beta. Are you ok?
Can you help us? We have nowhere to go, no one here, and have no papers.
This is Shameema and her son, Adhil.
They will stay with us until they find their own place.
I'll make a bed for the both of you.
Many, many months later...
Its been over a year and she is still here. We barely have any space!
She has no one here. We are her only family.
She's sorting her documents. Be patient, she will land on her feet soon enough.

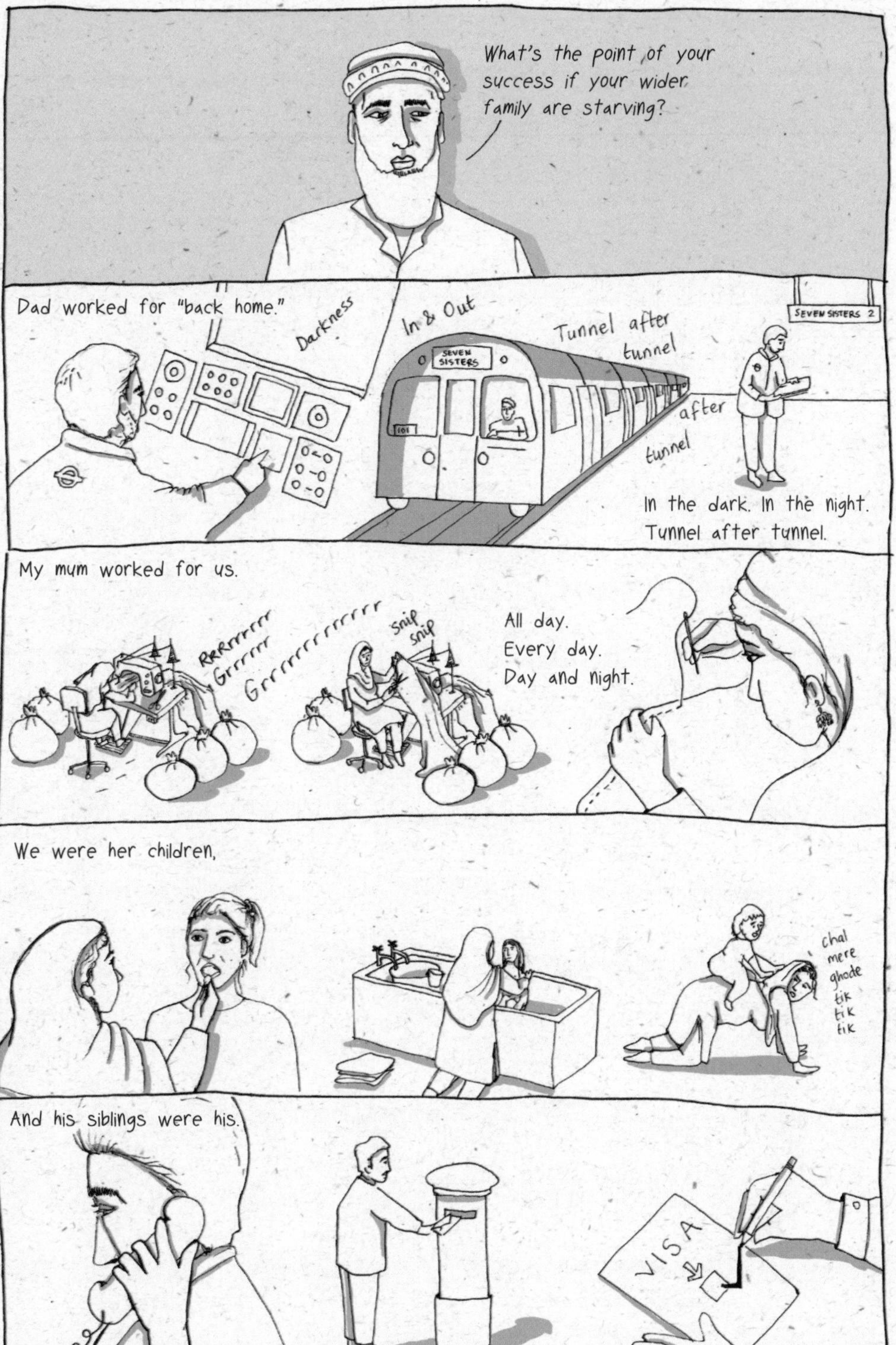
What's the point of your success if your wider family are starving?
Dad worked for "back home."
Darkness
In & Out
SEVEN SISTERS
Tunnel after tunnel
SEVEN SISTERS 2
after tunnel
In the dark. In the night. Tunnel after tunnel.
My mum worked for us.
Rrrrrrrrr Grrrrrr
Grrrrrrrrrrrrr
snip snip
All day.
Every day.
Day and night.
We were her children,
chal mere ghode tik tik tik
And his siblings were his.
VISA

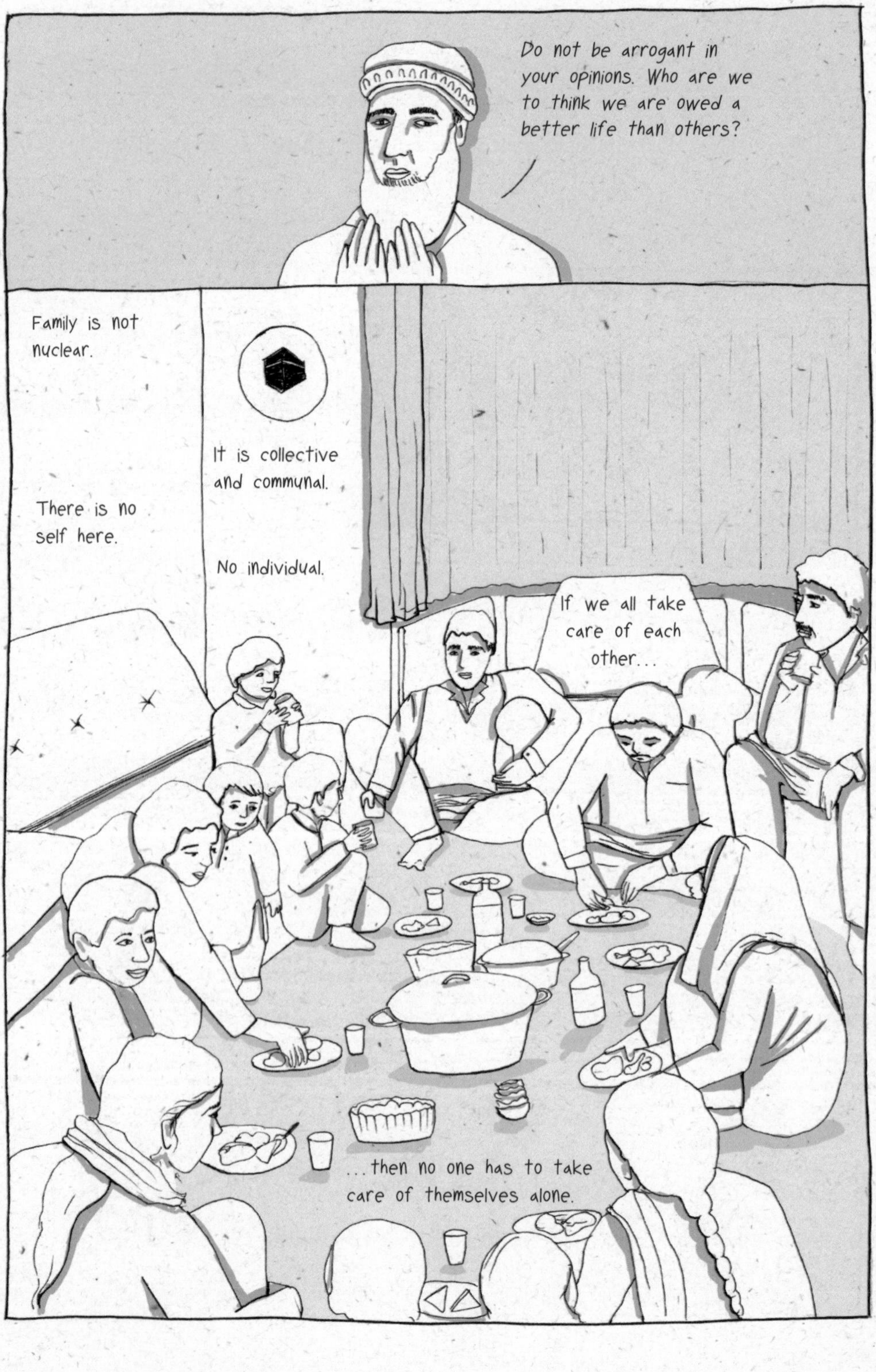
Do not be arrogant in your opinions. Who are we to think we are owed a better life than others?
Family is not nuclear.
There is no self here.
It is collective and communal.
No individual.
If we all take care of each other...
...then no one has to take care of themselves alone.

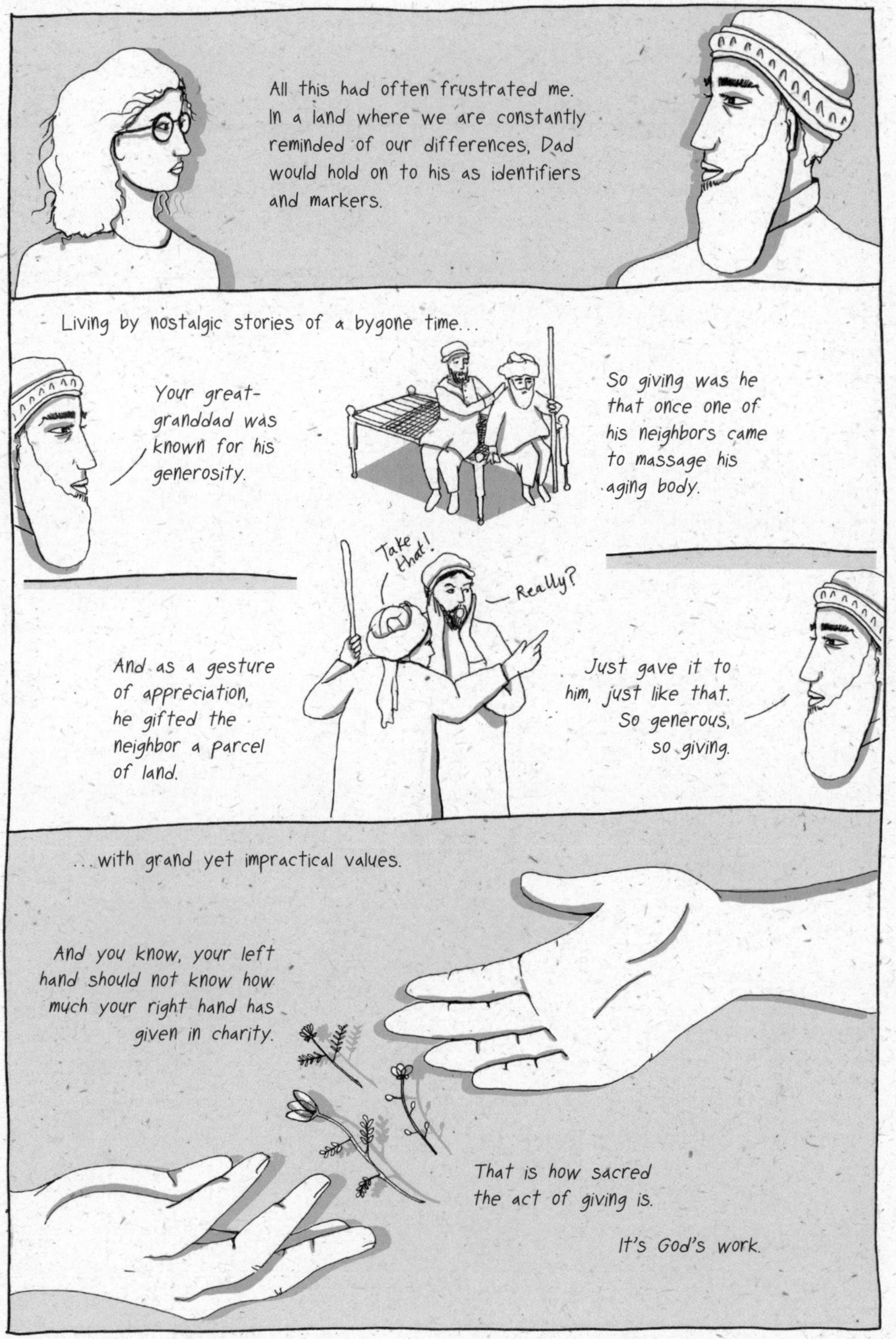
All this had often frustrated me. In a land where we are constantly reminded of our differences, Dad would hold on to his as identifiers and markers.
Living by nostalgic stories of a bygone time...
Your great-granddad was known for his generosity.
So giving was he that once one of his neighbors came to massage his aging body.
Take that!
Really?
And as a gesture of appreciation, he gifted the neighbor a parcel of land.
Just gave it to him, just like that. So generous, so giving.
...with grand yet impractical values.
And you know, your left hand should not know how much your right hand has given in charity.
That is how sacred the act of giving is.
It's God's work.

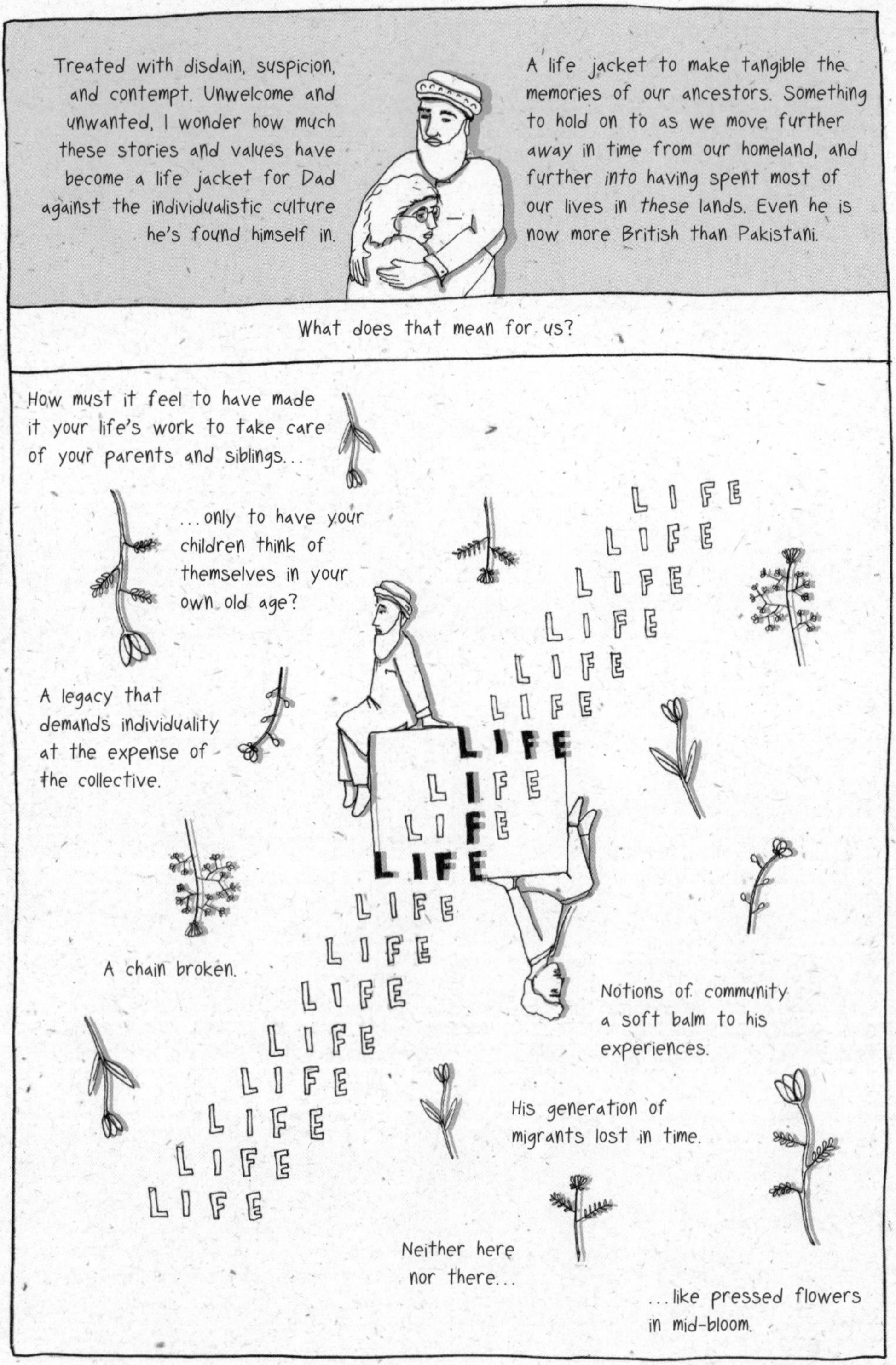
Treated with disdain, suspicion, and contempt. Unwelcome and unwanted, I wonder how much these stories and values have become a life jacket for Dad against the individualistic culture he's found himself in.
A life jacket to make tangible the memories of our ancestors. Something to hold on to as we move further away in time from our homeland, and further *into* having spent most of our lives in *these* lands. Even he is now more British than Pakistani.
What does that mean for us?
How must it feel to have made it your life's work to take care of your parents and siblings...
...only to have your children think of themselves in your own old age?
A legacy that demands individuality at the expense of the collective.
A chain broken.
LIFE
LIFE
LIFE
LIFE
LIFE
LIFE
LIFE
LIFE
LIFE
LIFE
LIFE
LIFE
LIFE
LIFE
LIFE
LIFE
LIFE
LIFE
Notions of community a soft balm to his experiences.
His generation of migrants lost in time.
Neither here nor there...
...like pressed flowers in mid-bloom.

The three-thousand-year-old Hindu caste system is perhaps the world's longest surviving social hierarchy. It's the idea that you are born into a social category that defines you until your death.

Despite the religious overtones, it's also practiced by many non-Hindu South Asians, including my family.

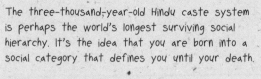

PUNJAB HILLS →

We are Mangral Rajputs.
Our ancestors were Hindu land owners who traveled from Rajasthan to the Punjab Hills (now called Kashmir) to set up the state of Kotli.

Since we are connected to the privilege of wealth and status, my family wear their caste proudly and as a badge of honor... especially our men.

RAJASTHAN

land
of
the
stepwells

Like my dad says,
"We marry from
within the caste."

The Mughal Empire saw the rise of Islam in South Asia. It was welcomed by many who saw it as an alternative to the rigid caste structure they were born into.

A promise of a more socially inclusive and equitable way forward.

I like to tell myself that is the reason why my ancestors converted, and not just to retain their wealth and power against the Mughal conquerors.

When the East India Company and subsequently the British Raj colonized South Asia, the caste system was used to their advantage. It was the perfect way to reinforce divisions, stir hatred, and cause chaos.

The Machiavellian approach of "divide and rule" pitted Hindus, Sikhs, and Muslims against each other.

Partition became a meager platitude in response to the hatred stirred up between the people.

The very history of Kashmir, our ancestral lands, tied to violent allegiances of caste and religion.

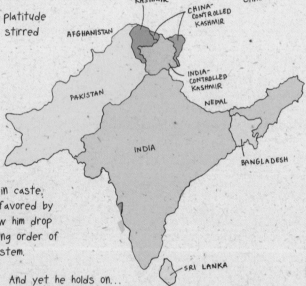

PAKISTAN-CONTROLLED KASHMIR

CHINA-CONTROLLED KASHMIR

CHINA

AFGHANISTAN

INDIA-CONTROLLED KASHMIR

PAKISTAN

NEPAL

INDIA

BANGLADESH

SRI LANKA

Second only to the Brahmans in caste, the Mangral Rajputs were not favored by migration. My dad's migration saw him drop right to the bottom of the pecking order of another elitist, classist system.

And yet he holds on... as a family we all hold on to the pride it gives us.

To this day, parents still seek a good, decent boy from within the caste for their daughters, and a respectful, dutiful girl for their sons.

What does it do other than keep us confined, narrow-minded, and willing to accept inequality, even when it is our own?

The characteristics that once defined our people now played out, like caricatures, in the gray, washed-out, and muted skies of the UK.

16 | LAYERS

♫ Alicia Keys "Fallin'"

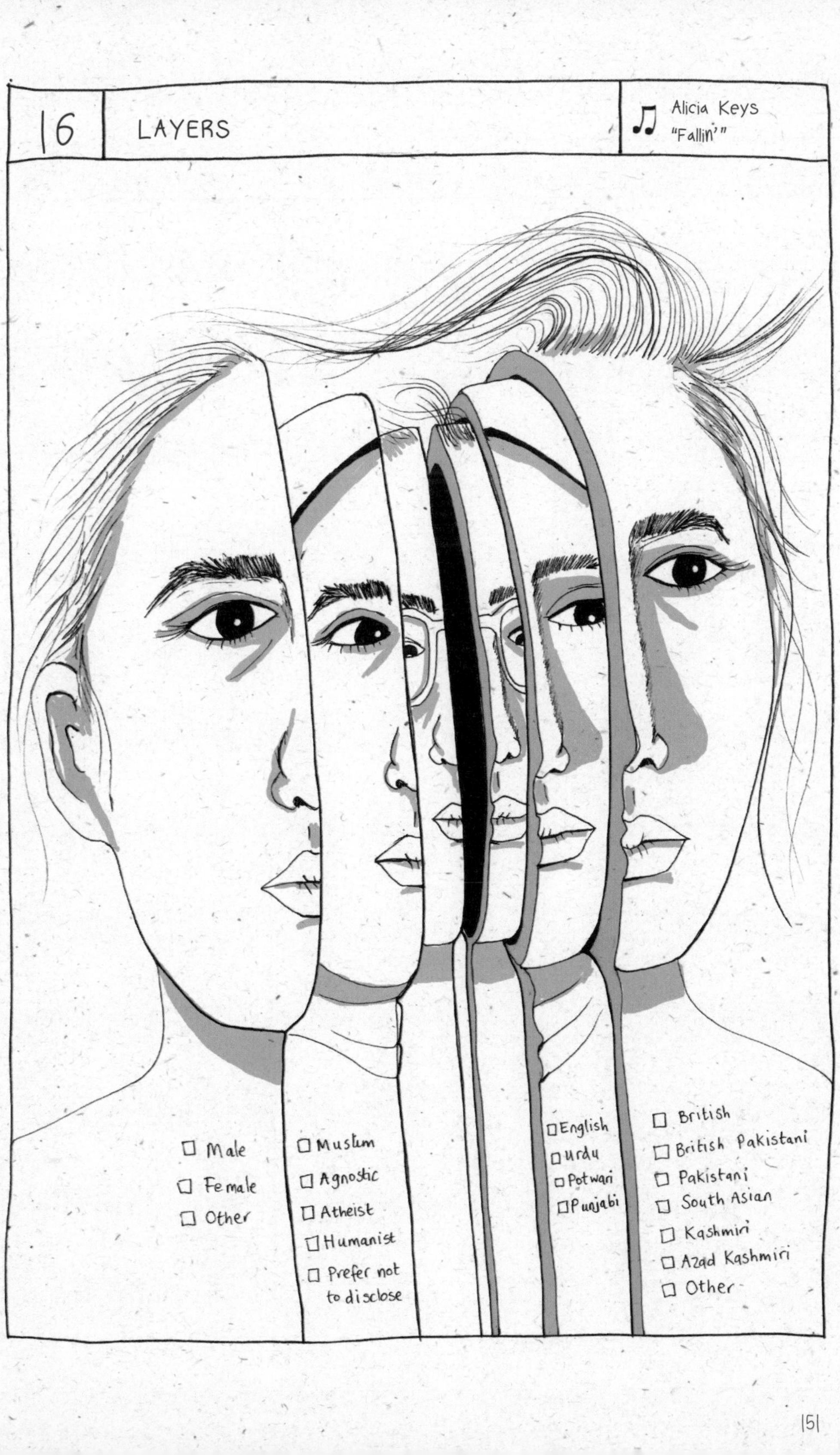
☐ Male
☐ Female
☐ Other
☐ Muslim
☐ Agnostic
☐ Atheist
☐ Humanist
☐ Prefer not to disclose
☐ English
☐ Urdu
☐ Potwari
☐ Punjabi
☐ British
☐ British Pakistani
☐ Pakistani
☐ South Asian
☐ Kashmiri
☐ Azad Kashmiri
☐ Other

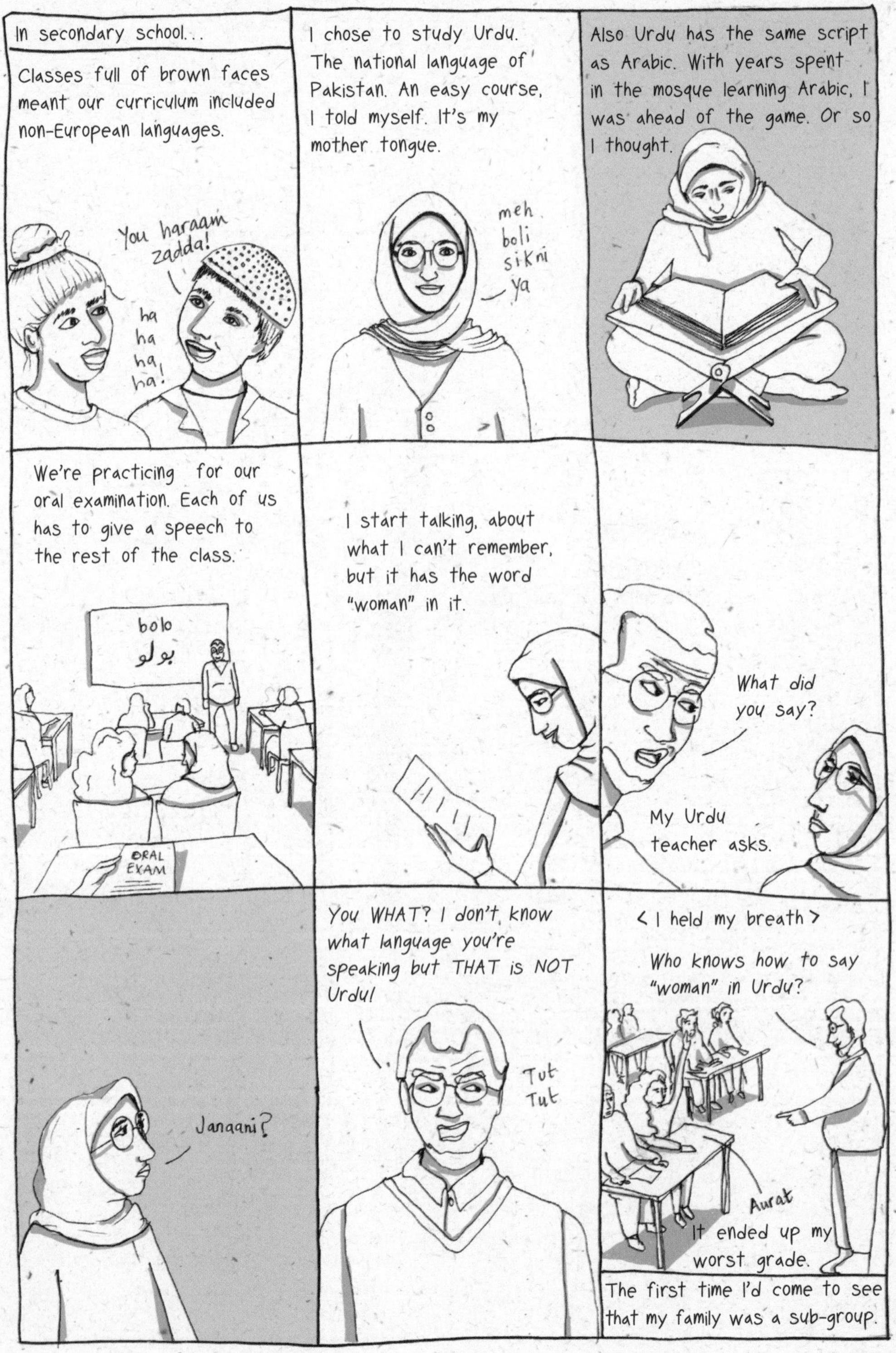
In secondary school...
Classes full of brown faces meant our curriculum included non-European languages.
You haraam zadda!
ha ha ha ha!
I chose to study Urdu. The national language of Pakistan. An easy course, I told myself. It's my mother tongue.
meh boli sikni ya
Also Urdu has the same script as Arabic. With years spent in the mosque learning Arabic, I was ahead of the game. Or so I thought.
We're practicing for our oral examination. Each of us has to give a speech to the rest of the class.
bolo
بولو
ORAL EXAM
I start talking, about what I can't remember, but it has the word "woman" in it.
What did you say?
My Urdu teacher asks.
Janaani?
You WHAT? I don't know what language you're speaking but THAT is NOT Urdu!
Tut Tut
< I held my breath >
Who knows how to say "woman" in Urdu?
Aurat
It ended up my worst grade.
The first time I'd come to see that my family was a sub-group.

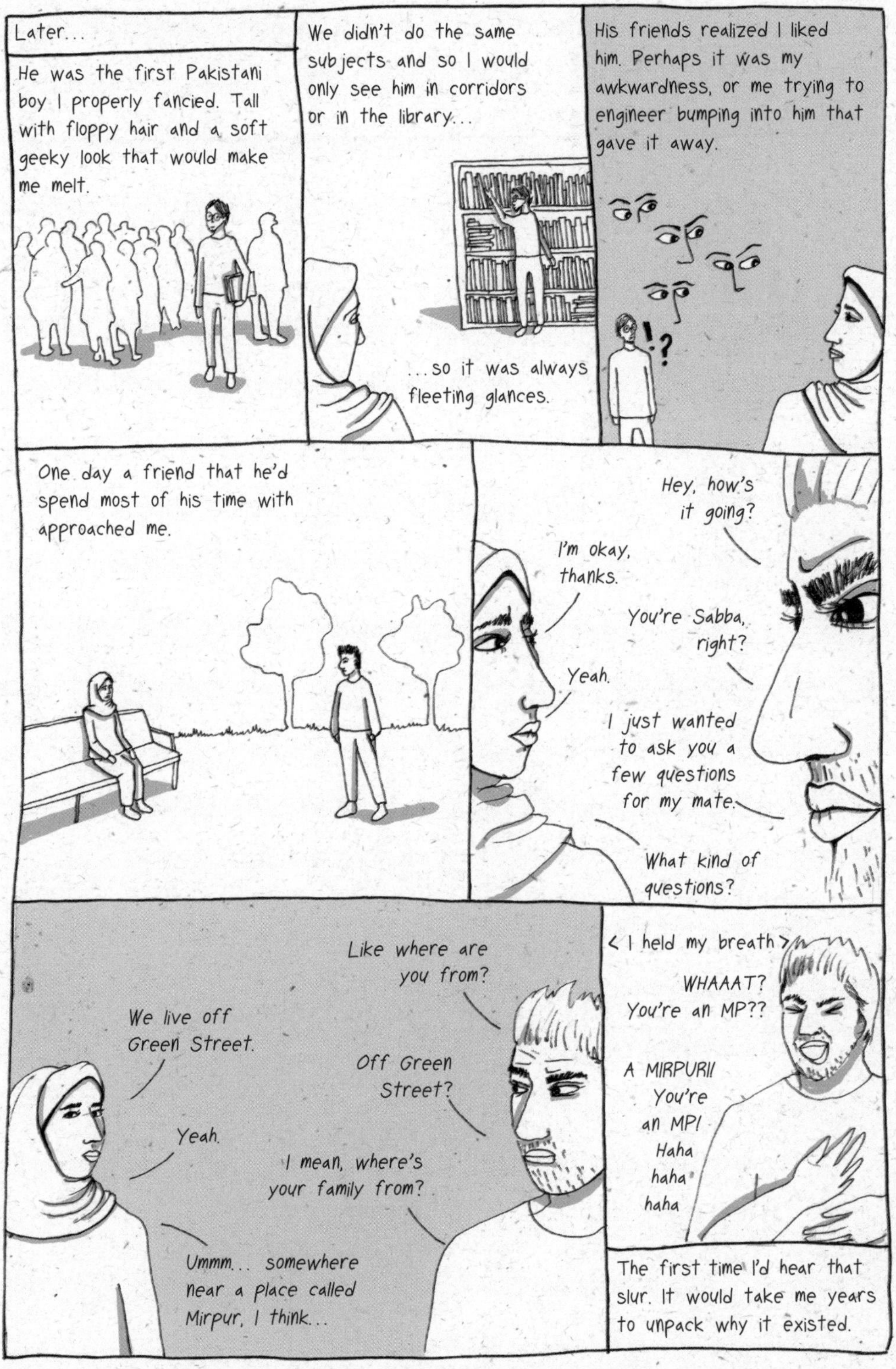
Later...
He was the first Pakistani boy I properly fancied. Tall with floppy hair and a soft geeky look that would make me melt.
We didn't do the same subjects and so I would only see him in corridors or in the library...
...so it was always fleeting glances.
His friends realized I liked him. Perhaps it was my awkwardness, or me trying to engineer bumping into him that gave it away.
!?
One day a friend that he'd spend most of his time with approached me.
Hey, how's it going?
I'm okay, thanks.
You're Sabba, right?
Yeah.
I just wanted to ask you a few questions for my mate.
What kind of questions?
Like where are you from?
We live off Green Street.
Off Green Street?
Yeah.
I mean, where's your family from?
Ummm... somewhere near a place called Mirpur, I think...
< I held my breath >
WHAAAT? You're an MP??
A MIRPURI! You're an MP! Haha haha haha
The first time I'd hear that slur. It would take me years to unpack why it existed.

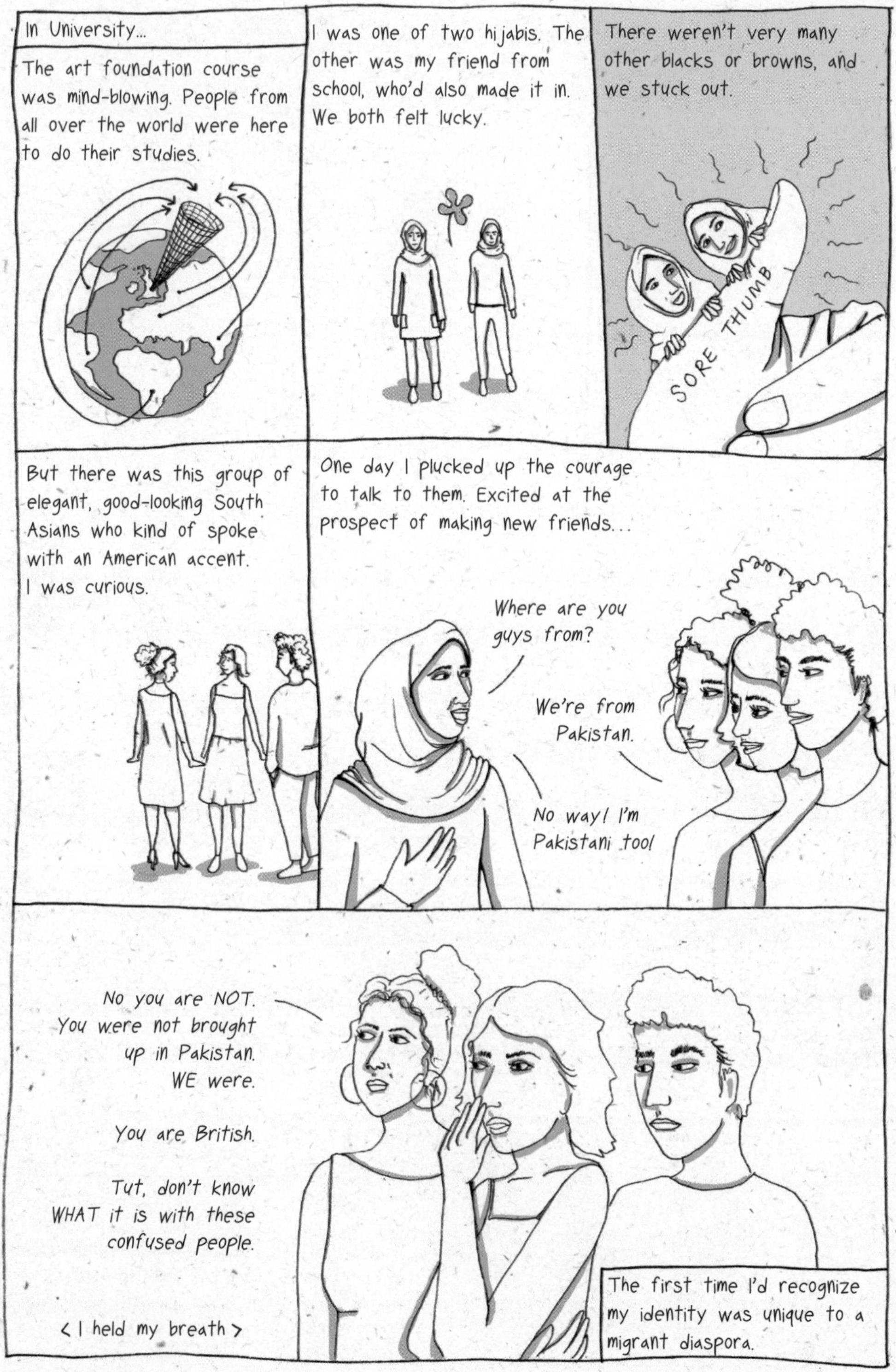

In University...
The art foundation course was mind-blowing. People from all over the world were here to do their studies.
I was one of two hijabis. The other was my friend from school, who'd also made it in. We both felt lucky.
There weren't very many other blacks or browns, and we stuck out.
SORE THUMB
But there was this group of elegant, good-looking South Asians who kind of spoke with an American accent. I was curious.
One day I plucked up the courage to talk to them. Excited at the prospect of making new friends...
Where are you guys from?
We're from Pakistan.
No way! I'm Pakistani too!
No you are NOT. You were not brought up in Pakistan. WE were.
You are British.
Tut, don't know WHAT it is with these confused people.
< I held my breath >
The first time I'd recognize my identity was unique to a migrant diaspora.

This is Kashmir.

TAJIKISTAN
AFGHANISTAN
CHINA
Shaksgam Valley
Siachin Glacier
Gilgit Baltistan
Aksai Chin
Ladakh
PAKISTAN
MANGLA DAM
Jammu & Kashmir
AZAD KASHMIR
INDIA

Split and broken, a tragic fall-out of Partition.

As the gateway to the Himalayas, it is geographically strategic for both India and Pakistan, therefore neither is prepared to let go.

Though many Kashmiris from both sides want independence.

It is one of the most militarized zones of conflict in the world, where one in every ten people is a soldier of war.

The construction of Mangla Dam, near the border with Pakistan, triggered a wave of migration to the UK...

ENGLAND
2% of the population is Pakistani

...where two thirds of England's Pakistanis are actually Kashmiris displaced by the dam.

When asked,

Where are you from?

We simply say,

We're from Pakistan.

Really to avoid recounting:

1. The history of Partition
2. The conflict of Kashmir
3. The water treaty
4. The dam
5. The migration
6. And even if we did call ourselves Kashmiri, would it just be Kashmiri or Azad (free) Kashmiri? Itself a loaded, politicized question.

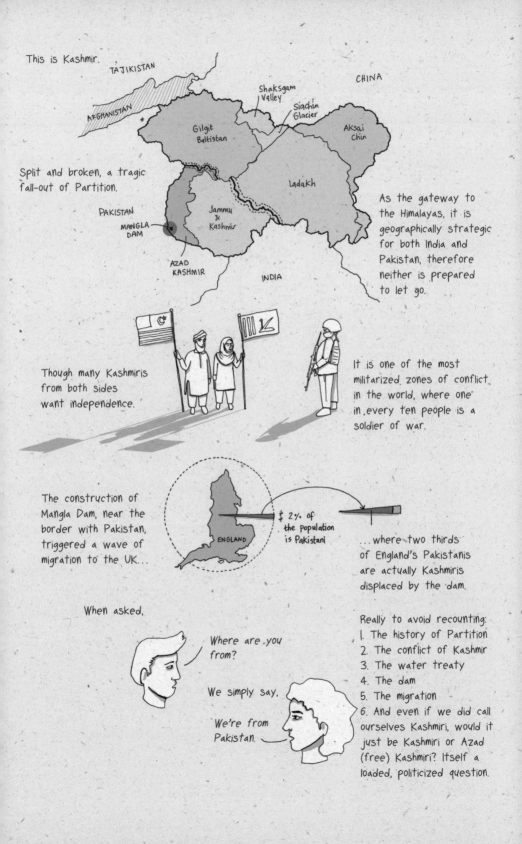

With years of disassociation and self-censorship from our own heritage, culture, roots, and language, I wonder...

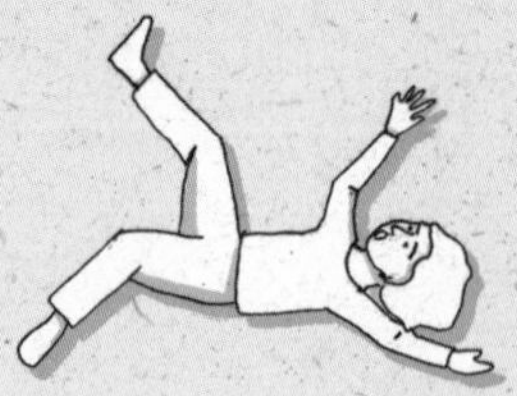

...have we fallen between the cracks?

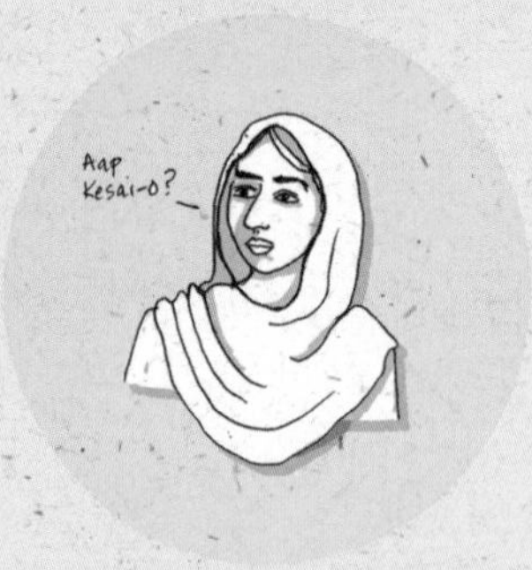
Aap Kesai-o?

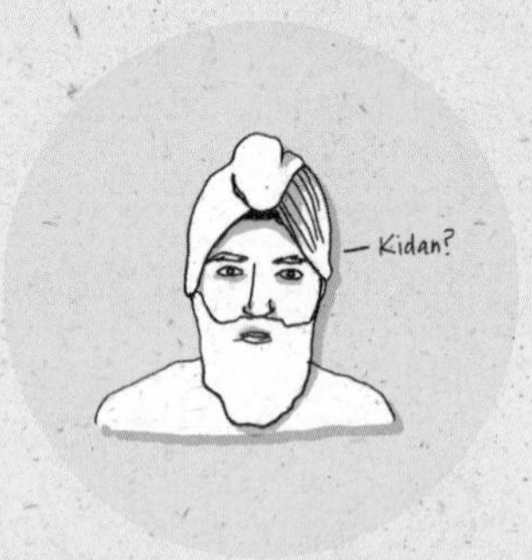
Kidan?

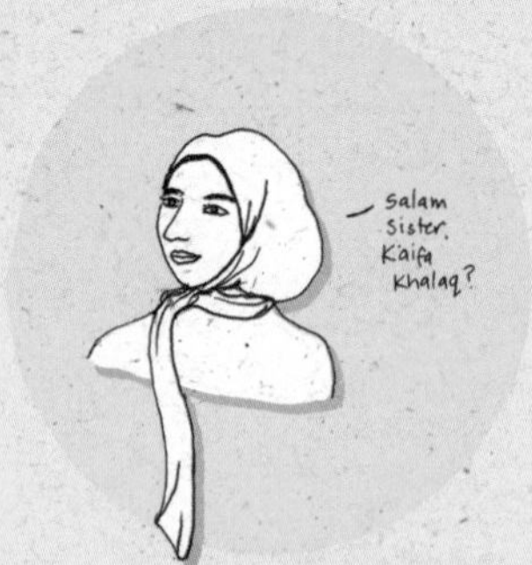
Salam Sister, Kaifa Khalaq?

Where we play out our version of Urdu in front of hostile and proud "actual" Pakistanis...

...put on a Frankenstein Punjabi for our Sikhi friends, whose cultural values (but not religious ones) align with ours...

...and read Arabic, the scripture of the one God, but have no idea what we recite.

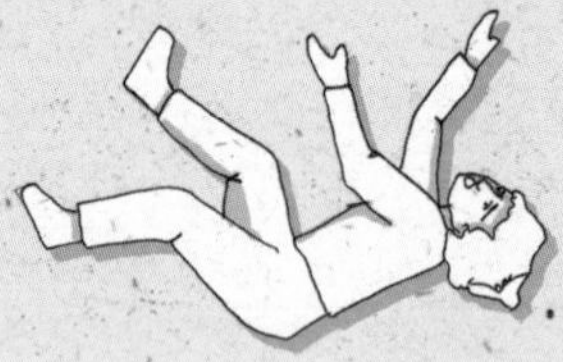

All the while, our own tongue, Pothwari, one of the oldest languages of the South Asian region, slowly erodes, left unrecognized as a language, without a script and without a definitive landscape to bind it.

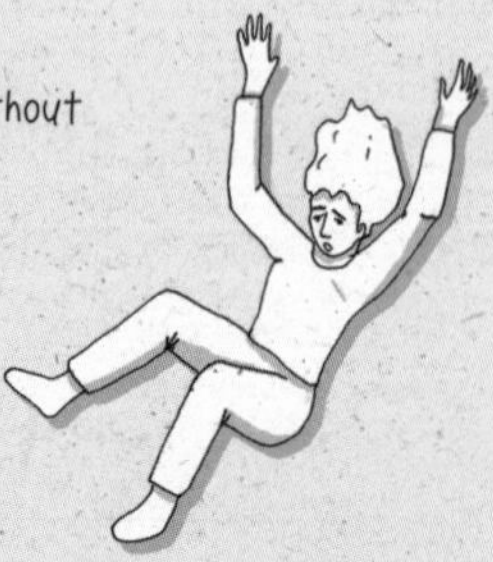

Some argue Pothwari is only a dialect.

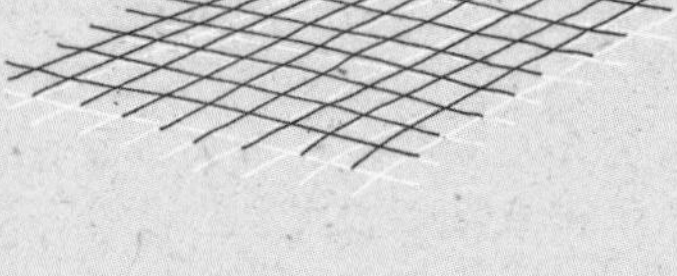

But when the overall majority of a group in the UK speaks Pothwari, who gets to dictate what is language and what is dialect?

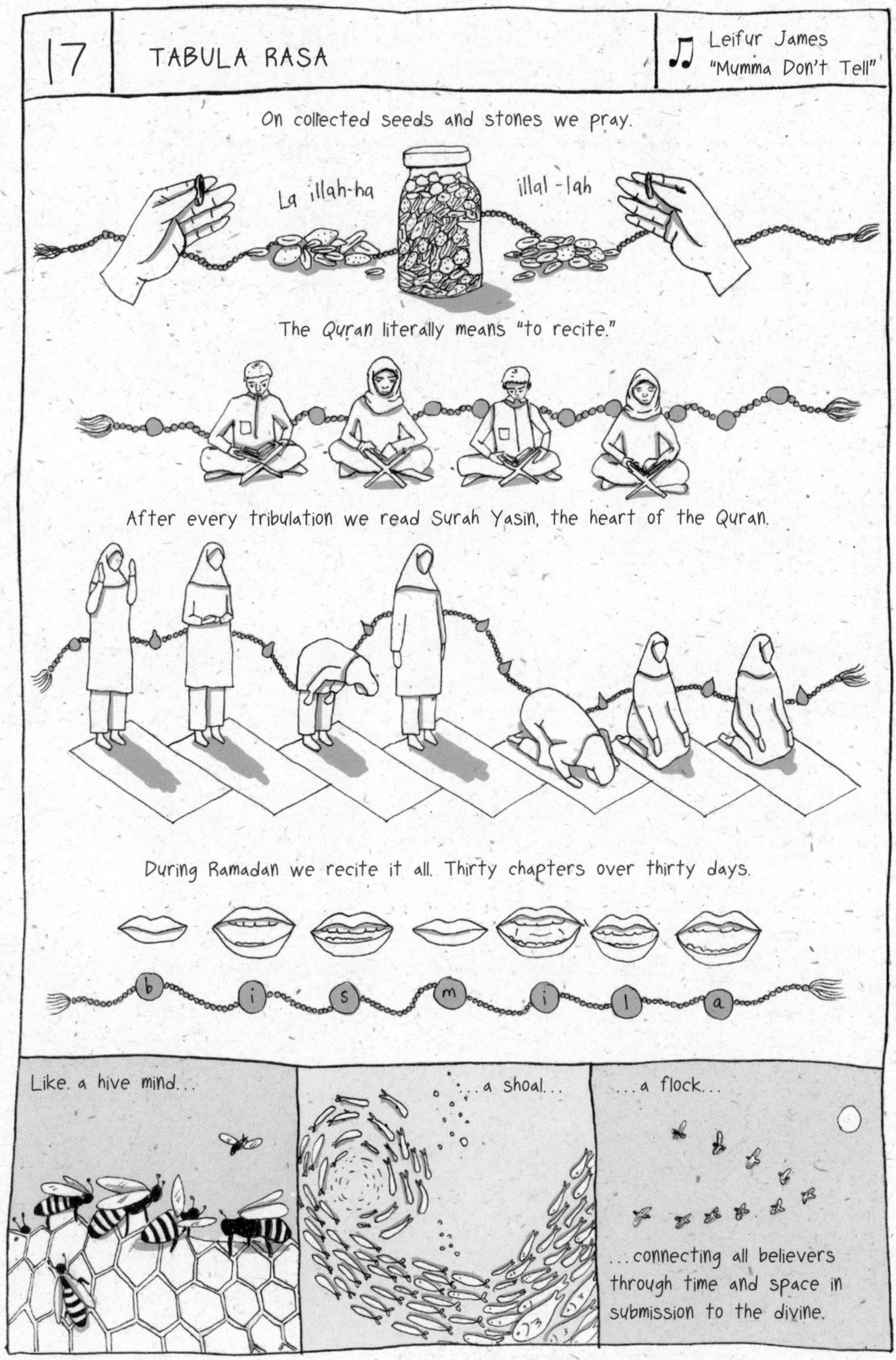
17
TABULA RASA
Leifur James
"Mumma Don't Tell"
On collected seeds and stones we pray.
La illah-ha
illal-lah
The *Quran* literally means "to recite."
After every tribulation we read Surah Yasin, the heart of the Quran.
During Ramadan we recite it all. Thirty chapters over thirty days.
b
i
s
m
i
l
a
Like a hive mind...
...a shoal...
...a flock...
...connecting all believers through time and space in submission to the divine.

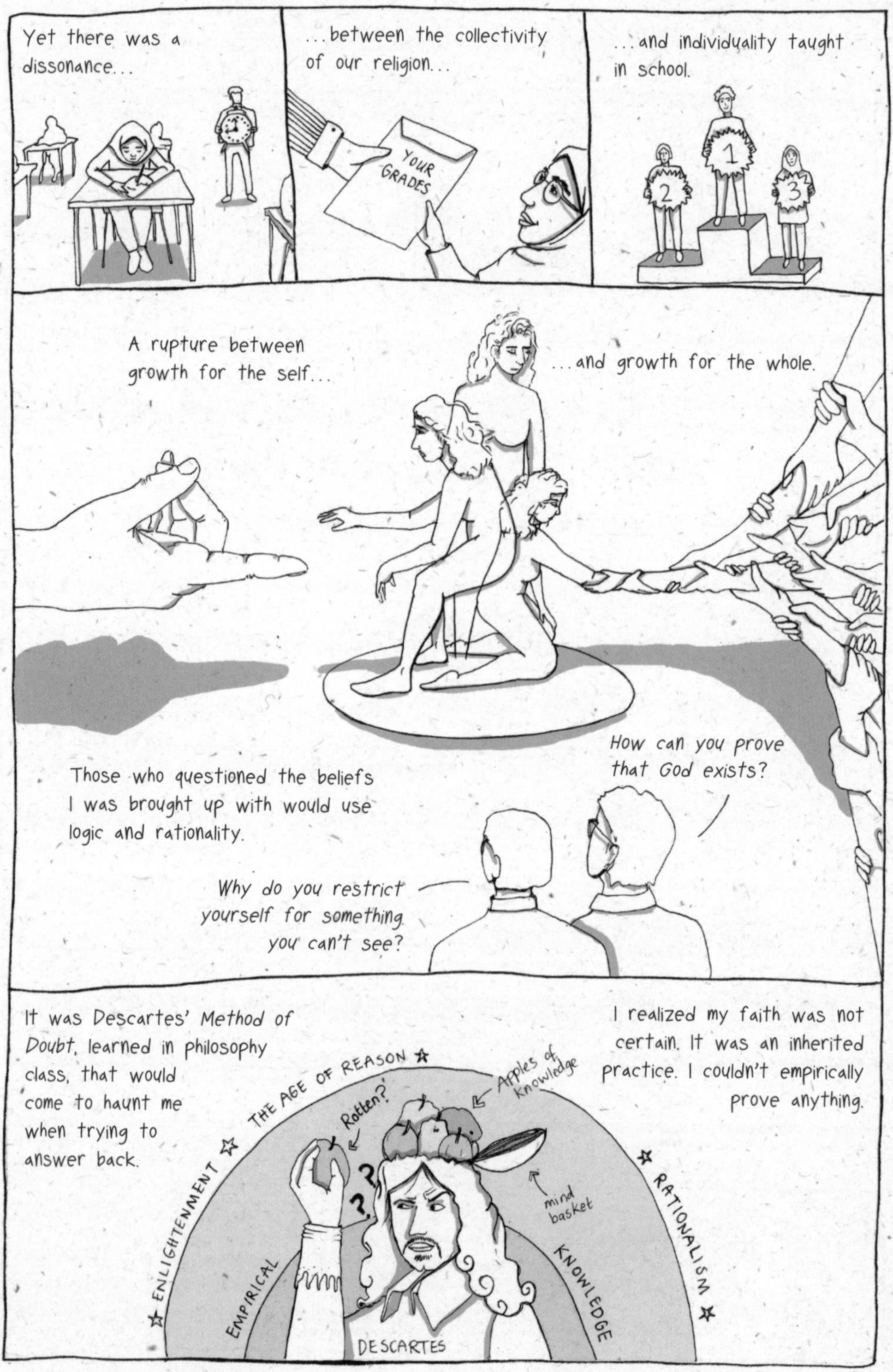
Yet there was a dissonance...
...between the collectivity of our religion...
YOUR GRADES
...and individuality taught in school.
1
2
3
A rupture between growth for the self...
...and growth for the whole.
Those who questioned the beliefs I was brought up with would use logic and rationality.
How can you prove that God exists?
Why do you restrict yourself for something you can't see?
It was Descartes' *Method of Doubt*, learned in philosophy class, that would come to haunt me when trying to answer back.
I realized my faith was not certain. It was an inherited practice. I couldn't empirically prove anything.
THE AGE OF REASON
Apples of Knowledge
Rotten?
mind basket
ENLIGHTENMENT
RATIONALISM
EMPIRICAL
KNOWLEDGE
DESCARTES

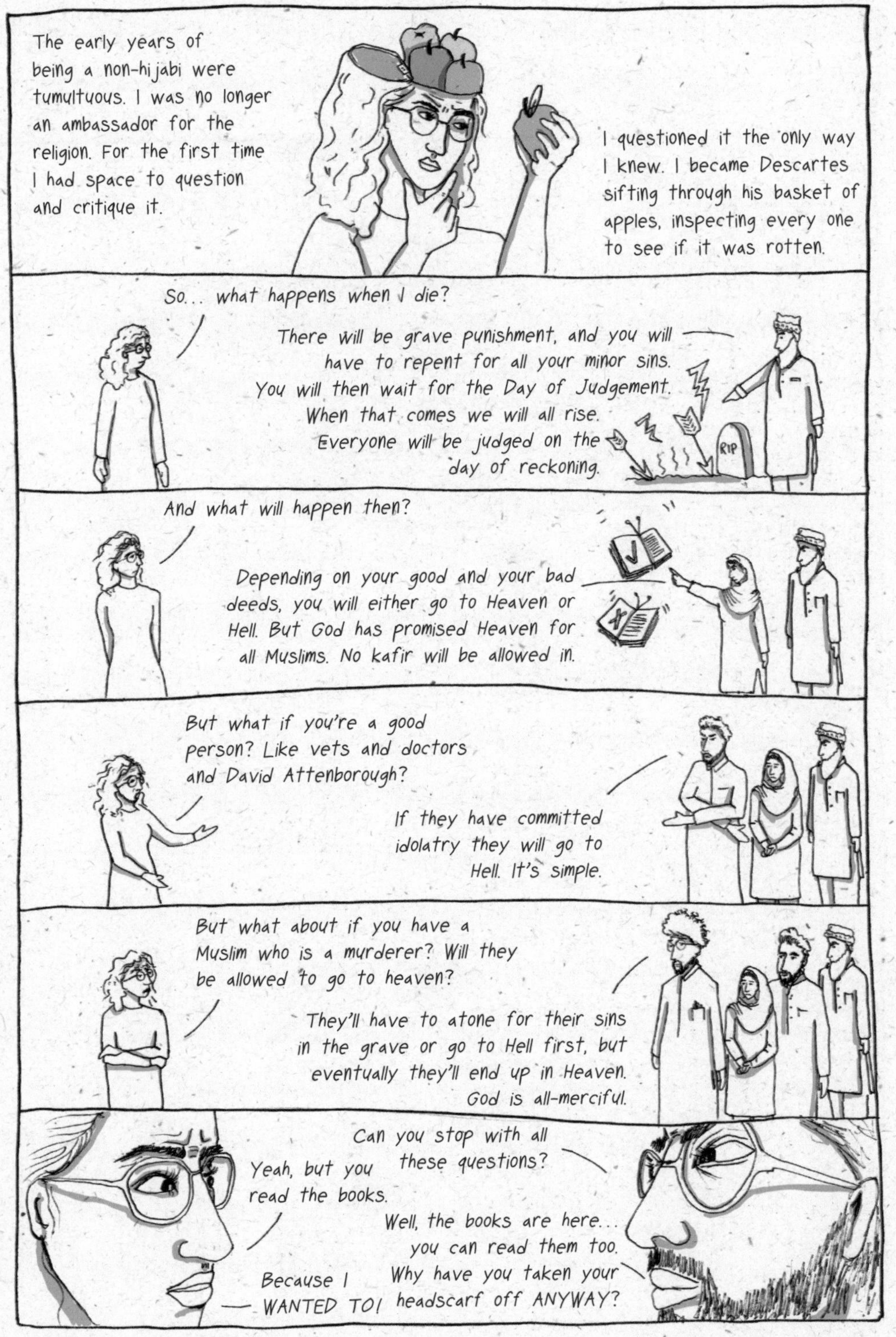

The early years of being a non-hijabi were tumultuous. I was no longer an ambassador for the religion. For the first time I had space to question and critique it.
I questioned it the only way I knew. I became Descartes sifting through his basket of apples, inspecting every one to see if it was rotten.
So... what happens when I die?
There will be grave punishment, and you will have to repent for all your minor sins. You will then wait for the Day of Judgement. When that comes we will all rise. Everyone will be judged on the day of reckoning.
RIP
And what will happen then?
Depending on your good and your bad deeds, you will either go to Heaven or Hell. But God has promised Heaven for all Muslims. No kafir will be allowed in.
But what if you're a good person? Like vets and doctors and David Attenborough?
If they have committed idolatry they will go to Hell. It's simple.
But what about if you have a Muslim who is a murderer? Will they be allowed to go to heaven?
They'll have to atone for their sins in the grave or go to Hell first, but eventually they'll end up in Heaven. God is all-merciful.
Can you stop with all these questions?
Yeah, but you read the books.
Well, the books are here... you can read them too. Why have you taken your headscarf off ANYWAY?
Because I WANTED TO!

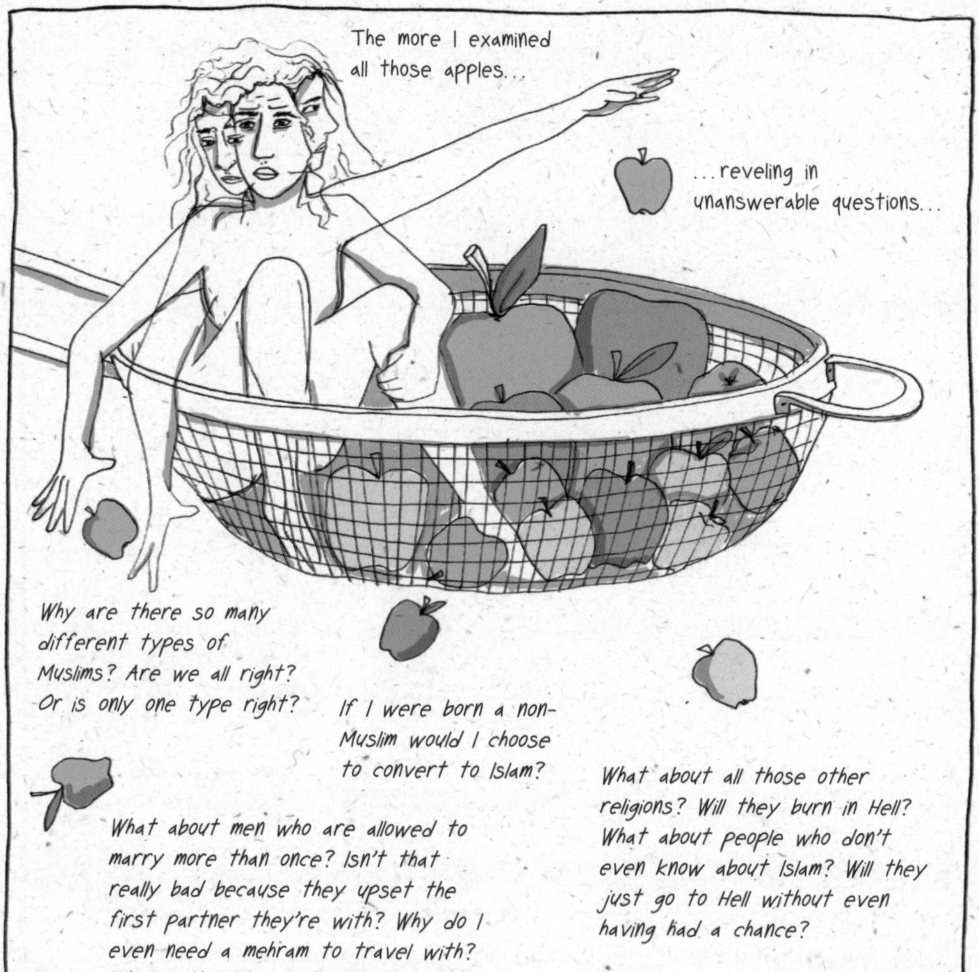
The more I examined all those apples...
...reveling in unanswerable questions...
Why are there so many different types of Muslims? Are we all right? Or is only one type right?
If I were born a non-Muslim would I choose to convert to Islam?
What about all those other religions? Will they burn in Hell? What about people who don't even know about Islam? Will they just go to Hell without even having had a chance?
What about men who are allowed to marry more than once? Isn't that really bad because they upset the first partner they're with? Why do I even need a mehram to travel with? Why can't I be a mehram? Why am I not allowed to drink alcohol in this life but in Heaven I'm promised wine?
Why am I the only one asking these questions? Does that mean everyone else has the answers? Or maybe they just refuse to ask? WHY am I asking all these questions? I won't get any answers. No one knows. But now that I've asked them, there's no going back.
Who even is this God who happens to be merciful and bountiful yet also so easy to anger, so controlling? If I don't remember him five times a day he gets really upset. Why is he even a He (capital HE)? Why? Can he really see everything, and if he can, why does he need two angels on my shoulders writing down all my good and bad deeds?
...the more friends and family withdrew.

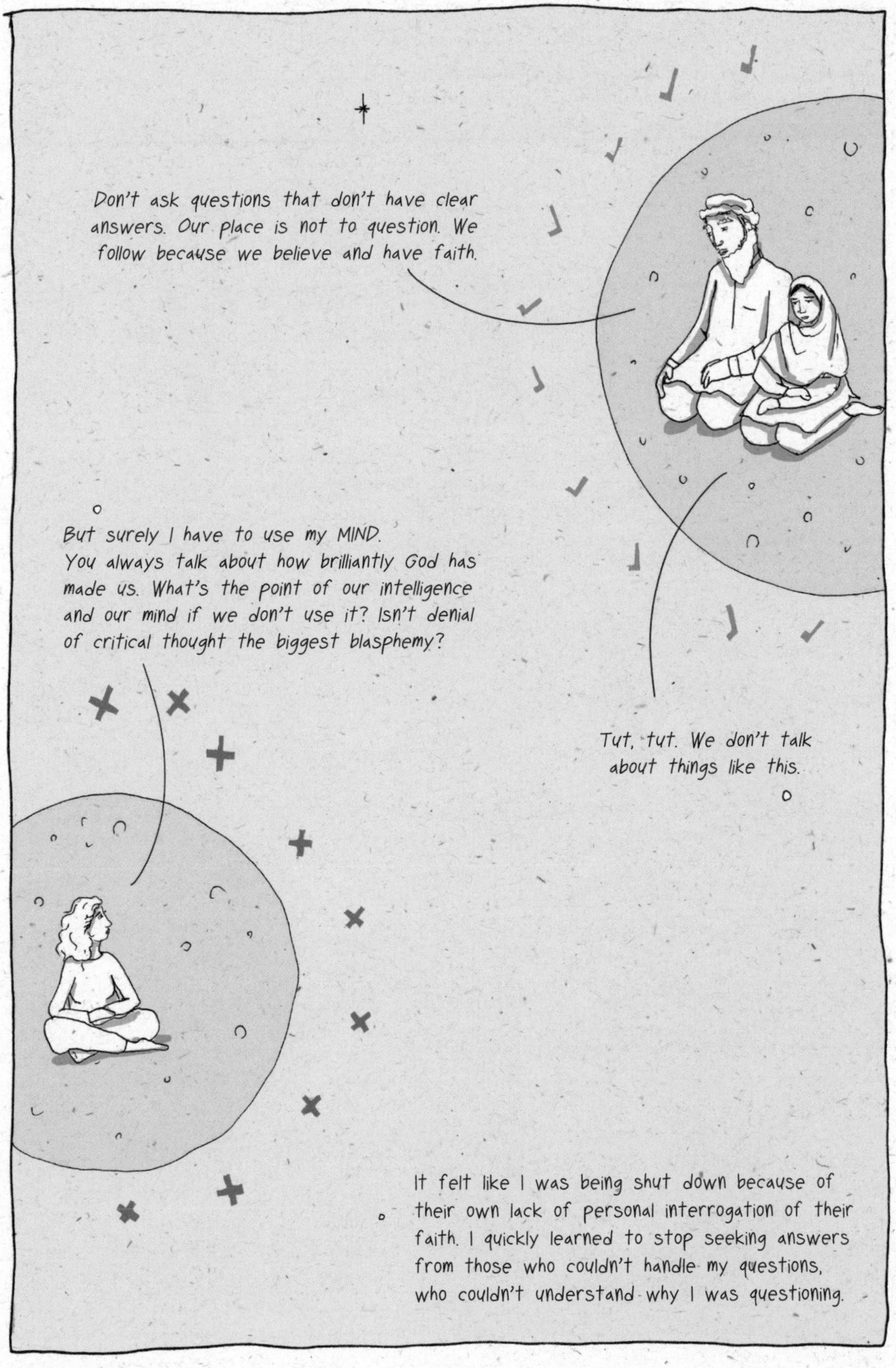
Don't ask questions that don't have clear answers. Our place is not to question. We follow because we believe and have faith.
But surely I have to use my MIND. You always talk about how brilliantly God has made us. What's the point of our intelligence and our mind if we don't use it? Isn't denial of critical thought the biggest blasphemy?
Tut, tut. We don't talk about things like this.
It felt like I was being shut down because of their own lack of personal interrogation of their faith. I quickly learned to stop seeking answers from those who couldn't handle my questions, who couldn't understand why I was questioning.

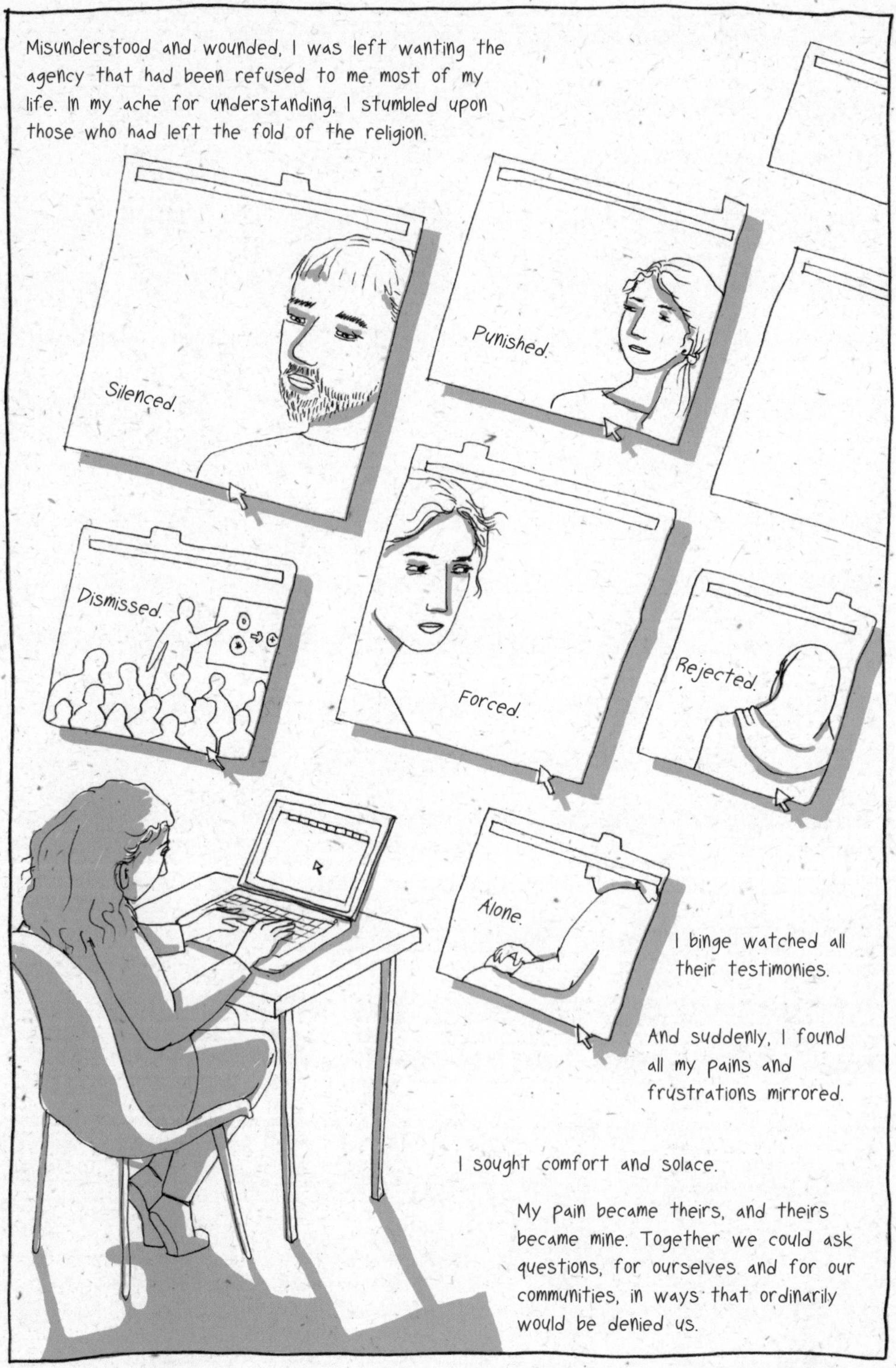
Misunderstood and wounded, I was left wanting the agency that had been refused to me most of my life. In my ache for understanding, I stumbled upon those who had left the fold of the religion.
Silenced.
Punished.
Dismissed.
Forced.
Rejected.
Alone.
I binge watched all their testimonies.
And suddenly, I found all my pains and frustrations mirrored.
I sought comfort and solace.
My pain became theirs, and theirs became mine. Together we could ask questions, for ourselves and for our communities, in ways that ordinarily would be denied us.

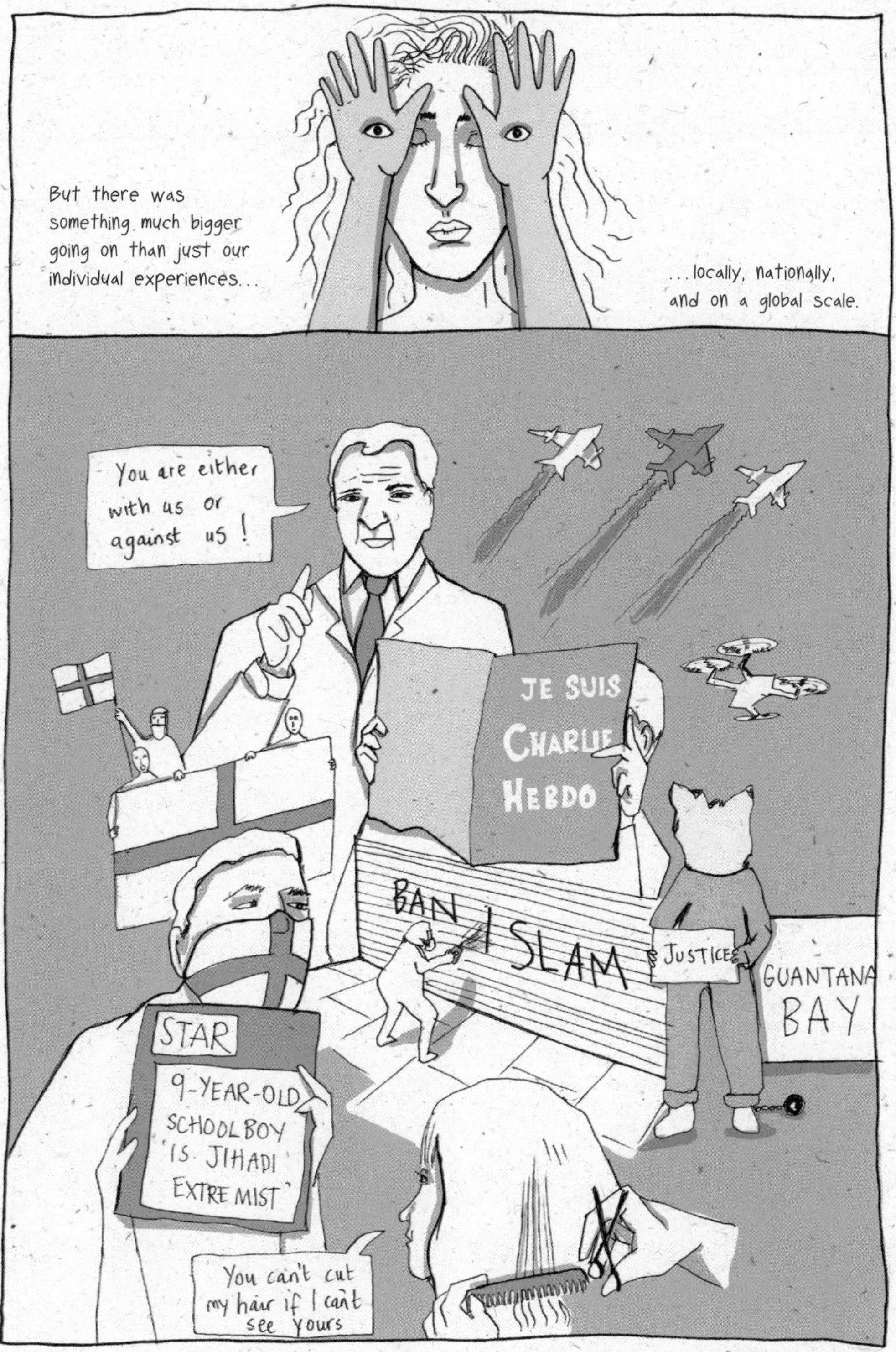
But there was something much bigger going on than just our individual experiences...
...locally, nationally, and on a global scale.
You are either with us or against us!
JE SUIS CHARLIE HEBDO
BAN ISLAM
JUSTICE
GUANTANA
BAY
STAR
9-YEAR-OLD SCHOOLBOY 'IS JIHADI EXTREMIST'
You can't cut my hair if I can't see yours

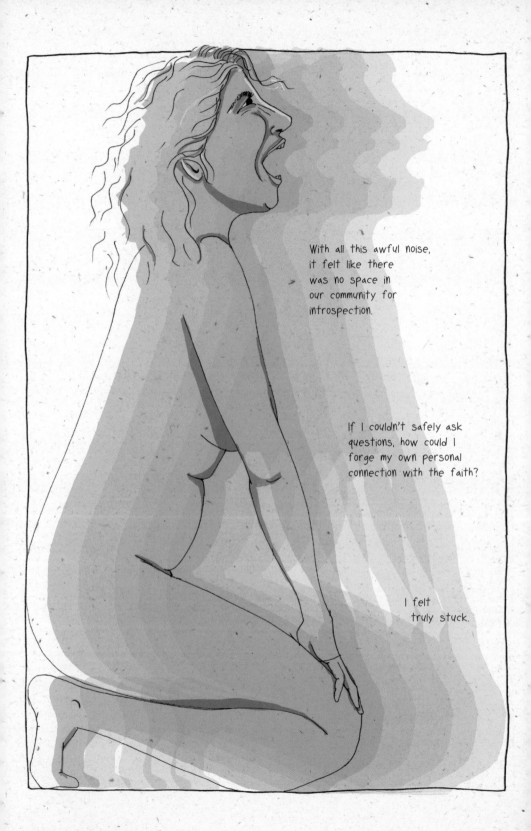

With all this awful noise, it felt like there was no space in our community for introspection.

If I couldn't safely ask questions, how could I forge my own personal connection with the faith?

I felt truly stuck.

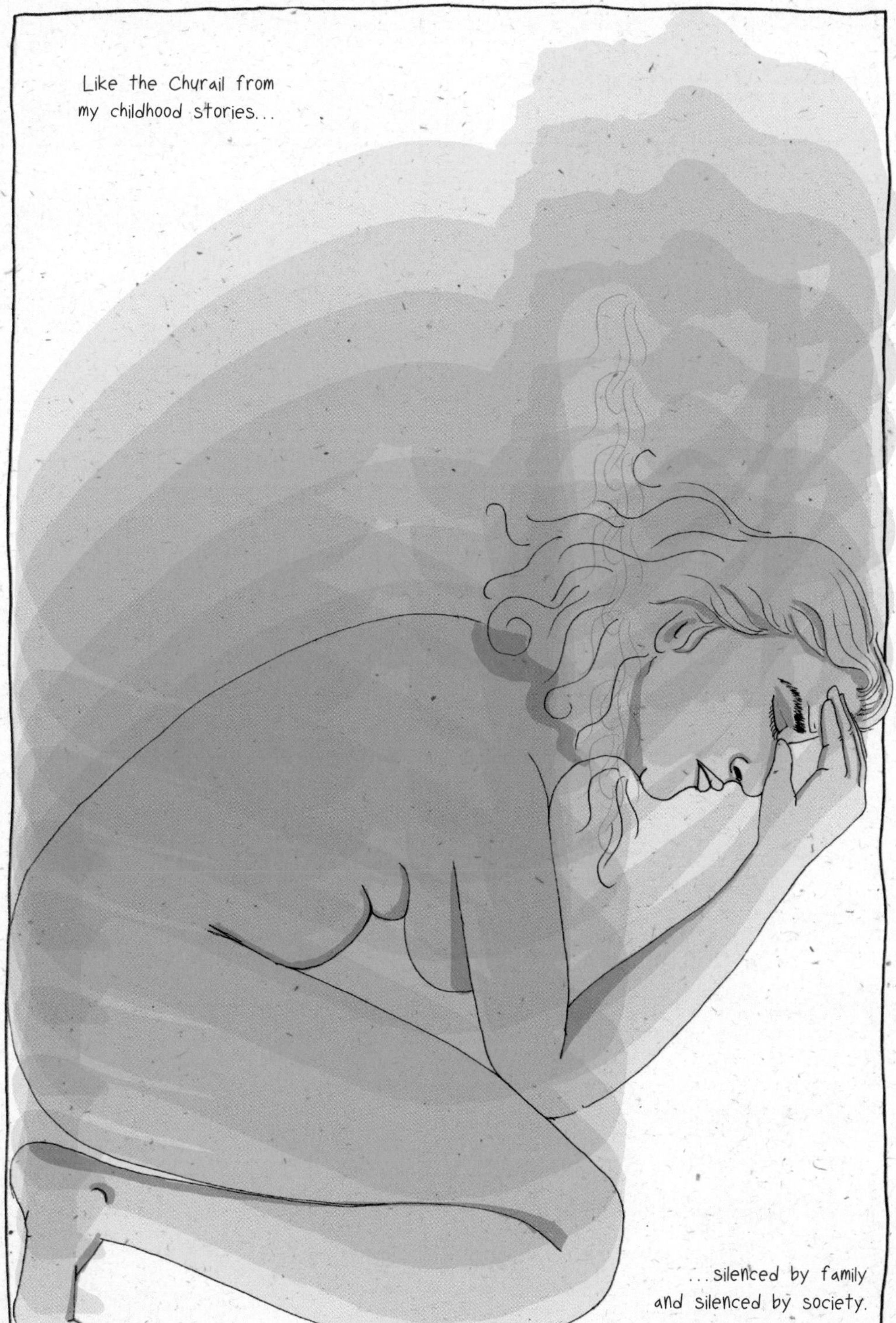
Like the Churail from
my childhood stories...
...silenced by family
and silenced by society.

So I did everything once denied me.

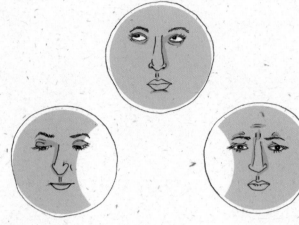

I became alienated from friends and family, lest a few loved ones saw through my anguish.

And though it gave me access to new ways of being, I continued to burn beneath it all.

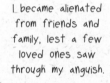

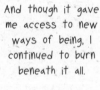

And like that, many moons of anger, frustration, and jealousy passed.

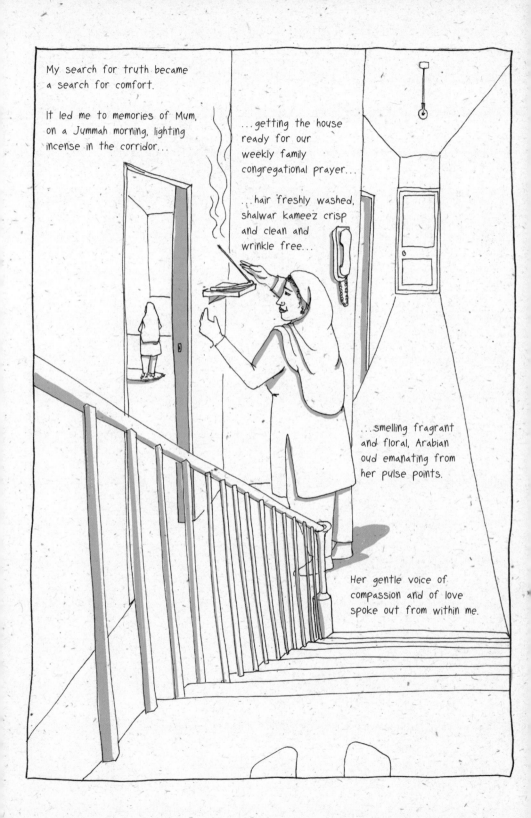

My search for truth became a search for comfort.

It led me to memories of Mum, on a Jummah morning, lighting incense in the corridor...

...getting the house ready for our weekly family congregational prayer...

...hair freshly washed, shalwar kameez crisp and clean and wrinkle free...

...smelling fragrant and floral, Arabian oud emanating from her pulse points.

Her gentle voice of compassion and of love spoke out from within me.

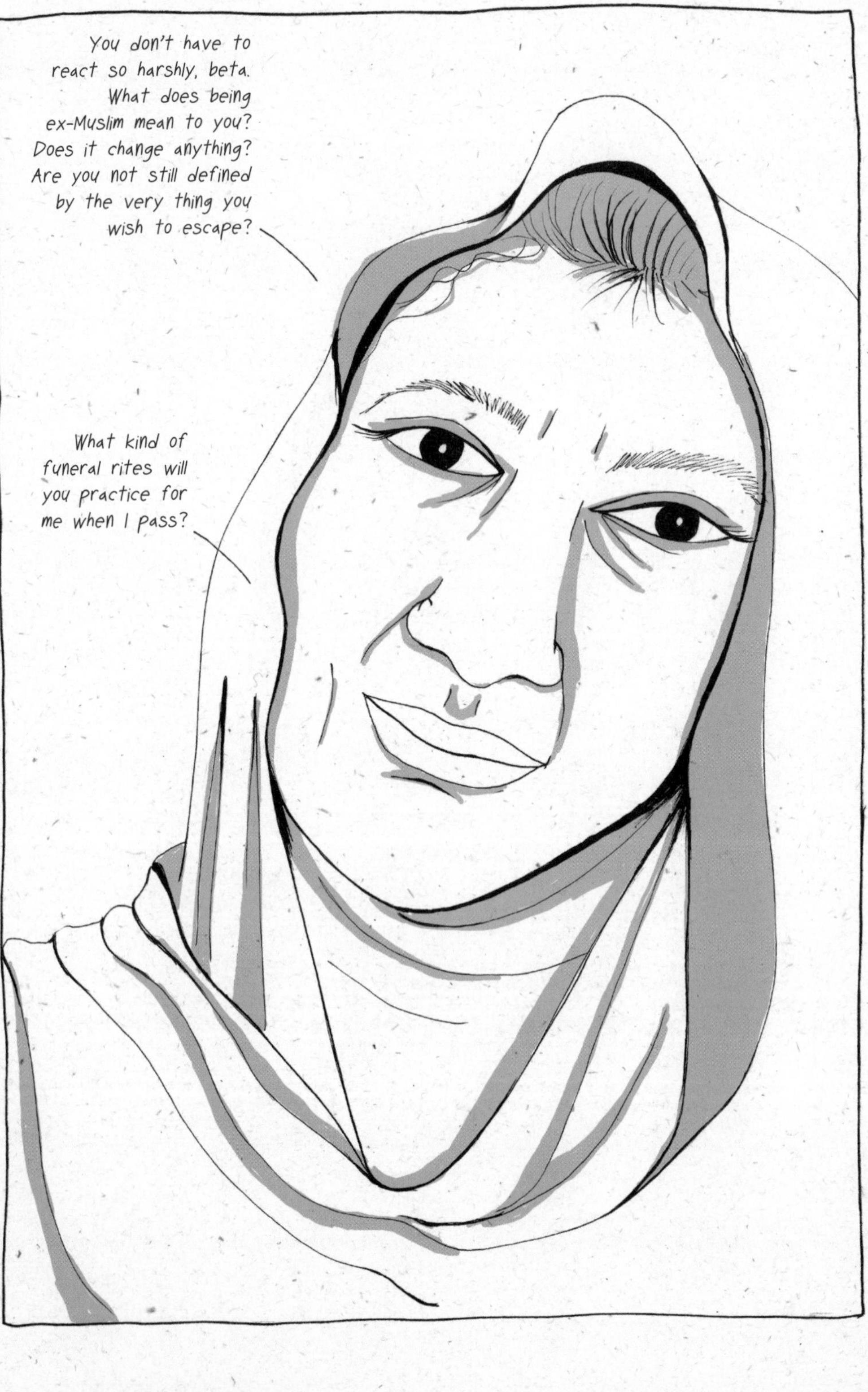
You don't have to react so harshly, beta. What does being ex-Muslim mean to you? Does it change anything? Are you not still defined by the very thing you wish to escape?
What kind of funeral rites will you practice for me when I pass?

What is life,
death,
grief,
loss,
if not something based
on the values of our
upbringing?

Could I really
rewrite it all
for myself?

And if I did, what
alternative belief system
would I base my new
values on?

How would I begin
to rewrite an entire
childhood's worth of
associations?

Or would I let go
of belief in the
unseen entirely?

Would I become an
echo of the scientific,
rational minds that
surrounded me in my
day-to-day life?

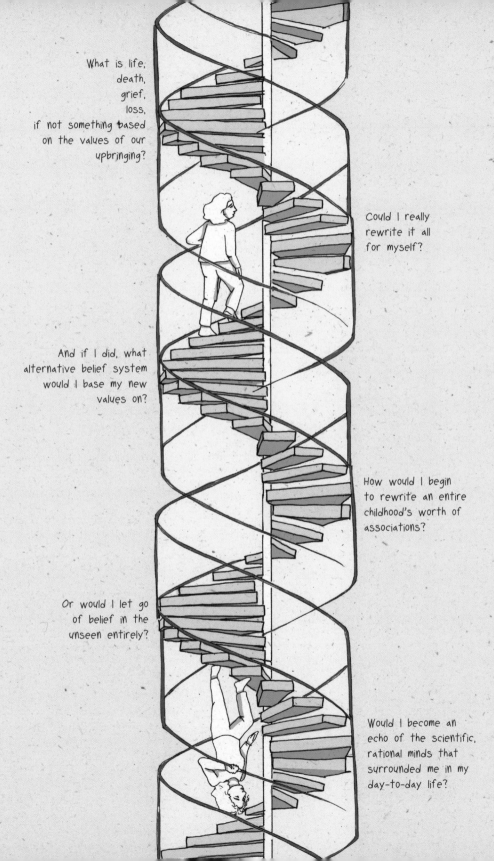

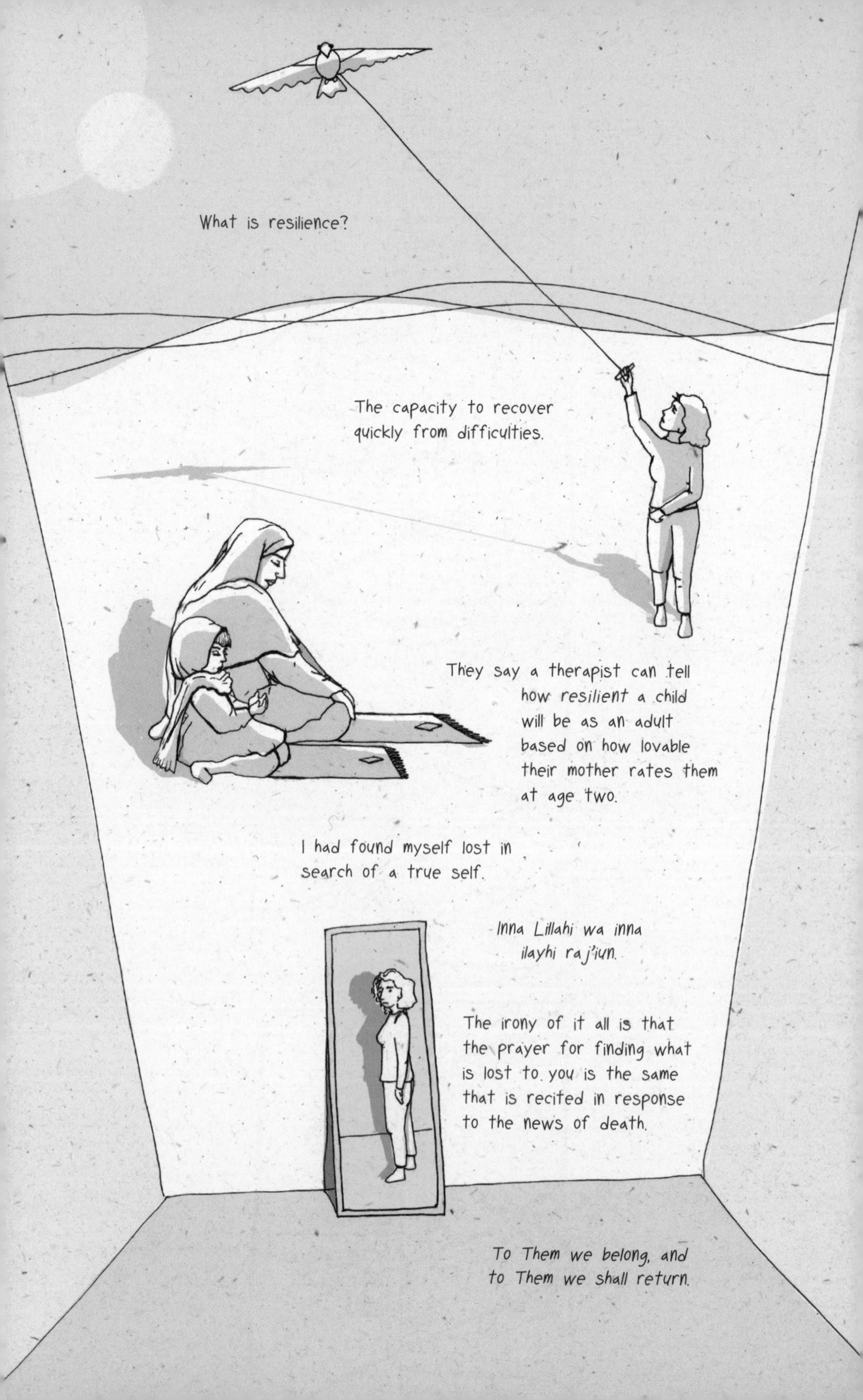
What is resilience?
The capacity to recover quickly from difficulties.
They say a therapist can tell how *resilient* a child will be as an adult based on how lovable their mother rates them at age two.
I had found myself lost in search of a true self.
Inna Lillahi wa inna ilayhi raj'iun.
The irony of it all is that the prayer for finding what is lost to you is the same that is recited in response to the news of death.
To Them we belong, and to Them we shall return.

18 SILENCE

♫ John Cage "4'33""

My last surviving grandparent. My mother's mother.
An old, wrinkled vessel of memories I am keen to tap into.
I ask her,
Nani-ama, tell me about your childhood days.
She looks into my eyes.
You look like my mother, you even behave like her.
What was she like?

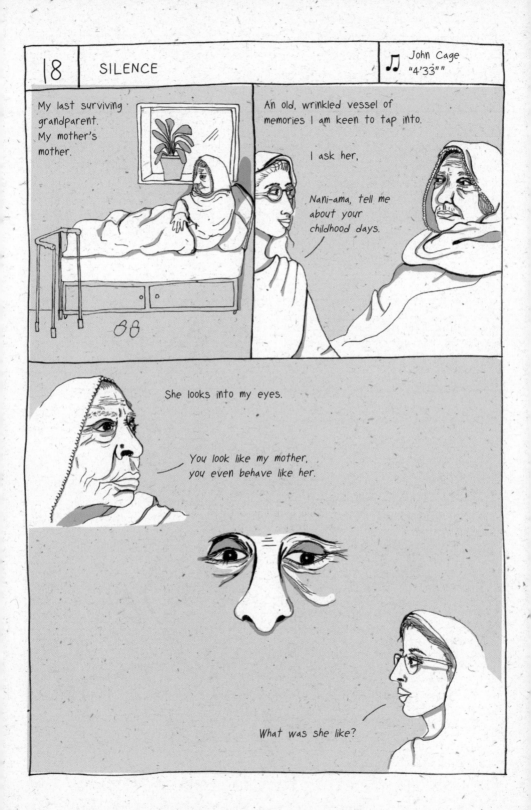

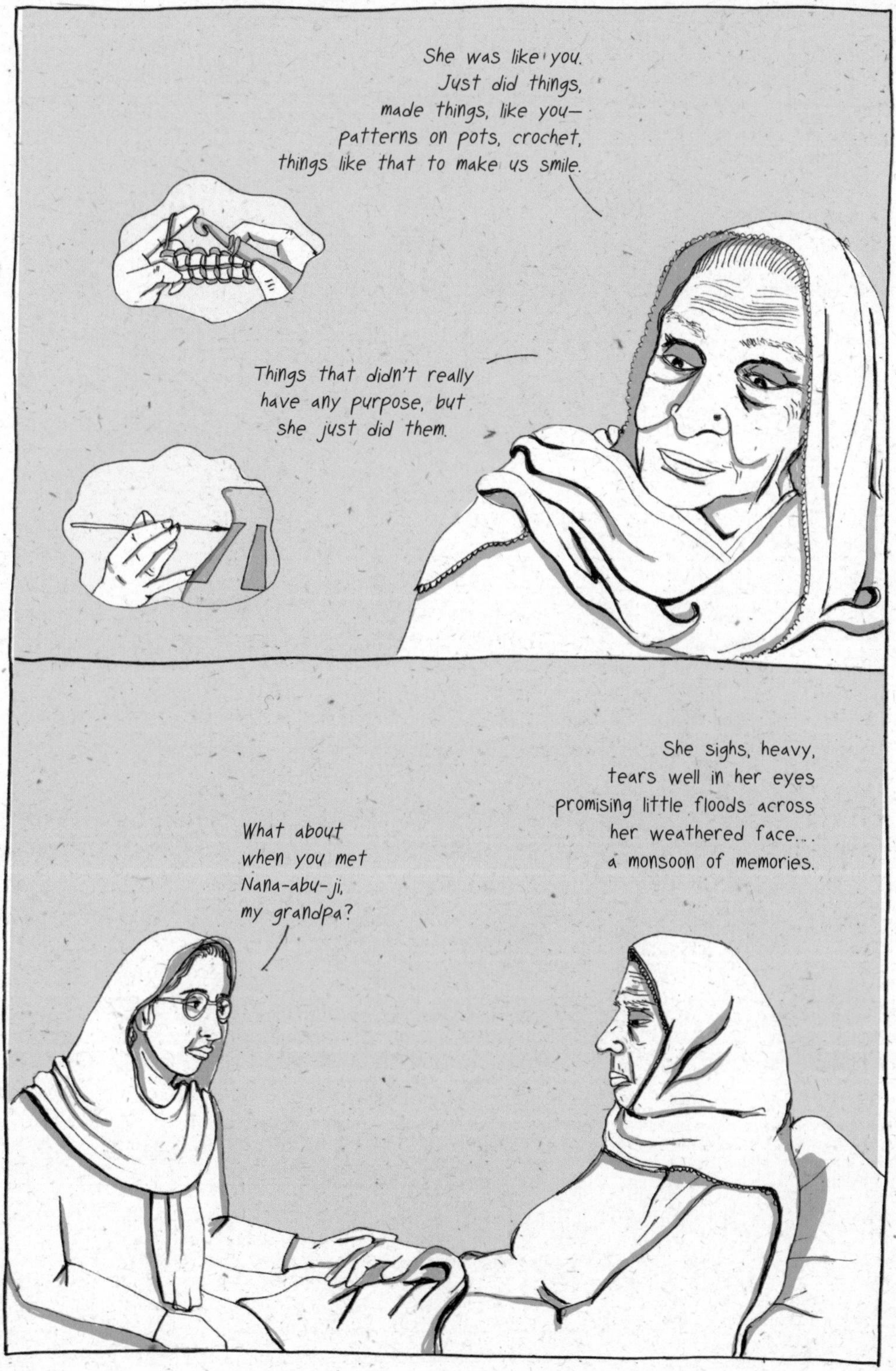
She was like you. Just did things, made things, like you— patterns on pots, crochet, things like that to make us smile.
Things that didn't really have any purpose, but she just did them.
She sighs, heavy, tears well in her eyes promising little floods across her weathered face... a monsoon of memories.
What about when you met Nana-abu-ji, my grandpa?

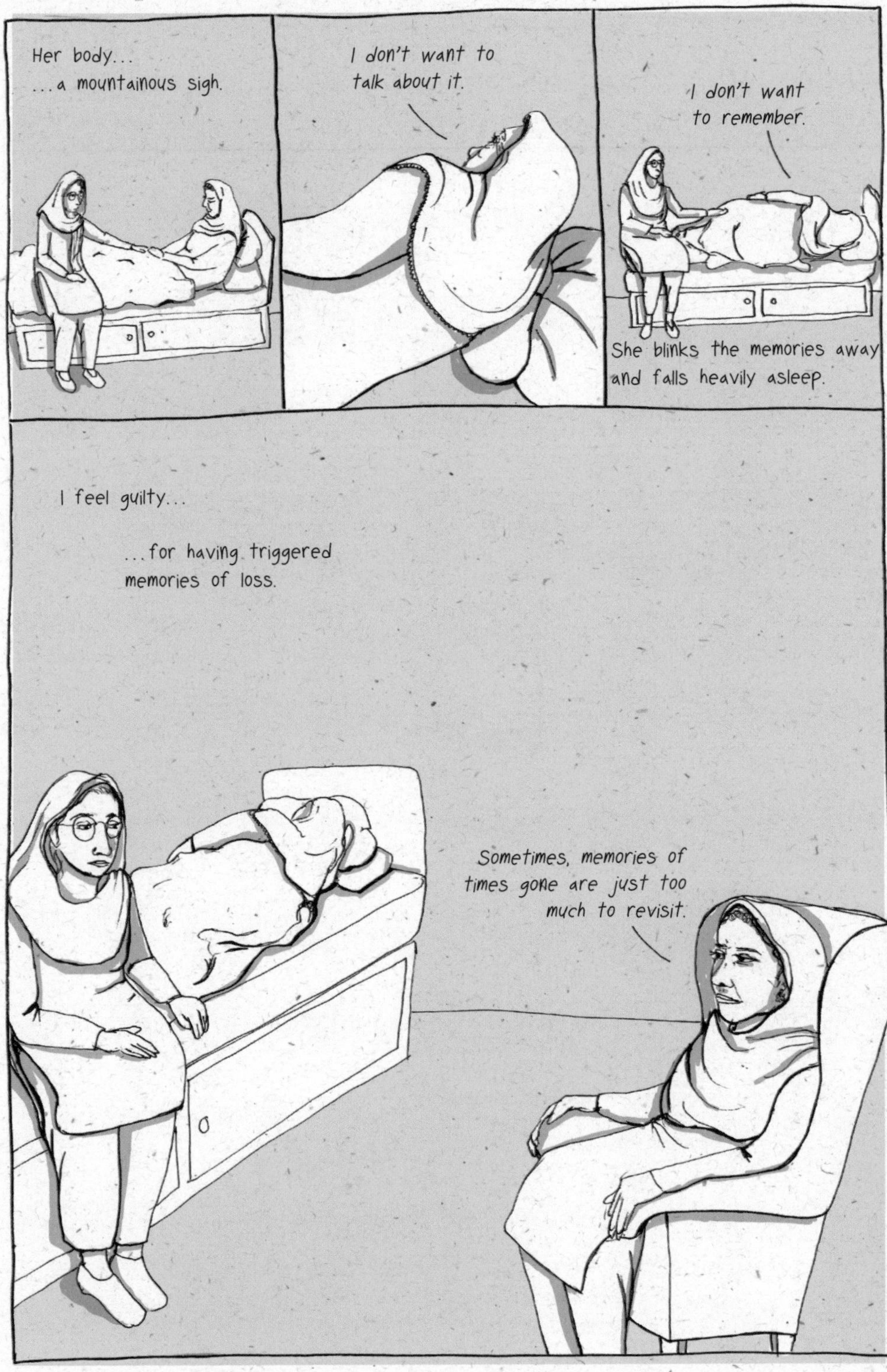
Her body...
...a mountainous sigh.
I don't want to talk about it.
I don't want to remember.
She blinks the memories away and falls heavily asleep.
I feel guilty...
...for having triggered memories of loss.
Sometimes, memories of times gone are just too much to revisit.

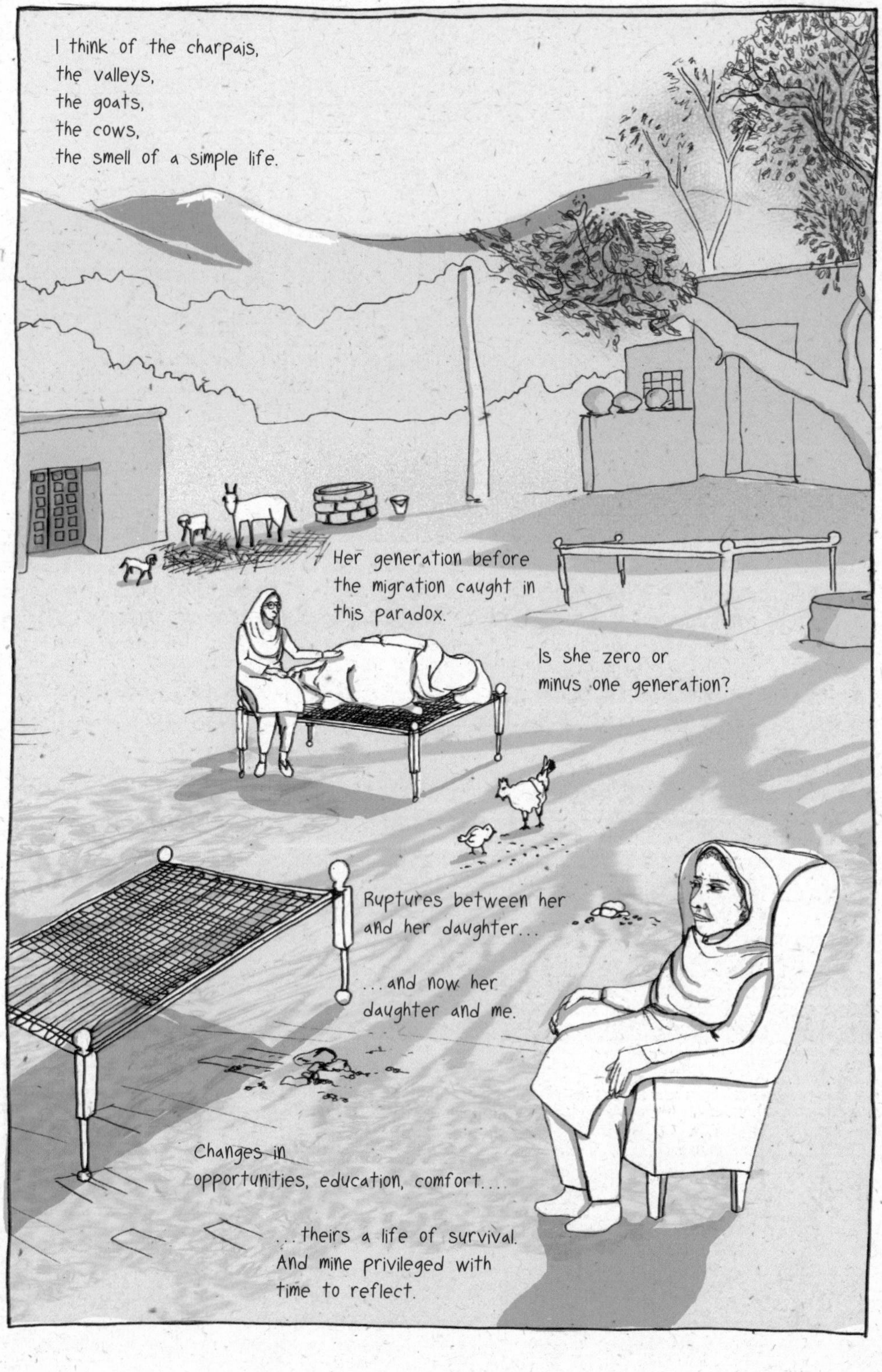
I think of the charpais,
the valleys,
the goats,
the cows,
the smell of a simple life.
Her generation before
the migration caught in
this paradox.
Is she zero or
minus one generation?
Ruptures between her
and her daughter...
...and now her
daughter and me.
Changes in
opportunities, education, comfort....
...theirs a life of survival.
And mine privileged with
time to reflect.

With generations of othering, how can we speak out for ourselves when we don't know what being treated with humanity looks like?

CAN'T SPEAK ENGLISH
BENEFITS SCROUNGERS
LACK OF INTEGRATION
UNDERCLASS
CHEAP LABOR
WORTHLESS IF NOT AT WORK
DODGY
NO DESIRE FOR ASSIMILATION
stay in this corner
keep working
the only place
stay silent
keep working
that will serve you
silent
complicit
stay small
stay silent
agreeable
grateful

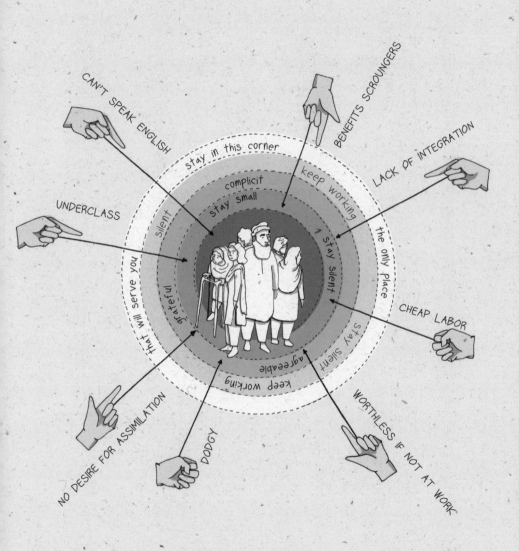

Cyclical and self-fulfilling.

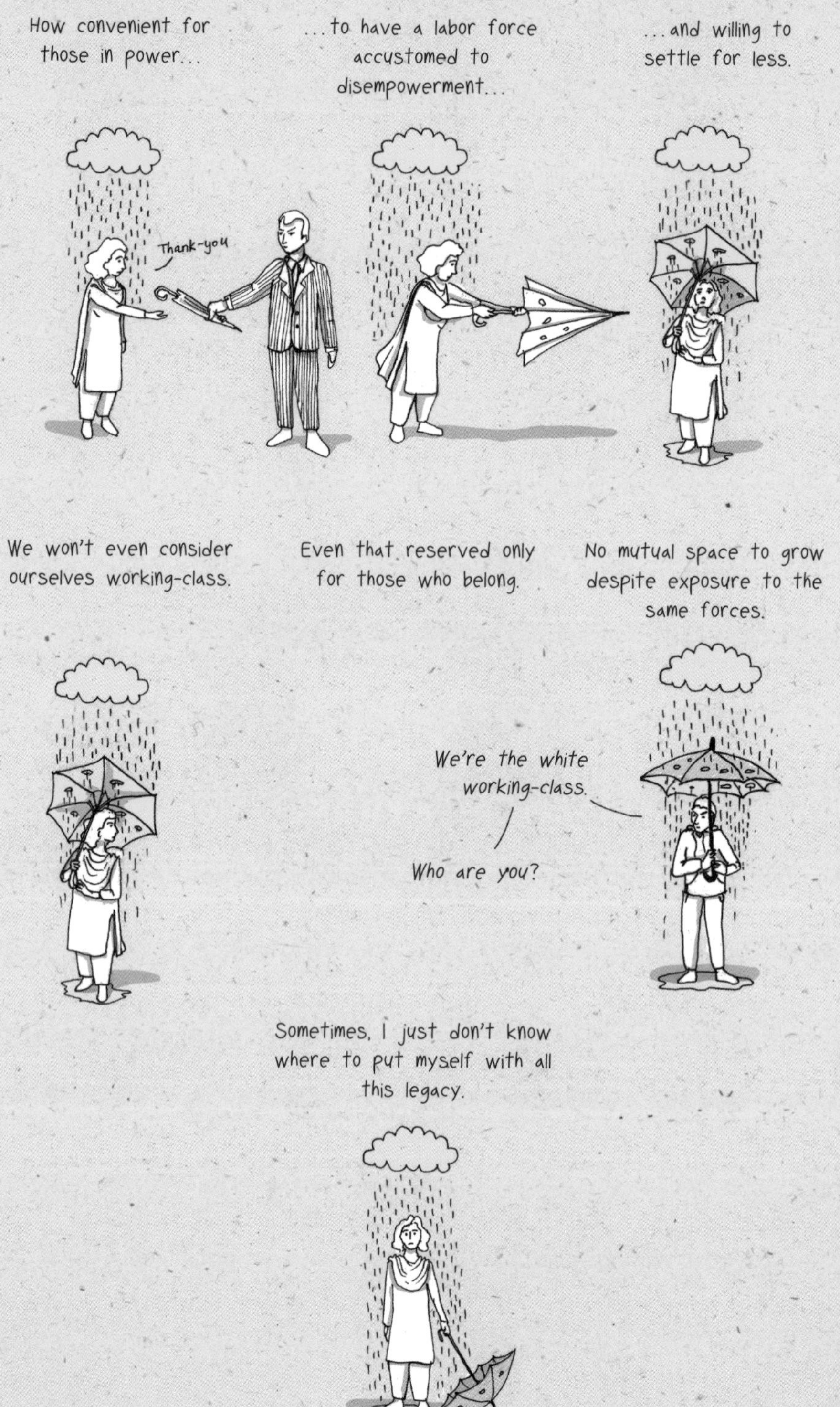
How convenient for those in power...
Thank-you
...to have a labor force accustomed to disempowerment...
...and willing to settle for less.
We won't even consider ourselves working-class.
Even that reserved only for those who belong.
No mutual space to grow despite exposure to the same forces.
We're the white working-class.
Who are you?
Sometimes, I just don't know where to put myself with all this legacy.

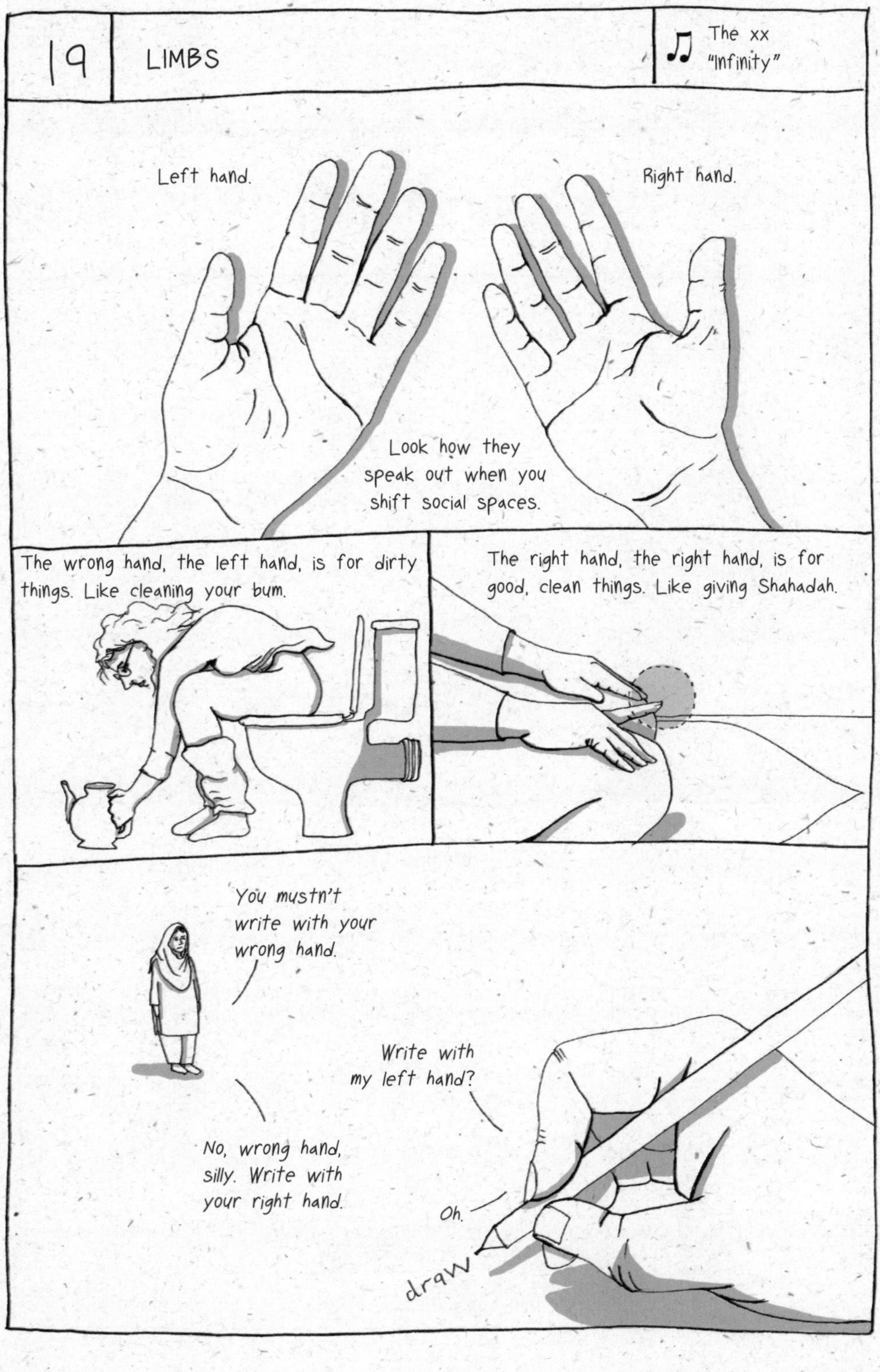
19
LIMBS
The xx "Infinity"
Left hand.
Right hand.
Look how they speak out when you shift social spaces.
The wrong hand, the left hand, is for dirty things. Like cleaning your bum.
The right hand, the right hand, is for good, clean things. Like giving Shahadah.
You mustn't write with your wrong hand.
Write with my left hand?
No, wrong hand, silly. Write with your right hand.
Oh.
draw

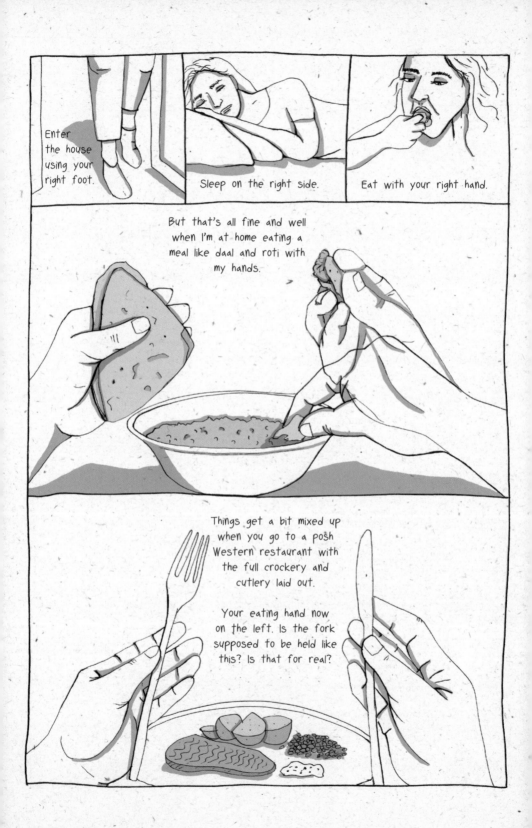

Enter the house using your right foot.

Sleep on the right side.

Eat with your right hand.

But that's all fine and well when I'm at home eating a meal like daal and roti with my hands.

Things get a bit mixed up when you go to a posh Western restaurant with the full crockery and cutlery laid out.

Your eating hand now on the left. Is the fork supposed to be held like this? Is that for real?

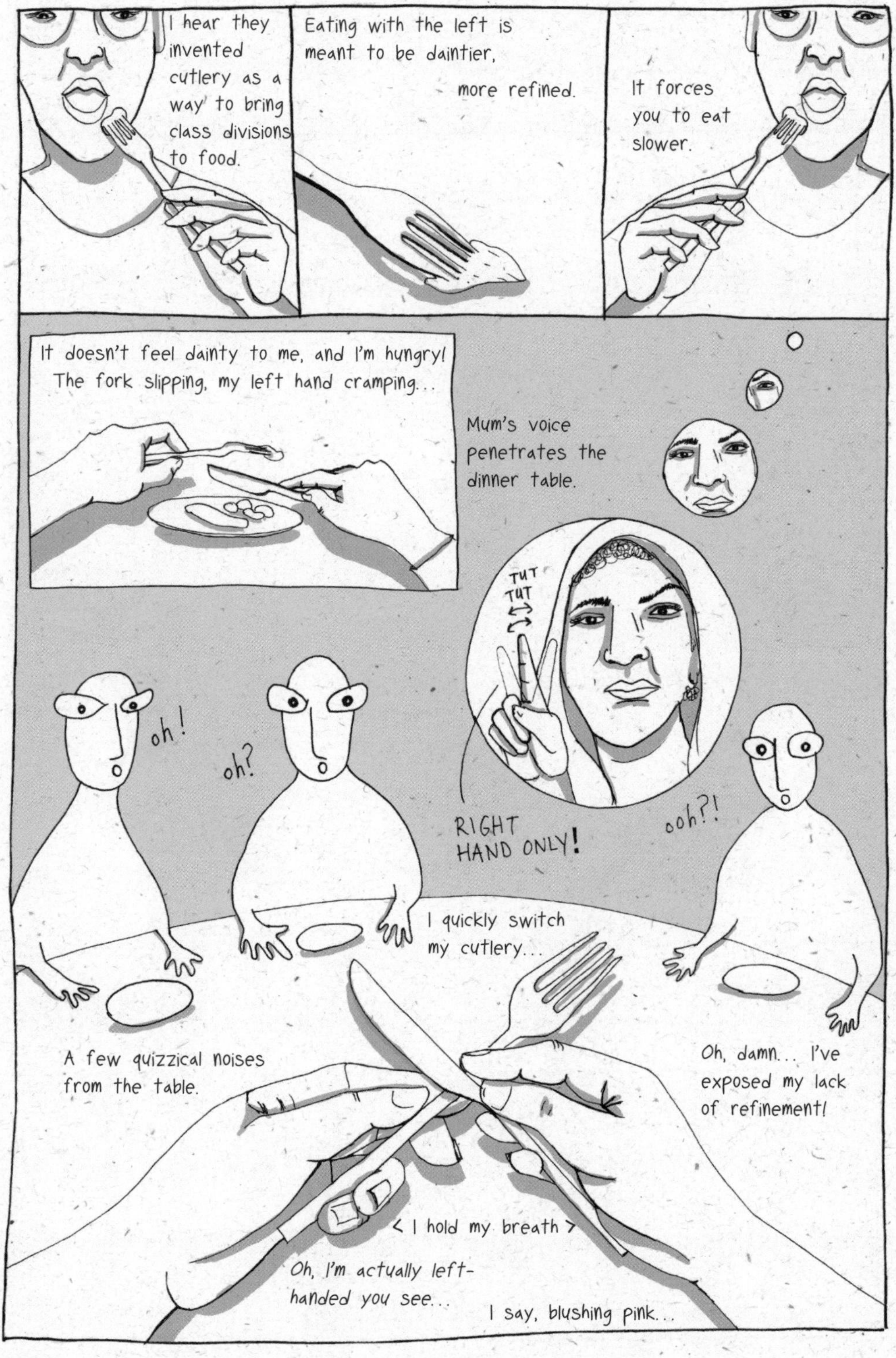
I hear they invented cutlery as a way to bring class divisions to food.
Eating with the left is meant to be daintier,
more refined.
It forces you to eat slower.
It doesn't feel dainty to me, and I'm hungry! The fork slipping, my left hand cramping...
Mum's voice penetrates the dinner table.
TUT TUT
RIGHT HAND ONLY!
oh!
oh?
ooh?!
I quickly switch my cutlery...
A few quizzical noises from the table.
Oh, damn... I've exposed my lack of refinement!
< I hold my breath >
Oh, I'm actually left-handed you see...
I say, blushing pink...

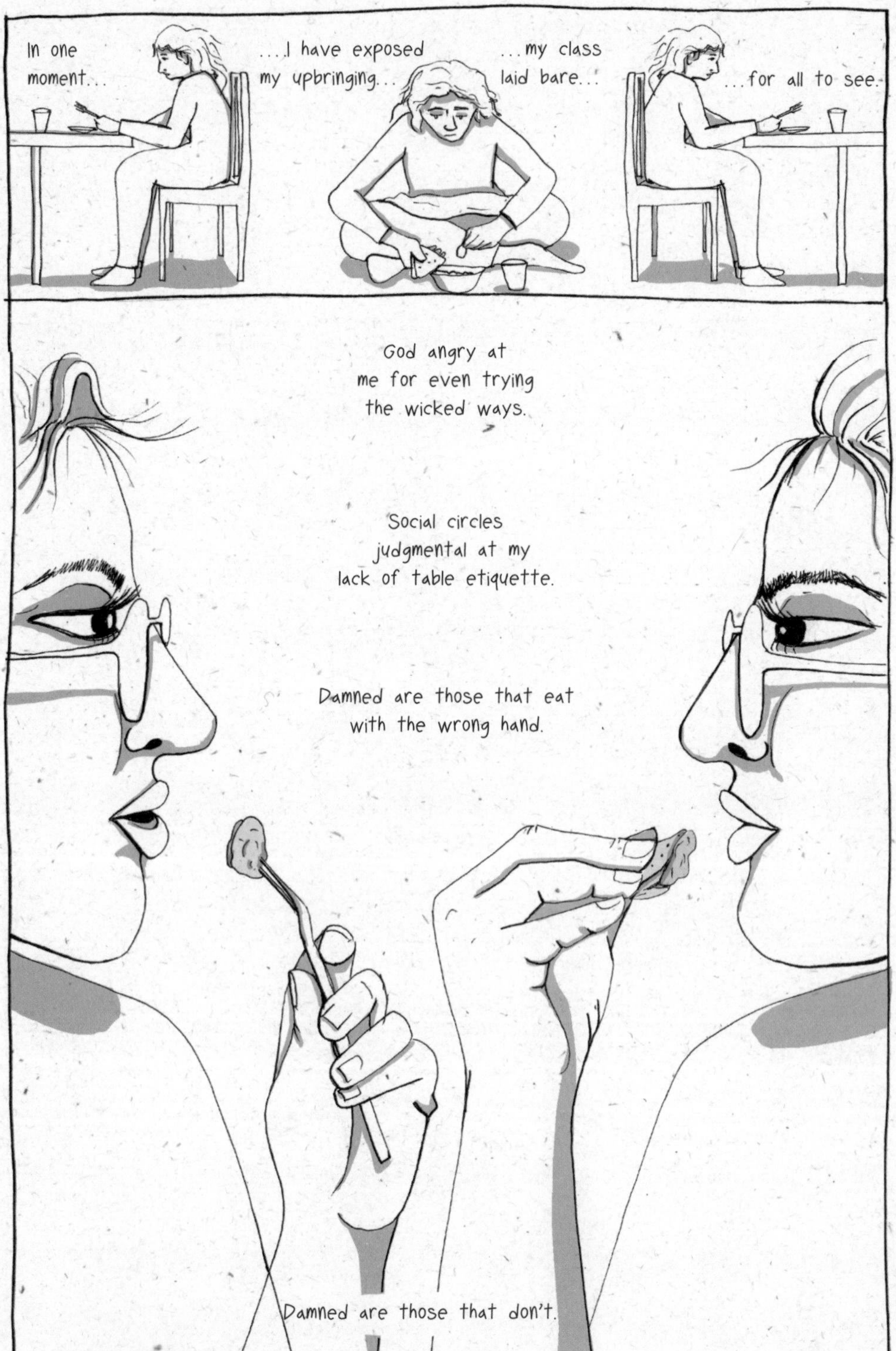
In one moment...
....I have exposed my upbringing...
...my class laid bare...
...for all to see.
God angry at me for even trying the wicked ways.
Social circles judgmental at my lack of table etiquette.
Damned are those that eat with the wrong hand.
Damned are those that don't.

How do we begin to negotiate all of these overlaps?

They call it acculturation. Four main methods an immigrant can adopt to adjust to a new cultural environment.

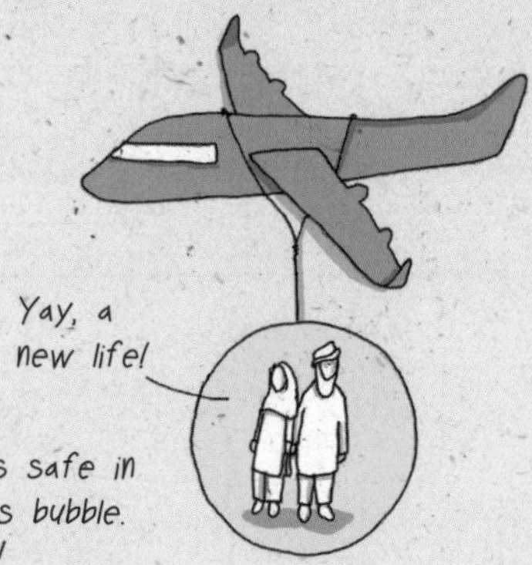
Yay, a new life!

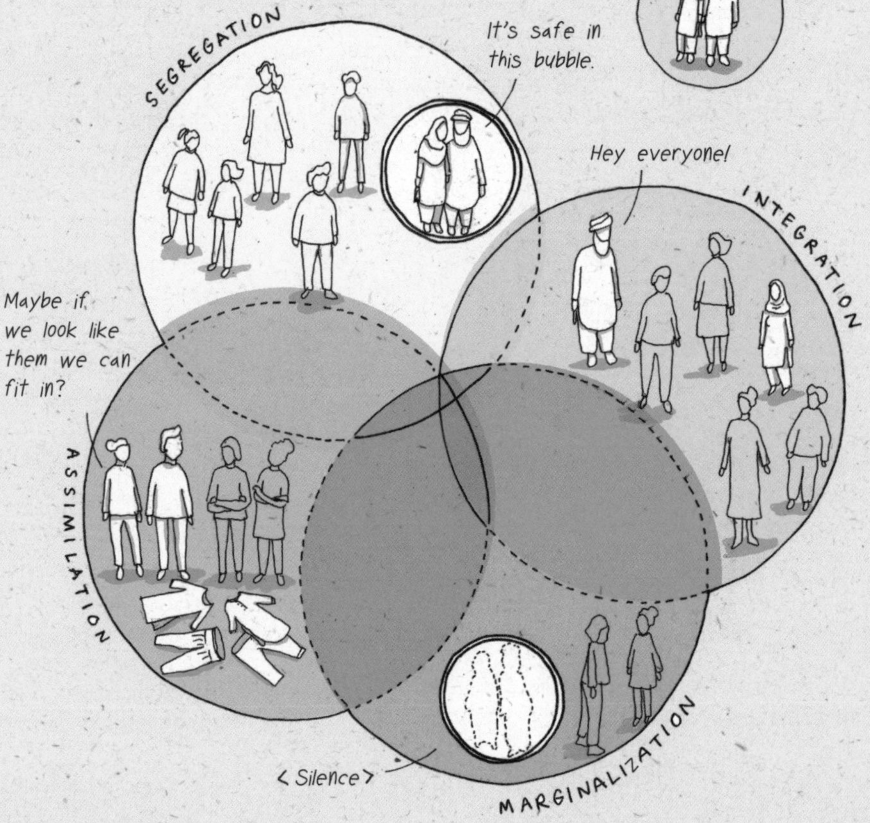
SEGREGATION
It's safe in this bubble.
Hey everyone!
INTEGRATION
Maybe if we look like them we can fit in?
ASSIMILATION
MARGINALIZATION
< Silence >

So many studies on how minorities conduct themselves within the host culture. But what about how the host culture affects the minority?

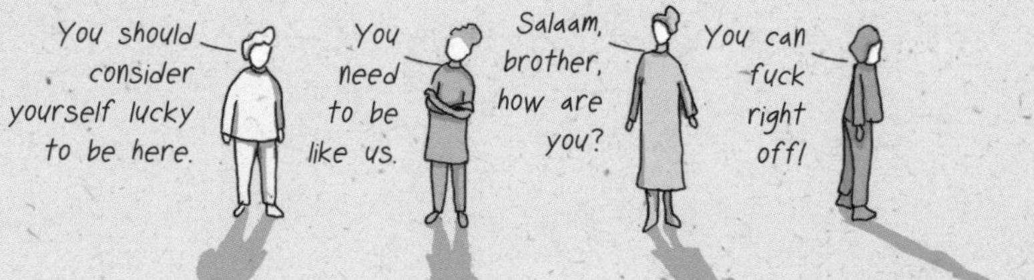
You should consider yourself lucky to be here.
You need to be like us.
Salaam, brother, how are you?
You can fuck right off!

Surely, the host culture is the one that sets the tone?

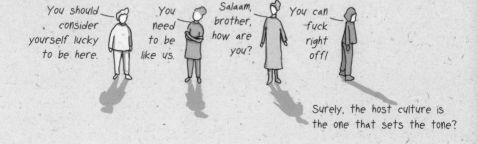

Will we be able to untangle from the
hundreds of years of imperialism and
how it shapes our place in this land?

Audre Lorde echoes in my mind:

"The master's tools will never
dismantle the master's house."

We are a displaced diaspora.
A scattered people whose origins now
lie only in passed-down memories.
Neither here nor there.

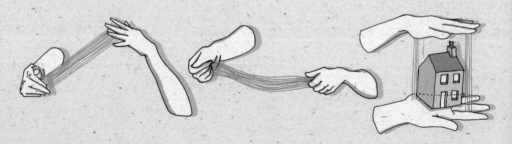

I clean, untangle, straighten...   ...wash, wipe, dust...   ...to feel this place,
                                                                      to wake up to it
                                                                      and call it Home.

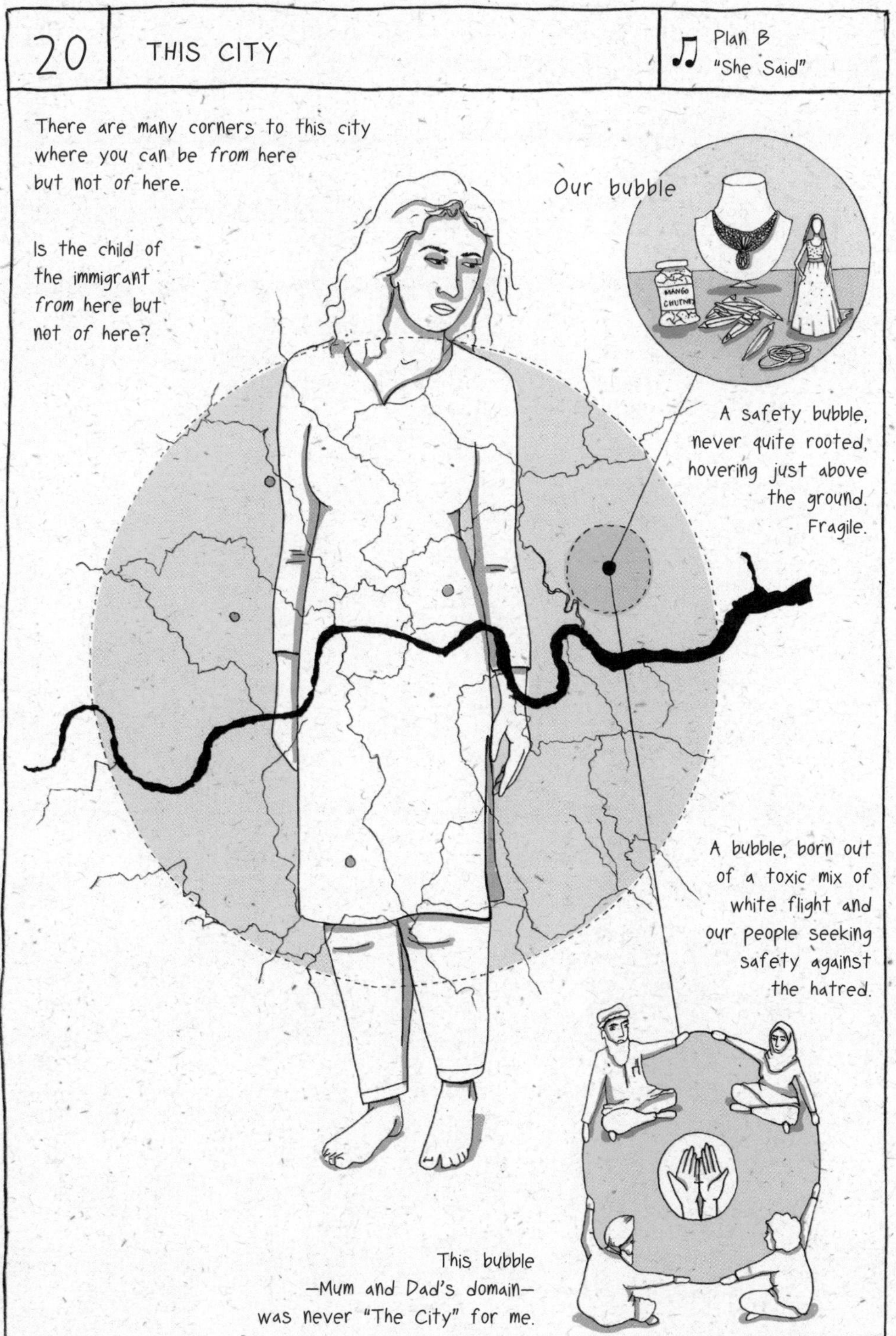
20
THIS CITY
♫ Plan B
"She Said"
There are many corners to this city where you can be *from* here but not *of* here.
Is the child of the immigrant *from* here but not *of* here?
Our bubble
A safety bubble, never quite rooted, hovering just above the ground. Fragile.
A bubble, born out of a toxic mix of white flight and our people seeking safety against the hatred.
This bubble
—Mum and Dad's domain—
was never "The City" for me.

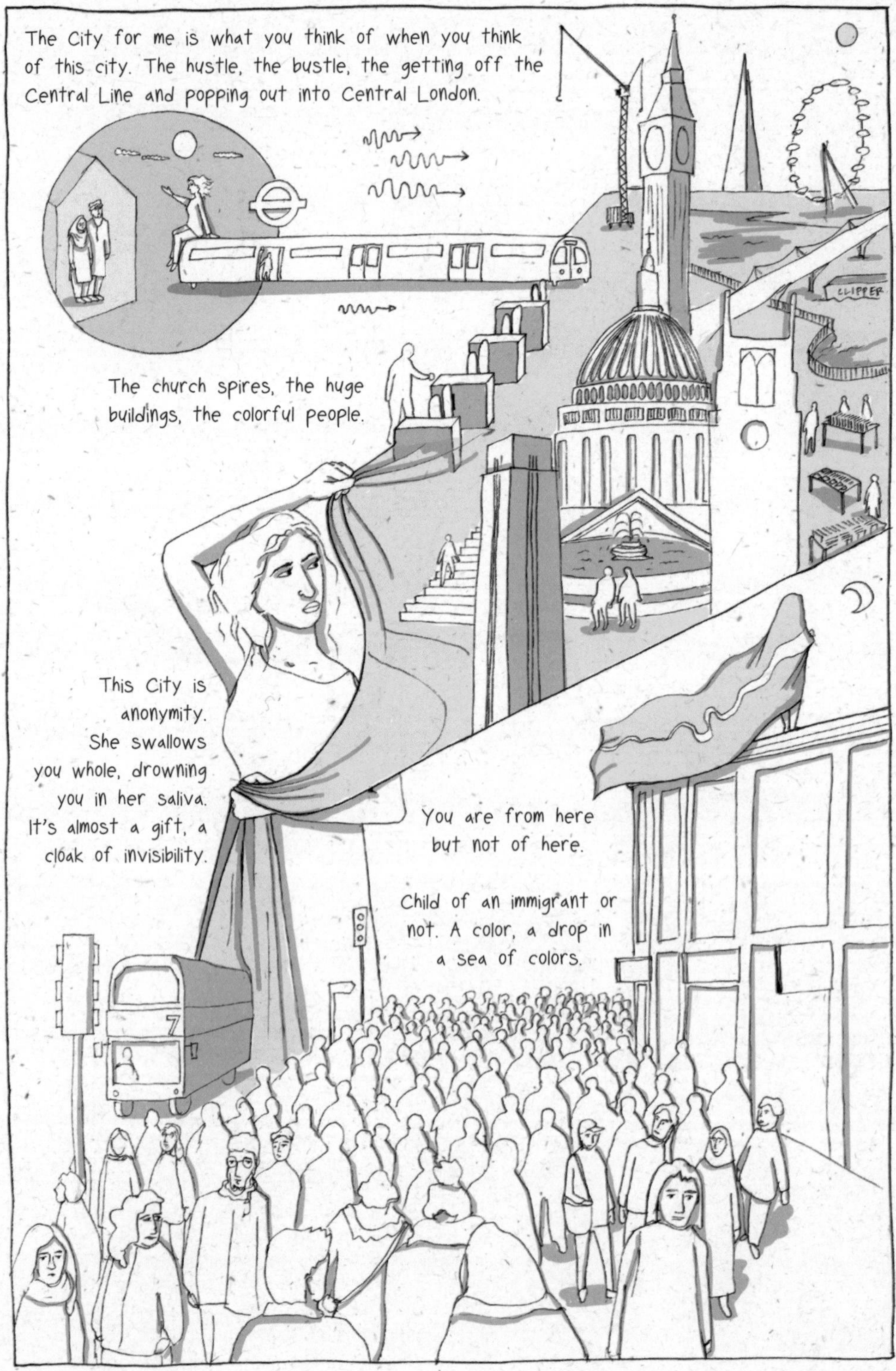

The City for me is what you think of when you think of this city. The hustle, the bustle, the getting off the Central Line and popping out into Central London.
CLIPPER
The church spires, the huge buildings, the colorful people.
This City is anonymity. She swallows you whole, drowning you in her saliva. It's almost a gift, a cloak of invisibility.
You are from here but not of here.
Child of an immigrant or not. A color, a drop in a sea of colors.

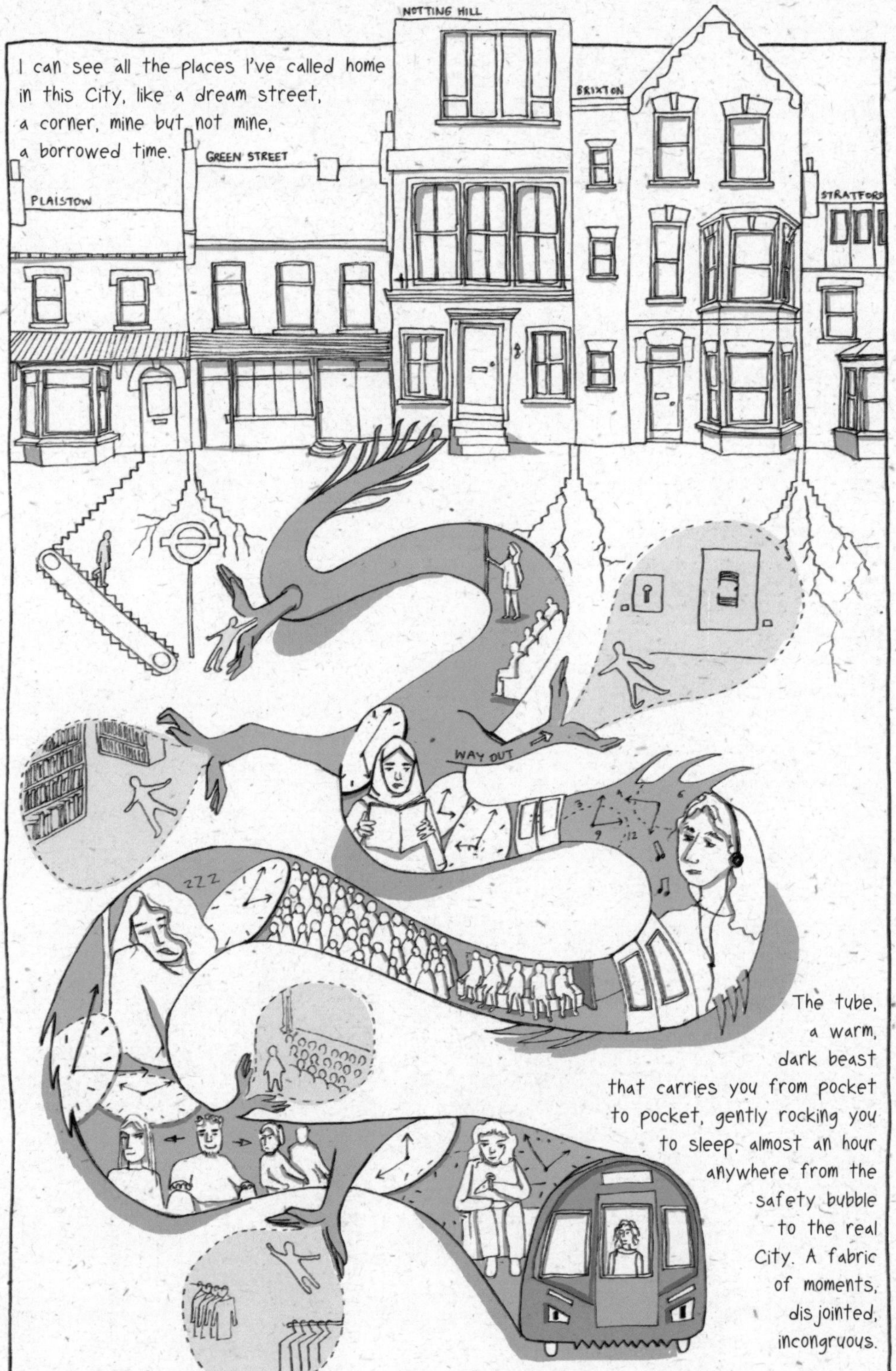
I can see all the places I've called home in this City, like a dream street, a corner, mine but not mine, a borrowed time.
NOTTING HILL
BRIXTON
GREEN STREET
PLAISTOW
STRATFORD
WAY OUT
zzz
The tube, a warm, dark beast that carries you from pocket to pocket, gently rocking you to sleep, almost an hour anywhere from the safety bubble to the real City. A fabric of moments, disjointed, incongruous.

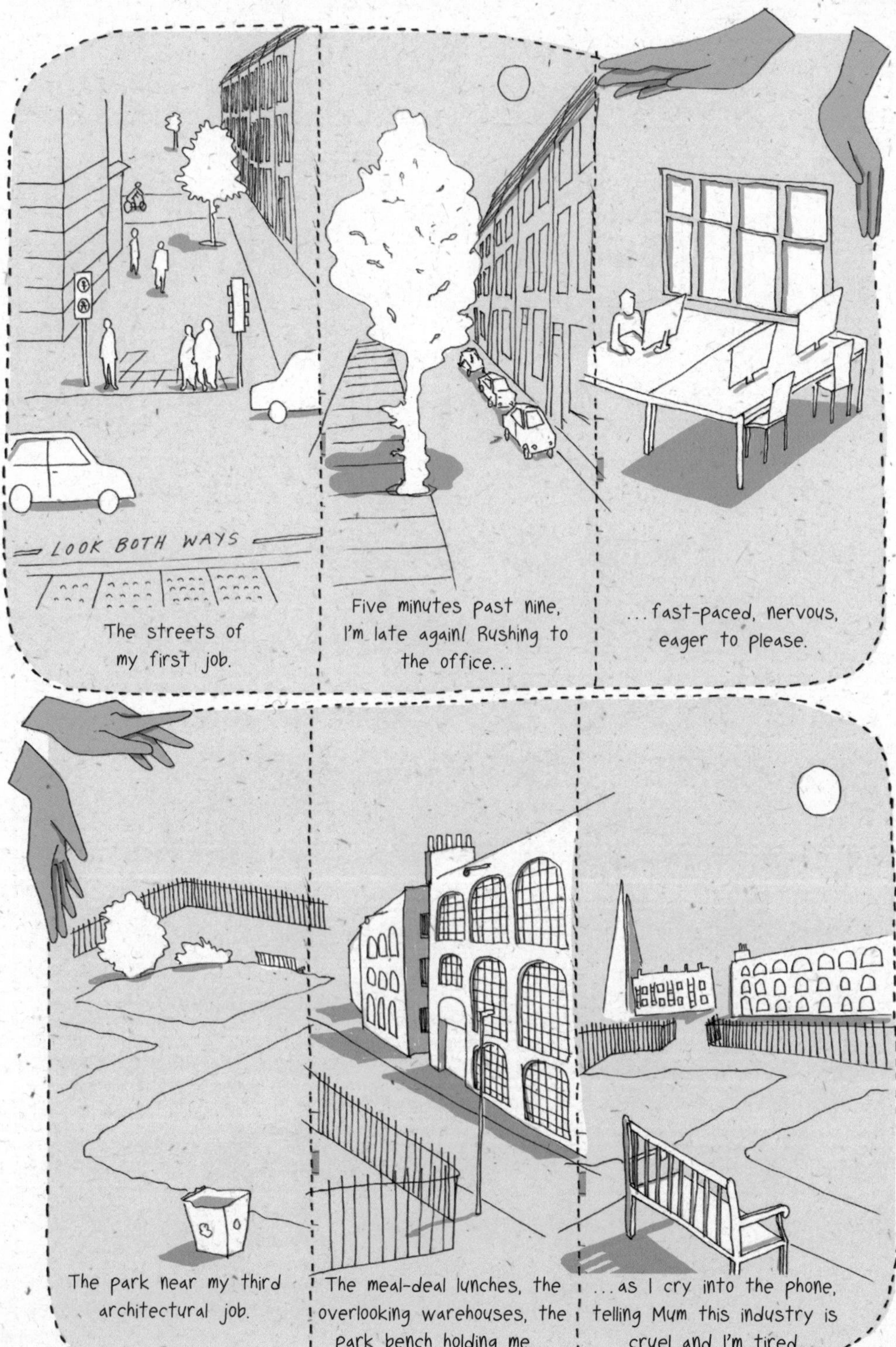
LOOK BOTH WAYS
The streets of my first job.
Five minutes past nine, I'm late again! Rushing to the office...
...fast-paced, nervous, eager to please.
The park near my third architectural job.
The meal-deal lunches, the overlooking warehouses, the park bench holding me...
...as I cry into the phone, telling Mum this industry is cruel and I'm tired.

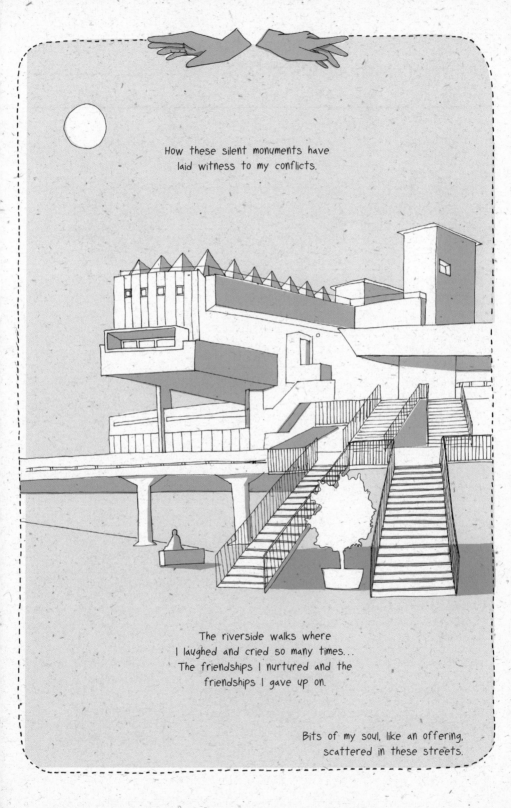

How these silent monuments have
laid witness to my conflicts.

The riverside walks where
I laughed and cried so many times...
The friendships I nurtured and the
friendships I gave up on.

Bits of my soul, like an offering,
scattered in these streets.

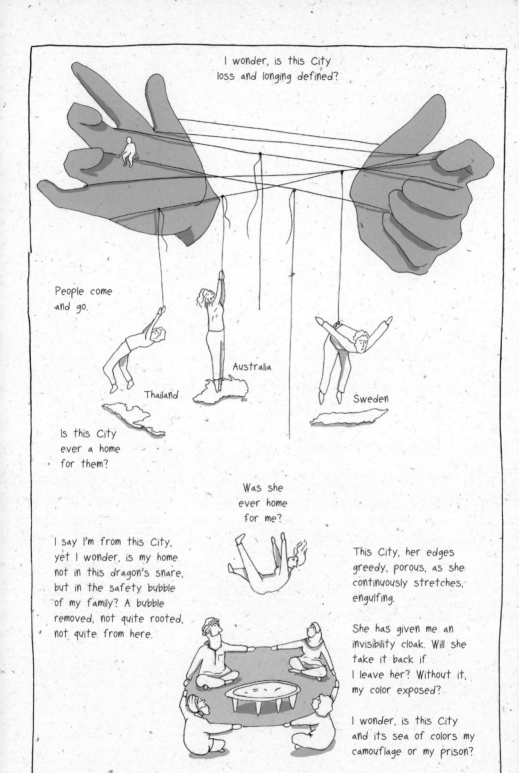

I wonder, is this City loss and longing defined?

People come and go.

Thailand

Australia

Sweden

Is this City ever a home for them?

Was she ever home for me?

I say I'm from this City, yet I wonder, is my home not in this dragon's snare, but in the safety bubble of my family? A bubble removed, not quite rooted, not quite from here.

This City, her edges greedy, porous, as she continuously stretches, engulfing.

She has given me an invisibility cloak. Will she take it back if I leave her? Without it, my color exposed?

I wonder, is this City and its sea of colors my camouflage or my prison?

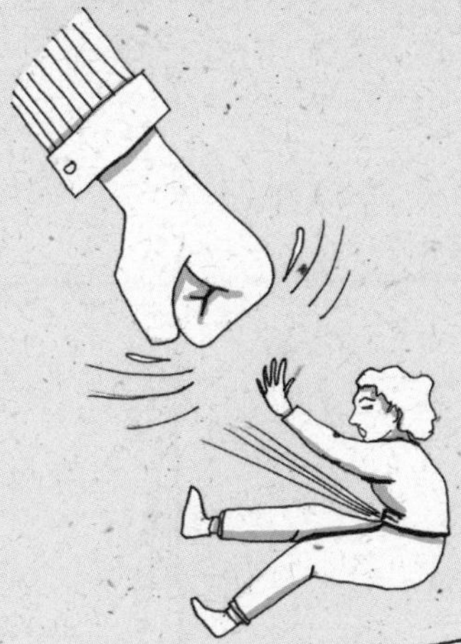

The outside bashes me in

to this interior world.

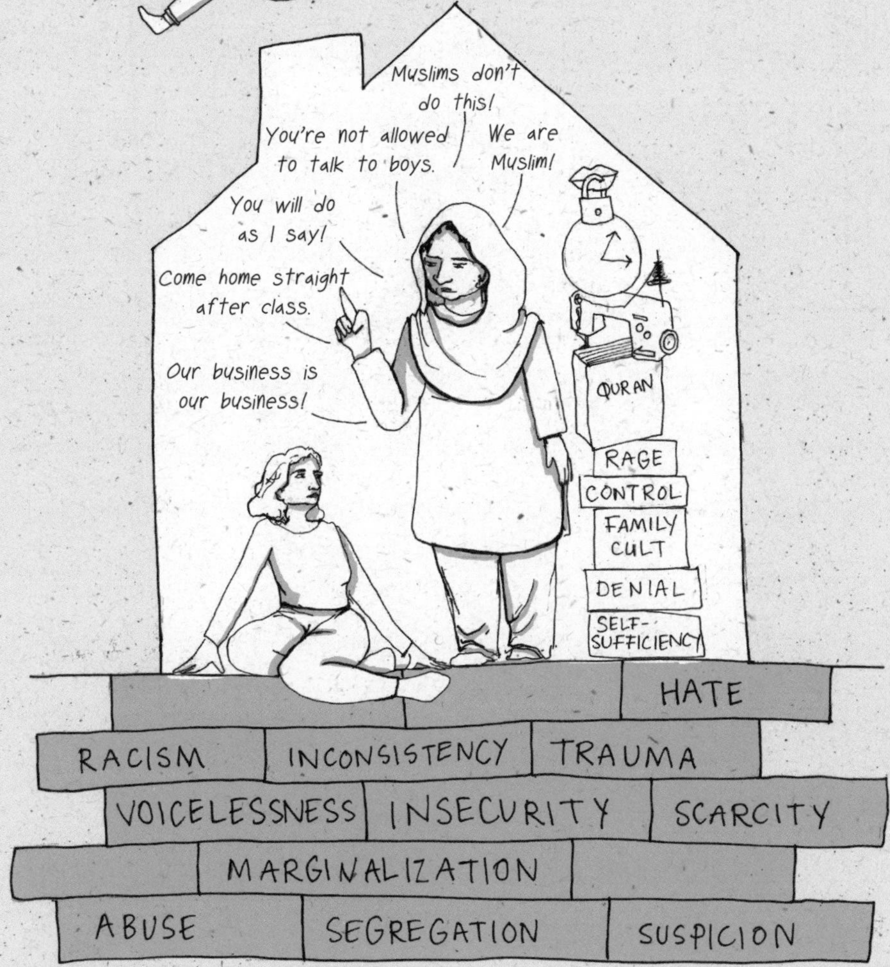
Muslims don't do this!
You're not allowed to talk to boys.
We are Muslim!
You will do as I say!
Come home straight after class.
Our business is our business!
QURAN
RAGE
CONTROL
FAMILY CULT
DENIAL
SELF-SUFFICIENCY
HATE
RACISM
INCONSISTENCY
TRAUMA
VOICELESSNESS
INSECURITY
SCARCITY
MARGINALIZATION
ABUSE
SEGREGATION
SUSPICION

This home with toxic foundations, where we tell ourselves this is what we do "back home." We convince ourselves it is our culture, but in essence it is born out of extremities, an absence of trust and an inability to grow safely.
A need to protect one's self becomes a fight for survival.

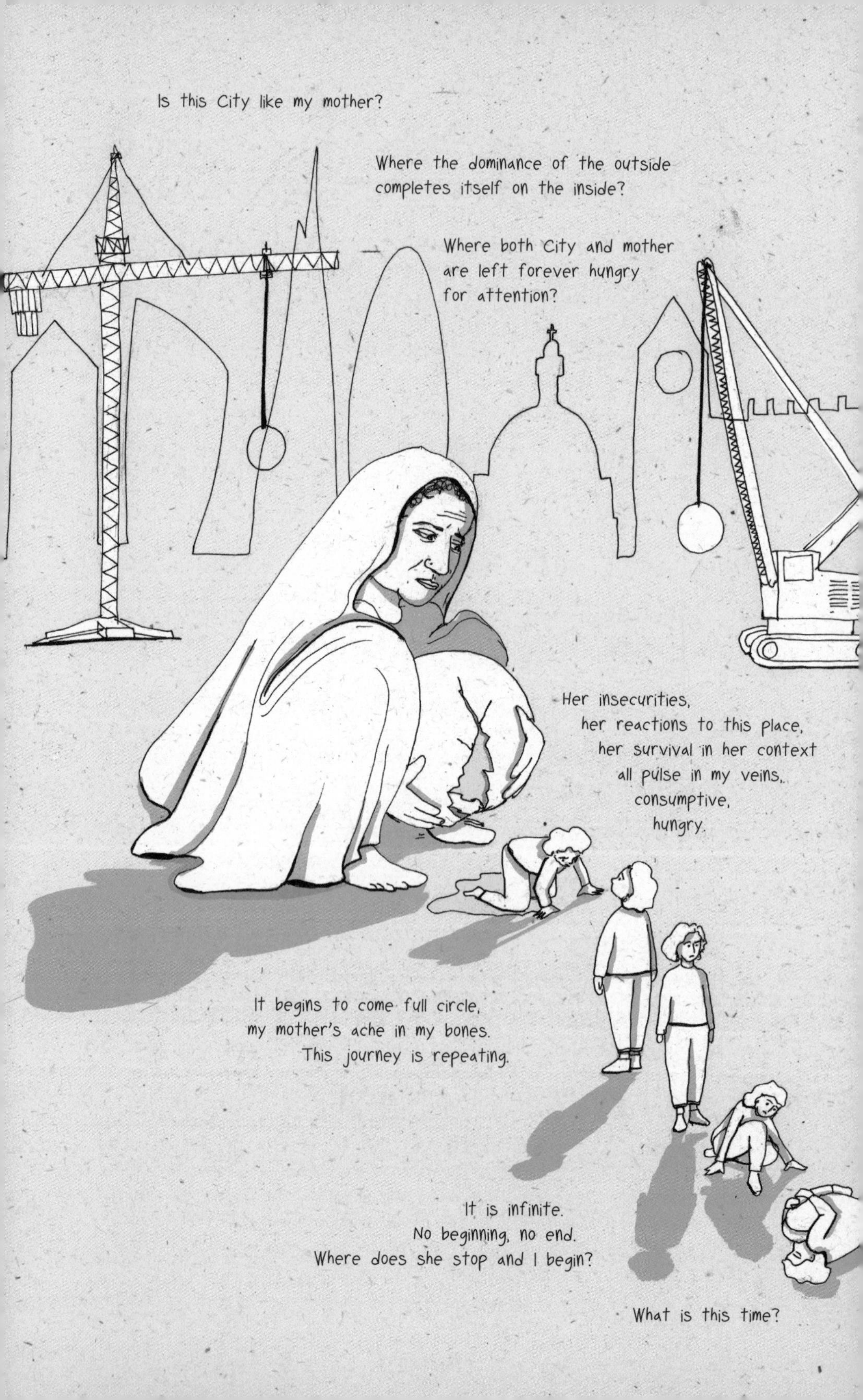
Is this City like my mother?
Where the dominance of the outside completes itself on the inside?
Where both City and mother are left forever hungry for attention?
Her insecurities,
her reactions to this place,
her survival in her context
all pulse in my veins,
consumptive,
hungry.
It begins to come full circle,
my mother's ache in my bones.
This journey is repeating.
It is infinite.
No beginning, no end.
Where does she stop and I begin?
What is this time?

three

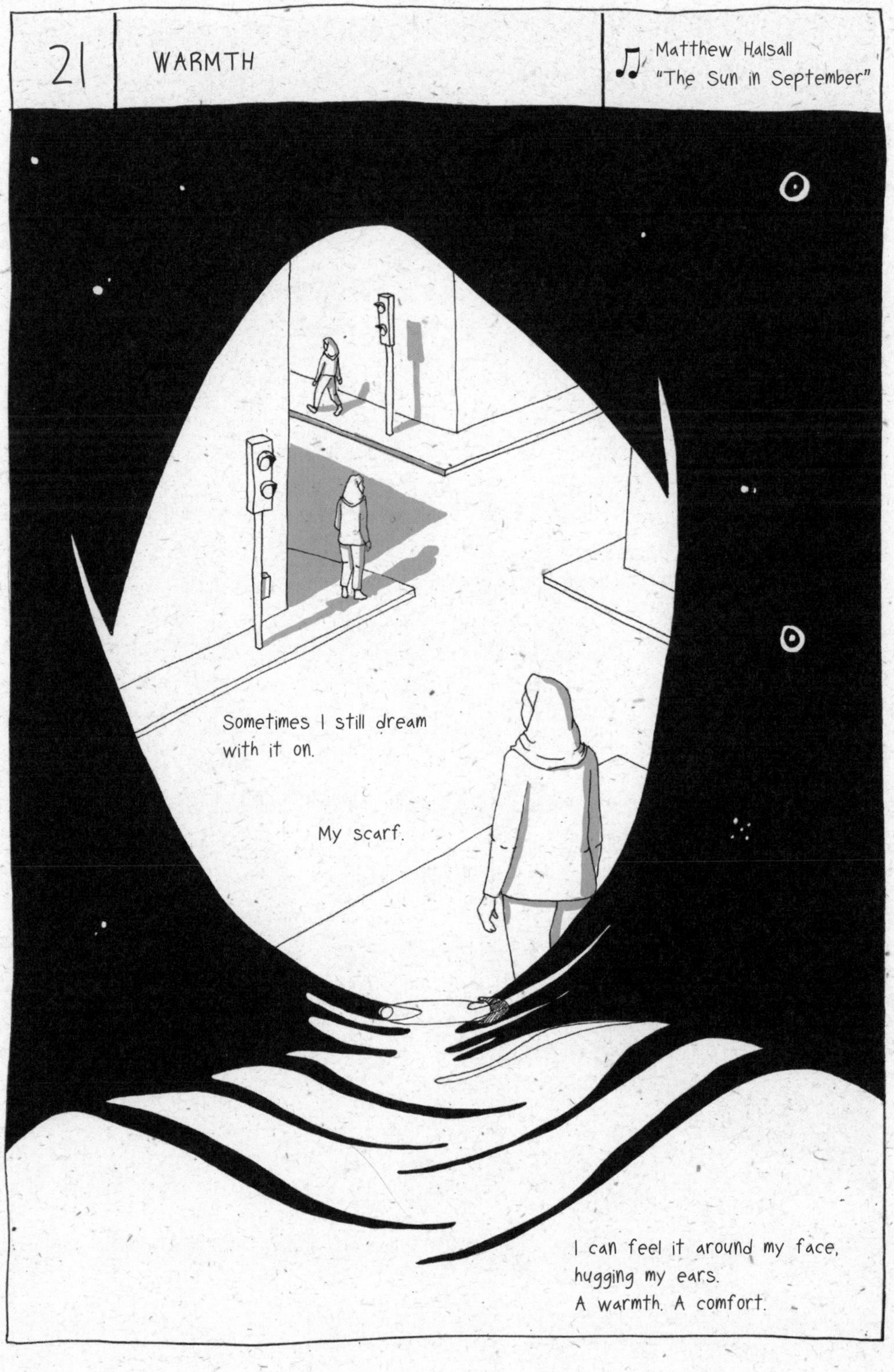
21
WARMTH
Matthew Halsall
"The Sun in September"
Sometimes I still dream with it on.
My scarf.
I can feel it around my face, hugging my ears.
A warmth. A comfort.

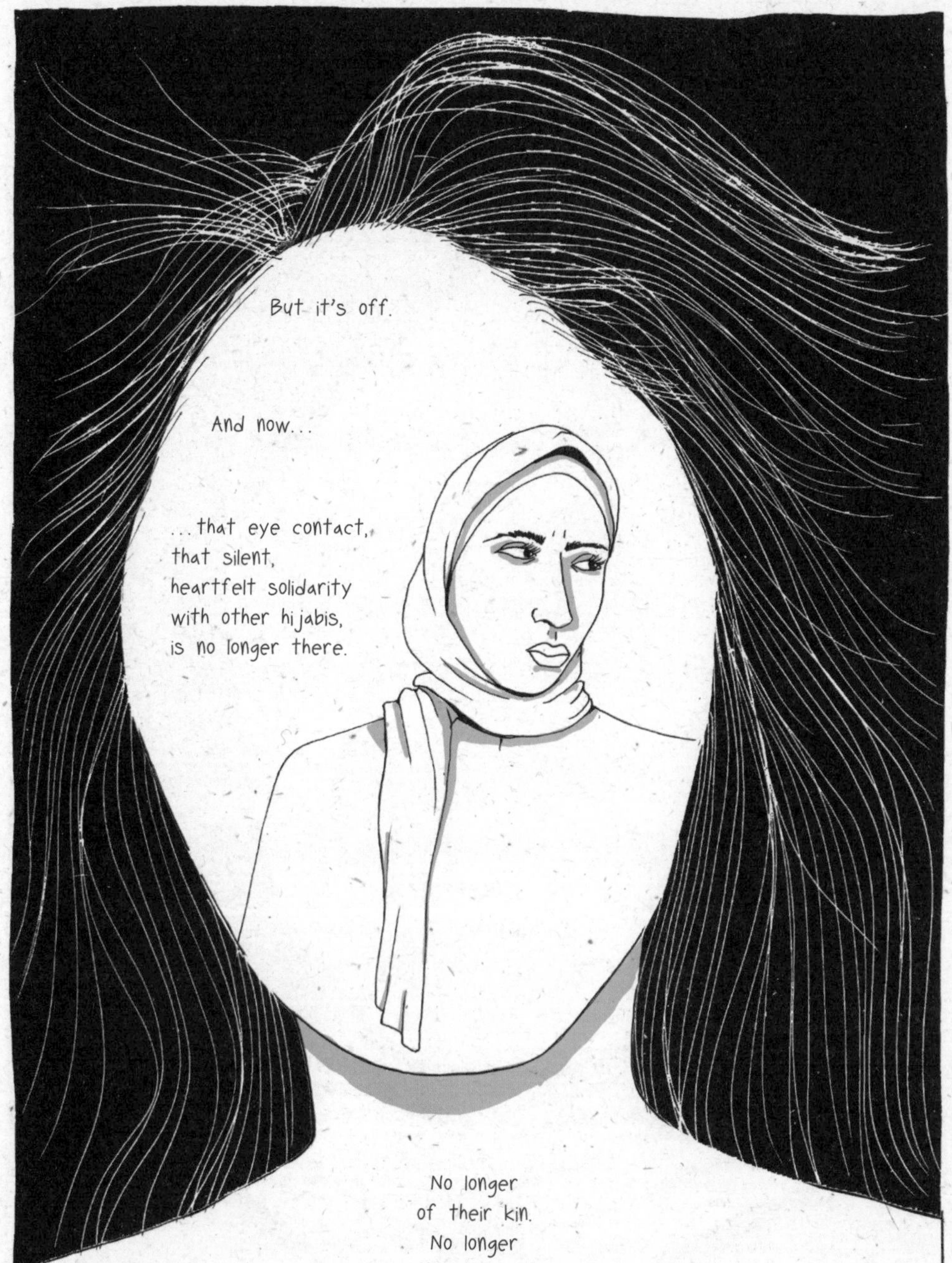
But it's off.
And now...
...that eye contact, that silent, heartfelt solidarity with other hijabis, is no longer there.
No longer of their kin. No longer their sister.
Just another person in this cold place.

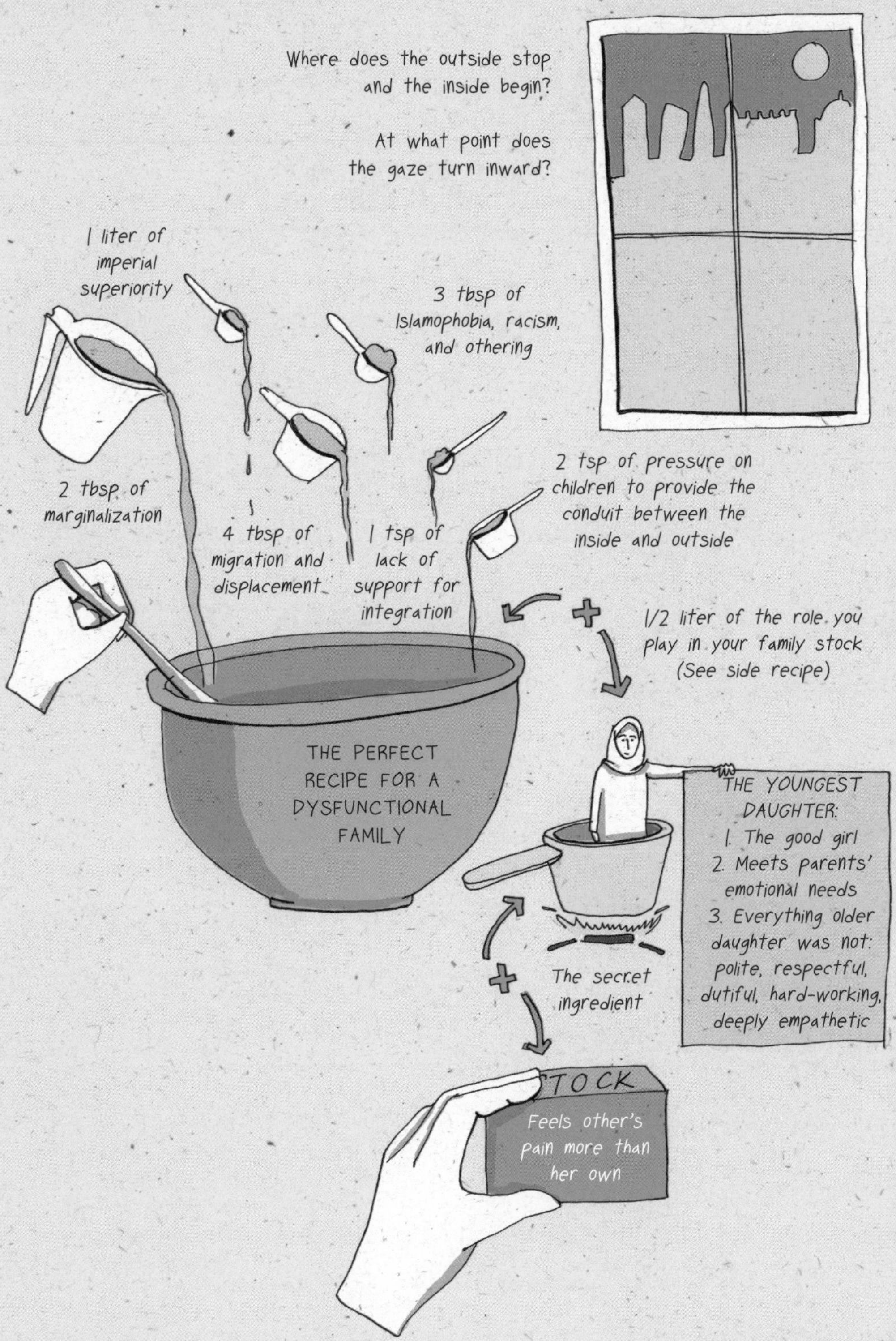
Where does the outside stop and the inside begin?
At what point does the gaze turn inward?
1 liter of imperial superiority
3 tbsp of Islamophobia, racism, and othering
2 tbsp of marginalization
4 tbsp of migration and displacement
1 tsp of lack of support for integration
2 tsp of pressure on children to provide the conduit between the inside and outside
1/2 liter of the role you play in your family stock (See side recipe)
THE PERFECT RECIPE FOR A DYSFUNCTIONAL FAMILY
THE YOUNGEST DAUGHTER:
1. The good girl
2. Meets parents' emotional needs
3. Everything older daughter was not: polite, respectful, dutiful, hard-working, deeply empathetic
The secret ingredient
STOCK
Feels other's pain more than her own

They call it codependency, this lost sense of self. A self that learns safety in accommodating the needs of others.

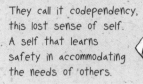

It seeks affection and approval from the outside because there is none from within.

The co-dependent gives and gives, attempting to fill and quench itself.

And then there is the one who takes and takes. The narcissist.

Who also has a lost sense of self, but instead seeks it in pursuit of prestige, superiority, and domination over others. An idealized sense of self.

Both giver and taker born from traumatic early experiences.

Both ultimately in need of external validation and approval.

In our efforts to survive, have we made a home for narcissism and co-dependency?

Are we feeding each other, triggering each other, consuming each other?

Is this the intergenerational trauma they speak of?
Will I become the taker with my own child, to quench the giver in me?
In this search for self, can I break the cycle?

♫ Queen
"Bohemian Rhapsody"

It's weird, the need to fit into certain boxes for people.
So they don't feel threatened.
So you are easily digestible.
Understandable.
Compartmentalizable.
Predictable.

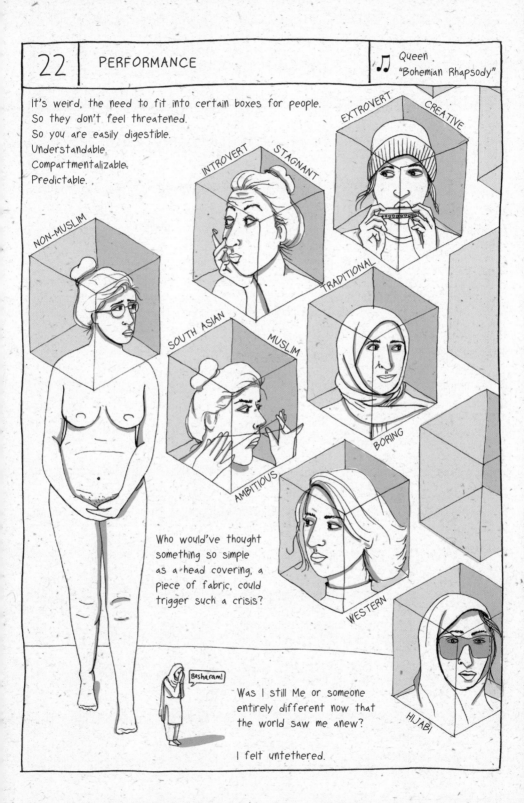

EXTROVERT

CREATIVE

INTROVERT

STAGNANT

NON-MUSLIM

TRADITIONAL

SOUTH ASIAN

MUSLIM

BORING

AMBITIOUS

Who would've thought something so simple as a head covering, a piece of fabric, could trigger such a crisis?

WESTERN

Besharam!

Was I still Me or someone entirely different now that the world saw me anew?

I felt untethered.

HIJABI

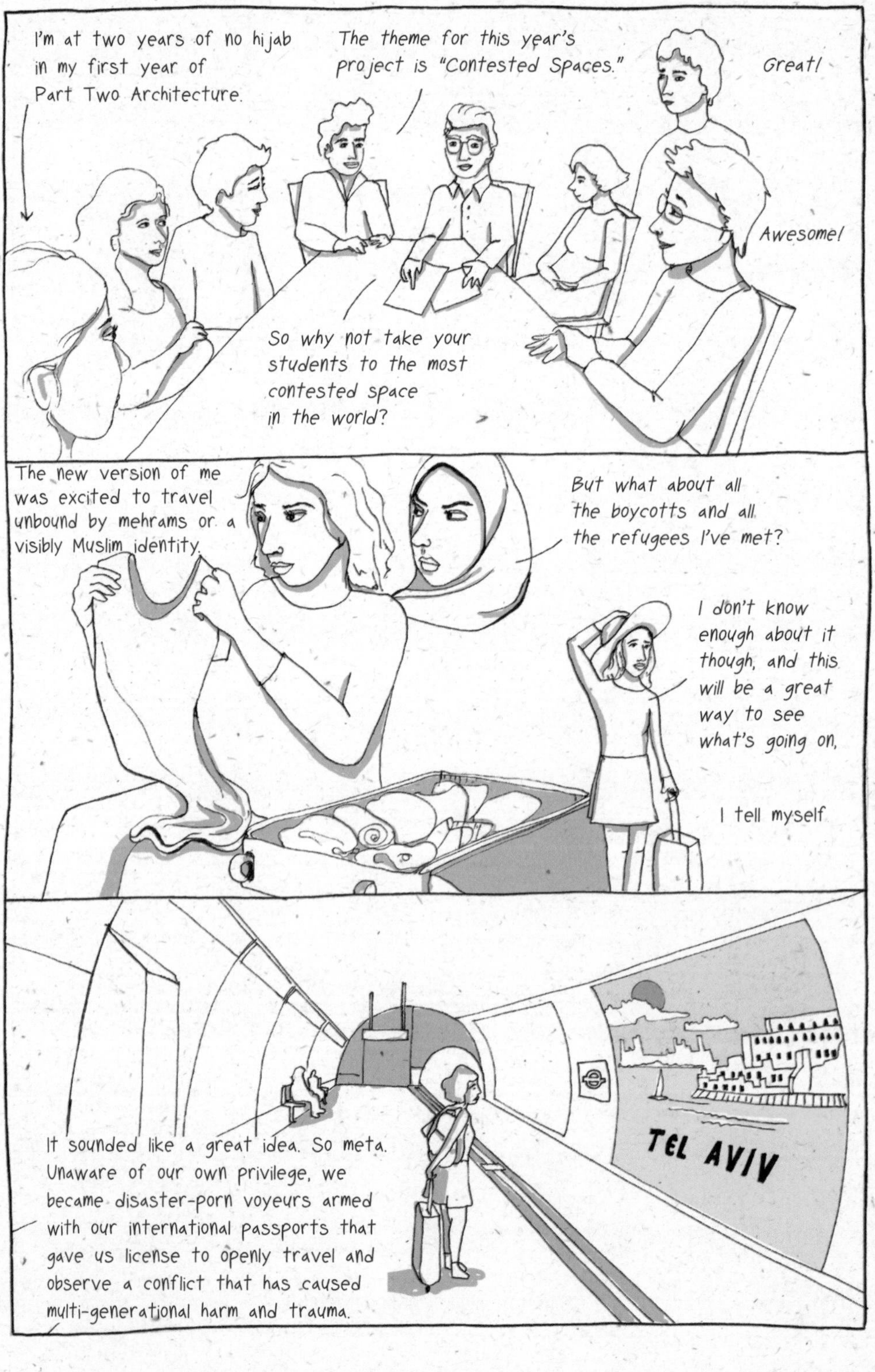
I'm at two years of no hijab in my first year of Part Two Architecture.
The theme for this year's project is "Contested Spaces."
Great!
Awesome!
So why not take your students to the most contested space in the world?
The new version of me was excited to travel unbound by mehrams or a visibly Muslim identity.
But what about all the boycotts and all the refugees I've met?
I don't know enough about it though, and this will be a great way to see what's going on,
I tell myself.
TEL AVIV
It sounded like a great idea. So meta. Unaware of our own privilege, we became disaster-porn voyeurs armed with our international passports that gave us license to openly travel and observe a conflict that has caused multi-generational harm and trauma.

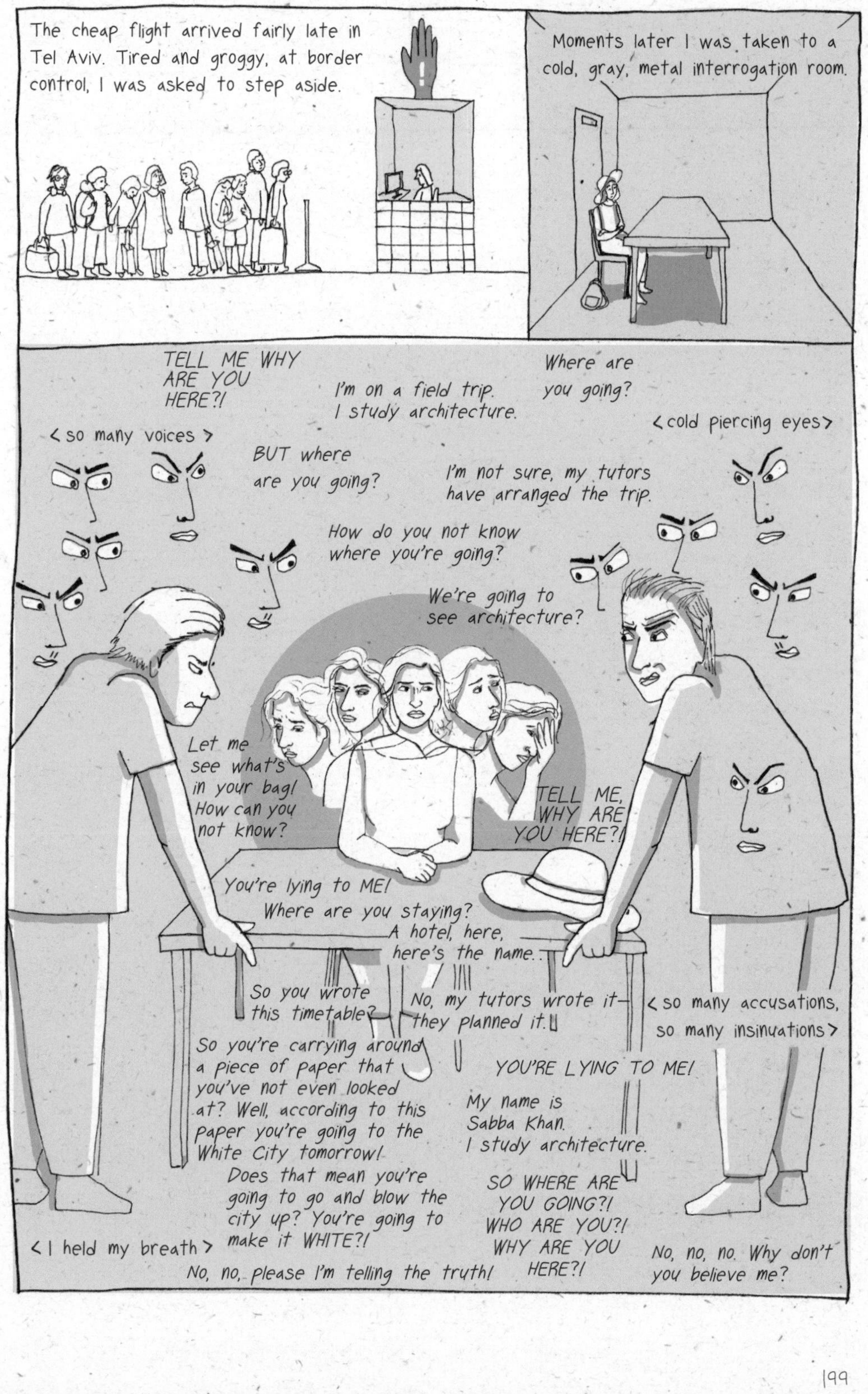
The cheap flight arrived fairly late in Tel Aviv. Tired and groggy, at border control, I was asked to step aside.
Moments later I was taken to a cold, gray, metal interrogation room.
TELL ME WHY ARE YOU HERE?!
I'm on a field trip. I study architecture.
Where are you going?
<so many voices>
BUT where are you going?
I'm not sure, my tutors have arranged the trip.
<cold piercing eyes>
How do you not know where you're going?
We're going to see architecture?
Let me see what's in your bag! How can you not know?
TELL ME, WHY ARE YOU HERE?!
You're lying to ME!
Where are you staying?
A hotel, here, here's the name.
So you wrote this timetable?
No, my tutors wrote it— they planned it.
<so many accusations, so many insinuations>
So you're carrying around a piece of paper that you've not even looked at? Well, according to this paper you're going to the White City tomorrow!
YOU'RE LYING TO ME!
My name is Sabba Khan. I study architecture.
Does that mean you're going to go and blow the city up? You're going to make it WHITE?!
SO WHERE ARE YOU GOING?! WHO ARE YOU?! WHY ARE YOU HERE?!
<I held my breath>
No, no, please I'm telling the truth!
No, no, no. Why don't you believe me?

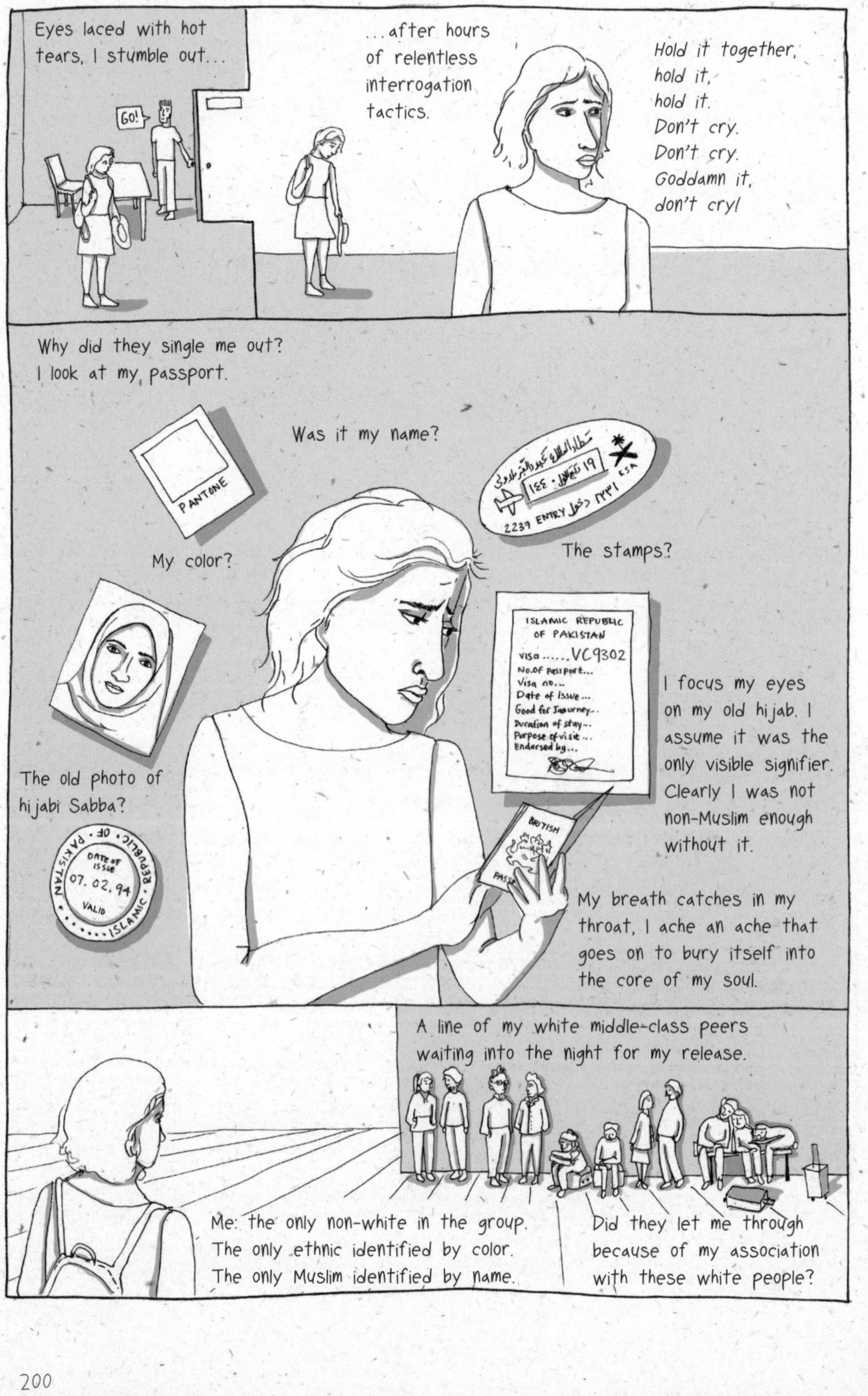
Eyes laced with hot tears, I stumble out...
GO!
...after hours of relentless interrogation tactics.
Hold it together,
hold it,
hold it.
Don't cry.
Don't cry.
Goddamn it,
don't cry!
Why did they single me out?
I look at my passport.
Was it my name?
PANTONE
My color?
2237 ENTRY
KSA
The stamps?
ISLAMIC REPUBLIC OF PAKISTAN
Visa......VC9302
No.of Passport...
Visa no...
Date of Issue...
Good for Journey...
Duration of stay...
Purpose of visit...
Endorsed by...
BRITISH
The old photo of hijabi Sabba?
ISLAMIC REPUBLIC OF PAKISTAN
DATE OF ISSUE
07.02.94
VALID
I focus my eyes on my old hijab. I assume it was the only visible signifier. Clearly I was not non-Muslim enough without it.
My breath catches in my throat, I ache an ache that goes on to bury itself into the core of my soul.
A line of my white middle-class peers waiting into the night for my release.
Me: the only non-white in the group. The only ethnic identified by color. The only Muslim identified by name.
Did they let me through because of my association with these white people?

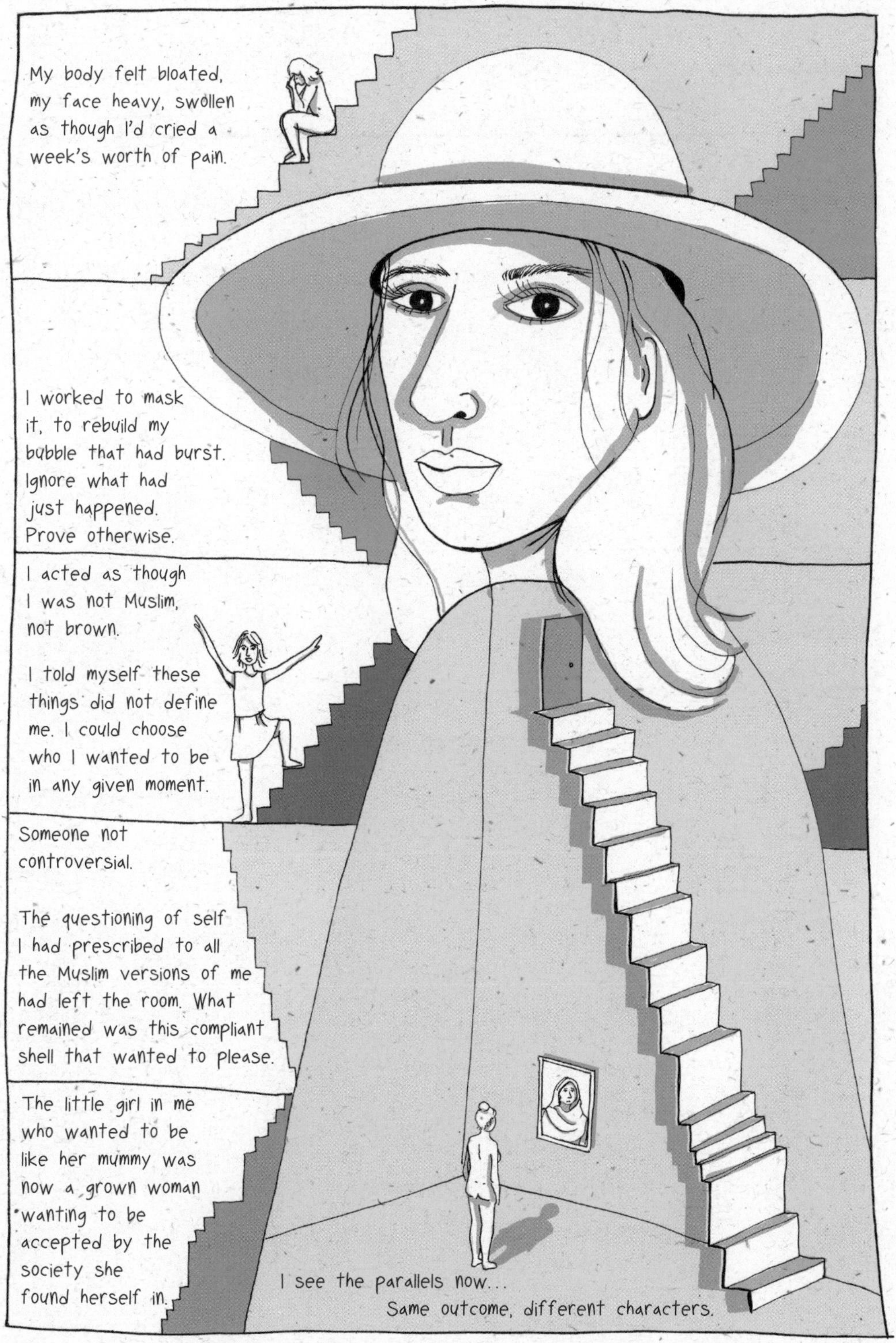

My body felt bloated, my face heavy, swollen as though I'd cried a week's worth of pain.
I worked to mask it, to rebuild my bubble that had burst. Ignore what had just happened. Prove otherwise.
I acted as though I was not Muslim, not brown.
I told myself these things did not define me. I could choose who I wanted to be in any given moment.
Someone not controversial.
The questioning of self I had prescribed to all the Muslim versions of me had left the room. What remained was this compliant shell that wanted to please.
The little girl in me who wanted to be like her mummy was now a grown woman wanting to be accepted by the society she found herself in.
I see the parallels now...
Same outcome, different characters.

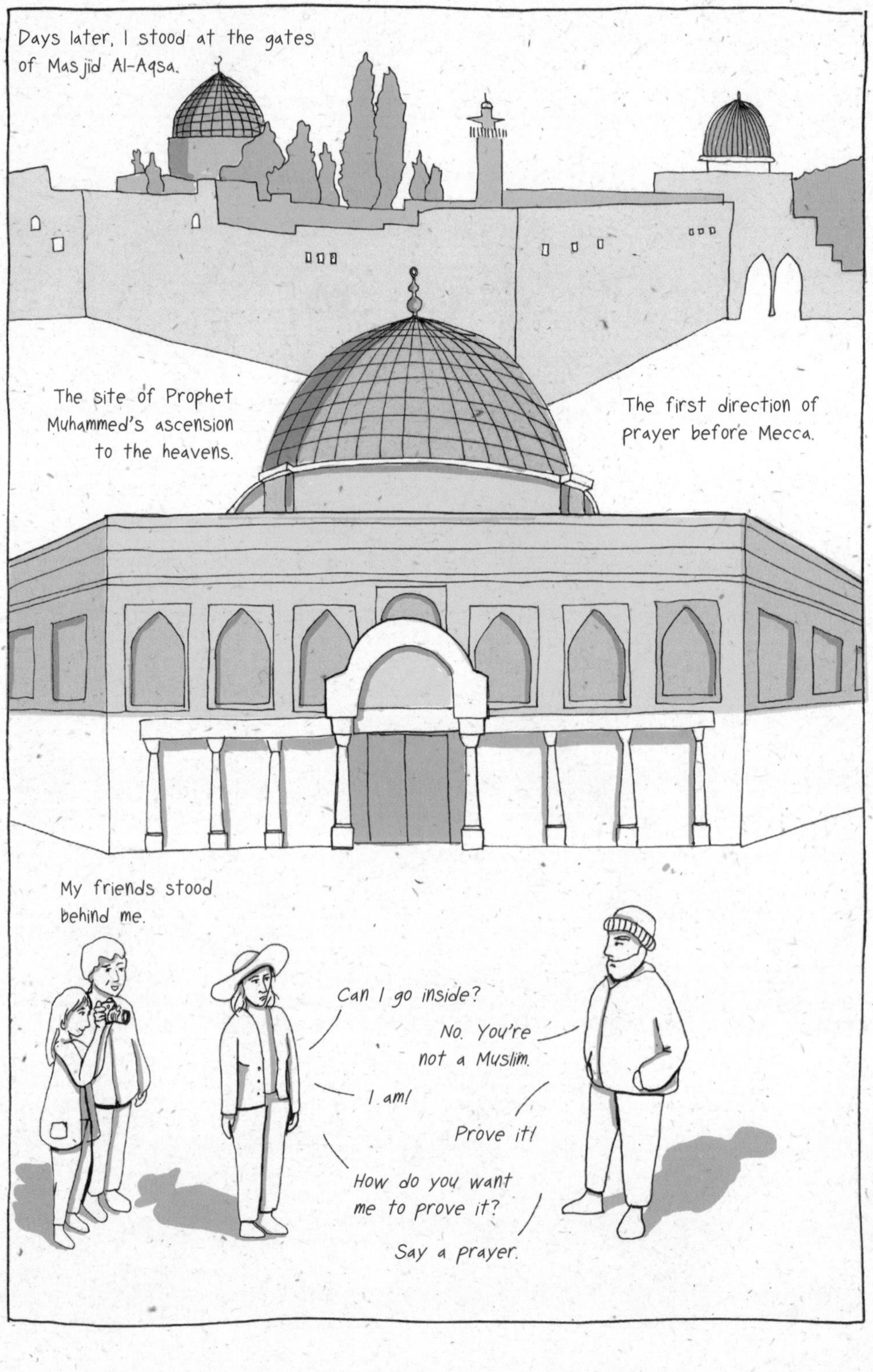

Days later, I stood at the gates of Masjid Al-Aqsa.
The site of Prophet Muhammed's ascension to the heavens.
The first direction of prayer before Mecca.
My friends stood behind me.
Can I go inside?
No. You're not a Muslim.
I am!
Prove it!
How do you want me to prove it?
Say a prayer.

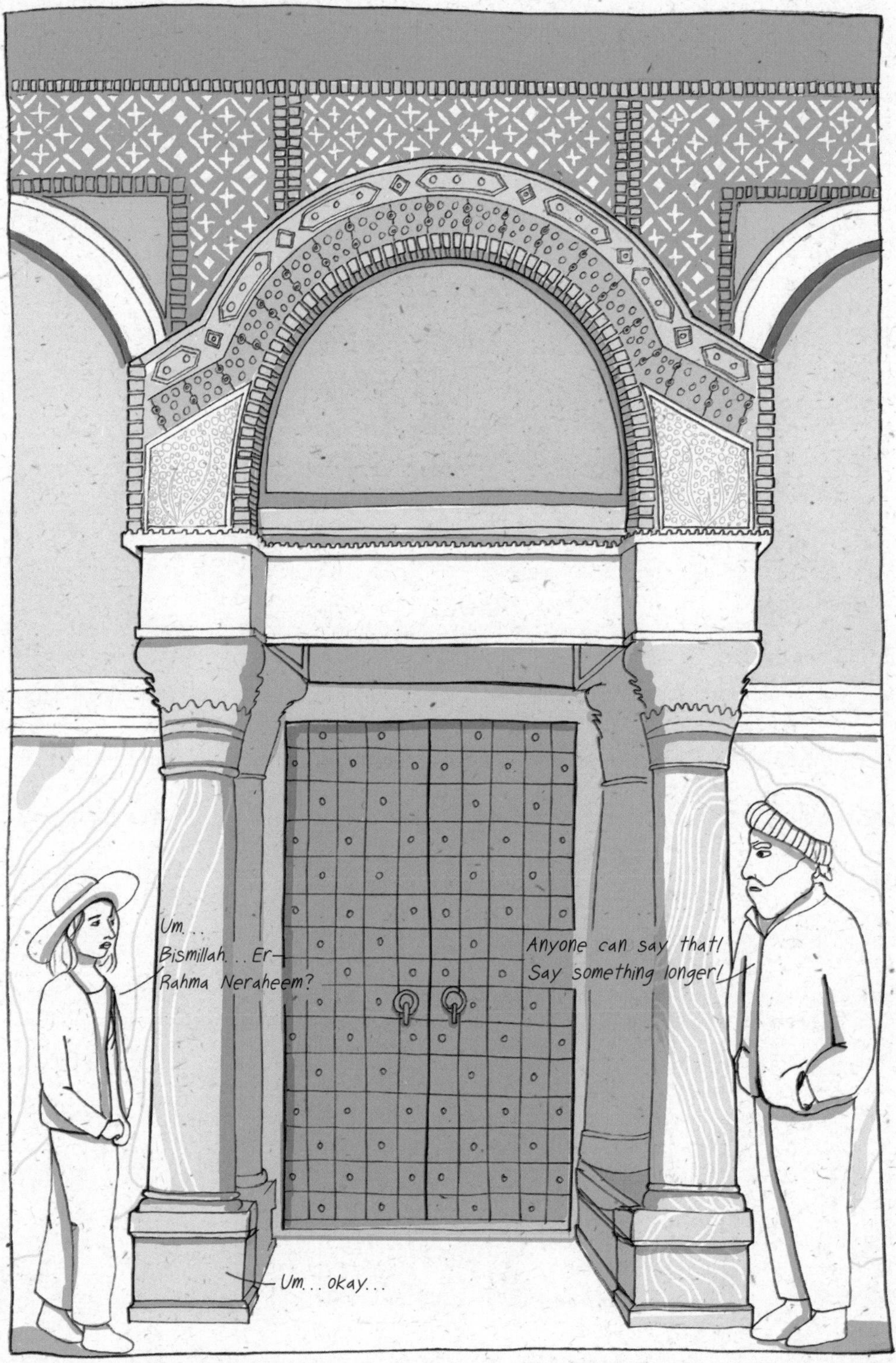
Um...
Bismillah... Er-
Rahma Neraheem?
Anyone can say that!
Say something longer!
Um... okay...

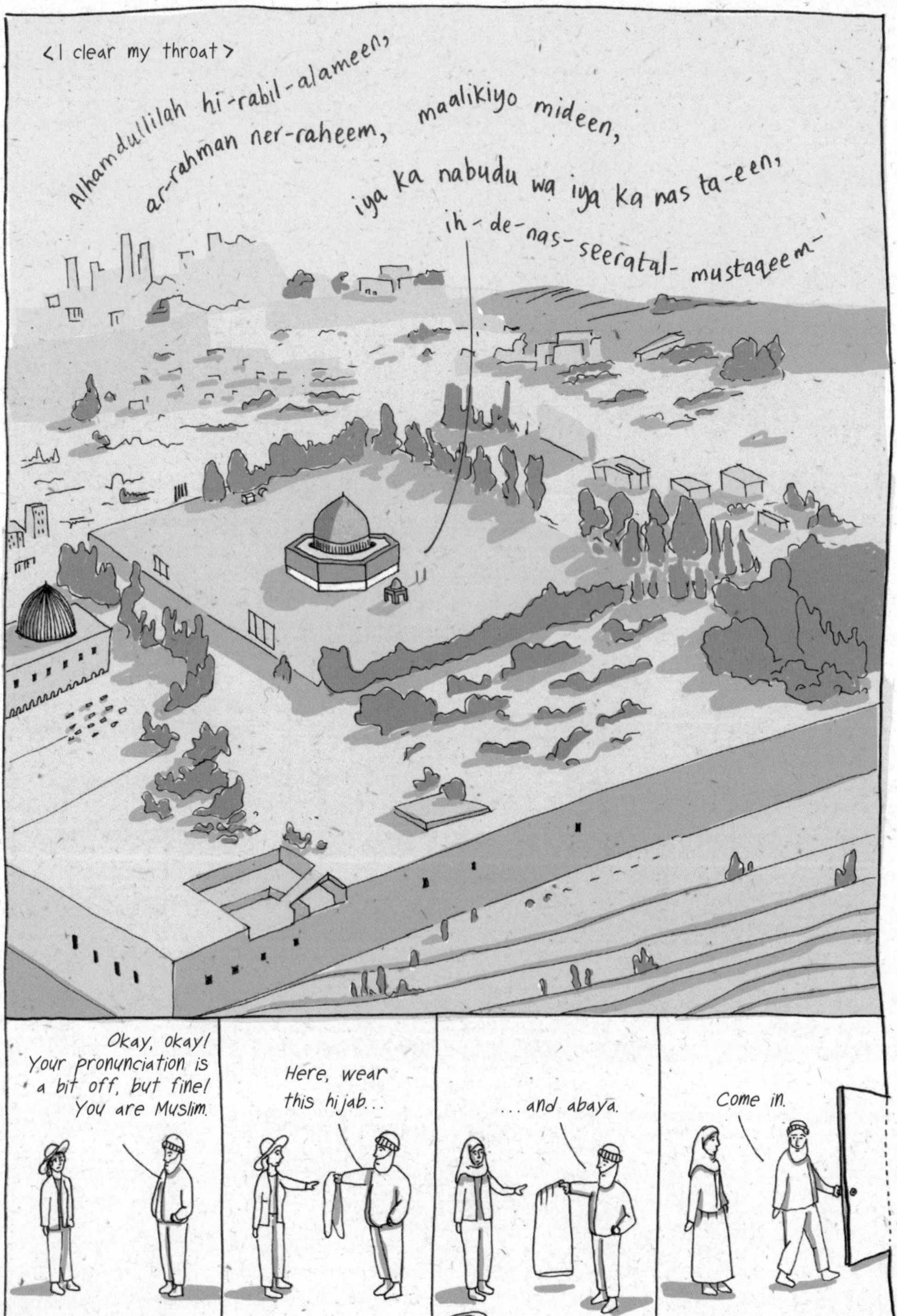
<I clear my throat>
Alhamdullilah hi-rabil-alameen,
ar-rahman ner-raheem, maalikiyo mideen,
iya ka nabudu wa iya ka nas ta-een,
ih-de-nas-seeratal-mustaqeem-
Okay, okay! Your pronunciation is a bit off, but fine! You are Muslim.
Here, wear this hijab...
...and abaya.
Come in.

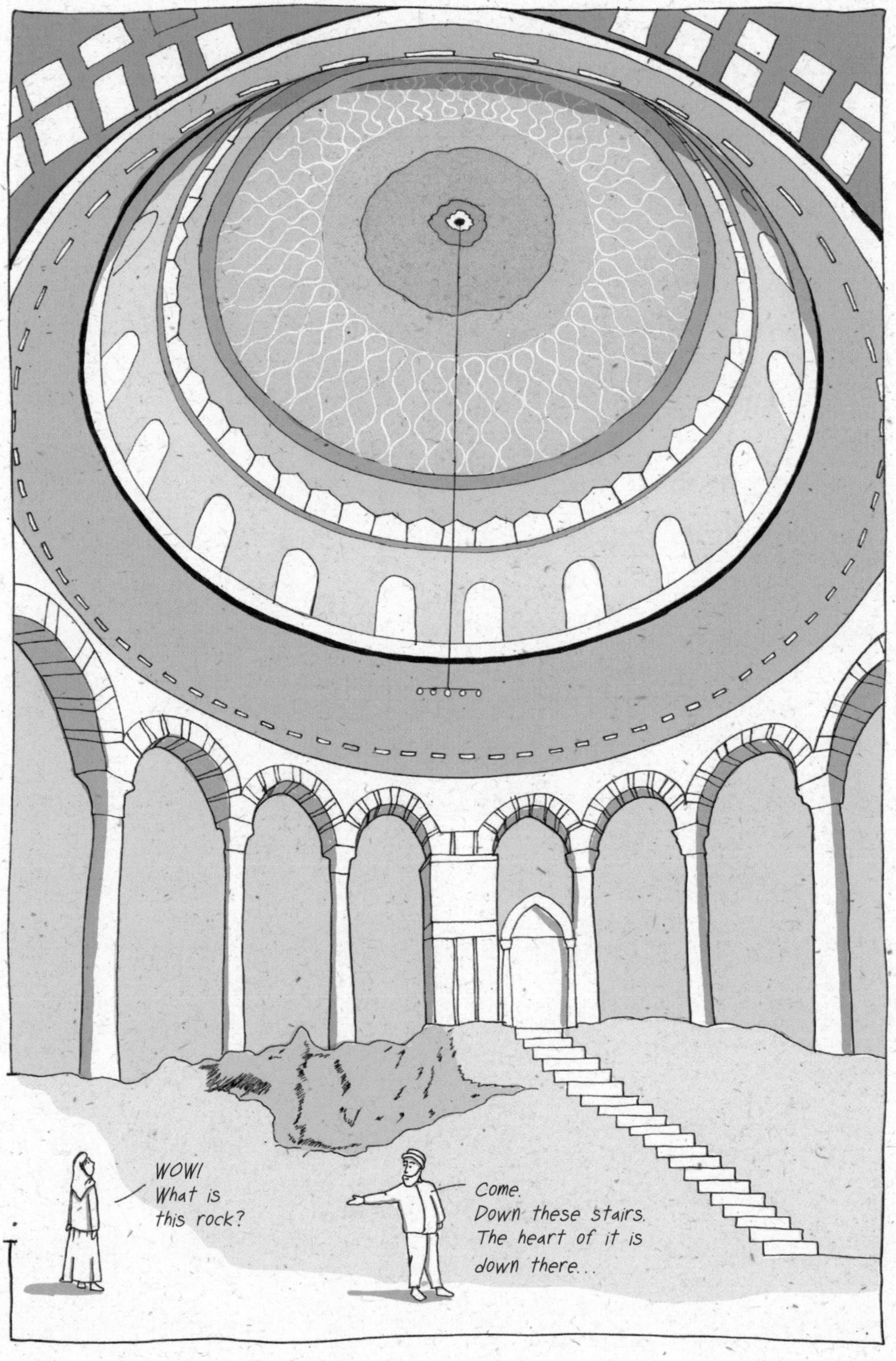
WOW!
What is
this rock?
Come.
Down these stairs.
The heart of it is
down there...

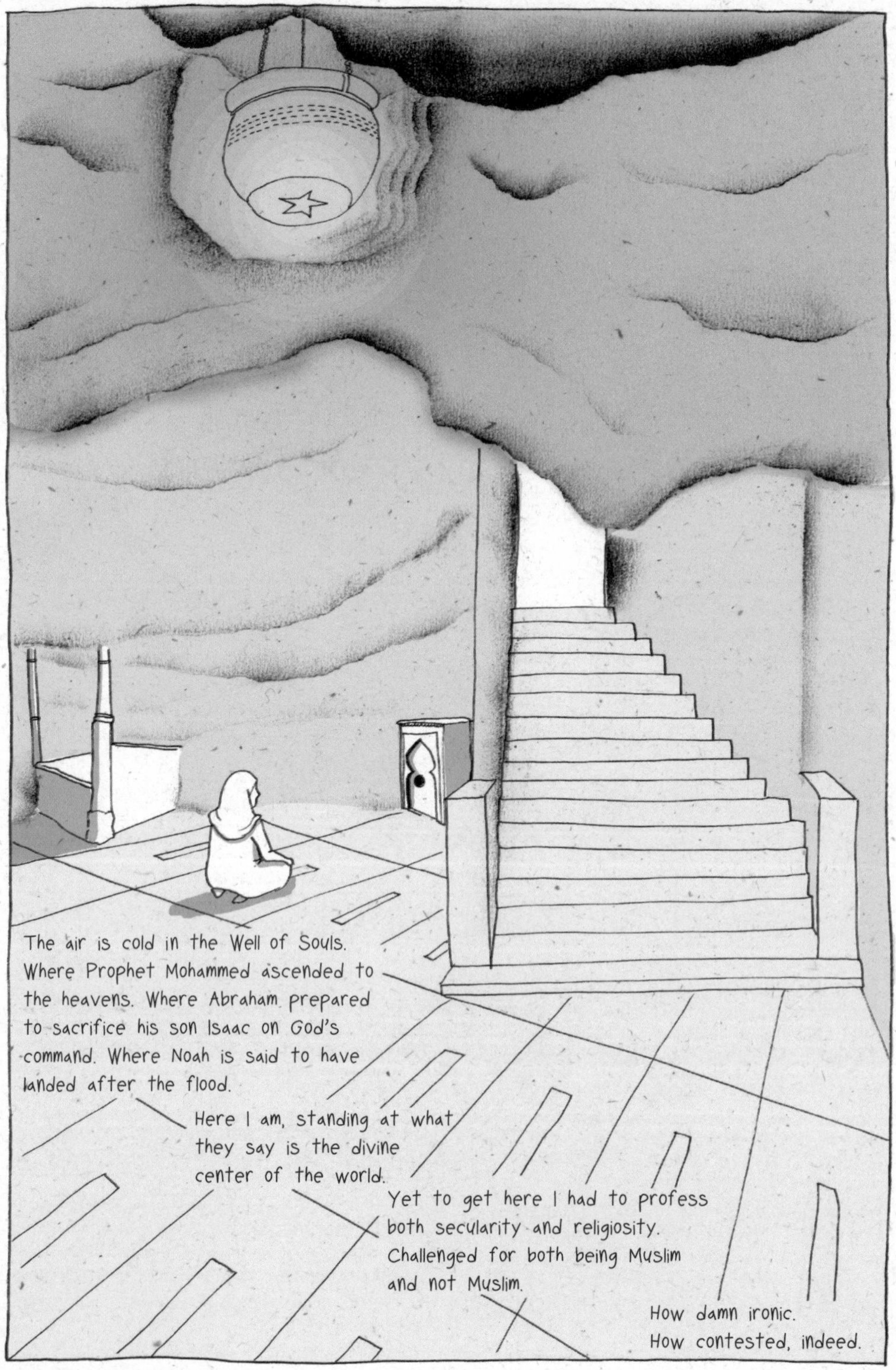
The air is cold in the Well of Souls. Where Prophet Mohammed ascended to the heavens. Where Abraham prepared to sacrifice his son Isaac on God's command. Where Noah is said to have landed after the flood.
Here I am, standing at what they say is the divine center of the world.
Yet to get here I had to profess both secularity and religiosity. Challenged for both being Muslim and not Muslim.
How damn ironic. How contested, indeed.

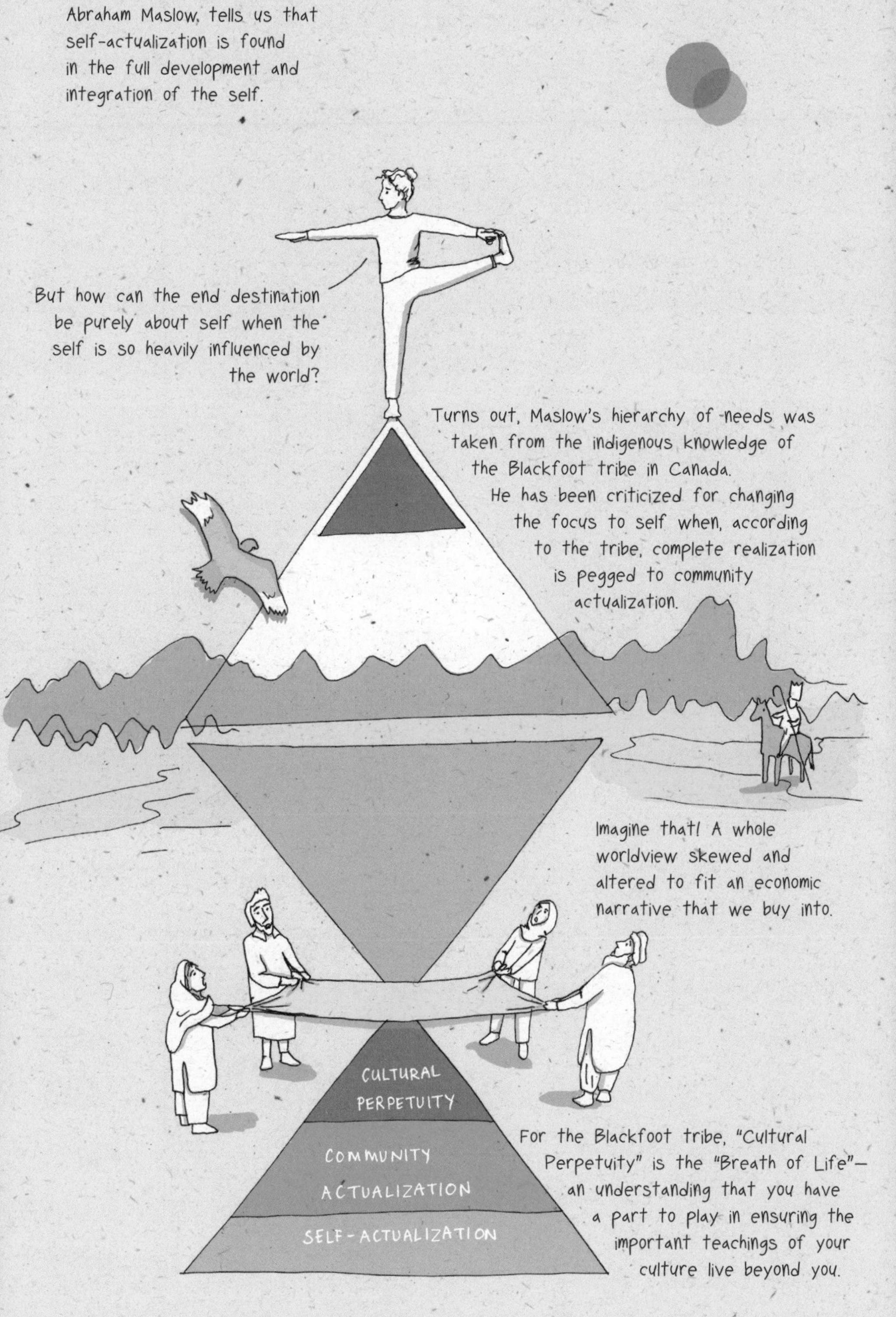
Abraham Maslow, tells us that self-actualization is found in the full development and integration of the self.
But how can the end destination be purely about self when the self is so heavily influenced by the world?
Turns out, Maslow's hierarchy of needs was taken from the indigenous knowledge of the Blackfoot tribe in Canada. He has been criticized for changing the focus to self when, according to the tribe, complete realization is pegged to community actualization.
Imagine that! A whole worldview skewed and altered to fit an economic narrative that we buy into.
CULTURAL PERPETUITY
COMMUNITY ACTUALIZATION
SELF-ACTUALIZATION
For the Blackfoot tribe, "Cultural Perpetuity" is the "Breath of Life"—an understanding that you have a part to play in ensuring the important teachings of your culture live beyond you.

How violent and possessive
for economic ideologies to
mold individuals to suit their purpose.

We are in need of a different
type of knowledge.

TEAR

SCRUNCH

One that is not born out of
imperial dominance.

SCRUNCH

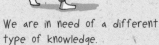

One that is not driven
by power and wealth.

Give me an archaic knowledge,
an old knowledge,
a knowledge that holds
all bodies and all minds.

One that serves inside and out.
Tangible and intangible.
Individual and collective.

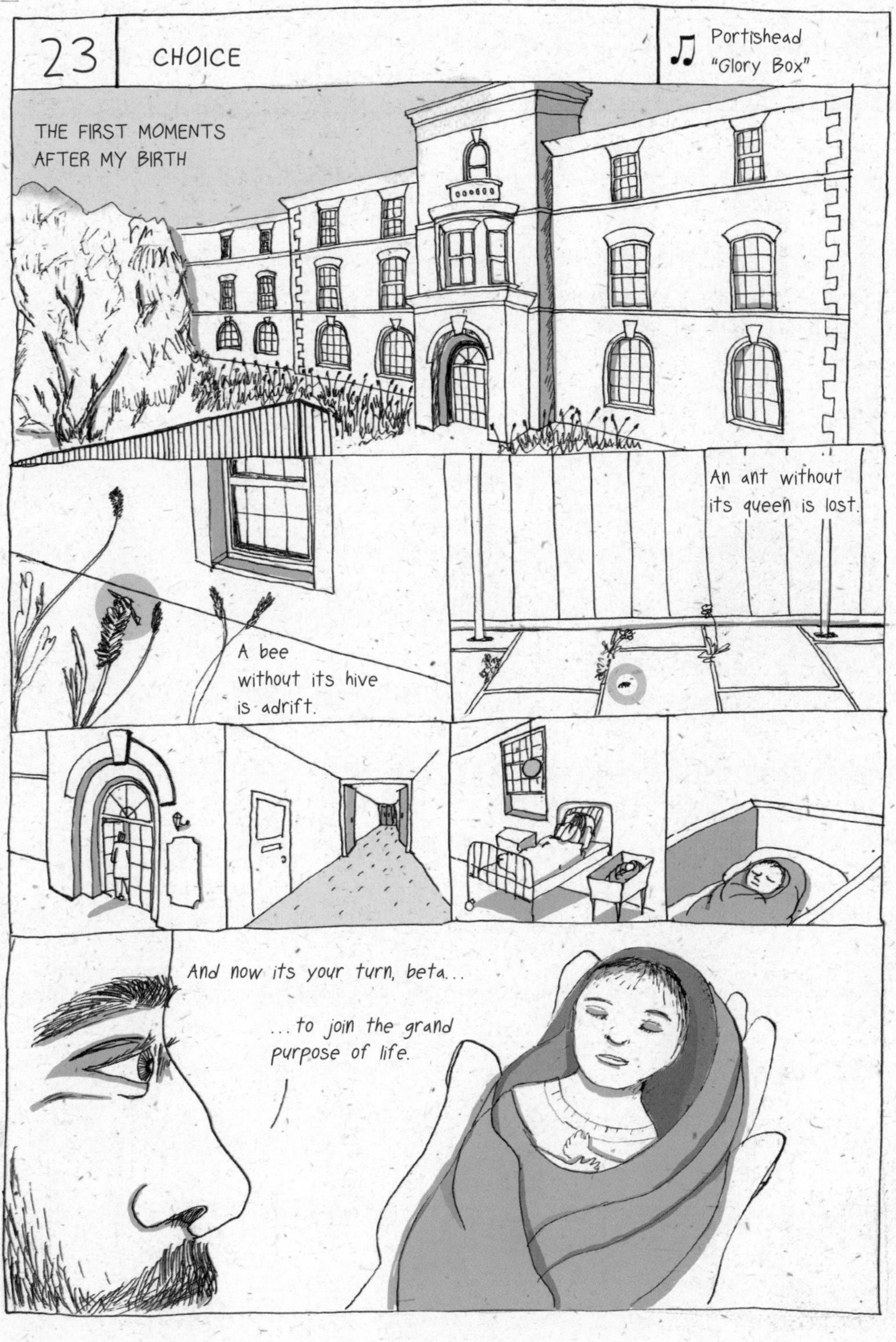
23
CHOICE
Portishead "Glory Box"
THE FIRST MOMENTS AFTER MY BIRTH
A bee without its hive is adrift.
An ant without its queen is lost.
And now its your turn, beta...
...to join the grand purpose of life.

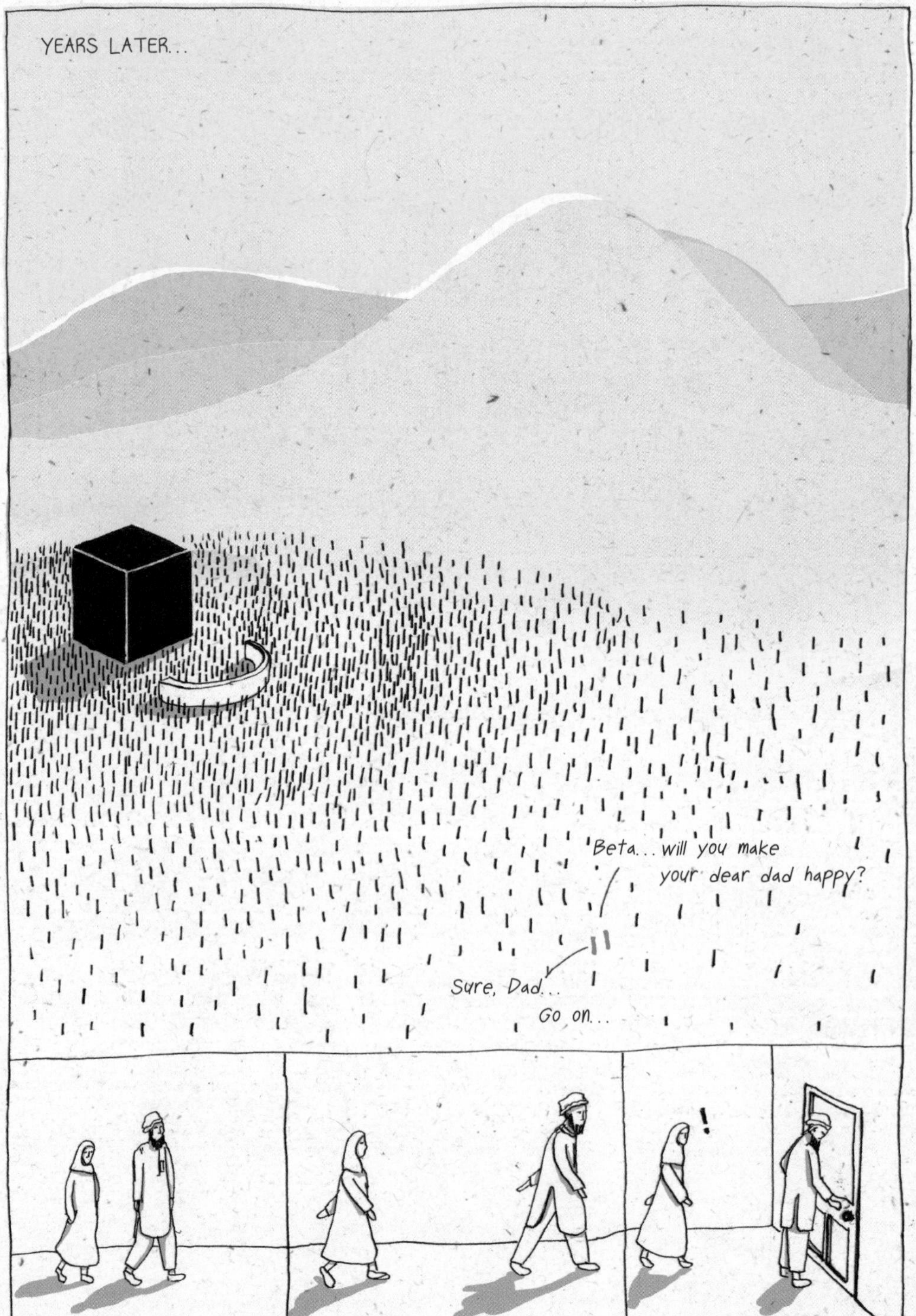
YEARS LATER...
Beta... will you make your dear dad happy?
Sure, Dad...
Go on...
!

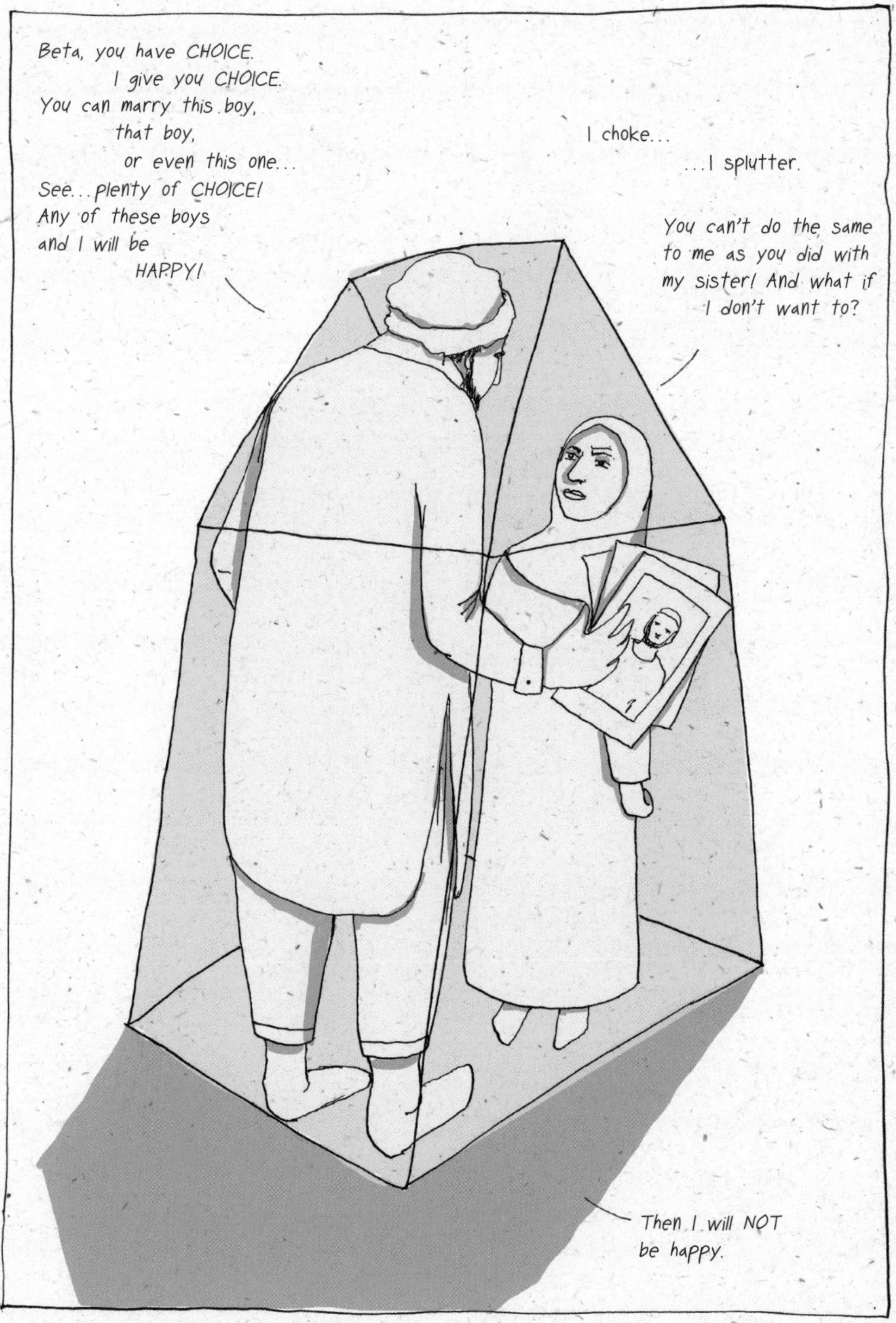
Beta, you have CHOICE. I give you CHOICE. You can marry this boy, that boy, or even this one... See... plenty of CHOICE! Any of these boys and I will be HAPPY!
I choke...
...I splutter.
You can't do the same to me as you did with my sister! And what if I don't want to?
Then I will NOT be happy.

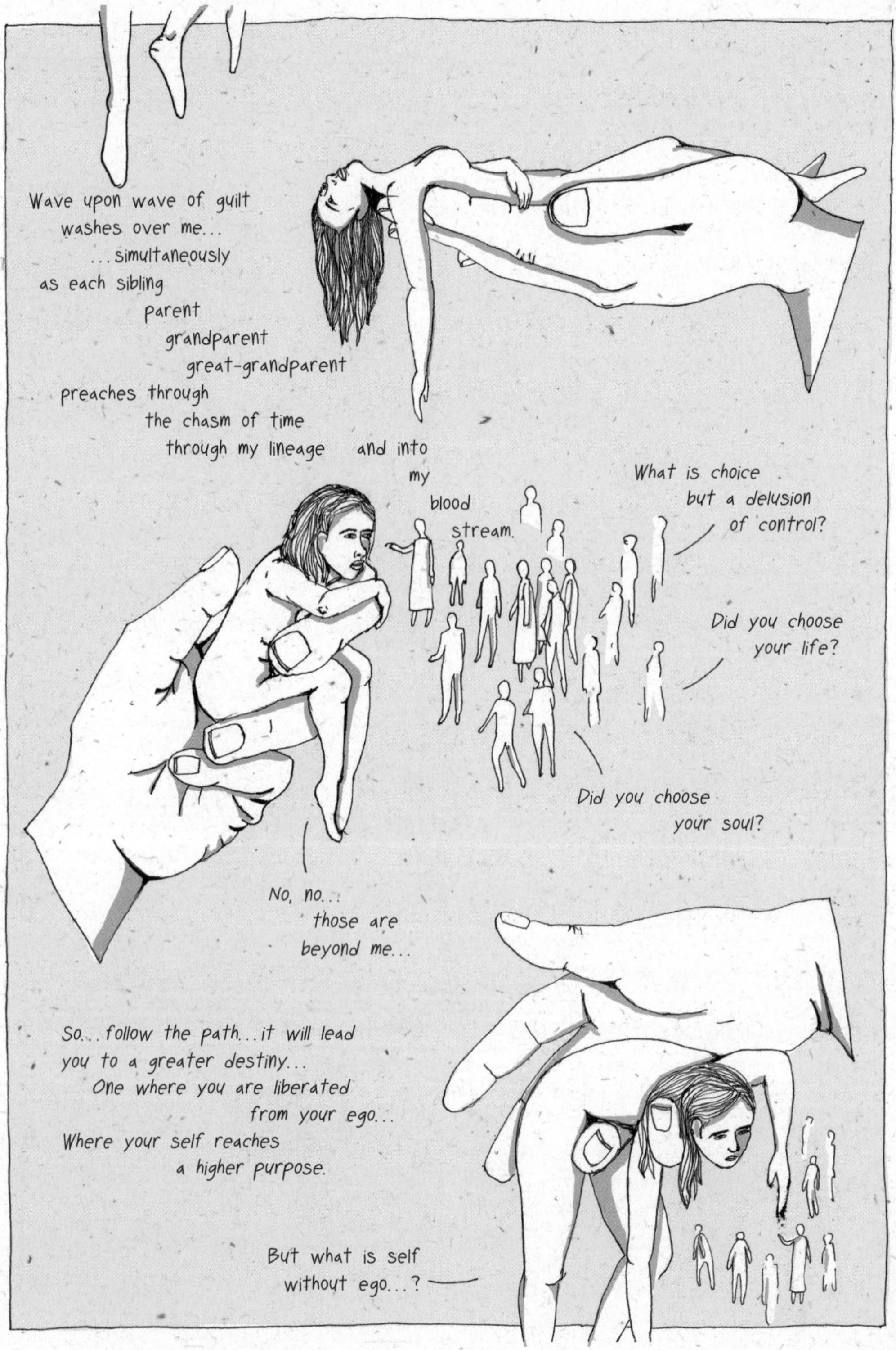

Wave upon wave of guilt
washes over me...
...simultaneously
as each sibling
parent
grandparent
great-grandparent
preaches through
the chasm of time
through my lineage and into
my
blood
stream.
What is choice
but a delusion
of control?
Did you choose
your life?
Did you choose
your soul?
No, no...
those are
beyond me...
So... follow the path... it will lead
you to a greater destiny...
One where you are liberated
from your ego...
Where your self reaches
a higher purpose.
But what is self
without ego...?

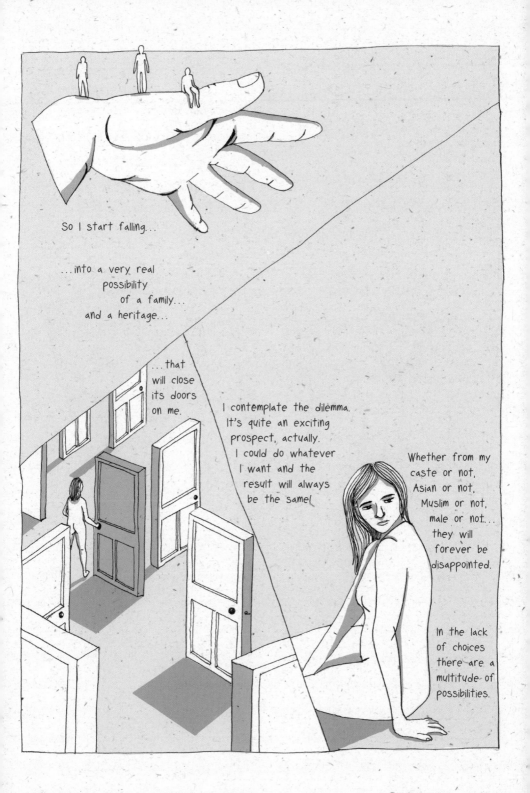

So I start falling...

...into a very real
possibility
of a family...
and a heritage...

...that
will close
its doors
on me.

I contemplate the dilemma.
It's quite an exciting
prospect, actually.
I could do whatever
I want and the
result will always
be the same!

Whether from my
caste or not,
Asian or not,
Muslim or not,
male or not...
they will
forever be
disappointed.

In the lack
of choices
there are a
multitude of
possibilities.

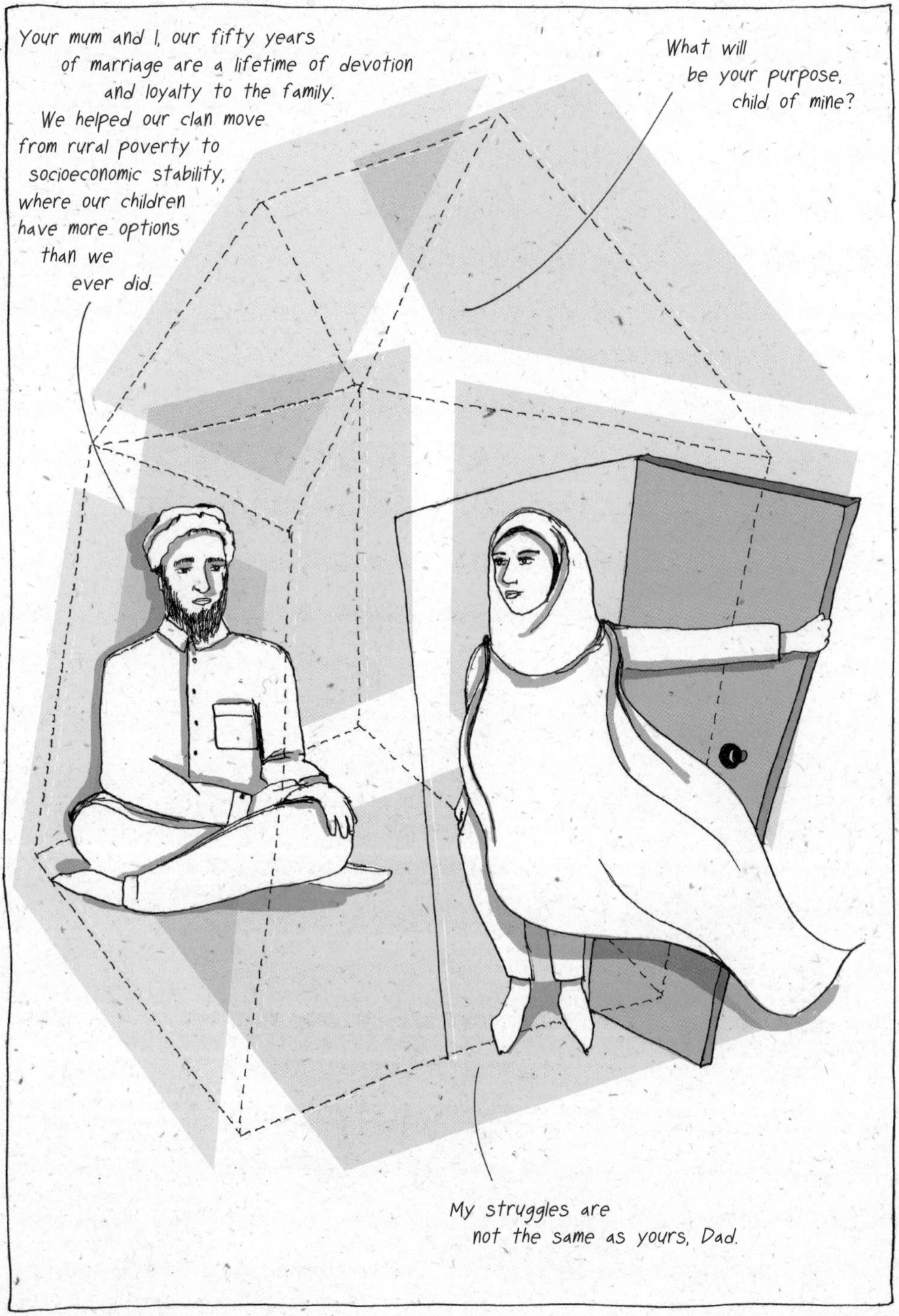
Your mum and I, our fifty years of marriage are a lifetime of devotion and loyalty to the family. We helped our clan move from rural poverty to socioeconomic stability, where our children have more options than we ever did.
What will be your purpose, child of mine?
My struggles are not the same as yours, Dad.

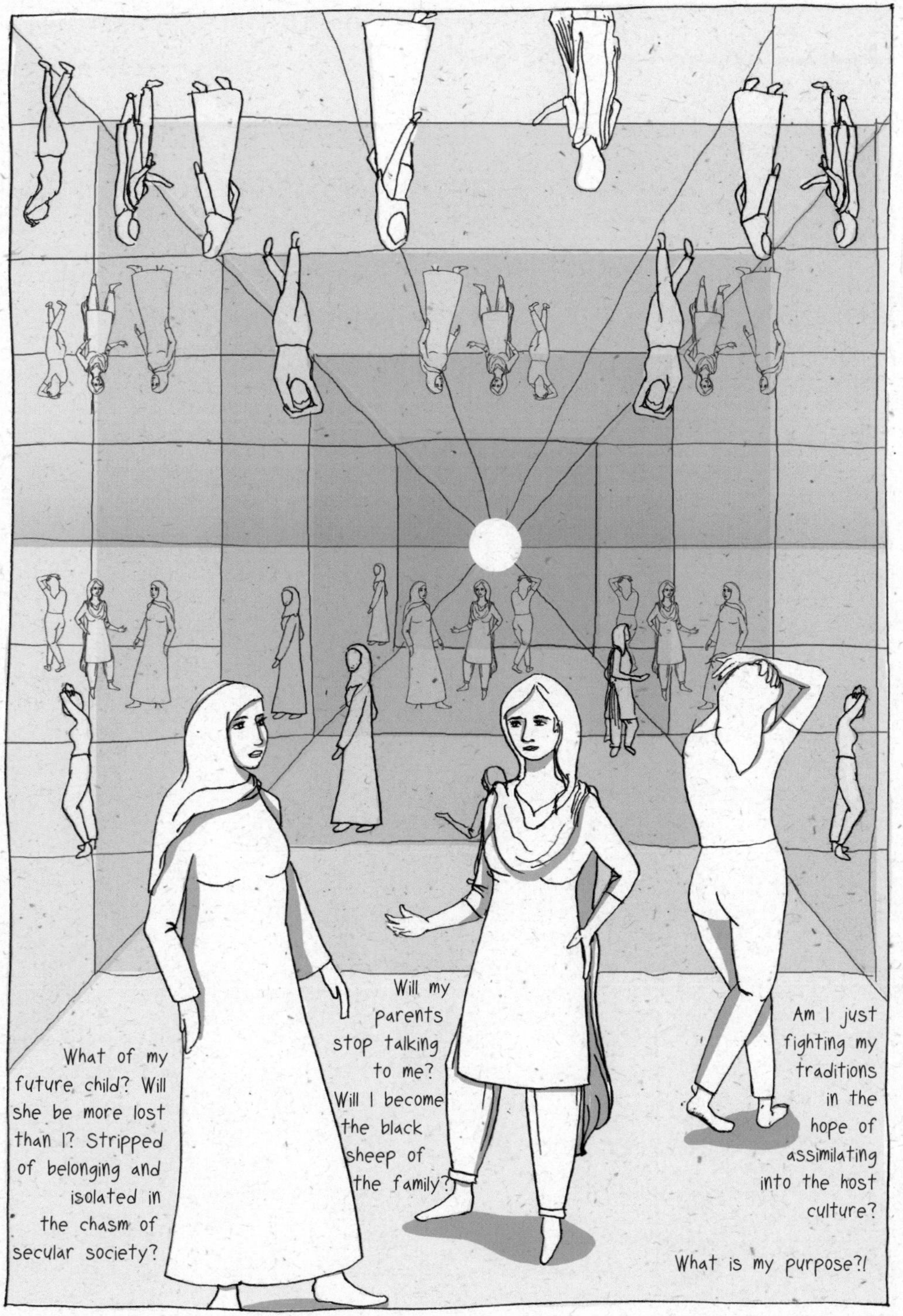
What of my future child? Will she be more lost than I? Stripped of belonging and isolated in the chasm of secular society?
Will my parents stop talking to me? Will I become the black sheep of the family?
Am I just fighting my traditions in the hope of assimilating into the host culture?
What is my purpose?!

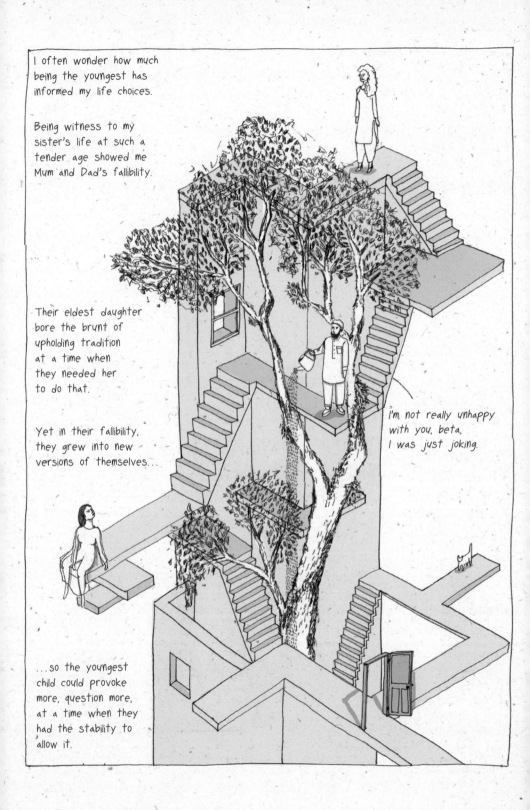

I often wonder how much being the youngest has informed my life choices.

Being witness to my sister's life at such a tender age showed me Mum and Dad's fallibility.

Their eldest daughter bore the brunt of upholding tradition at a time when they needed her to do that.

Yet in their fallibility, they grew into new versions of themselves...

I'm not really unhappy with you, beta, I was just joking.

...so the youngest child could provoke more, question more, at a time when they had the stability to allow it.

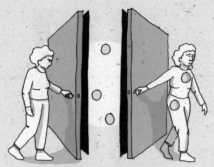

We all have roles we play,
but there is so much more
beyond that...

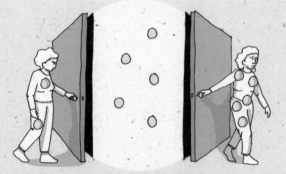

There is the higher self, the self
fueled by creativity, ambition,
aspiration, hopes, and desires.

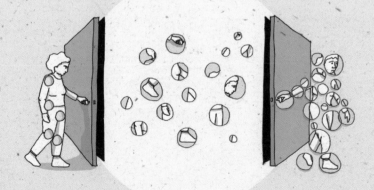

There is the lower self, fueled
by survival, taking care of self,
instincts, and food.

 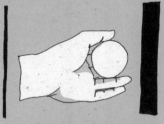 

There is the outer self. All the things that others know about you.

There is the inner self. The private self. Things only you know about you.

The soul is made up of all of these things plus another ingredient...

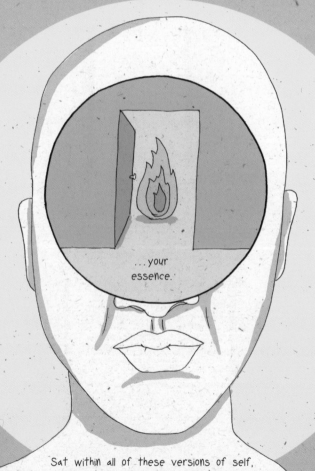

...your essence.

Sat within all of these versions of self, but ultimately untouched by tragedy, poverty, or hardship. Some say it is pure joy, love, or even the touch of the divine.

24 ILLUMINATIONS

♫ Mulatu Astatke "Tezeta (Nostalgia)"

This ain't no hunger strike.
I've been doing this for one whole month every year since I was seven. The age of responsibility.
Ramadan. The ninth month of the lunar calendar.
OUT OF SYNC WITH SOLAR CALENDAR
DEC
JAN
NOV
FULL MOON
FEB
OCT
SUN
MAR
SEP
EARTH
APR
AUG
MAY
JUNE
JULY
Each year the moon pushes forward fifteen days meaning no one Ramadan is the same as the last.

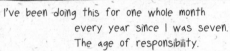

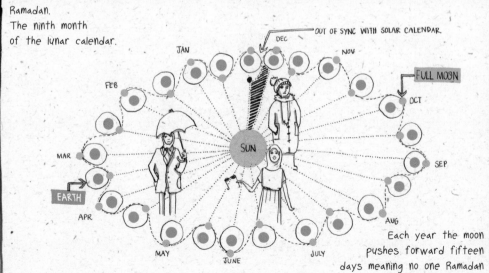

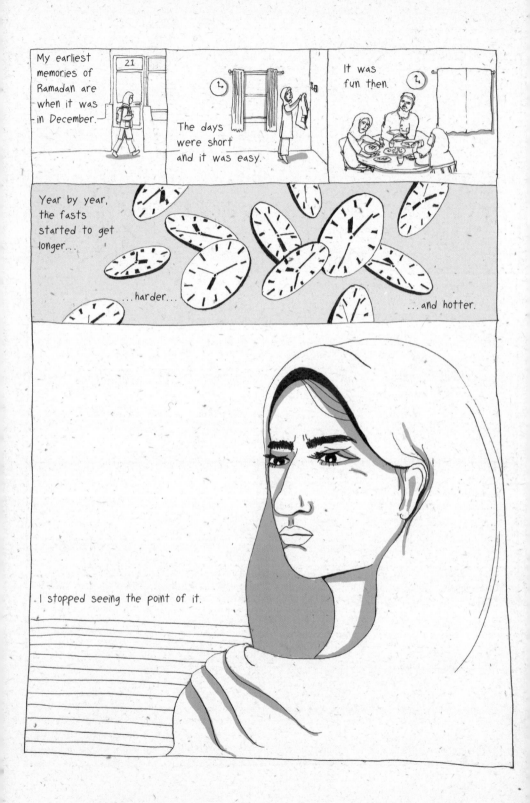

My earliest memories of Ramadan are when it was in December.

The days were short and it was easy.

It was fun then.

Year by year, the fasts started to get longer...

...harder...

...and hotter.

I stopped seeing the point of it.

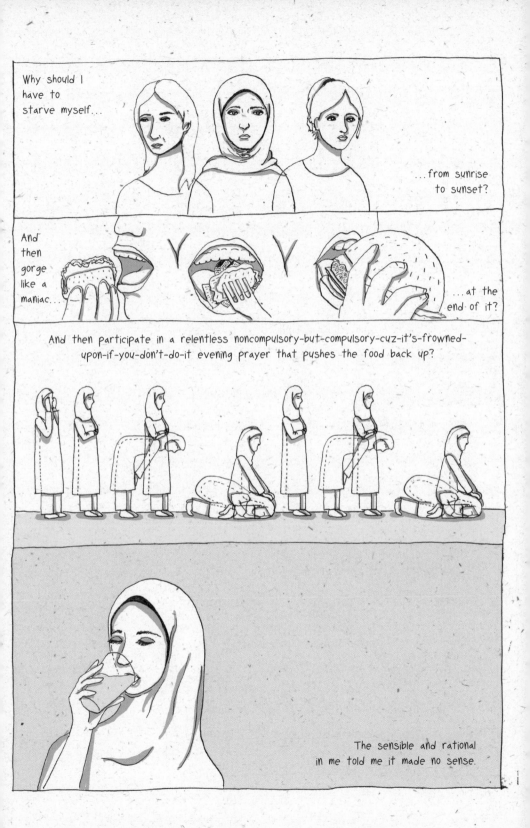

Why should I have to starve myself...

...from sunrise to sunset?

And then gorge like a maniac...

...at the end of it?

And then participate in a relentless noncompulsory-but-compulsory-cuz-it's-frowned-upon-if-you-don't-do-it evening prayer that pushes the food back up?

The sensible and rational in me told me it made no sense.

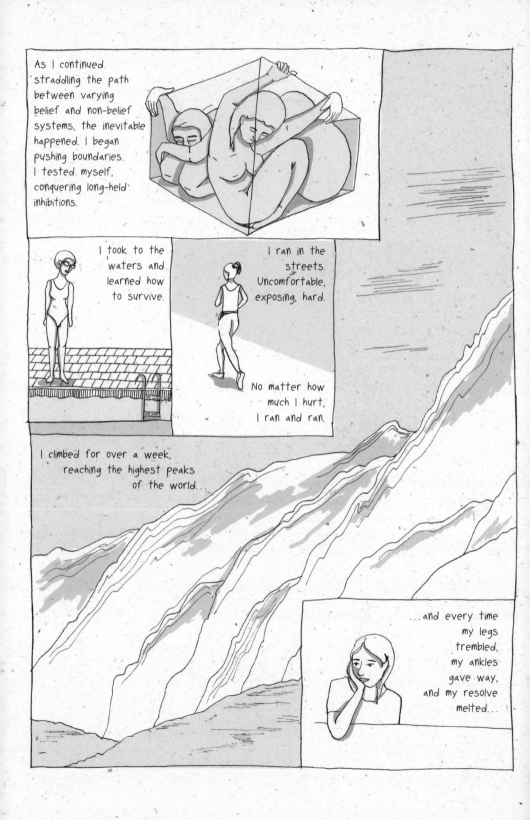

As I continued straddling the path between varying belief and non-belief systems, the inevitable happened. I began pushing boundaries. I tested myself, conquering long-held inhibitions.

I took to the waters and learned how to survive.

I ran in the streets. Uncomfortable, exposing, hard.

No matter how much I hurt, I ran and ran.

I climbed for over a week, reaching the highest peaks of the world...

...and every time my legs trembled, my ankles gave way, and my resolve melted...

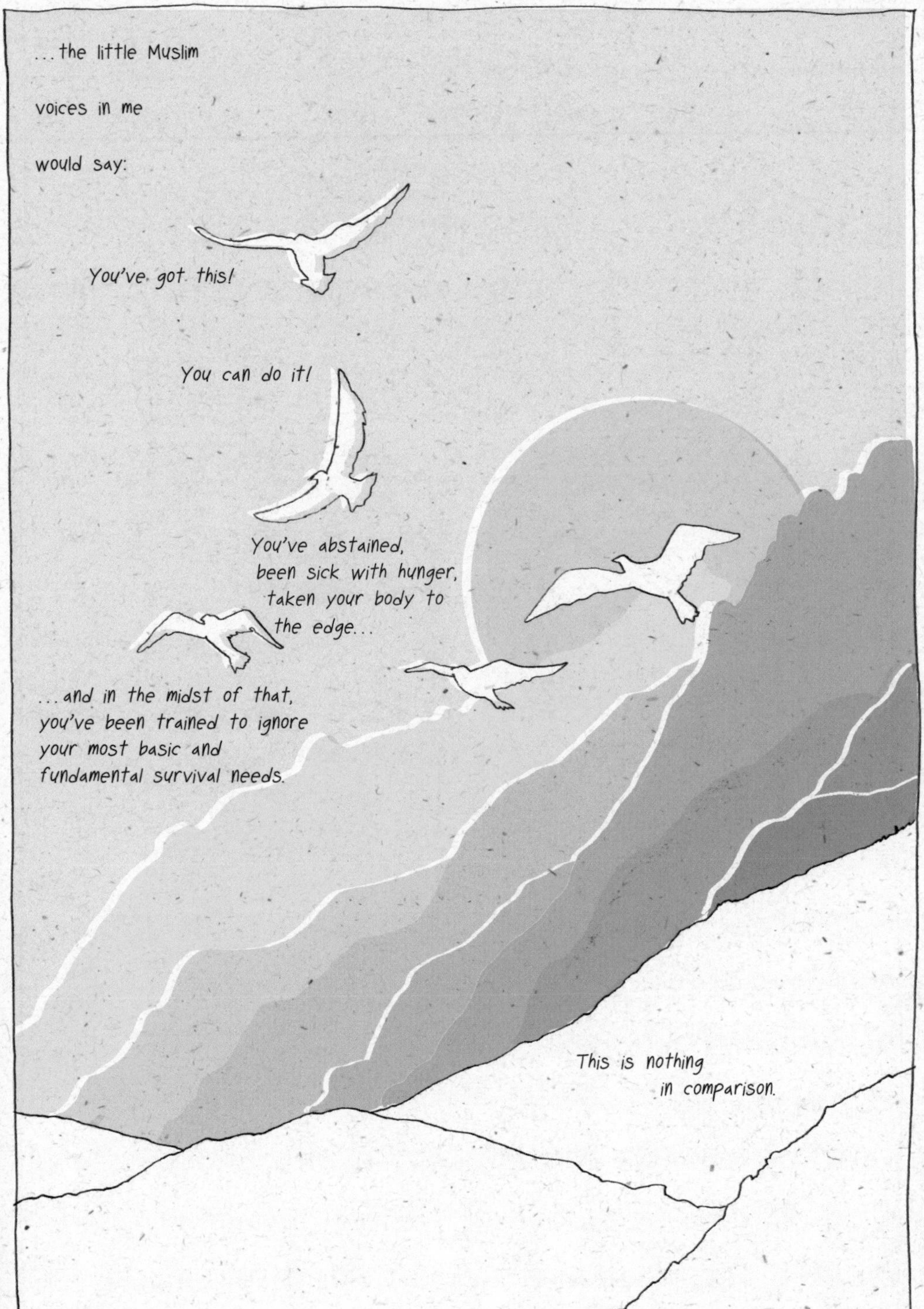
...the little Muslim
voices in me
would say:
You've got this!
You can do it!
You've abstained, been sick with hunger, taken your body to the edge...
...and in the midst of that, you've been trained to ignore your most basic and fundamental survival needs.
This is nothing in comparison.

When sustenance is disciplined,
and the physical desire
for consumption contained,
it is the mental,
the subconscious,
that conquers.

I face the reflections
of my soul,
and see what
those childhood days
have given me.

It was through my mum
that I learned prayer,
ablution rituals—
making myself clean and crisp,
for dialogue with the divine.

A consistency,
a commitment,
a loyalty.
Five times a day,
plus all the extras,
and the ones she'd missed as a child.
Every day, since I can remember.

But with it
came her guilt,
her shame, and
the burdens she'd carried.
The conflict of her love,
both respite and turmoil.

Reflected in how
the family would gather
for Jummah prayer:
some days quiet and still,
others raging and violent.
The paradox of the divine.

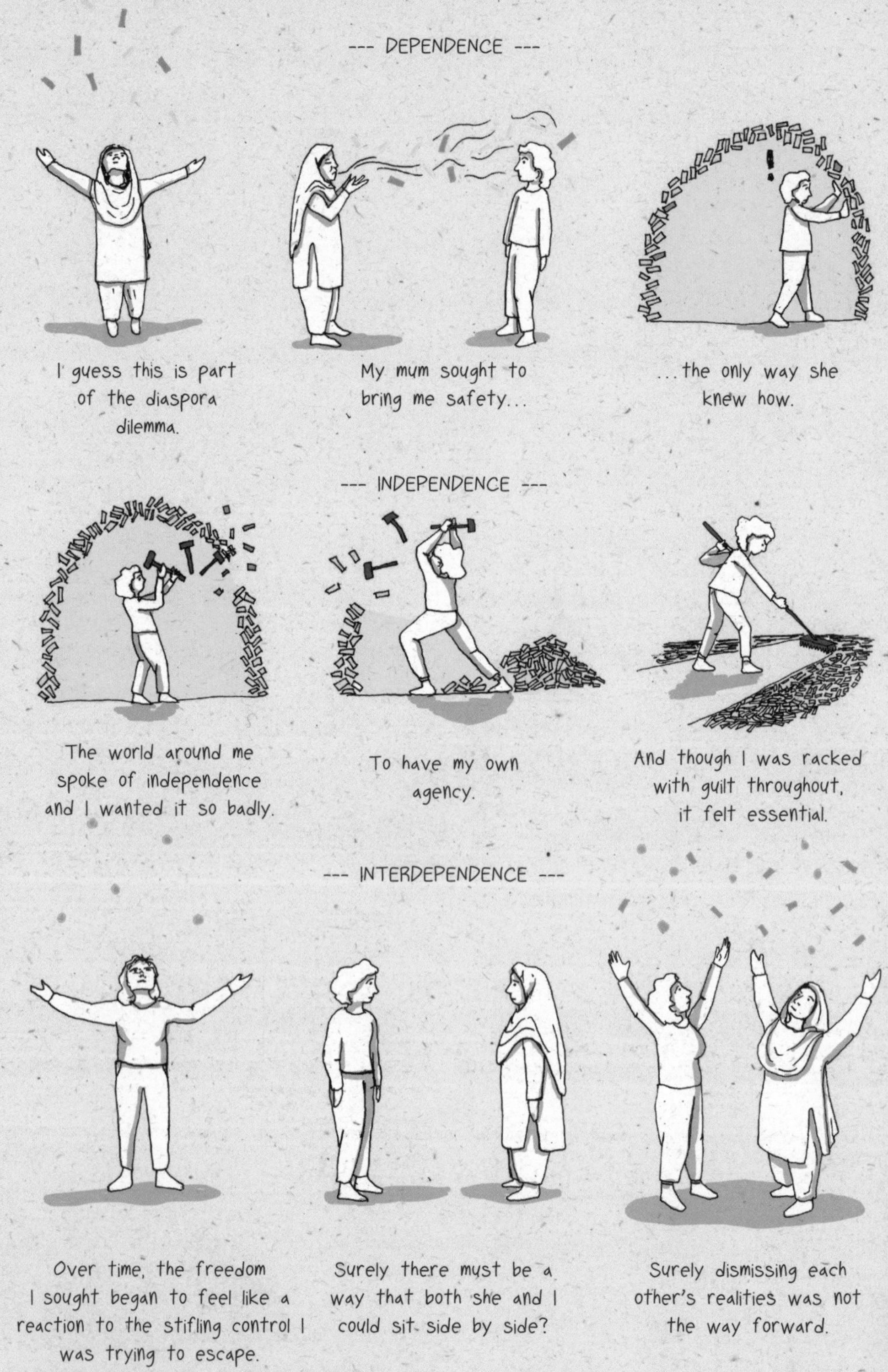
--- DEPENDENCE ---
I guess this is part of the diaspora dilemma.
My mum sought to bring me safety...
...the only way she knew how.
--- INDEPENDENCE ---
The world around me spoke of independence and I wanted it so badly.
To have my own agency.
And though I was racked with guilt throughout, it felt essential.
--- INTERDEPENDENCE ---
Over time, the freedom I sought began to feel like a reaction to the stifling control I was trying to escape.
Surely there must be a way that both she and I could sit side by side?
Surely dismissing each other's realities was not the way forward.

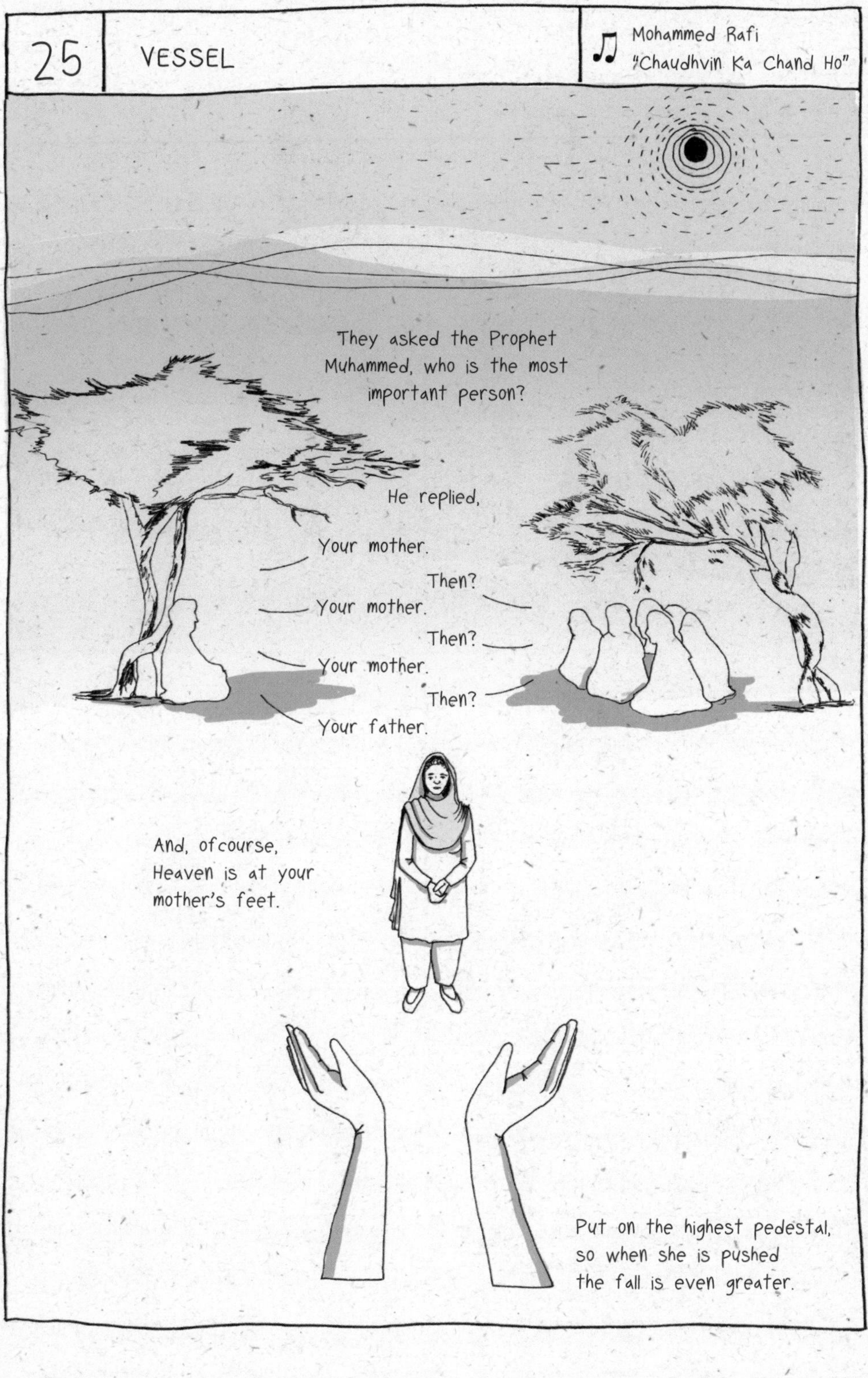
25
VESSEL
Mohammed Rafi
"Chaudhvin Ka Chand Ho"
They asked the Prophet Muhammed, who is the most important person?
He replied,
Your mother.
Then?
Your mother.
Then?
Your mother.
Then?
Your father.
And, ofcourse, Heaven is at your mother's feet.
Put on the highest pedestal, so when she is pushed the fall is even greater.

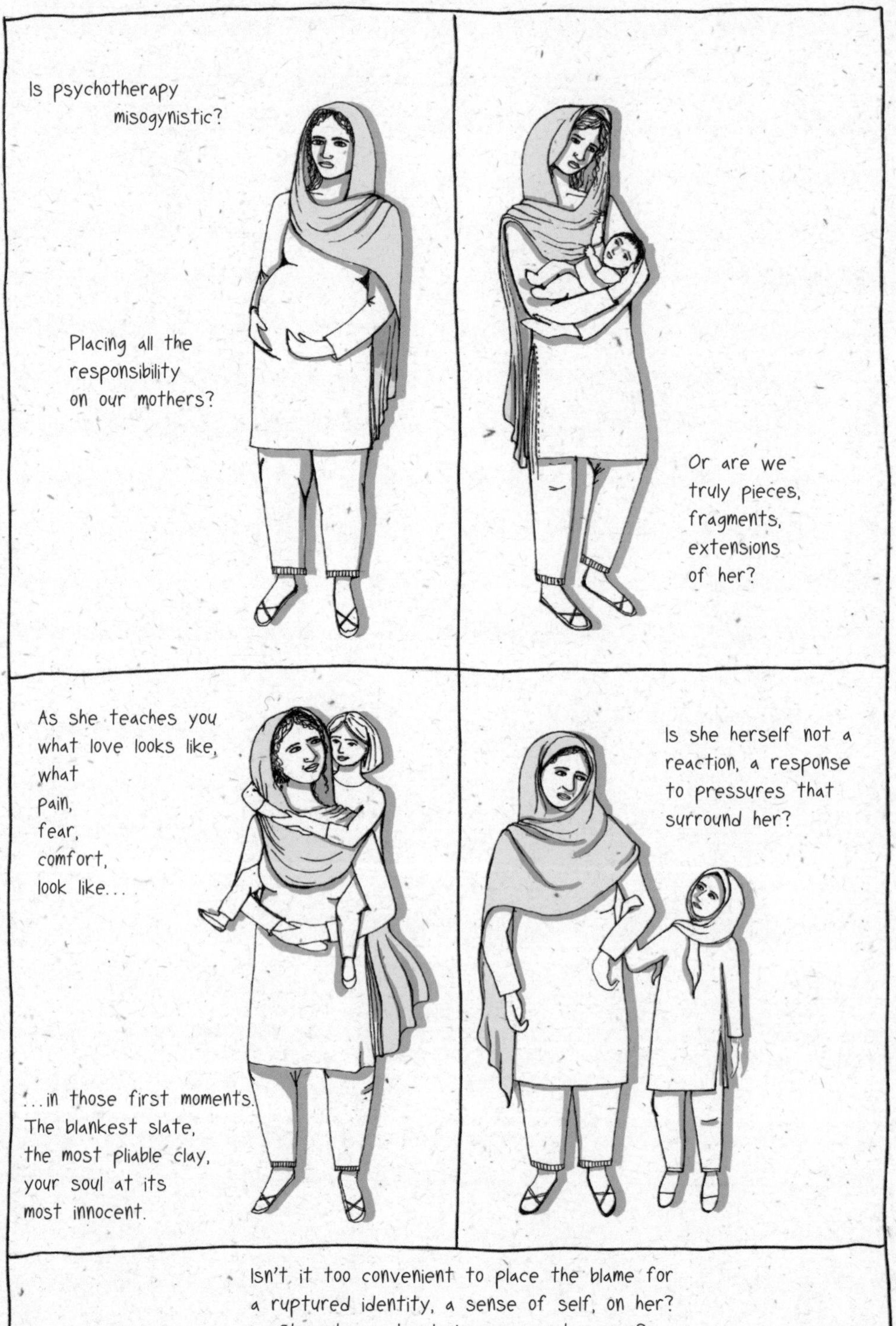
Is psychotherapy misogynistic?
Placing all the responsibility on our mothers?
Or are we truly pieces, fragments, extensions of her?
As she teaches you what love looks like, what pain, fear, comfort, look like...
...in those first moments. The blankest slate, the most pliable clay, your soul at its most innocent.
Is she herself not a reaction, a response to pressures that surround her?
Isn't it too convenient to place the blame for a ruptured identity, a sense of self, on her? She who so tenderly gave up her own?

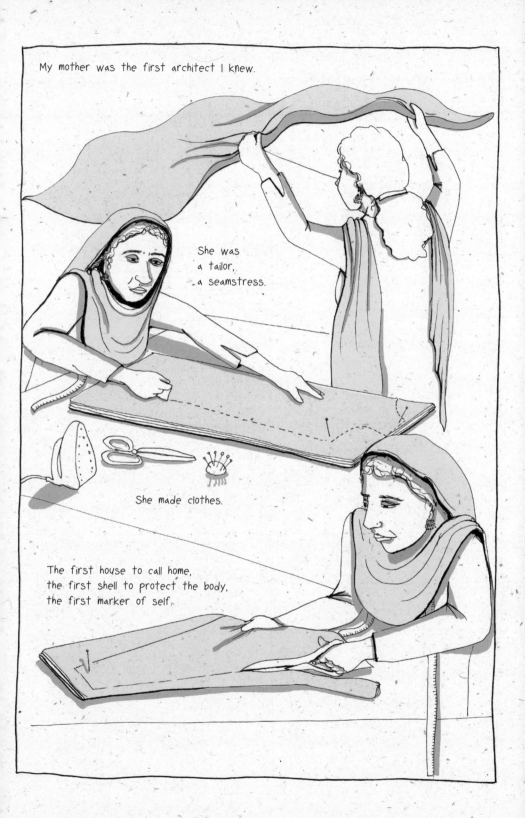

My mother was the first architect I knew.

She was
a tailor,
a seamstress.

She made clothes.

The first house to call home,
the first shell to protect the body,
the first marker of self.

229

Her Singer sewing machine etched into memory...

...the machine that kept her away from us...

...whirring into the early hours of Fajr.

She sewed for the textile warehouses in Whitechapel. Bags and bags of patterns to be stitched together.

She sewed to clothe us. Bags and bags of loose fabric from Queen's Market.

Her pedal worked the engine.

Prrrrrrr Prrrrrrr

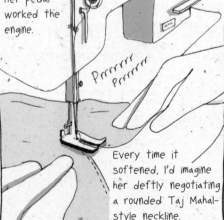

Every time it softened, I'd imagine her deftly negotiating a rounded Taj Mahal-style neckline.

Every time it roared, shaking the whole house with its pace...

GRRRR
RRR
Grrr

...I'd imagine the neatest, straightest, quickest edge.

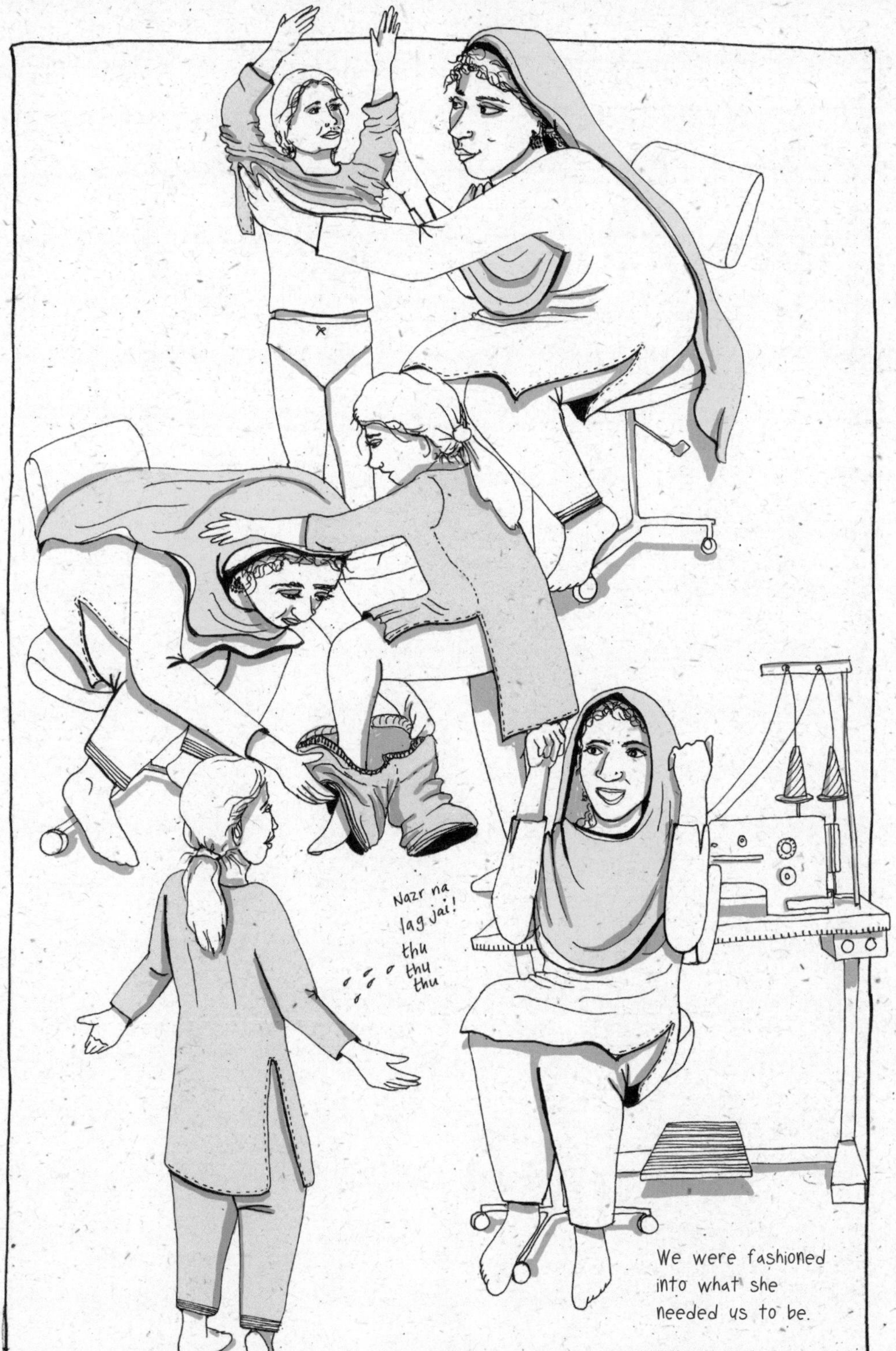
Nazr na lag jai!
thu thu thu
We were fashioned into what she needed us to be.

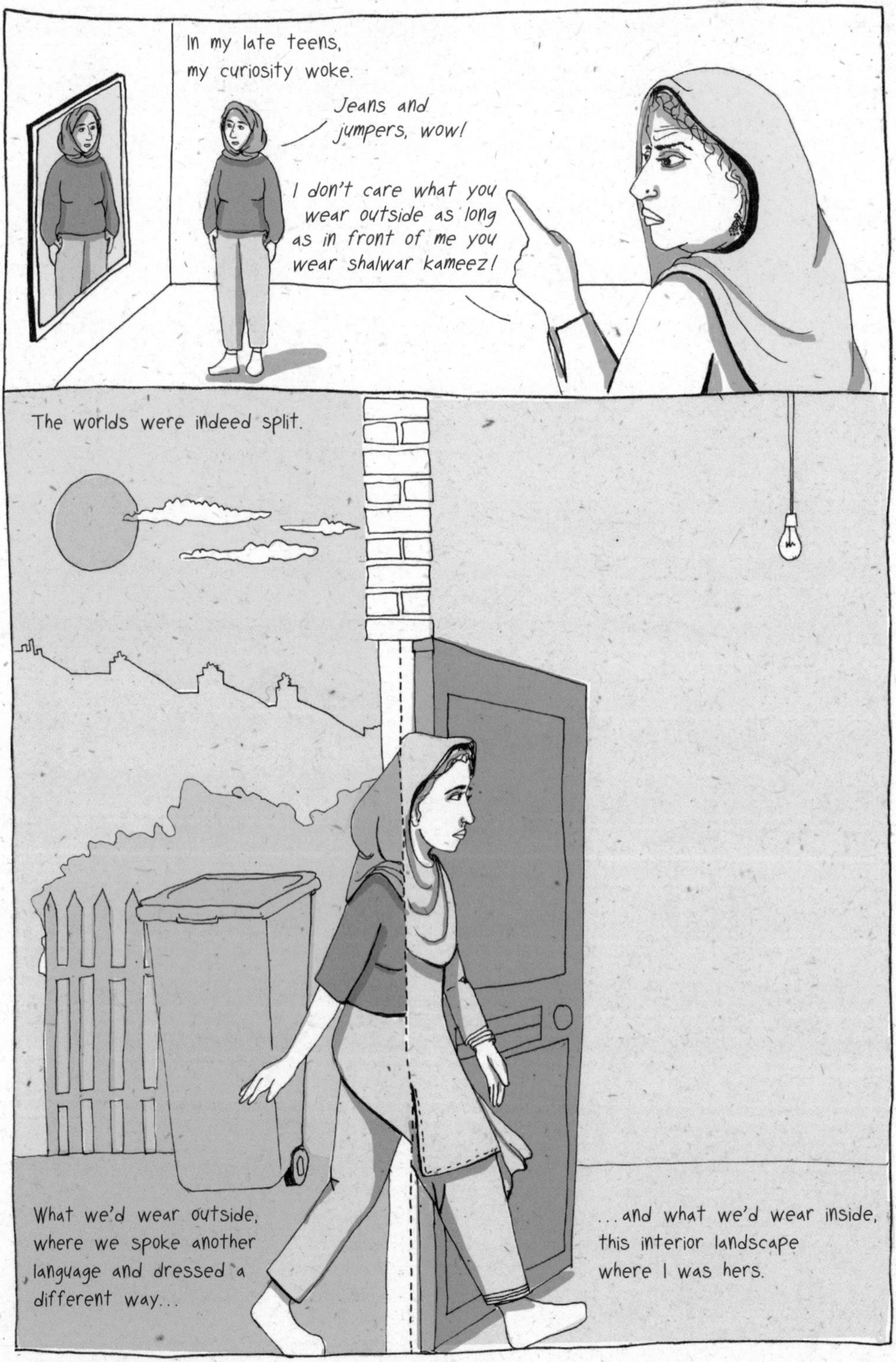
In my late teens, my curiosity woke.
Jeans and jumpers, wow!
I don't care what you wear outside as long as in front of me you wear shalwar kameez!
The worlds were indeed split.
What we'd wear outside, where we spoke another language and dressed a different way...
...and what we'd wear inside, this interior landscape where I was hers.

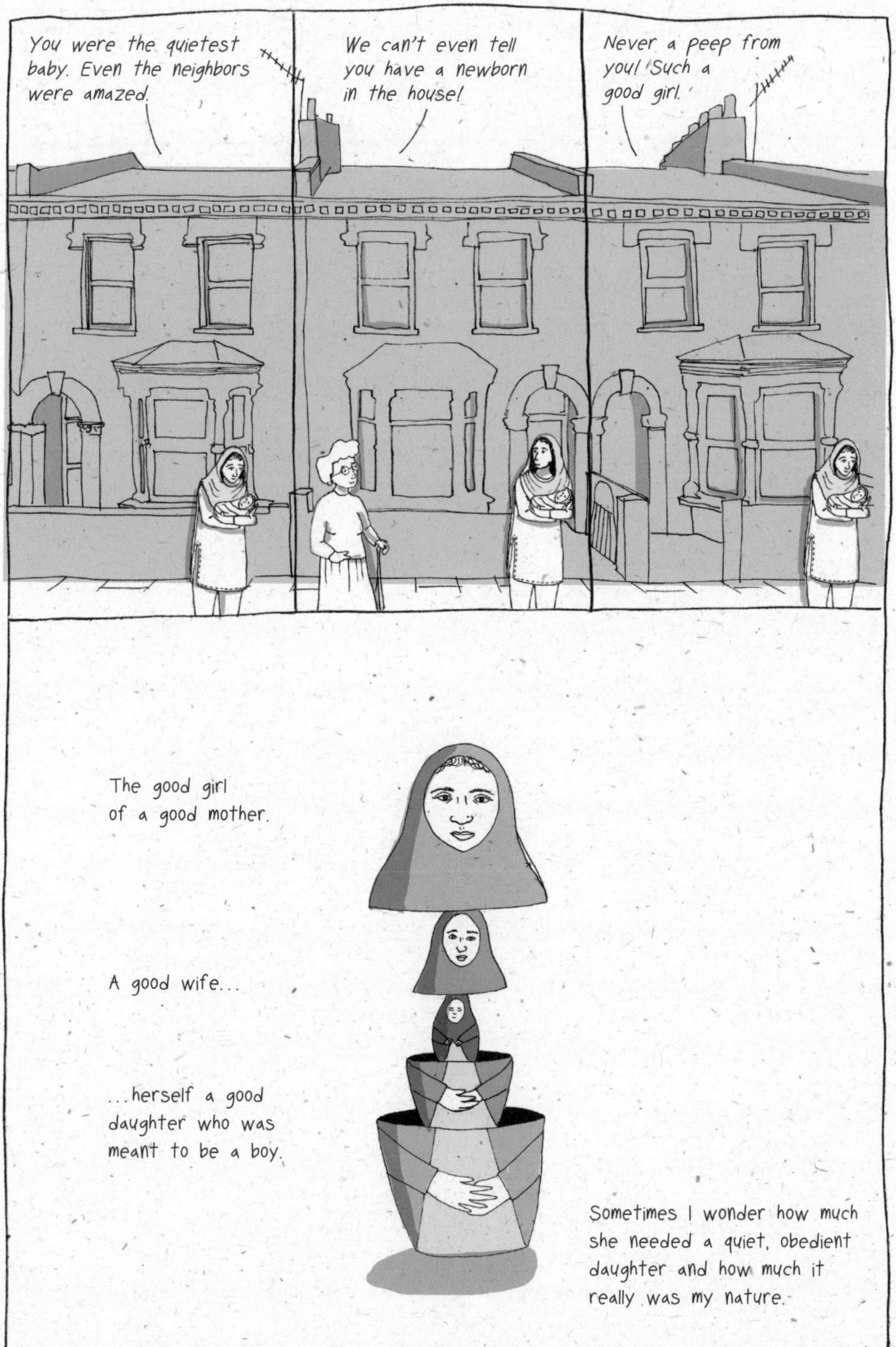
You were the quietest baby. Even the neighbors were amazed.
We can't even tell you have a newborn in the house!
Never a peep from you! Such a good girl.
The good girl of a good mother.
A good wife...
...herself a good daughter who was meant to be a boy.
Sometimes I wonder how much she needed a quiet, obedient daughter and how much it really was my nature.

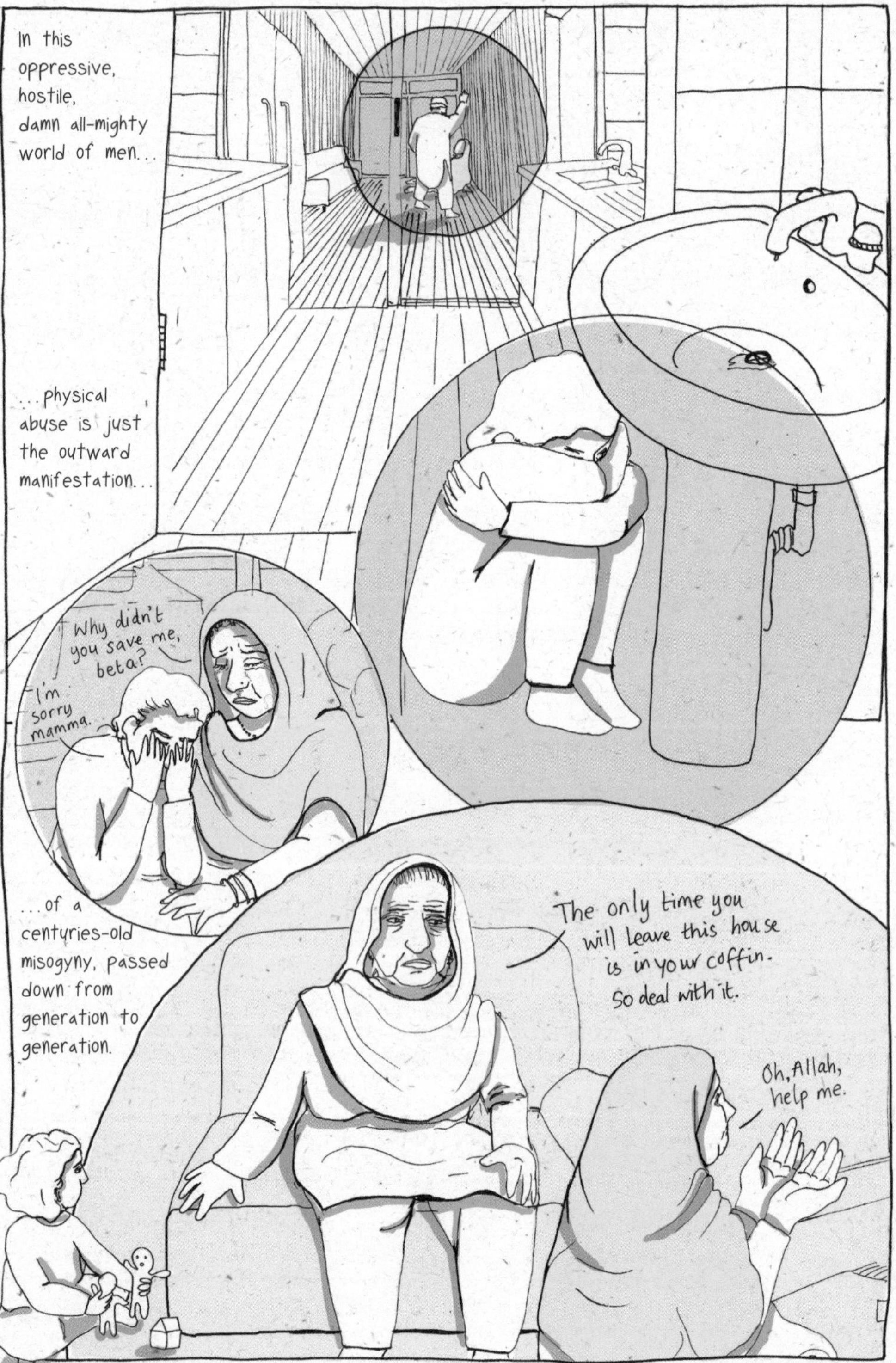

In this oppressive, hostile, damn all-mighty world of men...
...physical abuse is just the outward manifestation...
Why didn't you save me, beta?
I'm sorry mamma.
...of a centuries-old misogyny, passed down from generation to generation.
The only time you will leave this house is in your coffin. So deal with it.
Oh, Allah, help me.

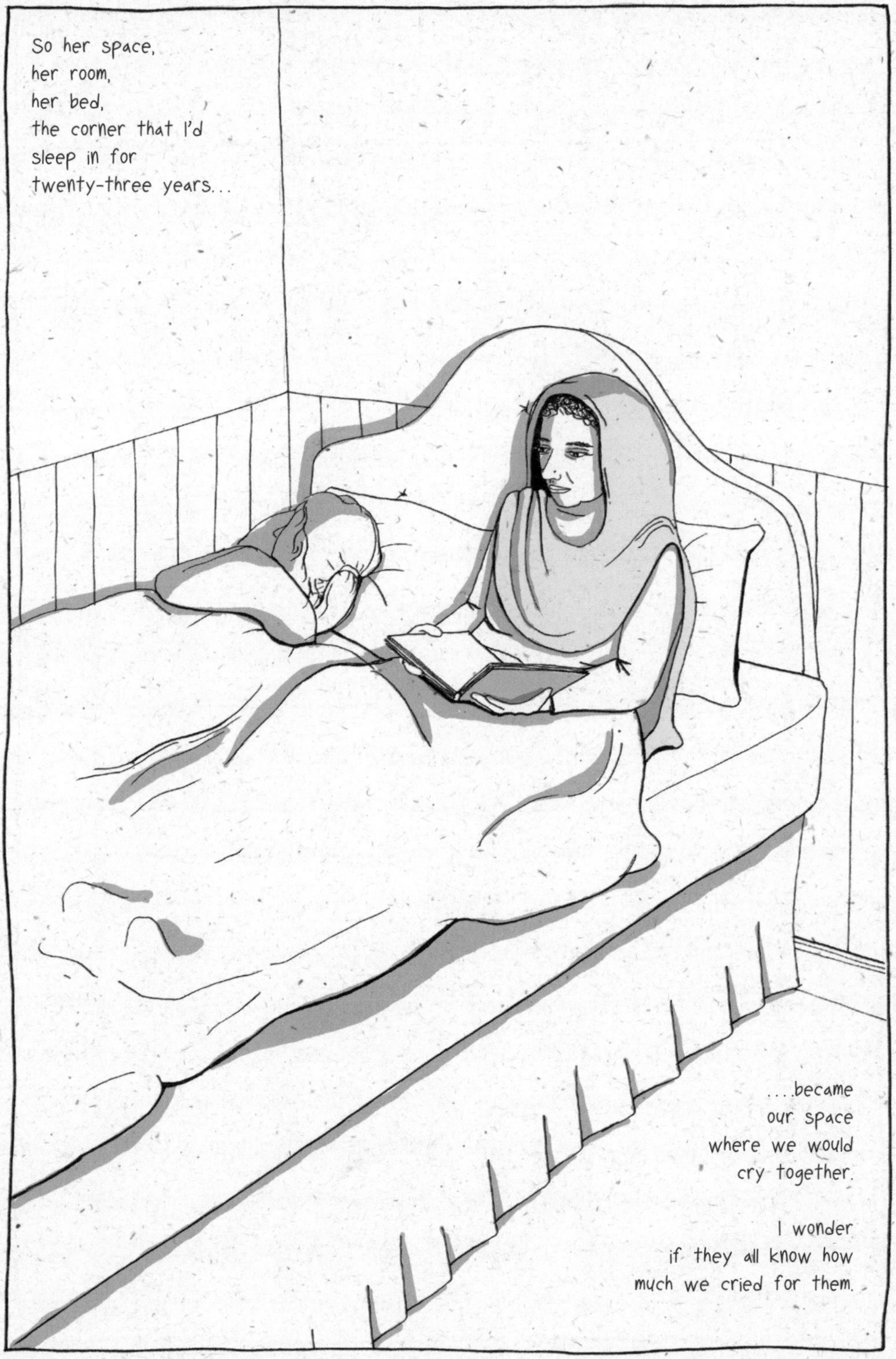
So her space,
her room,
her bed,
the corner that I'd
sleep in for
twenty-three years...
....became
our space
where we would
cry together.
I wonder
if they all know how
much we cried for them.

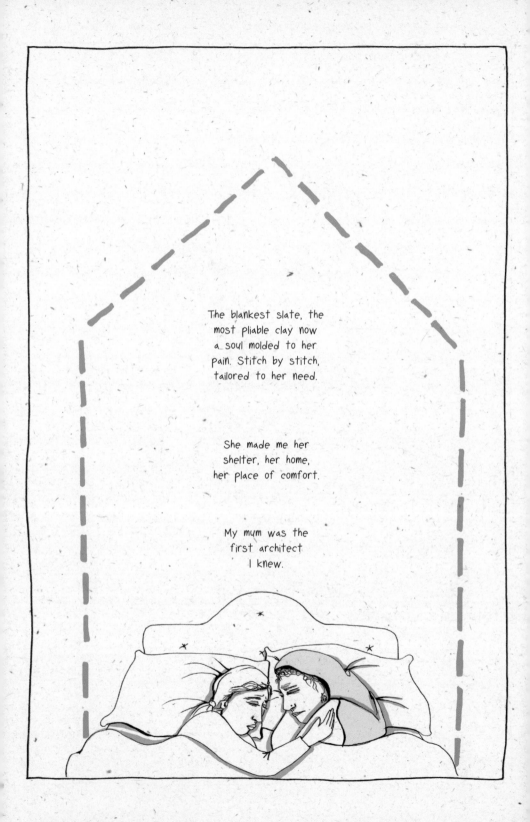

The blankest slate, the
most pliable clay now
a soul molded to her
pain. Stitch by stitch,
tailored to her need.

She made me her
shelter, her home,
her place of comfort.

My mum was the
first architect
I knew.

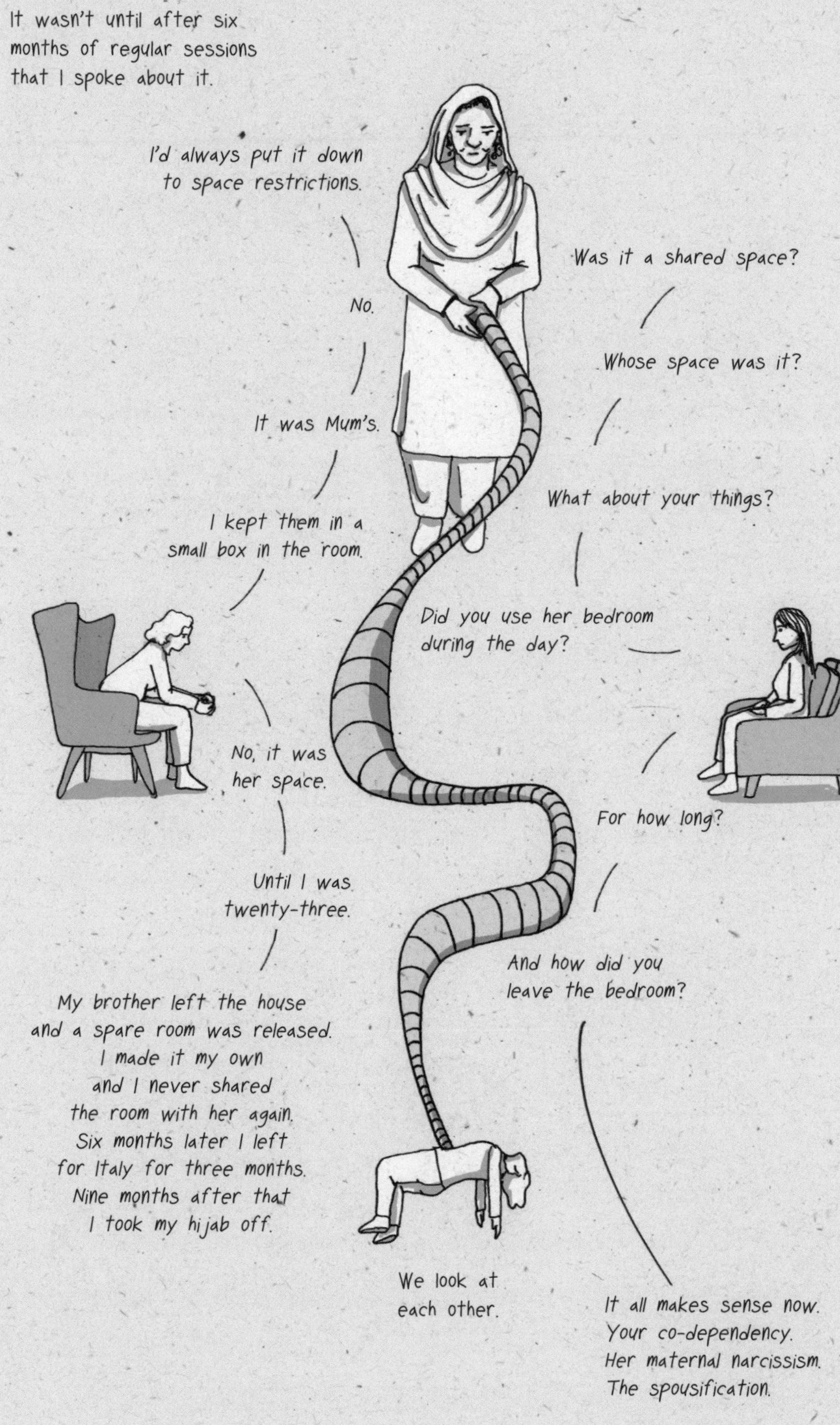
It wasn't until after six months of regular sessions that I spoke about it.
I'd always put it down to space restrictions.
Was it a shared space?
No.
Whose space was it?
It was Mum's.
What about your things?
I kept them in a small box in the room.
Did you use her bedroom during the day?
No, it was her space.
For how long?
Until I was twenty-three.
And how did you leave the bedroom?
My brother left the house and a spare room was released. I made it my own and I never shared the room with her again. Six months later I left for Italy for three months. Nine months after that I took my hijab off.
We look at each other.
It all makes sense now. Your co-dependency. Her maternal narcissism. The spousification.

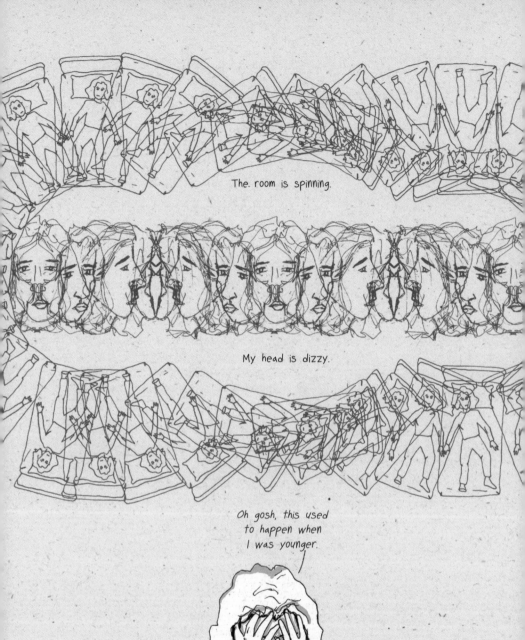

The room is spinning.

My head is dizzy.

Oh gosh, this used
to happen when
I was younger.

You're too in your mind.
You're disassociating.
Get back into your body.
Tap your foot on the floor.
Hug yourself.
Breathe.

26 FINITE

♫ Nick Cave & The Bad Seeds "As I Sat Sadly By Her Side"

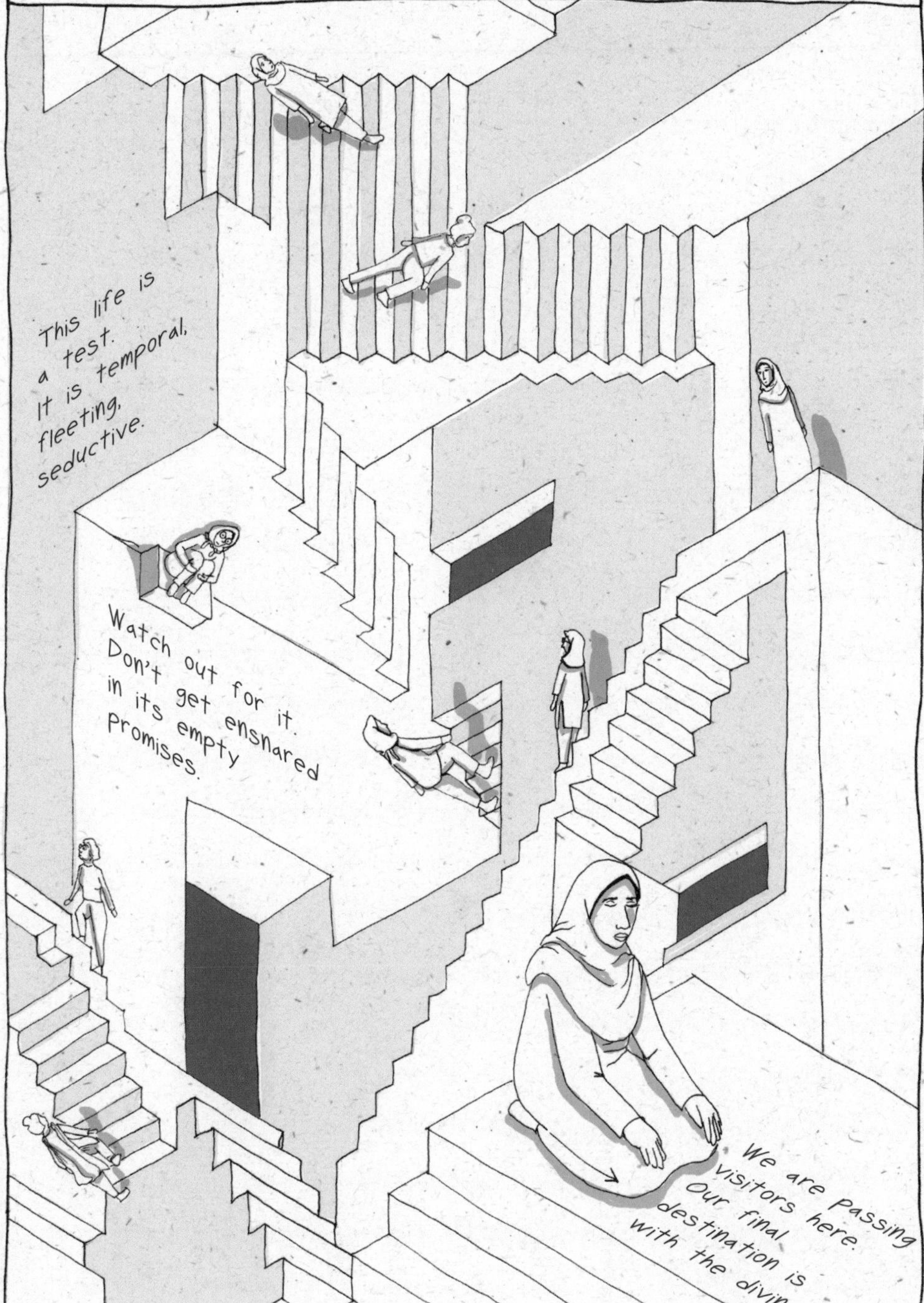
This life is a test. It is temporal, fleeting, seductive.
Watch out for it. Don't get ensnared in its empty promises.
We are passing visitors here. Our final destination is with the divine.

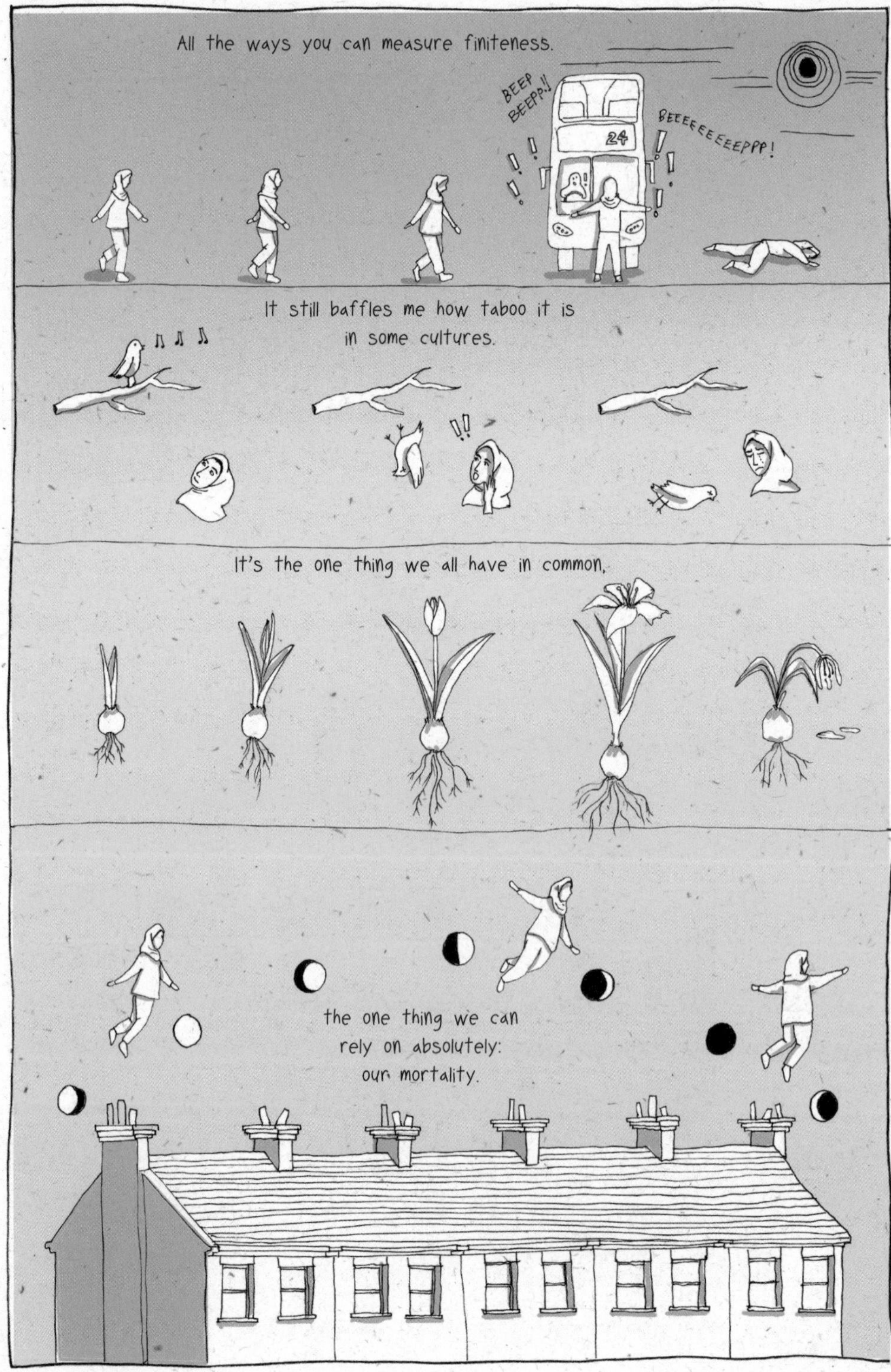
All the ways you can measure finiteness.
BEEP BEEPP!!
24
BEEEEEEEEEPPP!
It still baffles me how taboo it is in some cultures.
It's the one thing we all have in common,
the one thing we can rely on absolutely: our mortality.

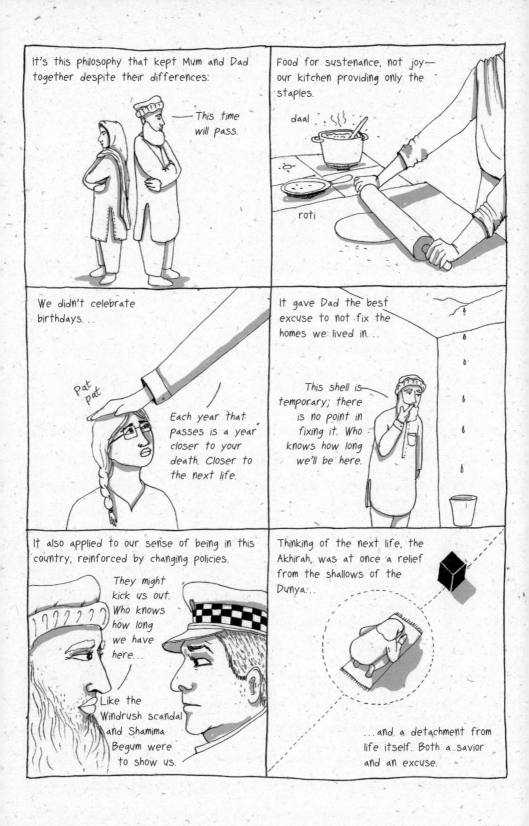

It's this philosophy that kept Mum and Dad together despite their differences:

This time will pass.

Food for sustenance, not joy— our kitchen providing only the staples.

daal

roti

We didn't celebrate birthdays...

Pat pat

Each year that passes is a year closer to your death. Closer to the next life.

It gave Dad the best excuse to not fix the homes we lived in...

This shell is temporary; there is no point in fixing it. Who knows how long we'll be here.

It also applied to our sense of being in this country, reinforced by changing policies.

They might kick us out. Who knows how long we have here...

Like the Windrush scandal and Shamima Begum were to show us.

Thinking of the next life, the Akhirah, was at once a relief from the shallows of the Dunya...

...and a detachment from life itself. Both a savior and an excuse.

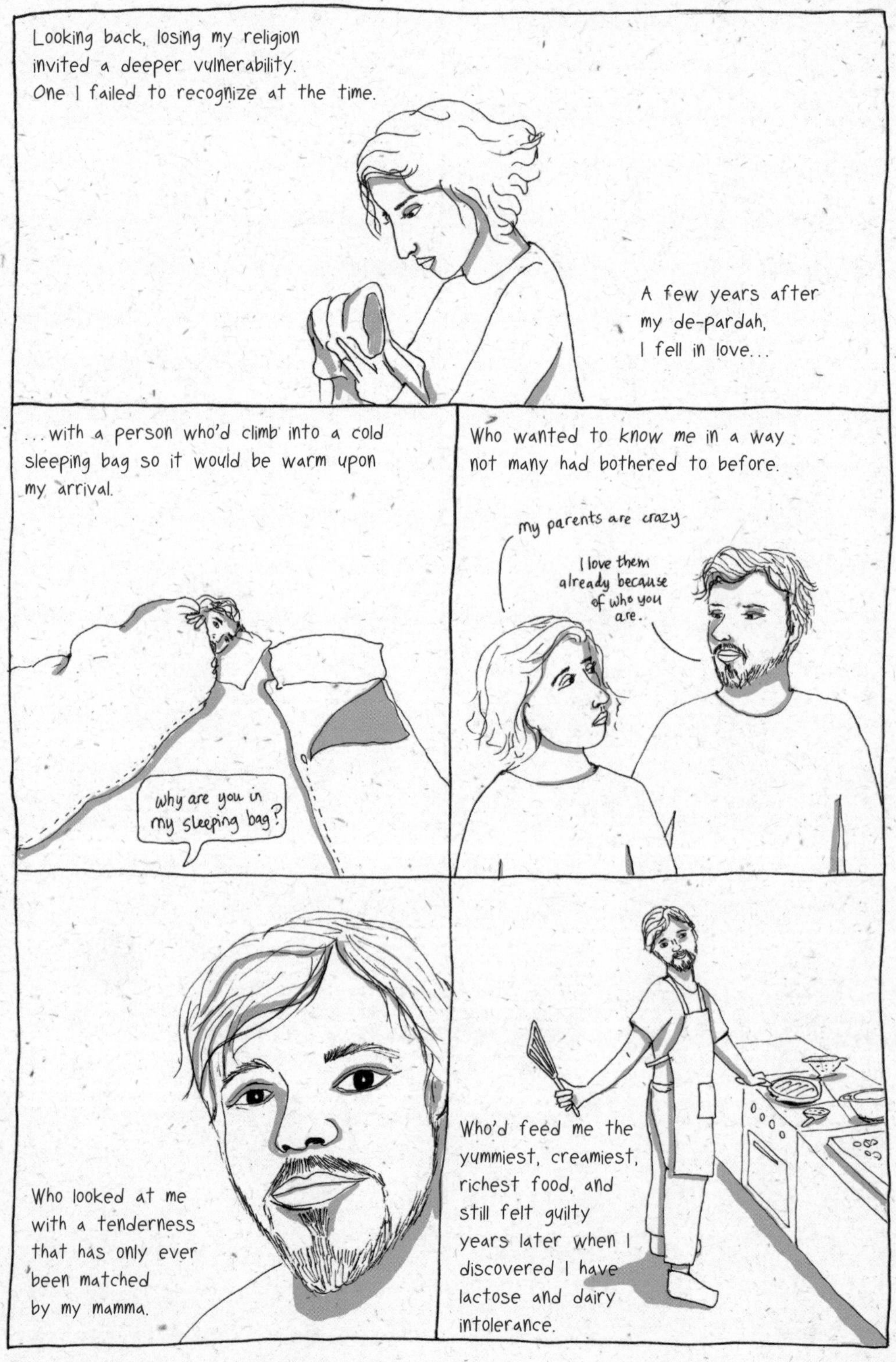
Looking back, losing my religion invited a deeper vulnerability. One I failed to recognize at the time.
A few years after my de-pardah, I fell in love...
...with a person who'd climb into a cold sleeping bag so it would be warm upon my arrival.
why are you in my sleeping bag?
Who wanted to know me in a way not many had bothered to before.
my parents are crazy
I love them already because of who you are.
Who looked at me with a tenderness that has only ever been matched by my mamma.
Who'd feed me the yummiest, creamiest, richest food, and still felt guilty years later when I discovered I have lactose and dairy intolerance.

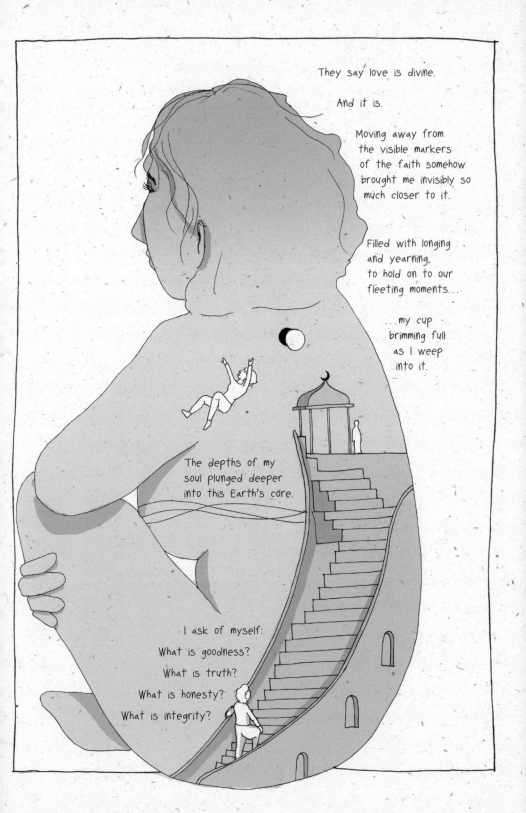

They say love is divine.

And it is.

Moving away from
the visible markers
of the faith somehow
brought me invisibly so
much closer to it.

Filled with longing
and yearning,
to hold on to our
fleeting moments...

...my cup
brimming full
as I weep
into it.

The depths of my
soul plunged deeper
into this Earth's core.

I ask of myself:
What is goodness?
What is truth?
What is honesty?
What is integrity?

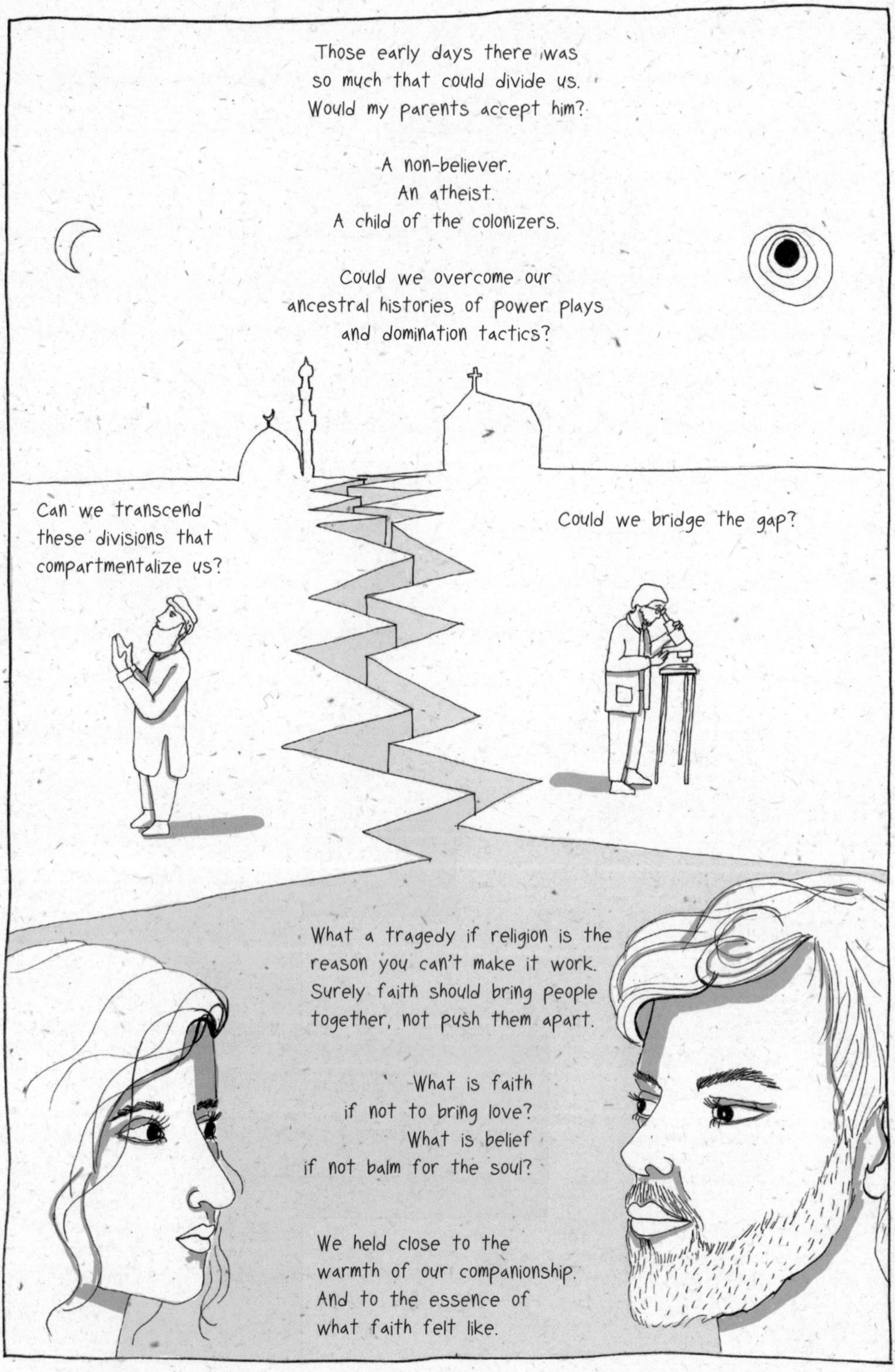

Those early days there was so much that could divide us. Would my parents accept him?
A non-believer.
An atheist.
A child of the colonizers.
Could we overcome our ancestral histories of power plays and domination tactics?
Can we transcend these divisions that compartmentalize us?
Could we bridge the gap?
What a tragedy if religion is the reason you can't make it work. Surely faith should bring people together, not push them apart.
What is faith if not to bring love? What is belief if not balm for the soul?
We held close to the warmth of our companionship. And to the essence of what faith felt like.

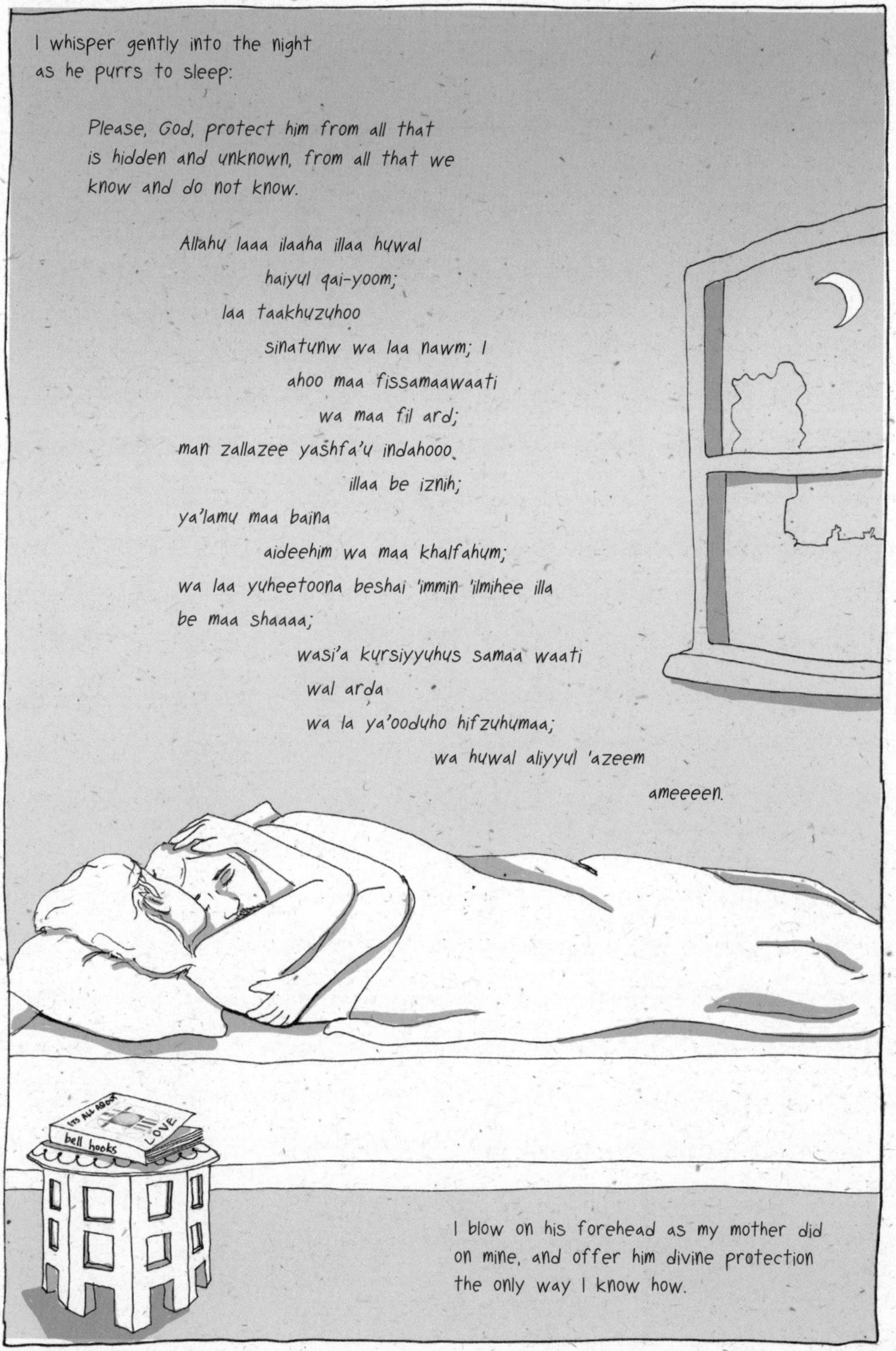
I whisper gently into the night
as he purrs to sleep:
Please, God, protect him from all that
is hidden and unknown, from all that we
know and do not know.
Allahu laaa ilaaha illaa huwal
haiyul qai-yoom;
laa taakhuzuhoo
sinatunw wa laa nawm; l
ahoo maa fissamaawaati
wa maa fil ard;
man zallazee yashfa'u indahooo
illaa be iznih;
ya'lamu maa baina
aideehim wa maa khalfahum;
wa laa yuheetoona beshai 'immin 'ilmihee illa
be maa shaaaa;
wasi'a kursiyyuhus samaa waati
wal arda
wa la ya'ooduho hifzuhumaa;
wa huwal aliyyul 'azeem
ameeeen.
IT'S ALL ABOUT LOVE
bell hooks
I blow on his forehead as my mother did
on mine, and offer him divine protection
the only way I know how.

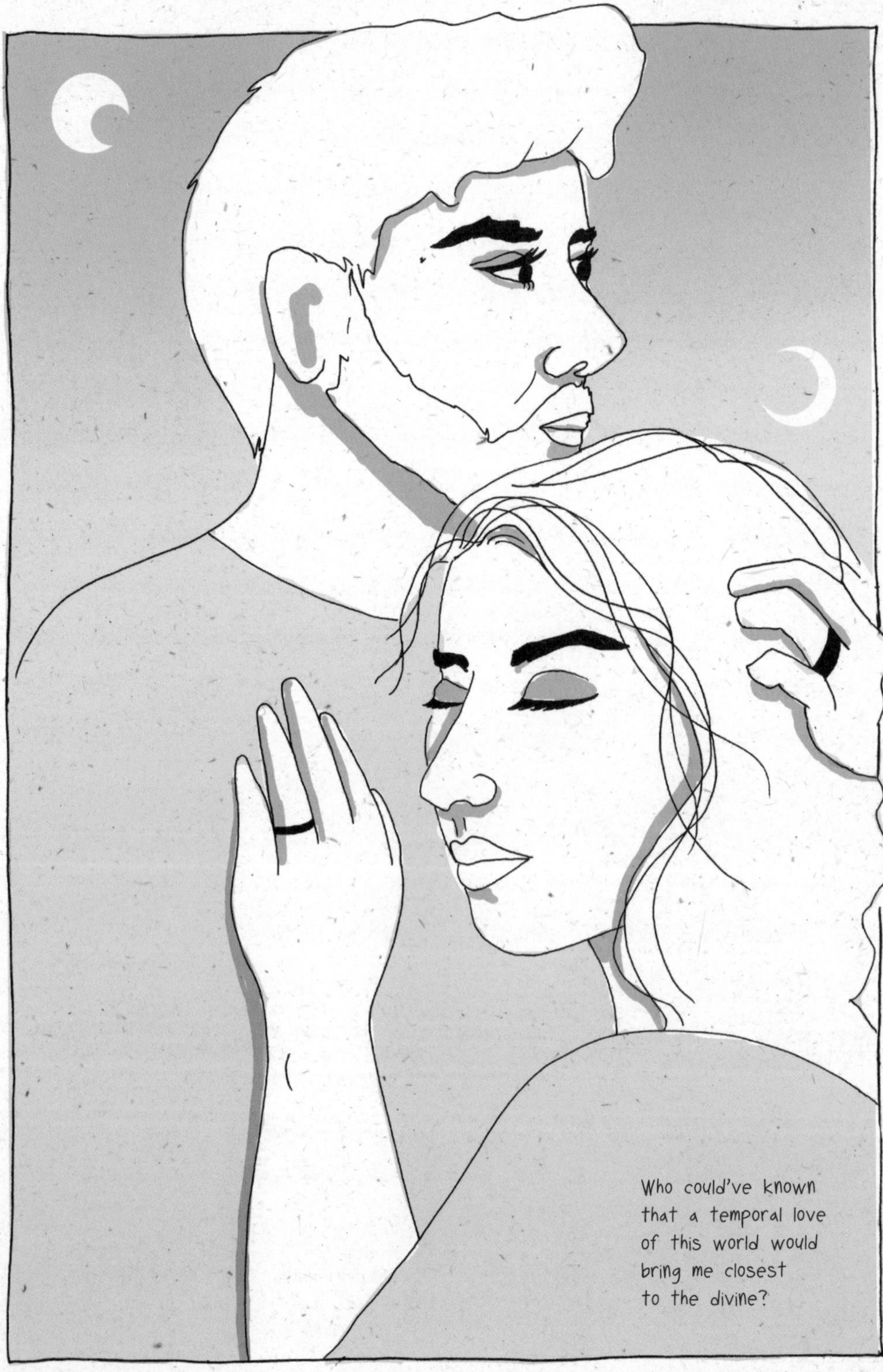
Who could've known
that a temporal love
of this world would
bring me closest
to the divine?

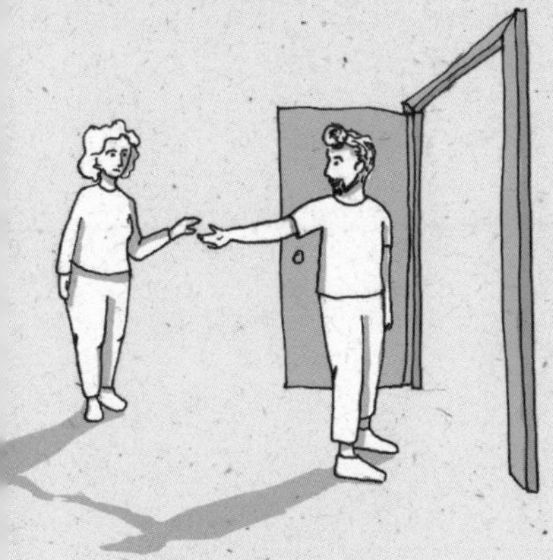

I'd never been in a relationship before,
let alone one with someone from a different culture,
a different race,
the race of belonging,
the dominating race.
Did I see him as a savior?
The connotations make me gulp.

I started noticing things,
like how he was
welcomed
accepted
loved
respected
by everyone...

...the corner-shop man,
the estate agents,
the neighbors.

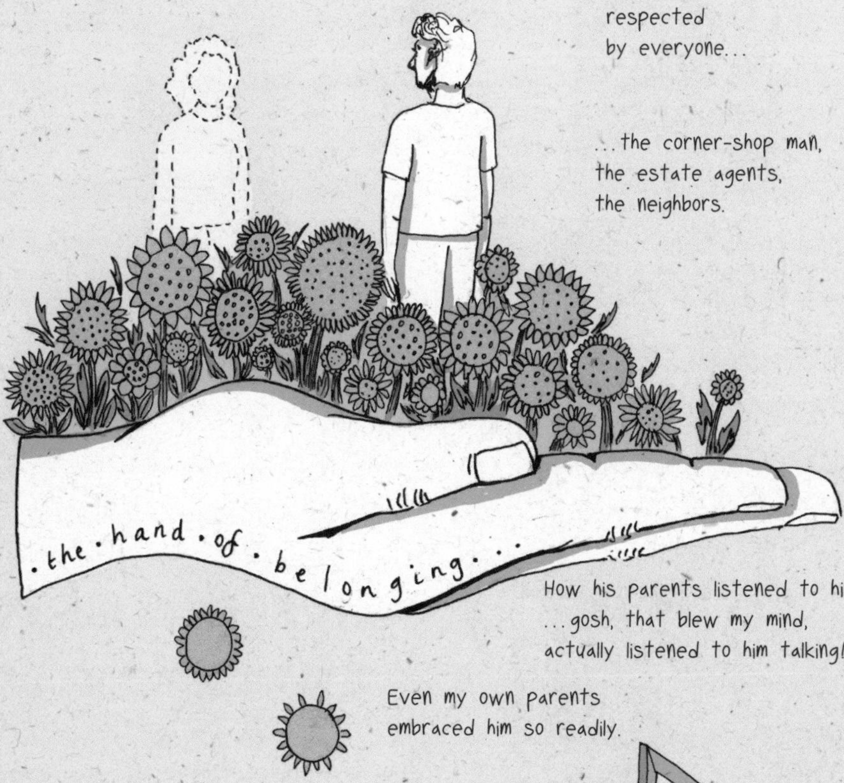
.the.hand.of.belonging...

How his parents listened to him...
...gosh, that blew my mind,
actually listened to him talking!

Even my own parents
embraced him so readily.

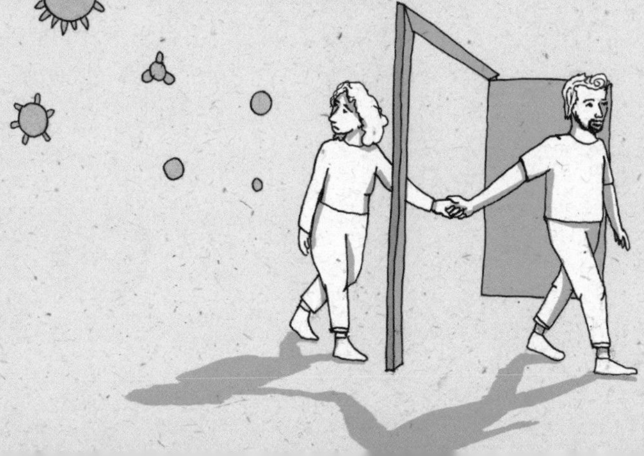

I'd tell myself it was down to
him, and his open and honest
soul. Yet I was so full of
conflict. I saw first hand
what belonging offers
to one who has always had it.
I felt jealous, and frustrated.
I wanted what he had.

What was it?
This magic stuff that
came so easily to him?

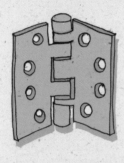

A childhood of consistency
that resulted in his own
secure attachment?

Developed social skills that meant
"getting along" with people just
came more easily to him?

A quality of life that
was a given for his
class, race, gender?

The more we grew with each
other, the more comfortable I'd
get in his ambient belonging.

But when not with him,
it returned, the jagged
edges of being other.

In his absence, I'd find myself
acting like him—perhaps that
would get me the instant
belonging that he had?

It didn't help.

I knew there was something
deeply unsettled within me
that I needed to resolve.

♪ Mohammed Rafi
"Yeh Duniya Yeh Mehfil"

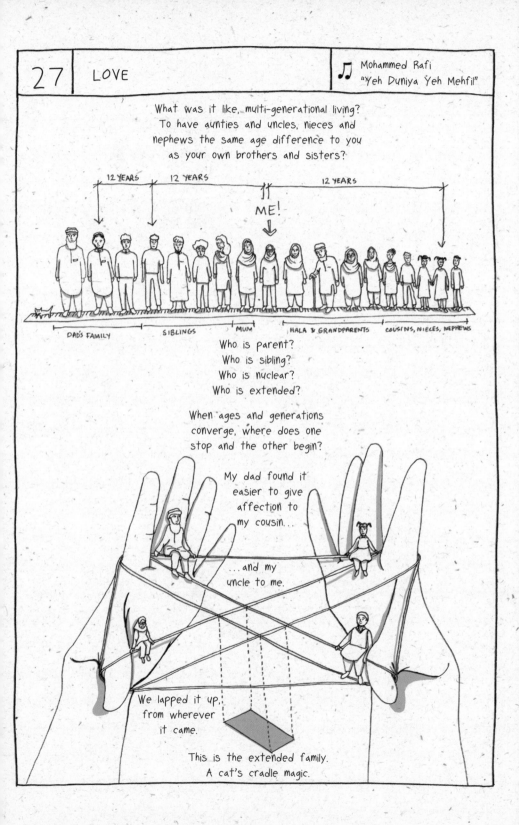

What was it like, multi-generational living?
To have aunties and uncles, nieces and
nephews the same age difference to you
as your own brothers and sisters?

12 YEARS   12 YEARS   12 YEARS

ME!

DAD'S FAMILY   SIBLINGS   MUM   HALA & GRANDPARENTS   COUSINS, NIECES, NEPHEWS

Who is parent?
Who is sibling?
Who is nuclear?
Who is extended?

When ages and generations
converge, where does one
stop and the other begin?

My dad found it
easier to give
affection to
my cousin...

...and my
uncle to me.

We lapped it up,
from wherever
it came.

This is the extended family.
A cat's cradle magic.

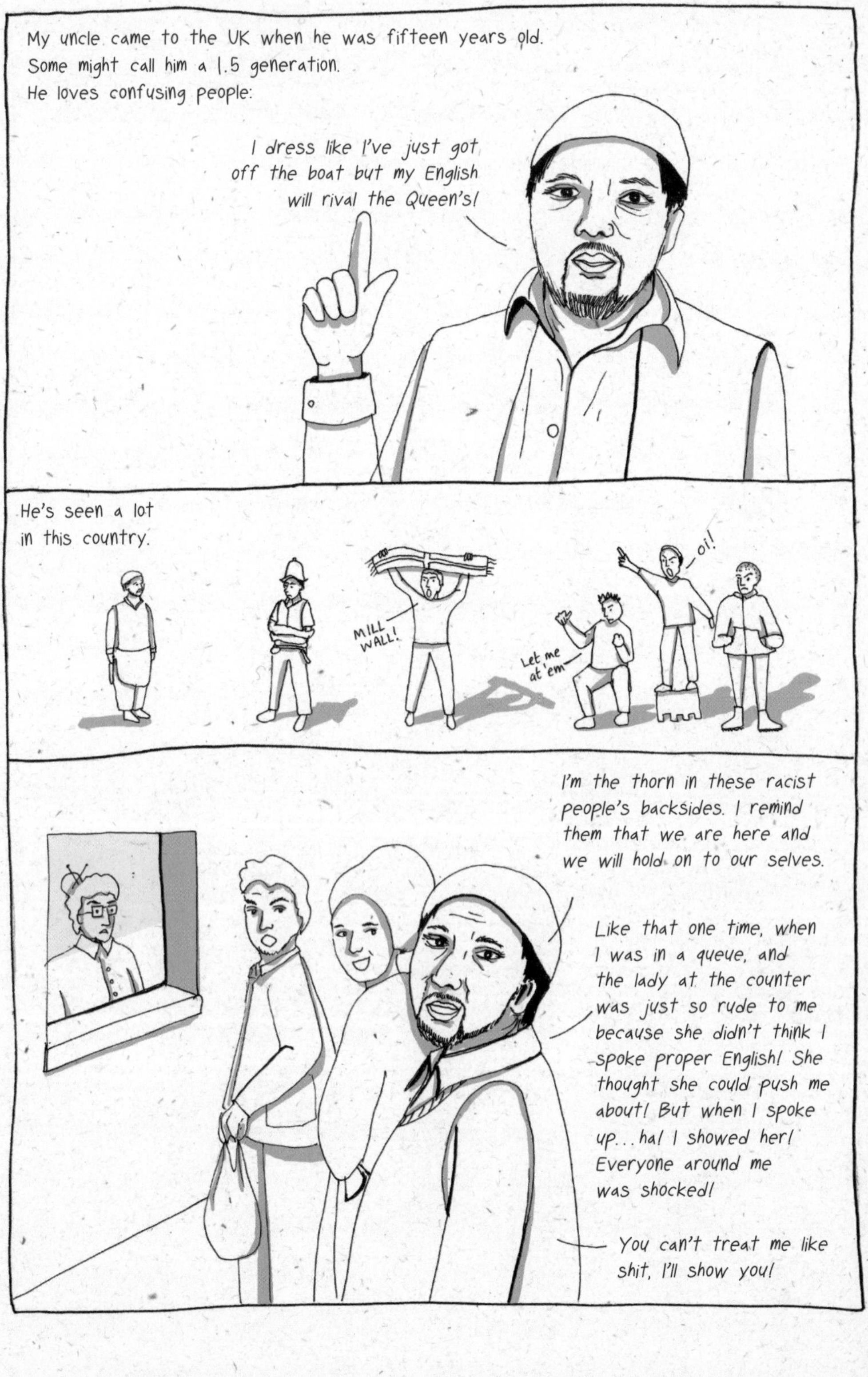
My uncle came to the UK when he was fifteen years old.
Some might call him a 1.5 generation.
He loves confusing people:
I dress like I've just got off the boat but my English will rival the Queen's!
He's seen a lot in this country.
MILL WALL!
Let me at 'em
Oi!
I'm the thorn in these racist people's backsides. I remind them that we are here and we will hold on to our selves.
Like that one time, when I was in a queue, and the lady at the counter was just so rude to me because she didn't think I spoke proper English! She thought she could push me about! But when I spoke up... ha! I showed her! Everyone around me was shocked!
You can't treat me like shit, I'll show you!

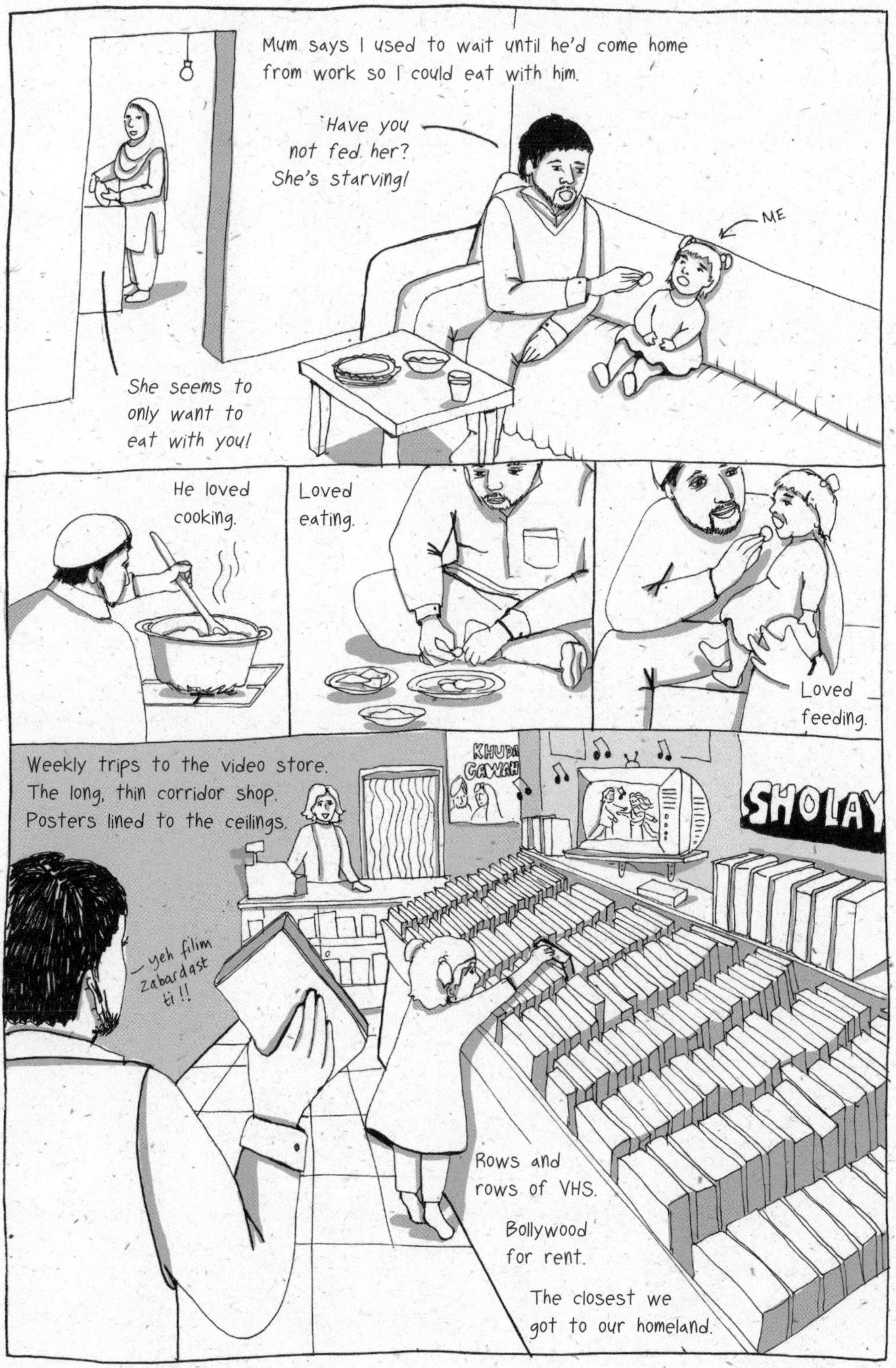
Mum says I used to wait until he'd come home from work so I could eat with him.
Have you not fed her? She's starving!
ME
She seems to only want to eat with you!
He loved cooking.
Loved eating.
Loved feeding.
Weekly trips to the video store. The long, thin corridor shop. Posters lined to the ceilings.
KHUDA GAWAH
SHOLAY
yeh filim zabardast ti!!
Rows and rows of VHS.
Bollywood for rent.
The closest we got to our homeland.

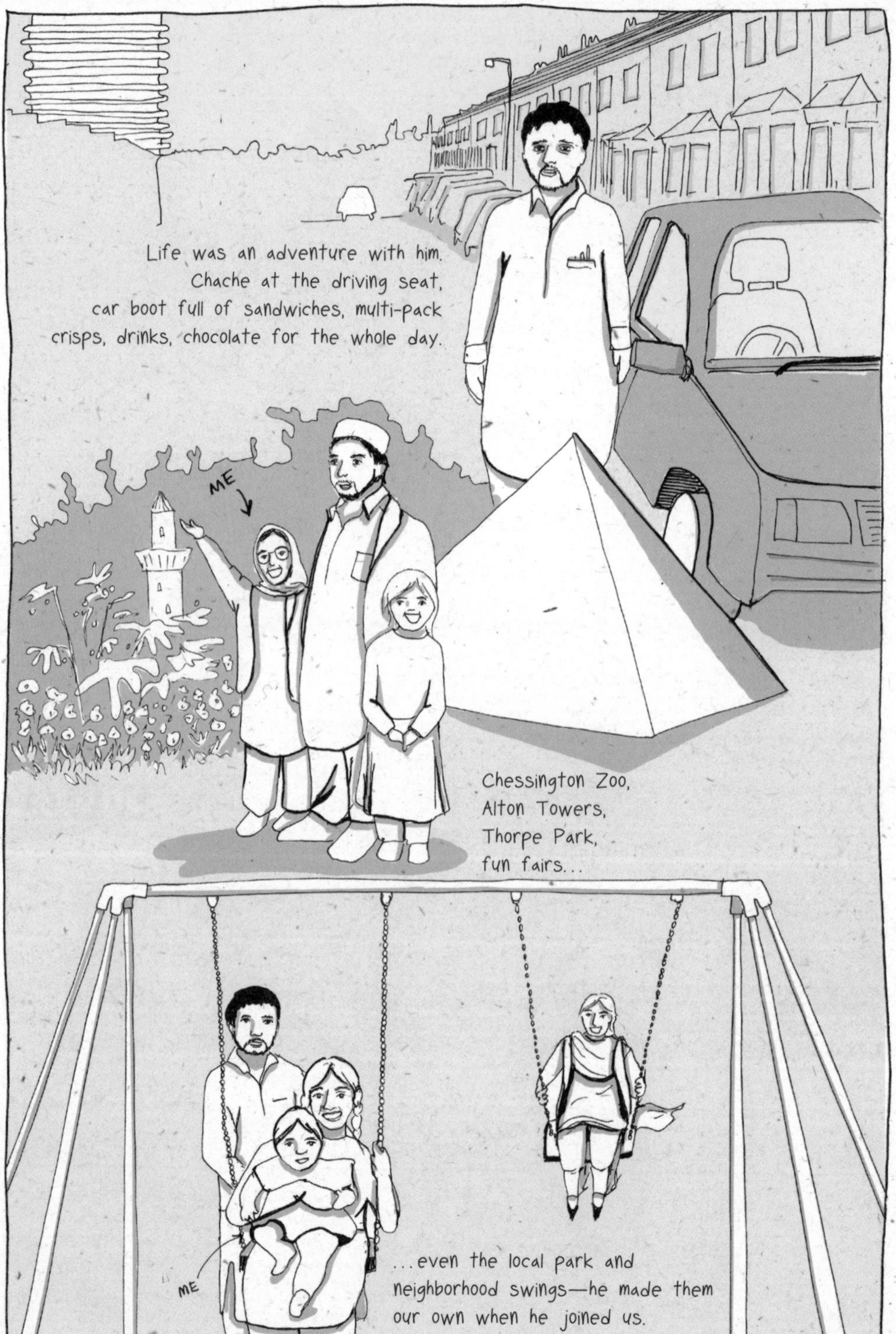
Life was an adventure with him.
Chache at the driving seat,
car boot full of sandwiches, multi-pack
crisps, drinks, chocolate for the whole day.
ME
Chessington Zoo,
Alton Towers,
Thorpe Park,
fun fairs...
ME
...even the local park and
neighborhood swings—he made them
our own when he joined us.

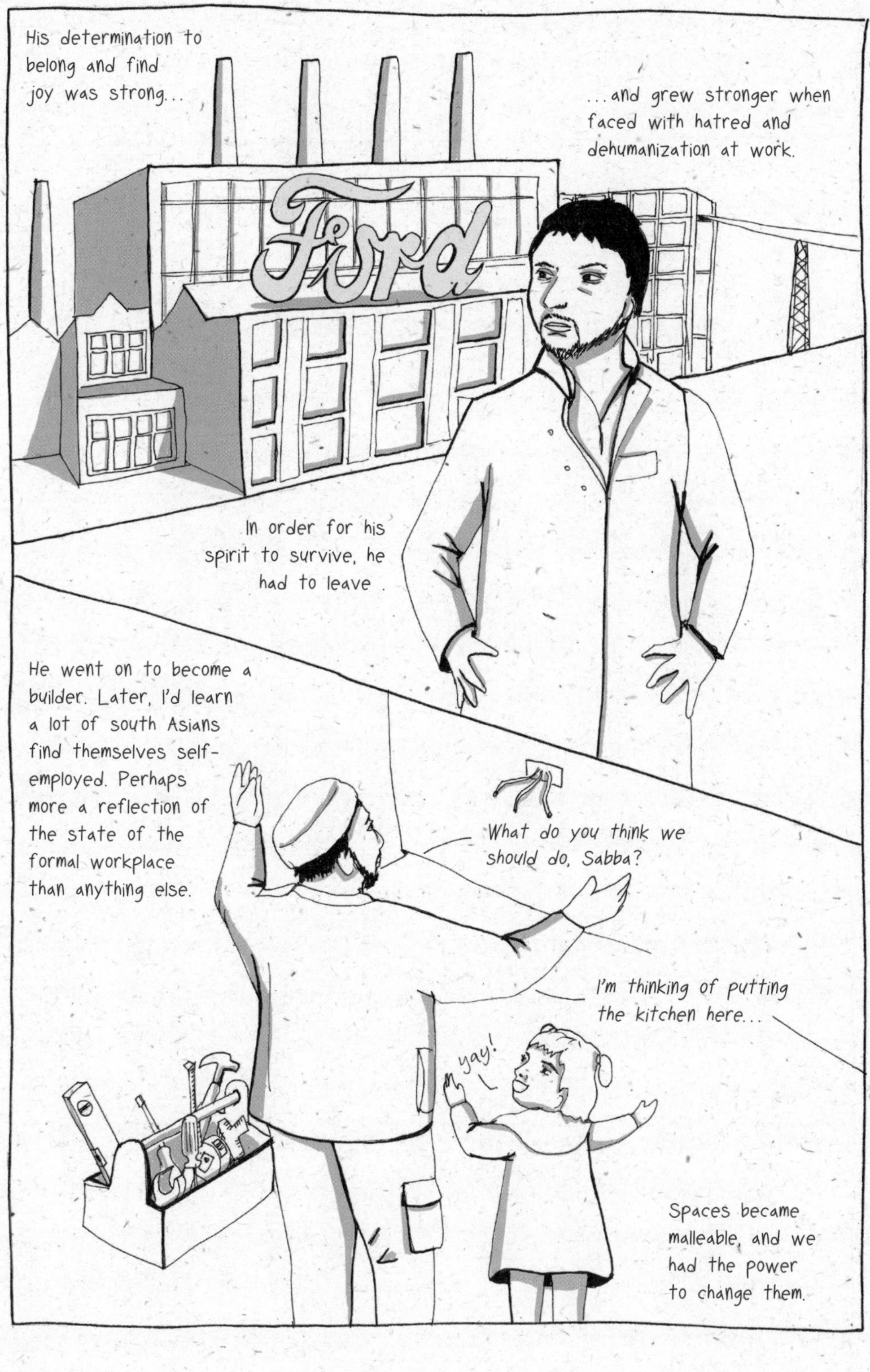
His determination to belong and find joy was strong...
...and grew stronger when faced with hatred and dehumanization at work.
Ford
In order for his spirit to survive, he had to leave .
He went on to become a builder. Later, I'd learn a lot of south Asians find themselves self-employed. Perhaps more a reflection of the state of the formal workplace than anything else.
What do you think we should do, Sabba?
I'm thinking of putting the kitchen here...
yay!
Spaces became malleable, and we had the power to change them.

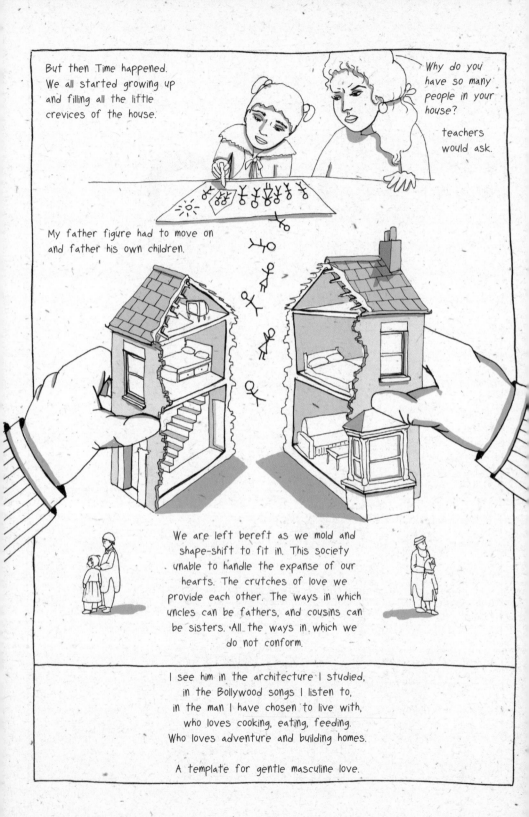

But then Time happened. We all started growing up and filling all the little crevices of the house.

Why do you have so many people in your house?

teachers would ask.

My father figure had to move on and father his own children.

We are left bereft as we mold and shape-shift to fit in. This society unable to handle the expanse of our hearts. The crutches of love we provide each other. The ways in which uncles can be fathers, and cousins can be sisters. All the ways in which we do not conform.

I see him in the architecture I studied, in the Bollywood songs I listen to, in the man I have chosen to live with, who loves cooking, eating, feeding. Who loves adventure and building homes.

A template for gentle masculine love.

They call it groupthink.
When a connected group of people makes irrational
or dysfunctional decisions because the desire to
maintain group harmony overrides logic or reason.

I often wonder what kind of life we would have
lived if Mum had left Dad during their difficult
days. Every couple has difficult days, for sure,
but are all as limited as she was?

They call it group-think.
But I do wonder, would the violence have stopped if
she'd left him? Would a different type of violence
have just filled its place? One of loneliness, financial
insecurity, and no support network?

I think of all the personal sacrifices she has made so she can maintain relations with her parents, her siblings, her children. People that would otherwise have been lost to her had she left the family system.

They call it group-think.
But is it fair to critique the group when the world beyond the group proves to be unsafe? It's hard to acknowledge this, but the years of angst toward my mum subside some as I realize that she really had no option other than to stay in line.

I realize I'd looked at her life with the lens of who I am. I'd applied my set of paths and options to her, and actually it isn't fair to do that. Her generation survived based on the options and knowledge available in their time.

I realize, the only sustainable way out of group-think is to, over generations, open up different ways of being, alternative options, and new possibilities for each other.

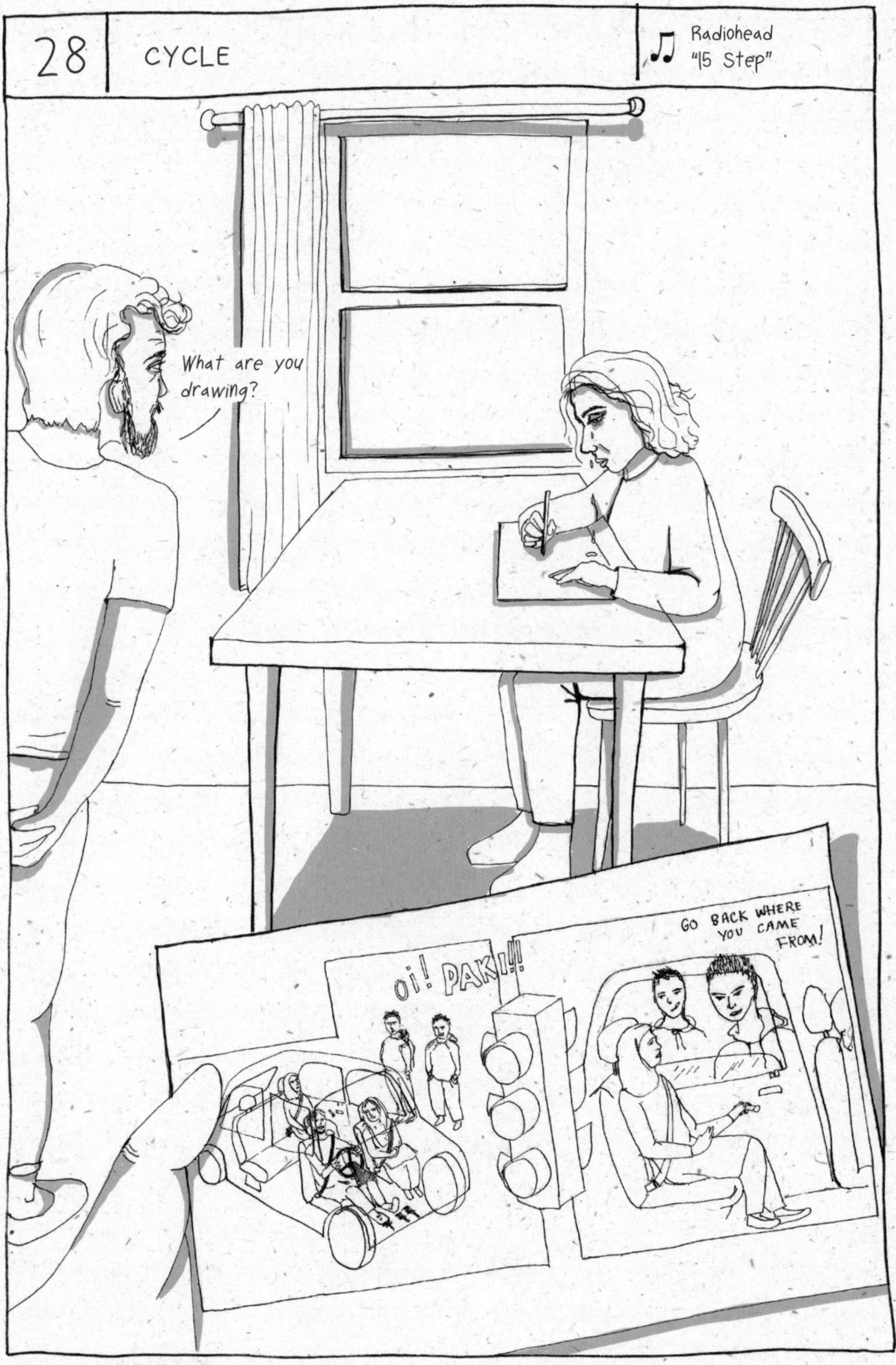
28
CYCLE
Radiohead
"15 Step"
What are you drawing?
oi! PAKI!!
GO BACK WHERE YOU CAME FROM!

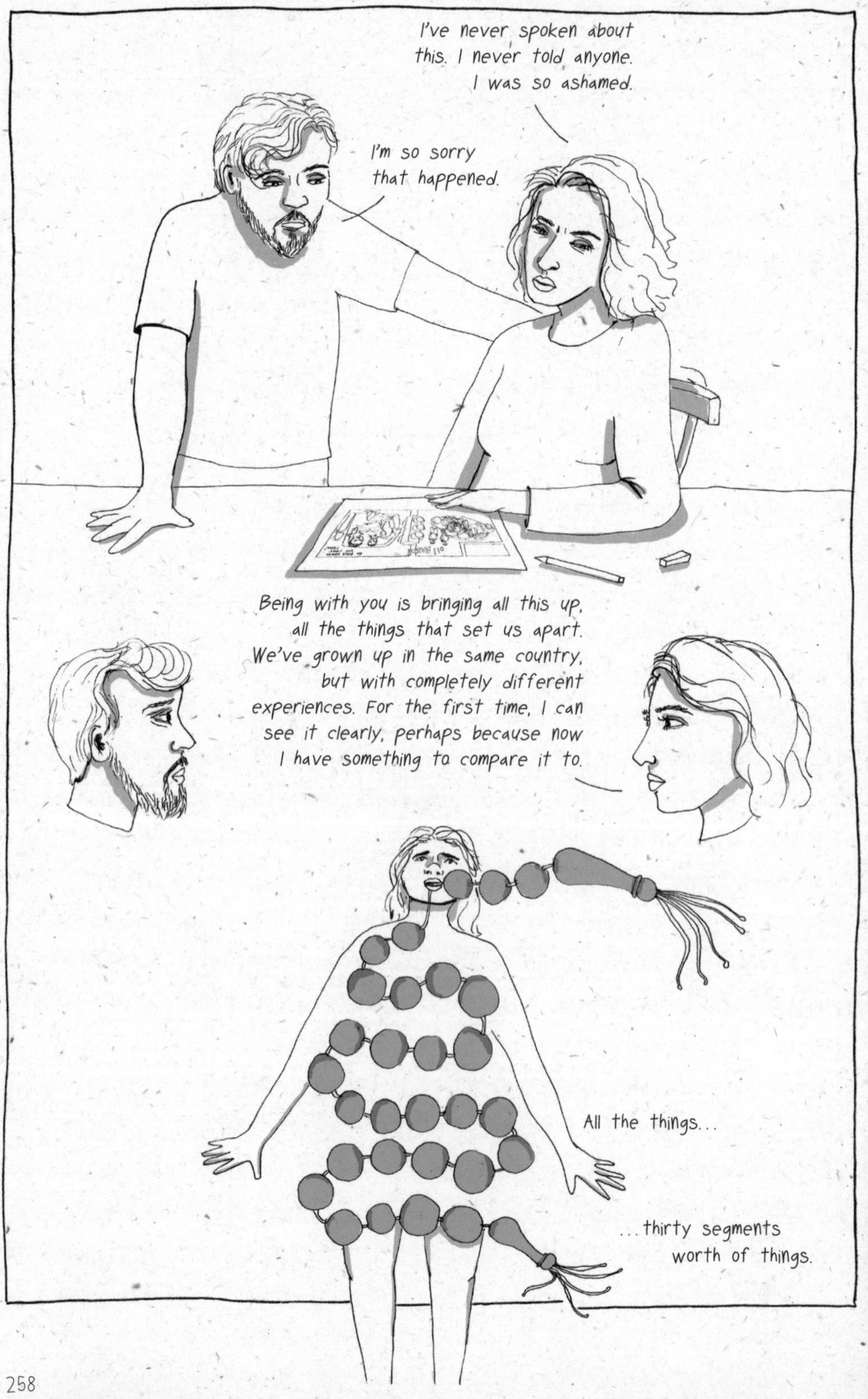
I've never spoken about this. I never told anyone. I was so ashamed.
I'm so sorry that happened.
Being with you is bringing all this up, all the things that set us apart. We've grown up in the same country, but with completely different experiences. For the first time, I can see it clearly, perhaps because now I have something to compare it to.
All the things...
...thirty segments worth of things.

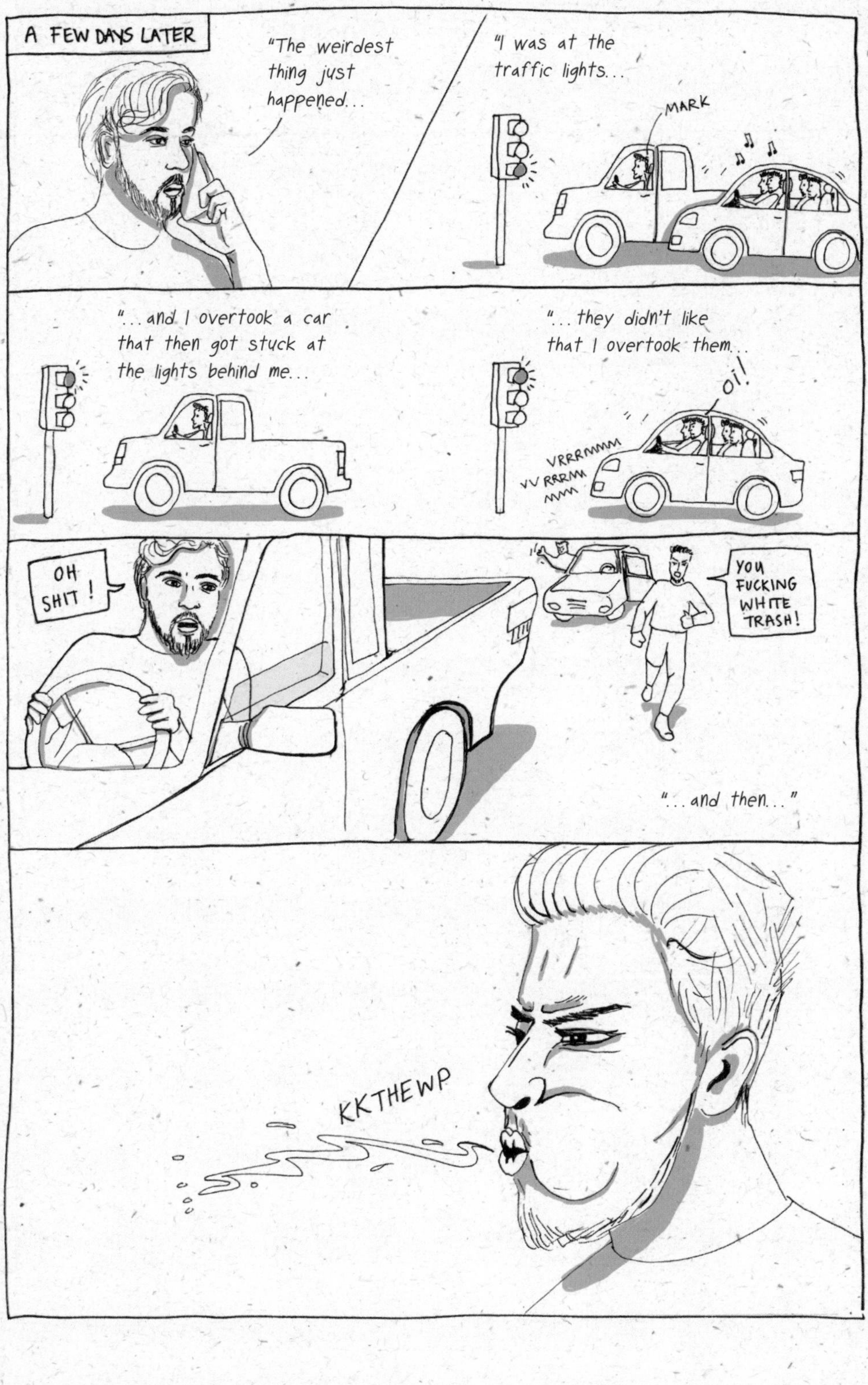
A FEW DAYS LATER
"The weirdest thing just happened...
"I was at the traffic lights...
MARK
"...and I overtook a car that then got stuck at the lights behind me...
"...they didn't like that I overtook them...
OI!
VRRRMMM
VV RRRM
MMM
OH SHIT!
YOU FUCKING WHITE TRASH!
"...and then..."
KKTHEWP

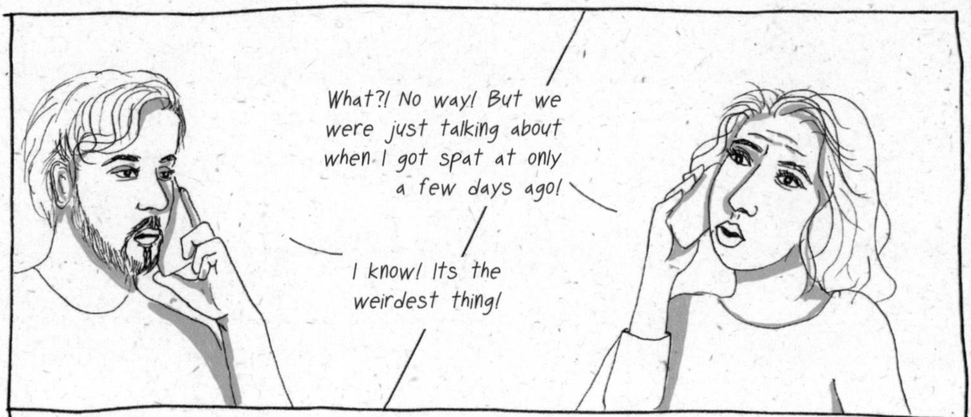
What?! No way! But we were just talking about when I got spat at only a few days ago!
I know! Its the weirdest thing!

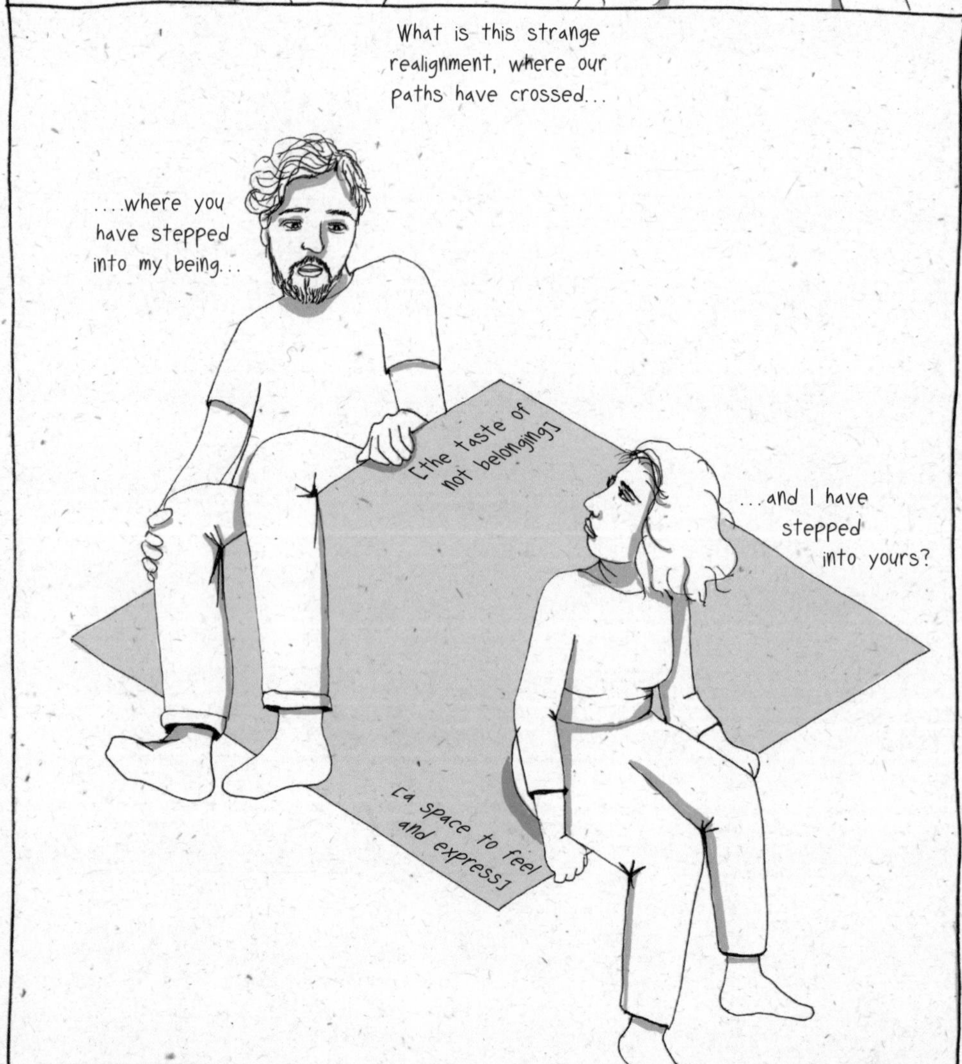
What is this strange realignment, where our paths have crossed...
....where you have stepped into my being...
[the taste of not belonging]
...and I have stepped into yours?
[a space to feel and express]

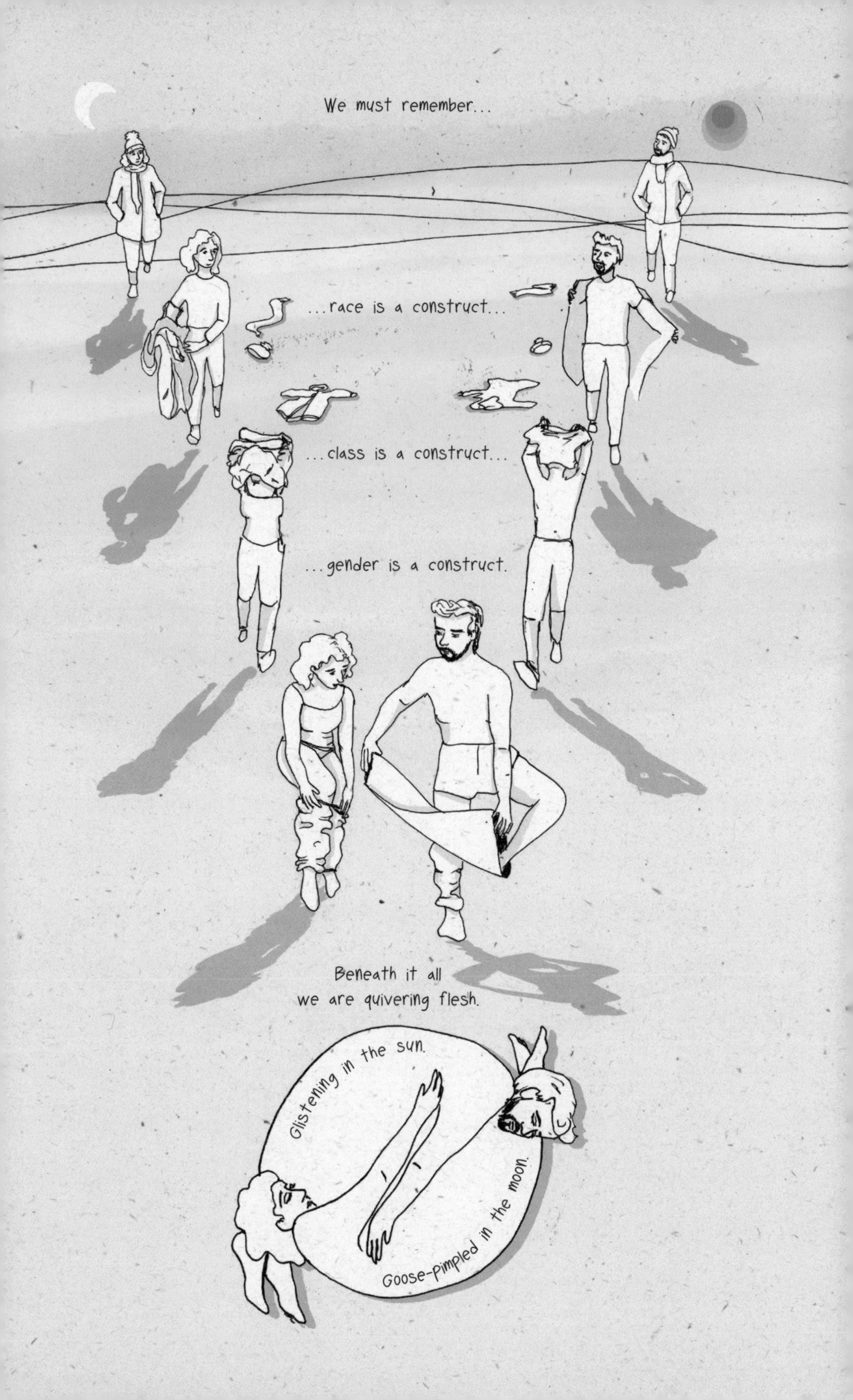
We must remember...
...race is a construct...
...class is a construct...
...gender is a construct.
Beneath it all
we are quivering flesh.
Glistening in the sun.
Goose-pimpled in the moon.

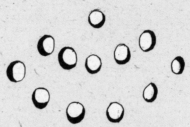

The power of vulnerability

to heal our souls

to fill the cracks with golden liquid.

Wabi sabi.

An imperfect beauty.

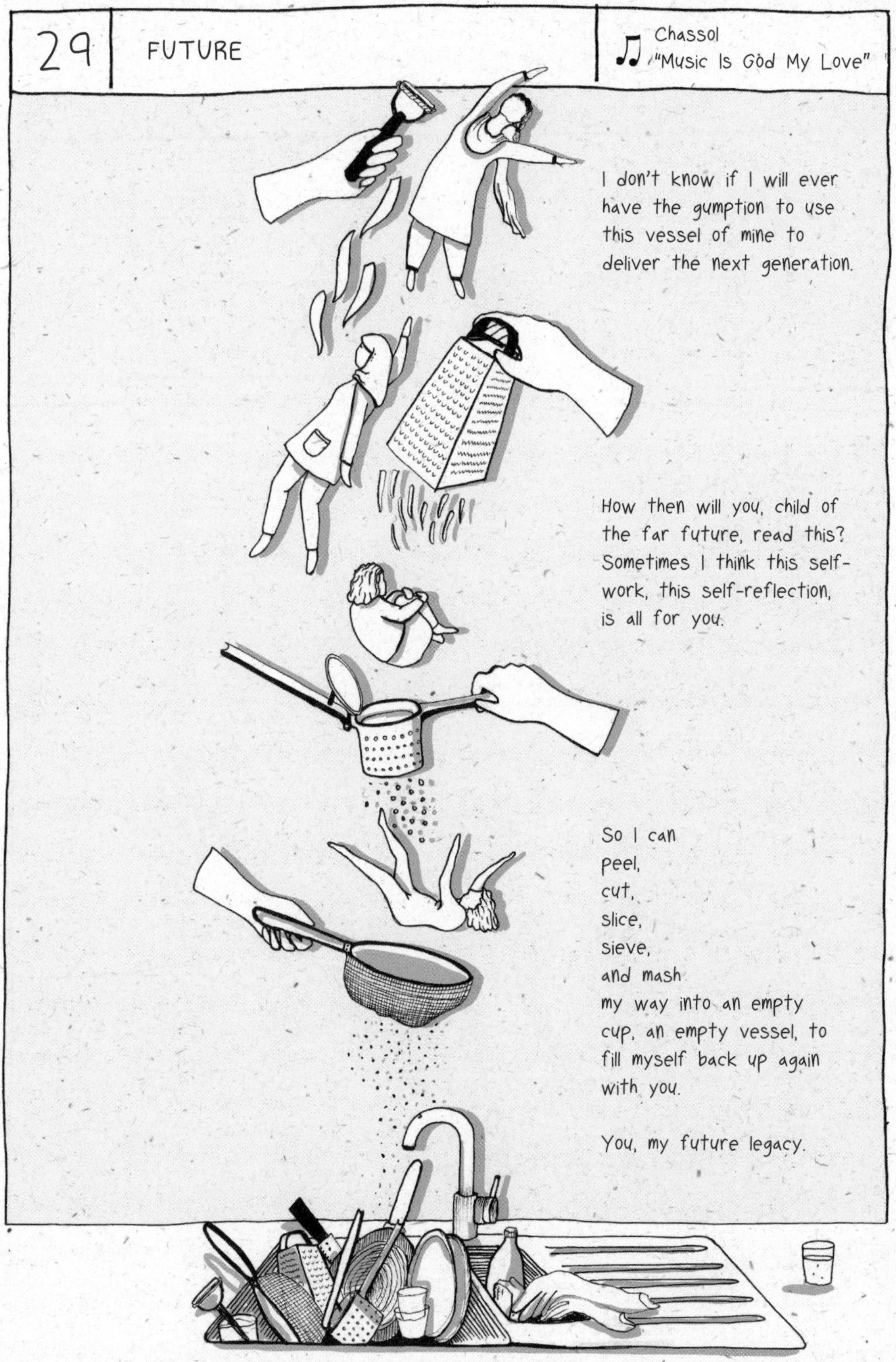
29
FUTURE
Chassol
"Music Is God My Love"
I don't know if I will ever have the gumption to use this vessel of mine to deliver the next generation.
How then will you, child of the far future, read this? Sometimes I think this self-work, this self-reflection, is all for you.
So I can
peel,
cut,
slice,
sieve,
and mash
my way into an empty cup, an empty vessel, to fill myself back up again with you.
You, my future legacy.

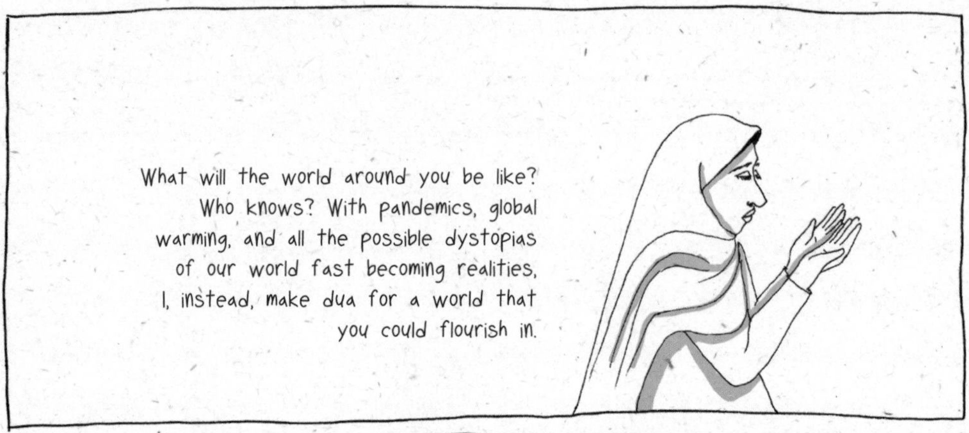
What will the world around you be like? Who knows? With pandemics, global warming, and all the possible dystopias of our world fast becoming realities, I, instead, make dua for a world that you could flourish in.

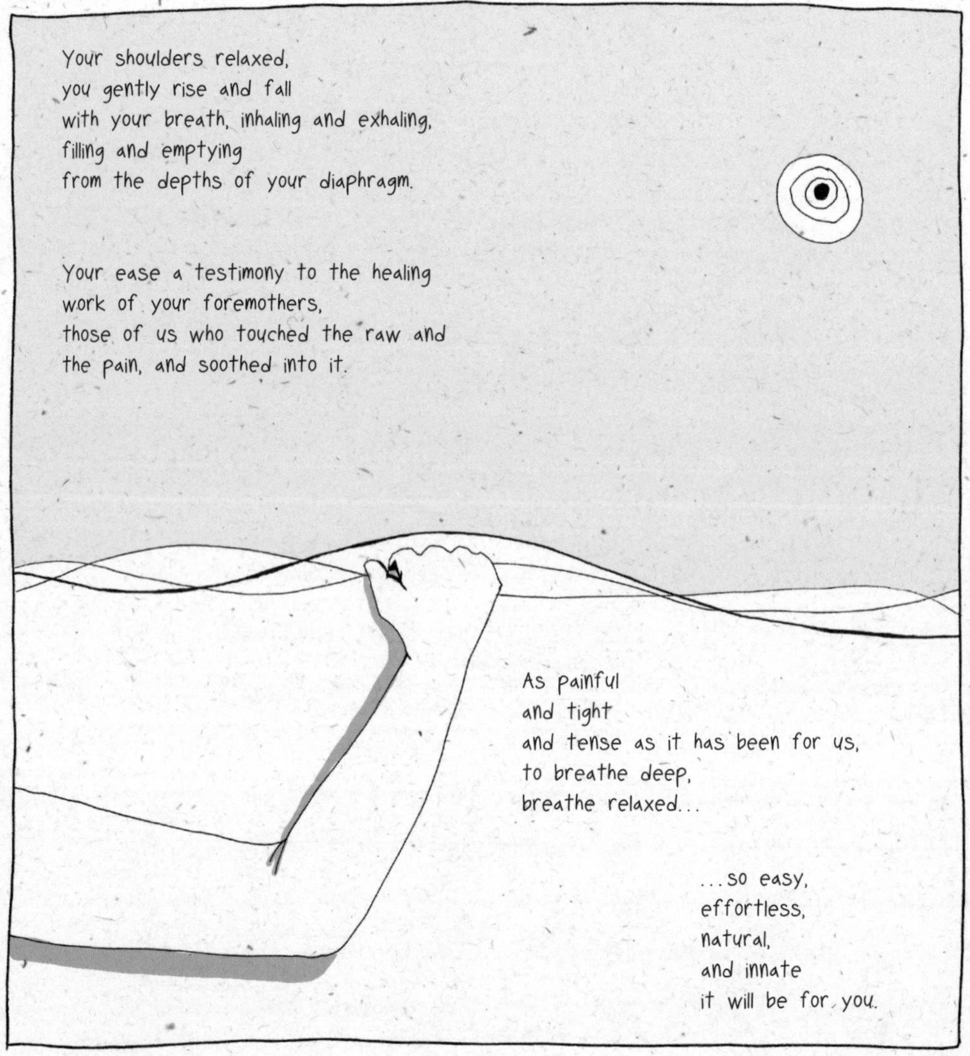
Your shoulders relaxed,
you gently rise and fall
with your breath, inhaling and exhaling,
filling and emptying
from the depths of your diaphragm.
Your ease a testimony to the healing
work of your foremothers,
those of us who touched the raw and
the pain, and soothed into it.
As painful
and tight
and tense as it has been for us,
to breathe deep,
breathe relaxed...
...so easy,
effortless,
natural,
and innate
it will be for you.

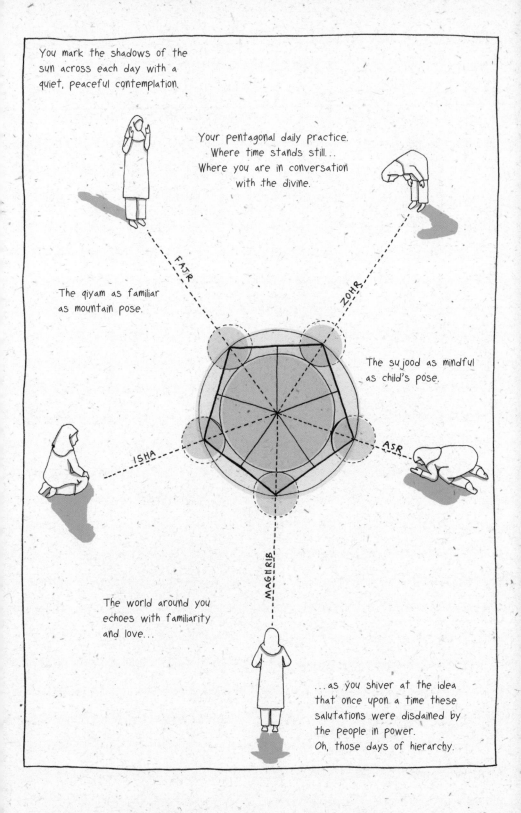

You mark the shadows of the sun across each day with a quiet, peaceful contemplation.

Your pentagonal daily practice. Where time stands still... Where you are in conversation with the divine.

The qiyam as familiar as mountain pose.

The sujood as mindful as child's pose.

FAJR

ZOHR

ISHA

ASR

MAGHRIB

The world around you echoes with familiarity and love...

...as you shiver at the idea that once upon a time these salutations were disdained by the people in power.
Oh, those days of hierarchy.

Each living vessel now...

...in pursuit of divine justice,
divine equilibrium...

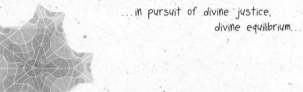

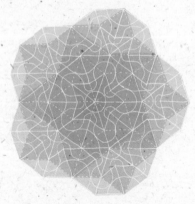

...shown to us in ninety-nine ways.

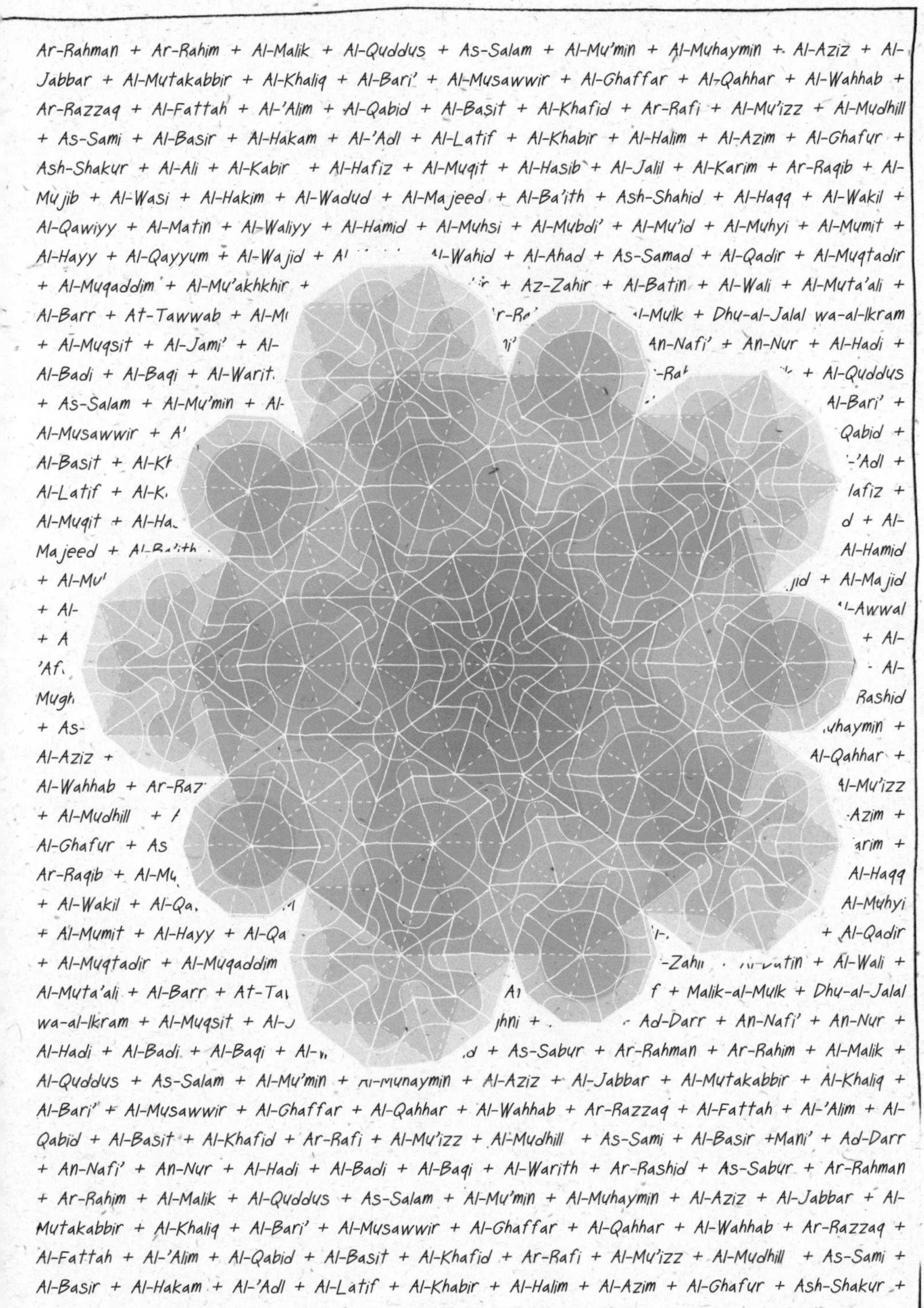

Ar-Rahman + Ar-Rahim + Al-Malik + Al-Quddus + As-Salam + Al-Mu'min + Al-Muhaymin + Al-Aziz + Al-Jabbar + Al-Mutakabbir + Al-Khaliq + Al-Bari' + Al-Musawwir + Al-Ghaffar + Al-Qahhar + Al-Wahhab + Ar-Razzaq + Al-Fattah + Al-'Alim + Al-Qabid + Al-Basit + Al-Khafid + Ar-Rafi + Al-Mu'izz + Al-Mudhill + As-Sami + Al-Basir + Al-Hakam + Al-'Adl + Al-Latif + Al-Khabir + Al-Halim + Al-Azim + Al-Ghafur + Ash-Shakur + Al-Ali + Al-Kabir + Al-Hafiz + Al-Muqit + Al-Hasib + Al-Jalil + Al-Karim + Ar-Raqib + Al-Mujib + Al-Wasi + Al-Hakim + Al-Wadud + Al-Majeed + Al-Ba'ith + Ash-Shahid + Al-Haqq + Al-Wakil + Al-Qawiyy + Al-Matin + Al-Waliyy + Al-Hamid + Al-Muhsi + Al-Mubdi' + Al-Mu'id + Al-Muhyi + Al-Mumit + Al-Hayy + Al-Qayyum + Al-Wajid + Al____ ____Al-Wahid + Al-Ahad + As-Samad + Al-Qadir + Al-Muqtadir + Al-Muqaddim + Al-Mu'akhkhir + ____ ____r + Az-Zahir + Al-Batin + Al-Wali + Al-Muta'ali + Al-Barr + At-Tawwab + Al-M____ ____r-Re____ ____l-Mulk + Dhu-al-Jalal wa-al-Ikram + Al-Muqsit + Al-Jami' + Al-____ ____ ____ ____An-Nafi' + An-Nur + Al-Hadi + Al-Badi + Al-Baqi + Al-Warit____ ____-Ra____ ____ + Al-Quddus + As-Salam + Al-Mu'min + Al-____ ____Al-Bari' + Al-Musawwir + A'____ ____Qabid + Al-Basit + Al-Kh____ ____-'Adl + Al-Latif + Al-K.____ ____lafiz + Al-Muqit + Al-Ha____ ____d + Al-Majeed + Al-Ba'ith____ ____Al-Hamid + Al-Mu'____ ____jid + Al-Majid + Al-____ ____'l-Awwal + A____ ____+ Al- + A____ ____+ Al- 'Af____ ____- Al- Mugh____ ____Rashid + As-____ ____uhaymin Al-Aziz +____ ____Al-Qahhar Al-Wahhab + Ar-Raz____ ____Al-Mu'izz + Al-Mudhill + /____ ____Azim + Al-Ghafur + As____ ____arim + Ar-Raqib + Al-Mu____ ____Al-Haqq + Al-Wakil + Al-Qa,____ ____Al-Muhyi + Al-Mumit + Al-Hayy + Al-Qa____ ____+ Al-Qadir + Al-Muqtadir + Al-Muqaddim____ ____-Zahir + Al-Batin + Al-Wali + Al-Muta'ali + Al-Barr + At-Ta____ ____f + Malik-al-Mulk + Dhu-al-Jalal wa-al-Ikram + Al-Muqsit + Al-J____ ____jhni +____ ____Ad-Darr + An-Nafi' + An-Nur + Al-Hadi + Al-Badi + Al-Baqi + Al-w____ ____d + As-Sabur + Ar-Rahman + Ar-Rahim + Al-Malik + Al-Quddus + As-Salam + Al-Mu'min + Al-Muhaymin + Al-Aziz + Al-Jabbar + Al-Mutakabbir + Al-Khaliq + Al-Bari' + Al-Musawwir + Al-Ghaffar + Al-Qahhar + Al-Wahhab + Ar-Razzaq + Al-Fattah + Al-'Alim + Al-Qabid + Al-Basit + Al-Khafid + Ar-Rafi + Al-Mu'izz + Al-Mudhill + As-Sami + Al-Basir + Mani' + Ad-Darr + An-Nafi' + An-Nur + Al-Hadi + Al-Badi + Al-Baqi + Al-Warith + Ar-Rashid + As-Sabur + Ar-Rahman + Ar-Rahim + Al-Malik + Al-Quddus + As-Salam + Al-Mu'min + Al-Muhaymin + Al-Aziz + Al-Jabbar + Al-Mutakabbir + Al-Khaliq + Al-Bari' + Al-Musawwir + Al-Ghaffar + Al-Qahhar + Al-Wahhab + Ar-Razzaq + Al-Fattah + Al-'Alim + Al-Qabid + Al-Basit + Al-Khafid + Ar-Rafi + Al-Mu'izz + Al-Mudhill + As-Sami + Al-Basir + Al-Hakam + Al-'Adl + Al-Latif + Al-Khabir + Al-Halim + Al-Azim + Al-Ghafur + Ash-Shakur + Al-Ali + Al-Kabir + Al-Hafiz + Al-Muqit + Al-Hasib + Al-Jalil + Al-Karim + Ar-Raqib

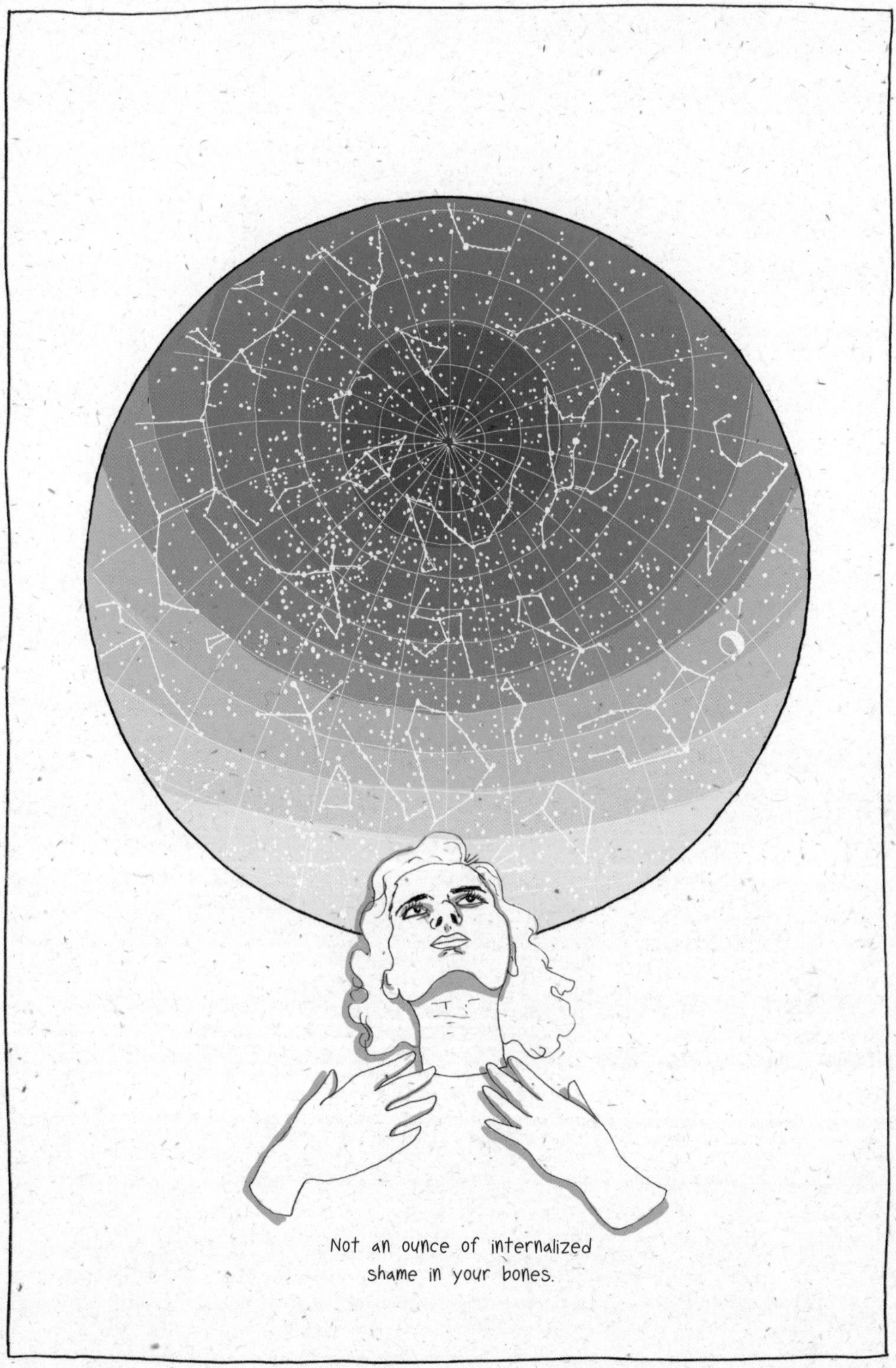
Not an ounce of internalized
shame in your bones.

منزل سے آگے بڑھ کر منزل تلاش کر

مل جائے تجھ کو دریا تو سمندر تلاش کر

Search for the path
beyond the path.

If you find a river
search for an ocean.

ہر شیشہ ٹوٹ جاتا ہے پتھر کی چوٹ سے

پتھر ہی ٹوٹ جائے وہ شیشہ تلاش کر

Every mirror shatters to pieces
when hurt by stone.

That the stone may shatter to pieces,
search for a mirror that has such power.

Poem by Allama Iqbal.
Translated by Shay Khan.

30 WATER

♫ Marlena Shaw
"Woman of the Ghetto (Live)"

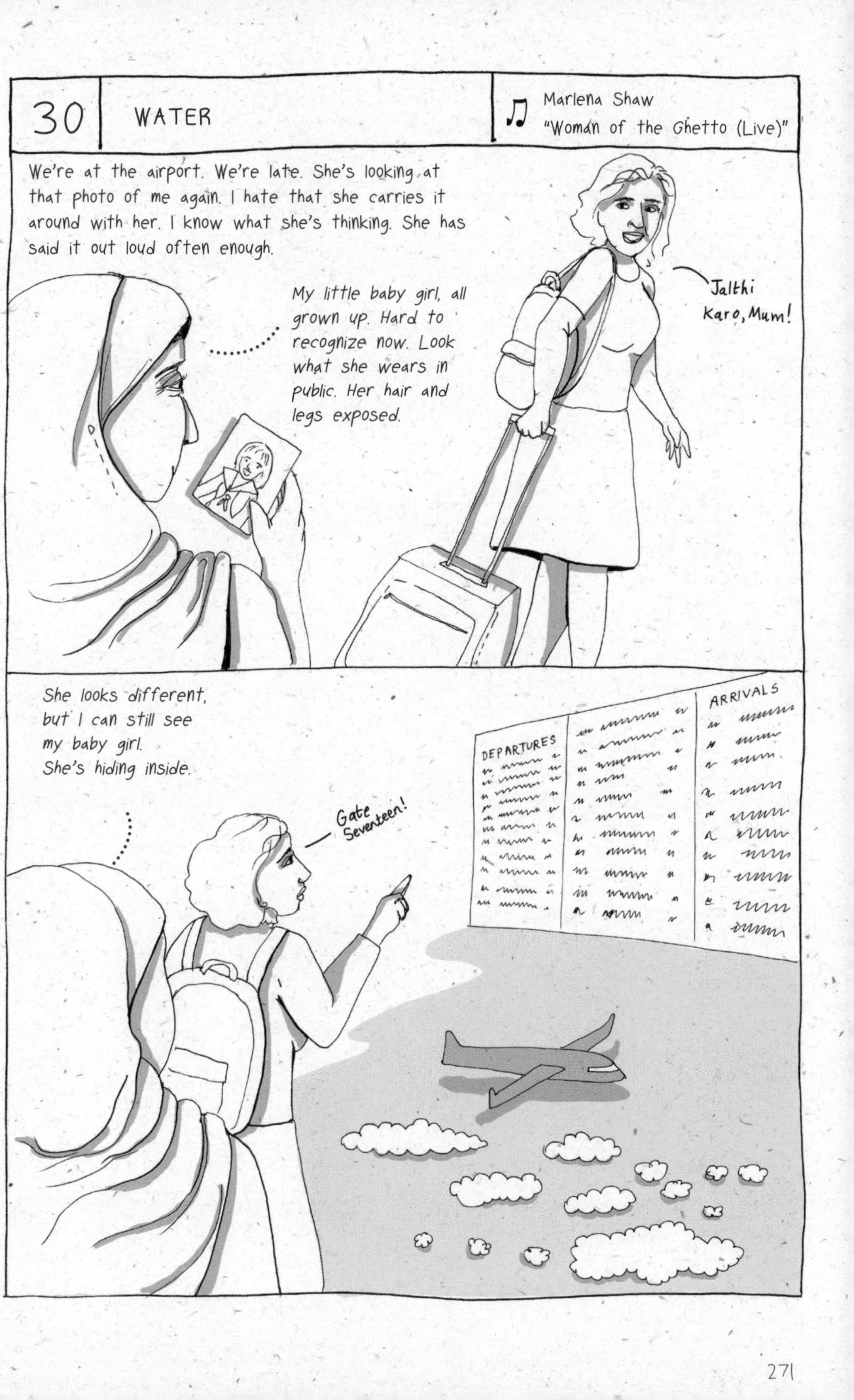

We're at the airport. We're late. She's looking at that photo of me again. I hate that she carries it around with her. I know what she's thinking. She has said it out loud often enough.
My little baby girl, all grown up. Hard to recognize now. Look what she wears in public. Her hair and legs exposed.
Jalthi Karo, Mum!
She looks different, but I can still see my baby girl. She's hiding inside.
Gate Seventeen!
DEPARTURES
ARRIVALS

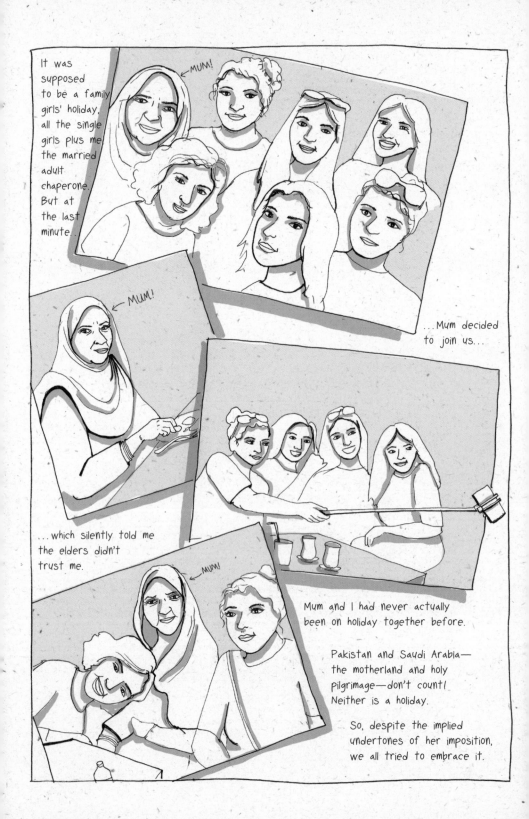

It was supposed to be a family girls' holiday, all the single girls plus me the married adult chaperone. But at the last minute...

← MUM!

← MUM!

...Mum decided to join us...

...which silently told me the elders didn't trust me.

← MUM!

Mum and I had never actually been on holiday together before.

Pakistan and Saudi Arabia— the motherland and holy pilgrimage—don't count! Neither is a holiday.

So, despite the implied undertones of her imposition, we all tried to embrace it.

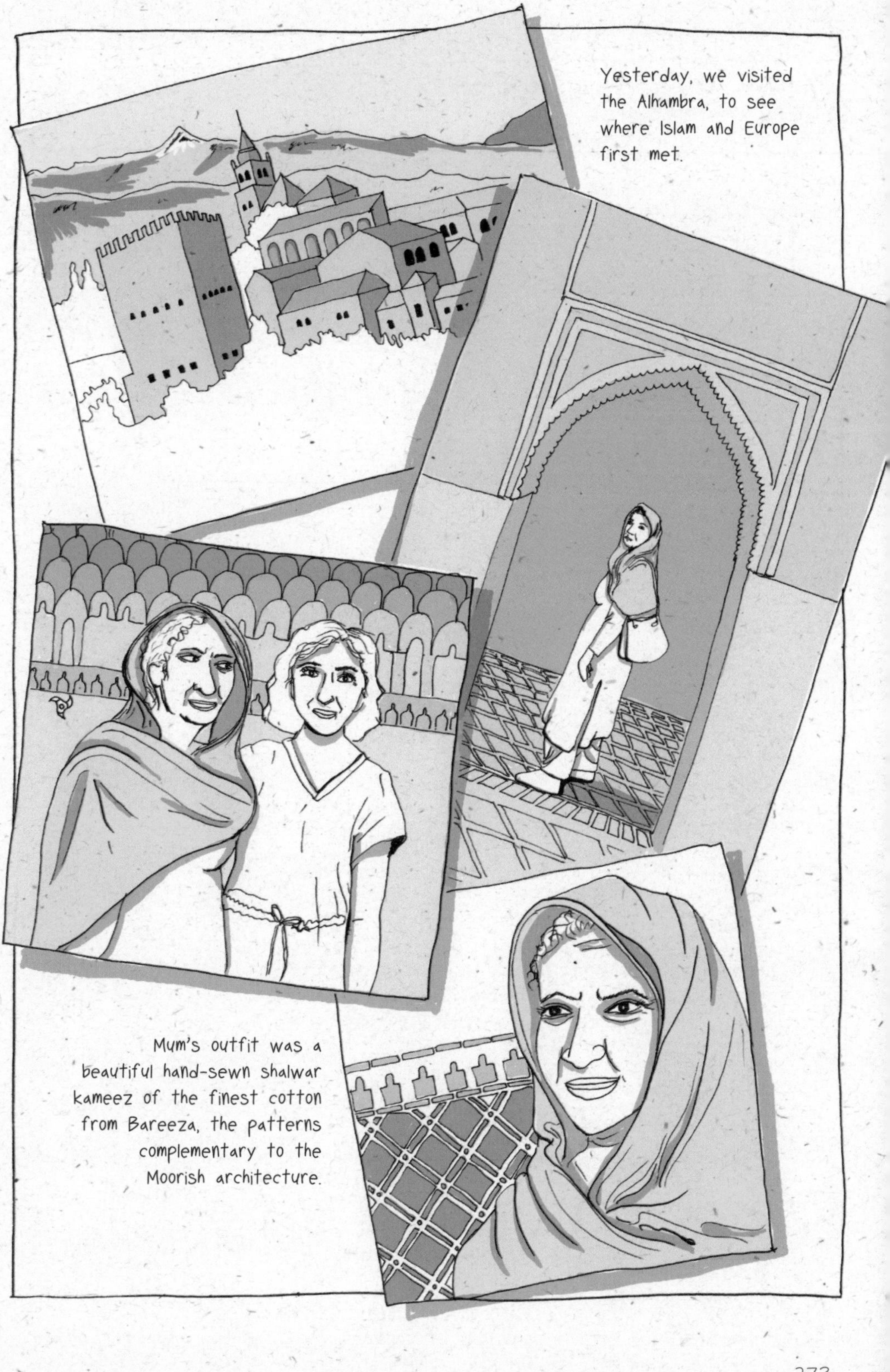
Yesterday, we visited the Alhambra, to see where Islam and Europe first met.
Mum's outfit was a beautiful hand-sewn shalwar kameez of the finest cotton from Bareeza, the patterns complementary to the Moorish architecture.

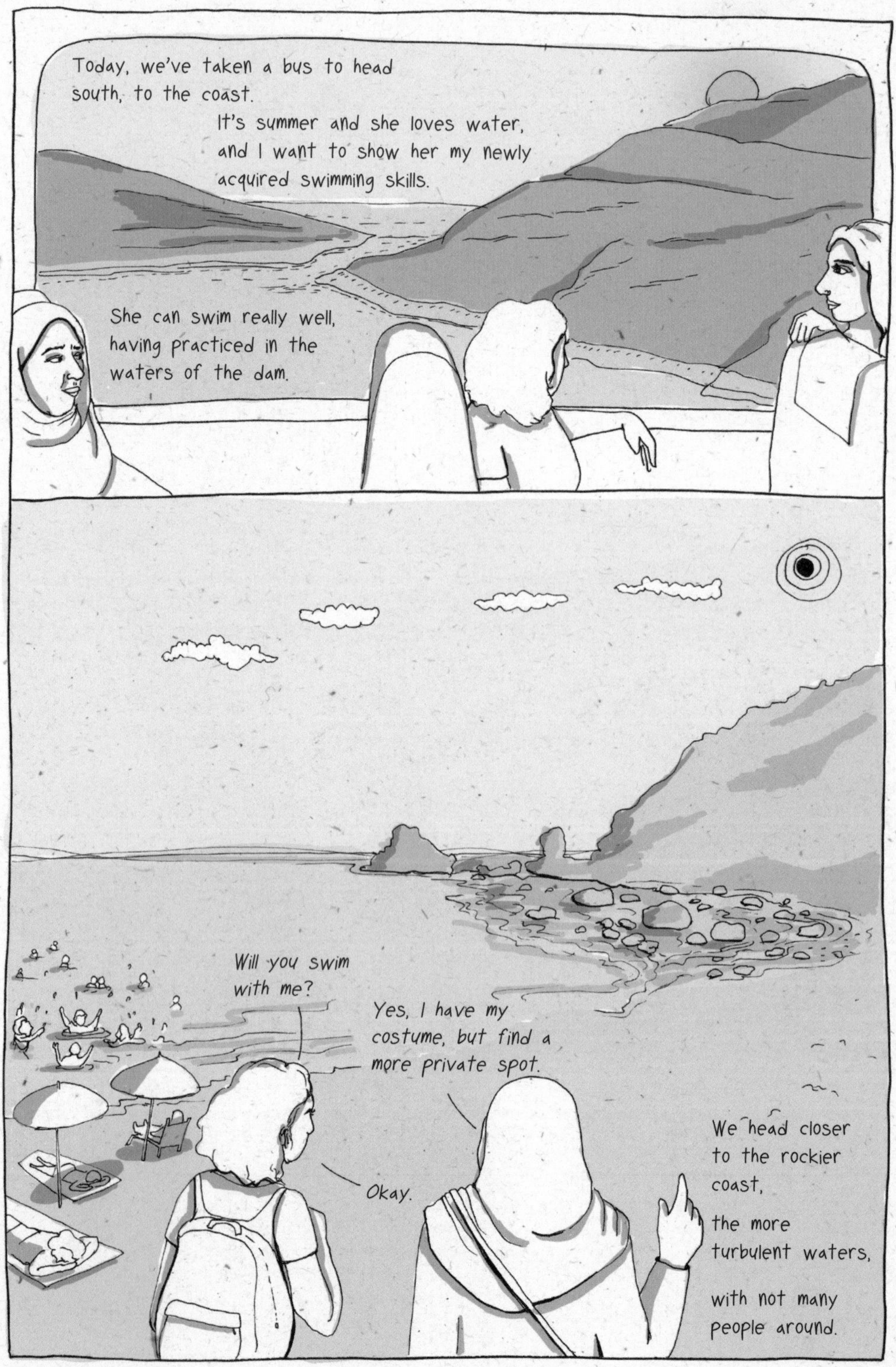
Today, we've taken a bus to head south, to the coast.
It's summer and she loves water, and I want to show her my newly acquired swimming skills.
She can swim really well, having practiced in the waters of the dam.
Will you swim with me?
Yes, I have my costume, but find a more private spot.
Okay.
We head closer to the rockier coast,
the more turbulent waters,
with not many people around.

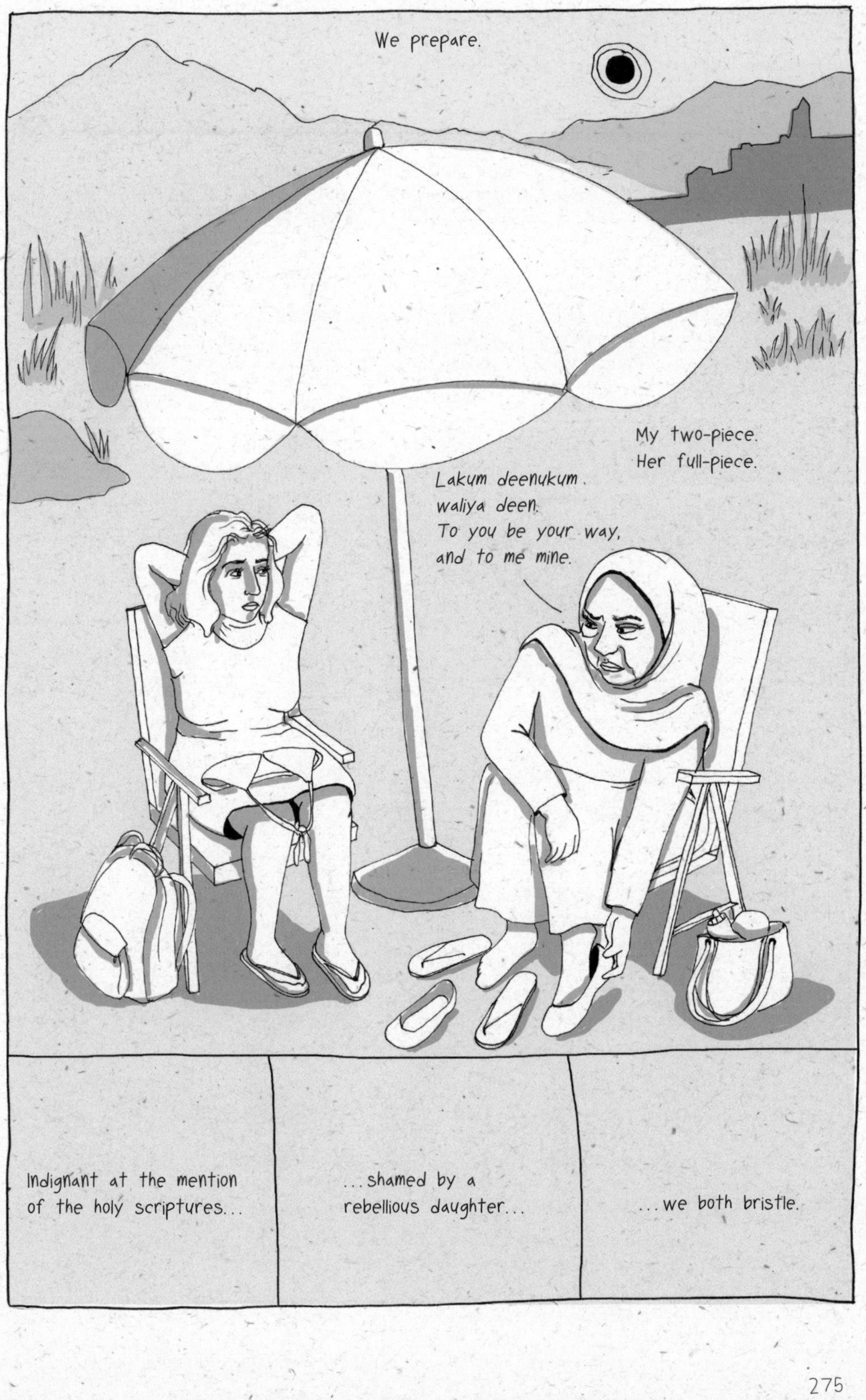
We prepare.
My two-piece.
Her full-piece.
Lakum deenukum waliya deen. To you be your way, and to me mine.
Indignant at the mention of the holy scriptures...
...shamed by a rebellious daughter...
...we both bristle.

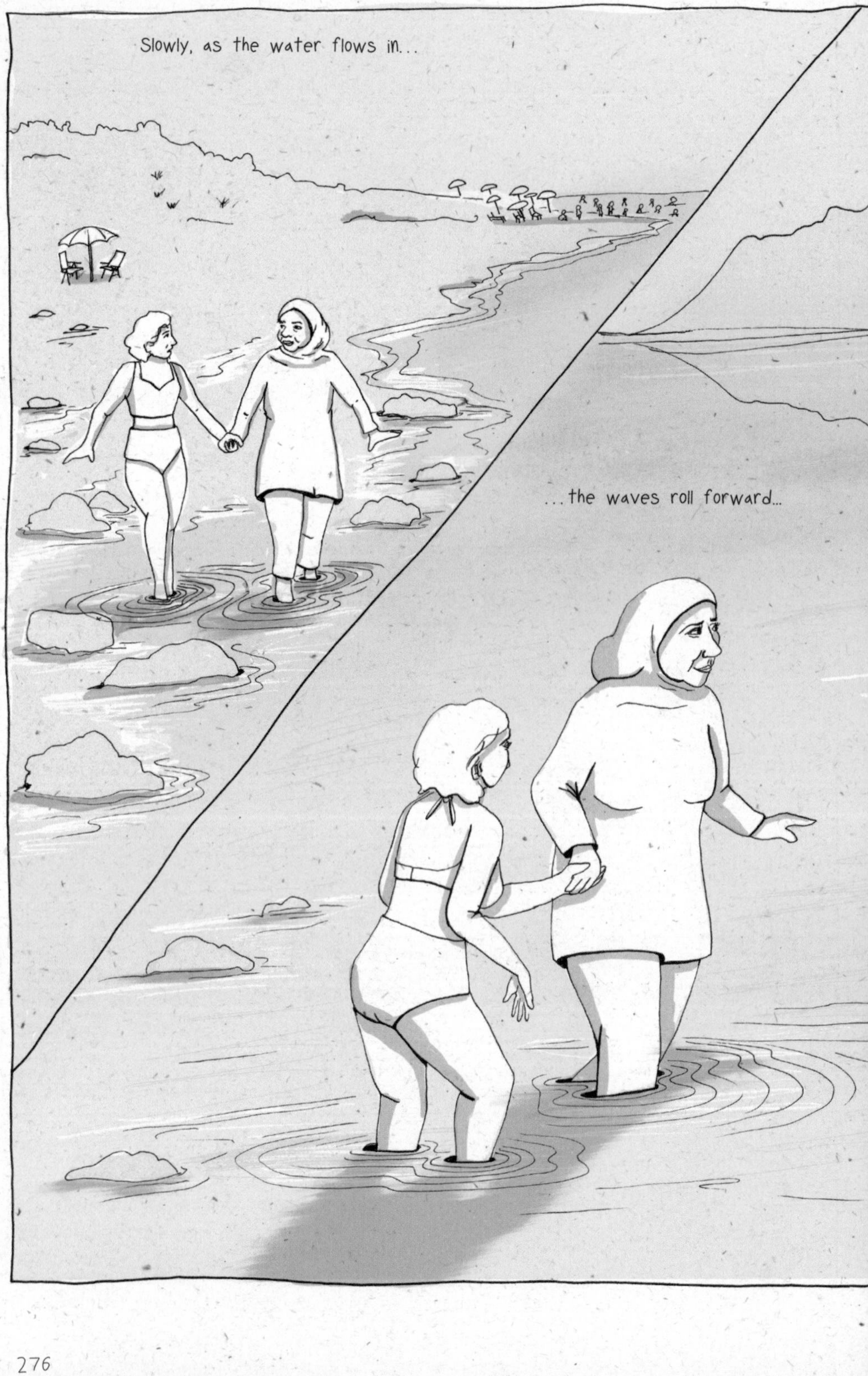
Slowly, as the water flows in...
...the waves roll forward...

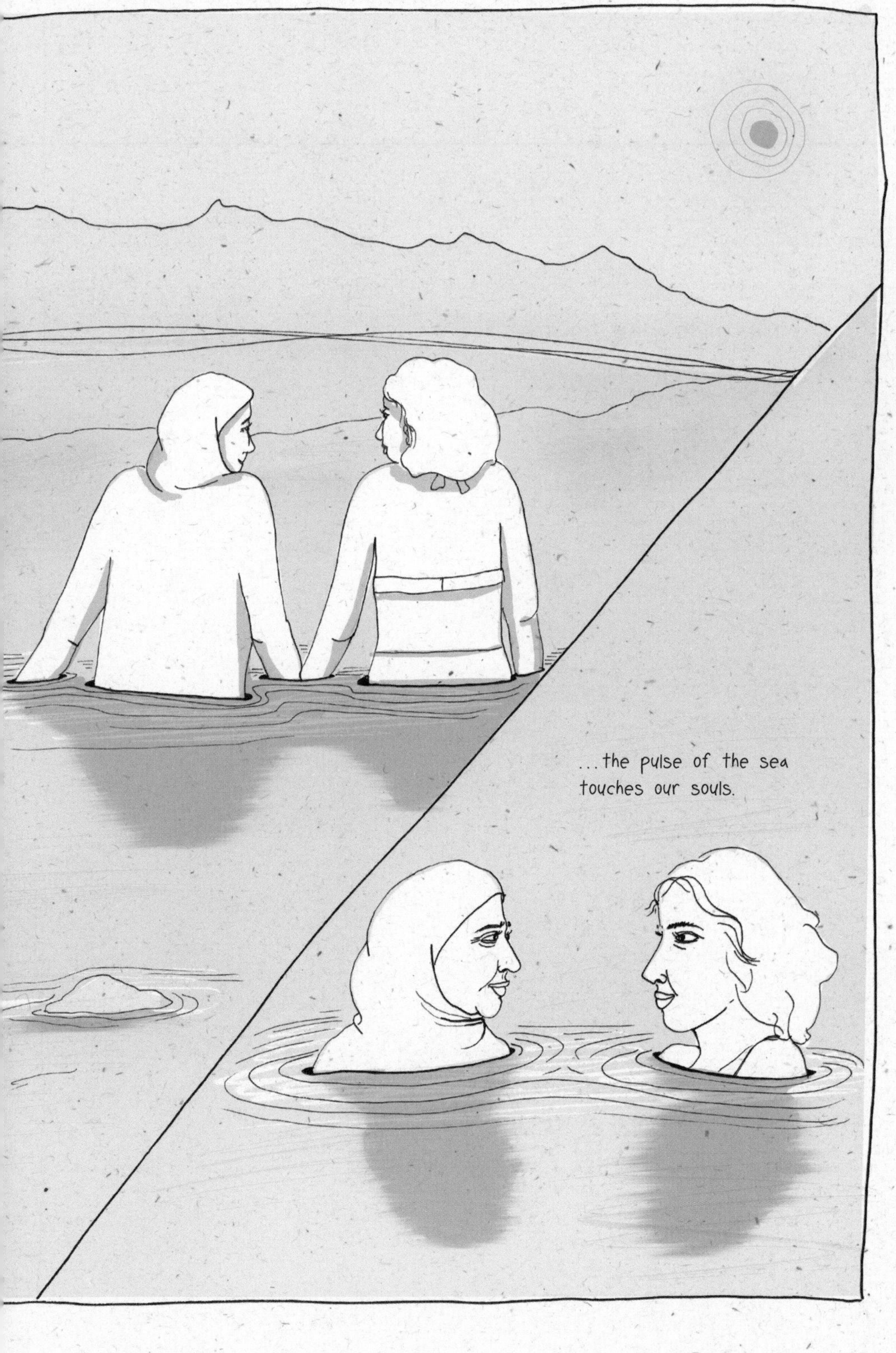
...the pulse of the sea
touches our souls.

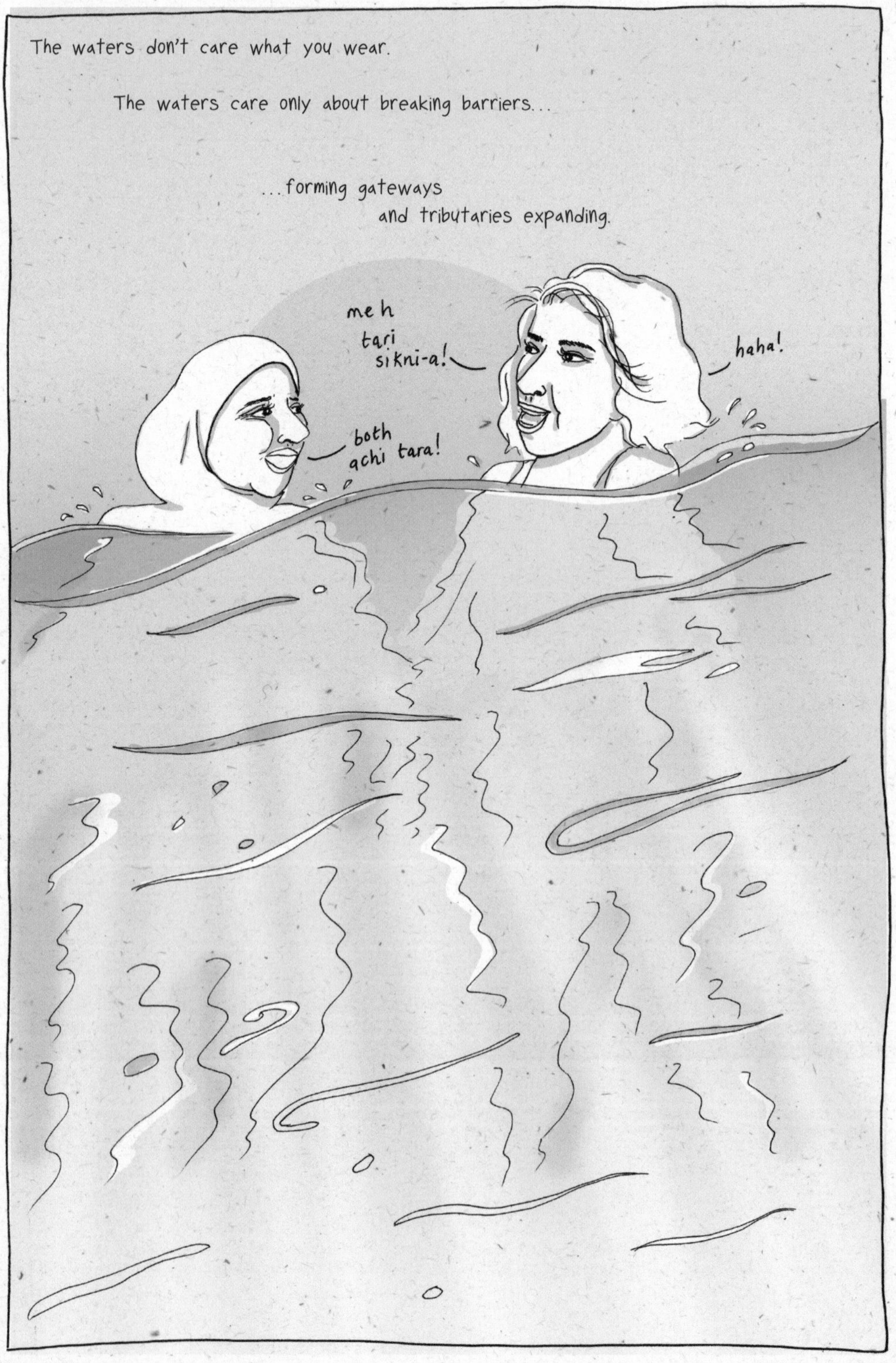
The waters don't care what you wear.
The waters care only about breaking barriers...
...forming gateways
and tributaries expanding.
meh tari sikni-a!
both achi tara!
haha!

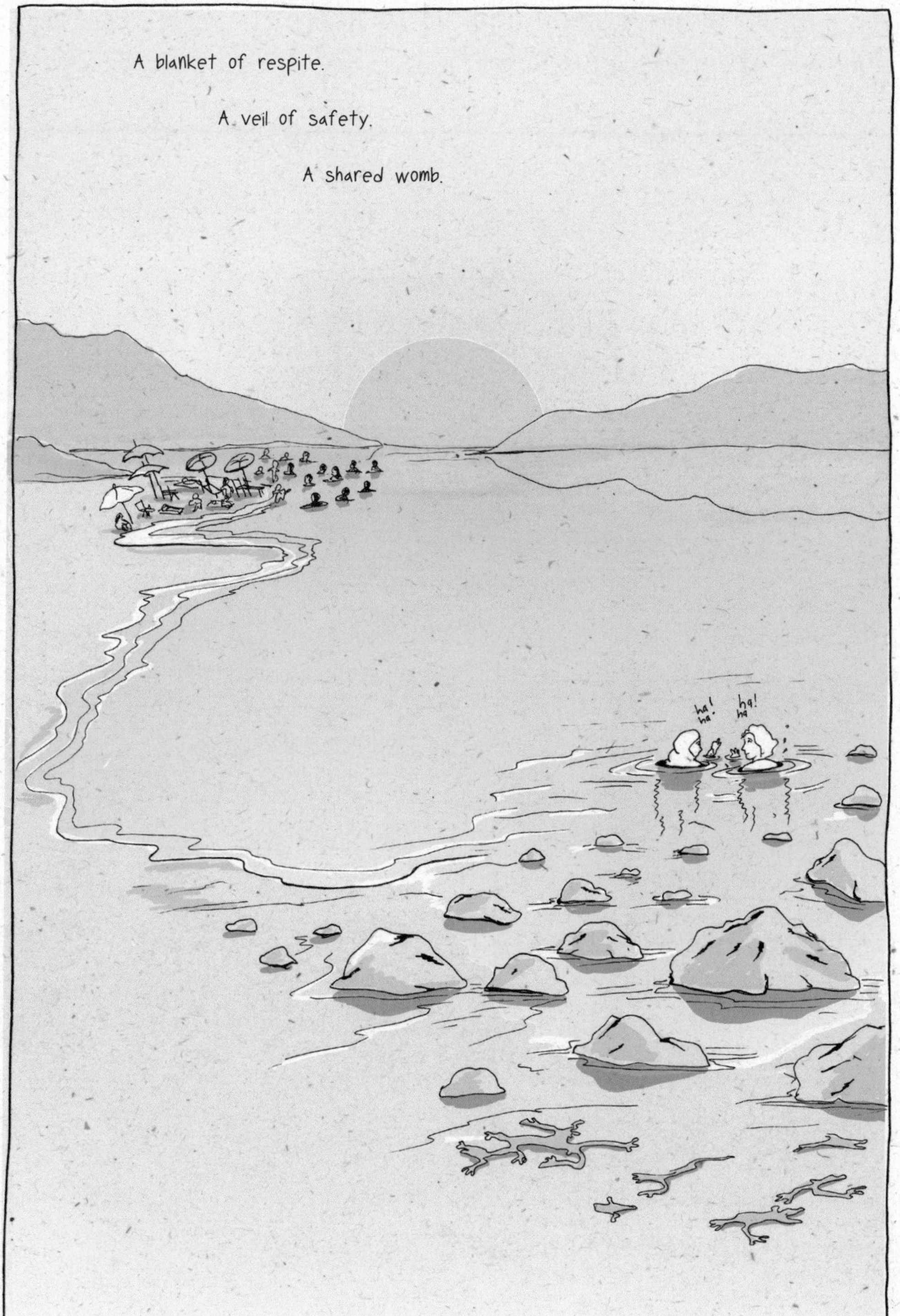
A blanket of respite.
A veil of safety.
A shared womb.
ha! ha.
ha! ha

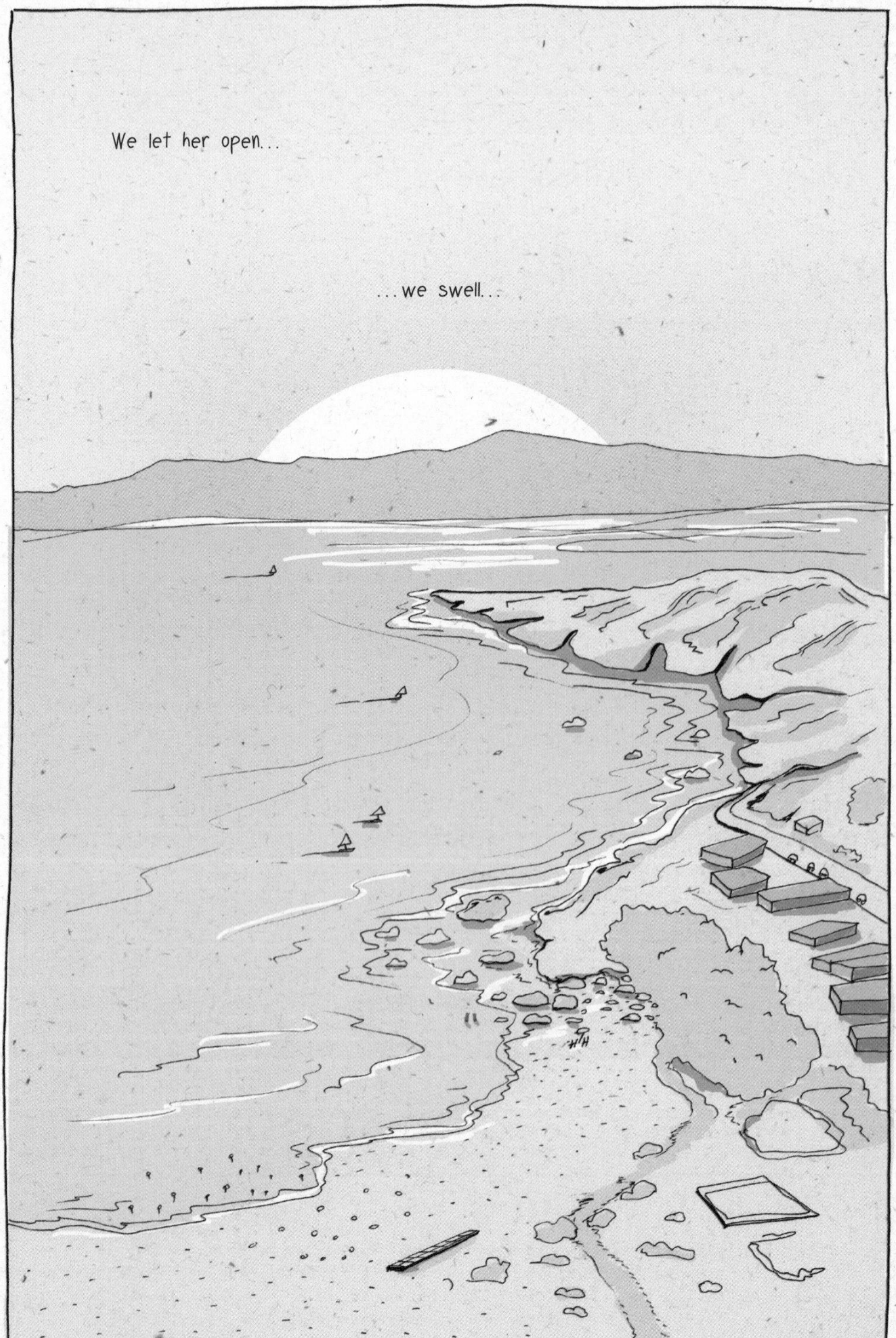
We let her open...
...we swell...